CW00432666

HOUSE (

European Union Committee

6th Report of Session 2005-06

Completing the Internal Market in Services

Report with Evidence

Ordered to be printed 5 July and published 21 July 2005

Published by the Authority of the House of Lords

London : The Stationery Office Limited
£23.00

HL Paper 23

The European Union Committee

The European Union Committee is appointed by the House of Lords "to consider European Union documents and other matters relating to the European Union". The Committee has seven Sub-Committees which are:

Economic and Financial Affairs, and International Trade (Sub-Committee A)
Internal Market (Sub-Committee B)
Foreign Affairs, Defence and Development Policy (Sub-Committee C)
Environment and Agriculture (Sub-Committee D)
Law and Institutions (Sub-Committee E)
Home Affairs (Sub-Committee F)
Social and Consumer Affairs (Sub-Committee G)

Our Membership

The Members of the European Union Committee are:

Lord Blackwell
Lord Bowness
Lord Brown of Eaton-under-Heywood
Lord Dubs
Lord Geddes
Lord Grenfell (Chairman)
Lord Goodhart
Lord Hannay of Chiswick
Lord Harrison

Lord Maclennan of Rogart
Lord Marlesford
Lord Neill of Bladen
Lord Radice
Lord Renton of Mount Harry
Baroness Thomas of Walliswood
Lord Tomlinson
Lord Woolmer of Leeds
Lord Wright of Richmond

The Members of the Sub-Committee which carried out this inquiry (Sub-Committee B: Internal Market) are:

Baroness Cohen of Pimlico
Baroness Eccles of Moulton
Lord Fearn
Lord Fyfe of Fairfield
Lord Geddes
Lord Haskel

Lord Roper
Lord Shutt of Greetland
Lord St John of Bletso
Lord Swinfen
Lord Walpole
Lord Woolmer of Leeds (Chairman)

Information about the Committee

The reports and evidence of the Committee are published by and available from The Stationery Office. For information freely available on the web, our homepage is:

http://www.parliament.uk/parliamentary_committees/lords_eu_select_committee.cfm

There you will find many of our publications, along with press notices, details of membership and forthcoming meetings, and other information about the ongoing work of the Committee and its Sub-Committees, each of which has its own homepage.

General Information

General information about the House of Lords and its Committees, including guidance to witnesses, details of current inquiries and forthcoming meetings is on the internet at
http://www.parliament.uk/about_lords/about_lords.cfm

Contacts for the European Union Committee

Contact details for individual Sub-Committees are given on the website.

General correspondence should be addressed to the Clerk of the European Union Committee, Committee Office, House of Lords, London, SW1A OPW
The telephone number for general enquiries is 020 7219 5791.
The Committee's email address is euclords@parliament.uk

CONTENTS

Note: Pages of the report are numbered in bold type; pages of evidence re numbered in ordinary type. References in the text of the report are as follows:

(Q) refers to a question in oral evidence

ABSTRACT

The European Union has long accepted that a single market in manufactured goods is fundamental to the EU, creating a market of 450 million people, bringing greater competition and increased choice for consumers. But trade in services across the EU remains subject to a large number of restrictions, limiting choice for consumers and businesses, holding back growth, output and employment. The Council of Ministers says that this must change if the Lisbon goals of improved growth in output and employment are to be realised.

The Commission has therefore proposed a Directive which seeks to encourage greater cross-border trade in services by providing a legal framework that will eliminate obstacles to:

• The freedom for service providers to establish their business in any Member State; and

• The free movement of services between Member States.

It seeks to give "both providers and recipients of services the legal certainty they need in order to exercise these two fundamental freedoms enshrined in the Treaty."[1]

Our Report concentrates on the second objective, namely the free movement of services between Member States. This subject has raised the most controversy, much of which arises from the Country of Origin Principle. Under this, a business which provides services in the Member State in which it is established is qualified to provide services on a temporary basis in any other Member State according to the regulations of its home Member State. The draft Directive proposes a substantial number of exceptions to the application of the Principle and of derogations from the draft Directive which meet many of the concerns that might arise.

Even so the Commission's proposal has been criticised. Our Report considers these criticisms. In our view, the draft Services Directive does not pose a threat to the health and safety of employees or consumers. It does not pose a threat to environmental standards, nor does it pose a threat to consumer protection. Services of general economic interest should not be excluded from the Directive. Many of the arguments raised against the draft Directive appear to be either based upon misunderstanding or seek to obstruct change and the effective operation of the free movement of services in the EU. The effect of such obstructions will be to hold back the dynamic contribution of a single market in services which would bring with it greater competition and innovation, increased choice and lower prices for consumers and business.

The draft Directive offers opportunities for small businesses in all 25 Member States of the European Union. The thrust of the draft Directive should be supported. The Services Directive is essential to remove unnecessary and unjustified obstacles to trade and to flexible markets thereby making the European Union more competitive in a global economy.

---

[1] Proposal for a Directive of the European Parliament and of the Council on Services in the Internal Market SEC (2004) 21

Completing the Internal Market in Services

CHAPTER 1: INTRODUCTION

1. The four fundamental freedoms on which the European Community has been based since its beginnings just under fifty years ago are the free movement of capital, goods, persons and services. Therefore, in principle businesses and self-employed individuals have had since then the freedom to offer their services in any Member State of the European Union.

2. As a result, one might expect flourishing European Union cross border trade in services. Yet this is not the case. Whilst services account for around 54% of European Union Gross Value Added, in 2001 cross border trade in services amounted to only 20% of total trade in the Internal Market[1]. There is a large potential for a functioning Internal Market in services which would contribute to driving forward the renewed Lisbon Agenda[2] goals of greater economic growth and more jobs in the European Union.

3. The Commission has therefore proposed a Directive which seeks to encourage greater cross-border trade in services by providing a legal framework that will eliminate obstacles to:

   - The freedom for service providers to establish their business in any Member State; and

   - The free movement of services between Member States.

4. It seeks to give "both providers and recipients of services the legal certainty they need in order to exercise these two fundamental freedoms enshrined in the Treaty."[3]

5. Our Report concentrates on the second objective, namely the free movement of services between Member States. This subject has raised the most controversy. In order to eliminate obstacles to the free movement of services the draft Directive provides for:

   - The application of the Country of Origin Principle;

   - The rights of recipients to use services from businesses established in other Member States; and

   - In the case of posting of workers, an allocation of tasks between the Member State of origin and the Member State of destination.

---

[1] Commission Extended Impact Assessment of Proposal for a Directive on Services in the Internal Market, SEC(2004)21.

[2] At the March 2000 Lisbon European Council, Member States agreed a ten year goal and accompanying strategy to modernise the EU economy and social model by 2010. This became known as the "Lisbon Agenda". In 2005, after it had become clear that the original Lisbon goals would not be achieved by 2010, the programme was refocused on greater economic growth and more jobs.

[3] Proposal for a Directive of the European Parliament and of the Council on Services in the Internal Market SEC(2004)21

6. In order to establish mutual trust between Member States so that obstacles to trade can be overcome, the draft Directive provides for harmonisation of legislation to guarantee protection in certain areas such as consumer protection, stronger mutual assistance between national authorities, measures to promote the quality of services and encouragement of codes of business conduct at Community level.

7. The Commission's Proposal has been criticised. Opponents argue, for example, that if the new EU Member States can compete in the market for services on an equal basis without applying the often higher social rights as well as health and safety and environmental standards of some of the EU 15, the lowest level of standards in the European Union will become the norm. Other opponents of the draft Directive argue that its scope is too wide and that sector specific legislation would be more suitable. Others fear that consumer protection rights will be weakened.

8. We analyse these concerns in this report and conclude that, in the main, they are unfounded. The thrust of the draft Directive should be supported. The Services Directive is essential to remove unnecessary and unjustified obstacles to trade thereby making the European Union more competitive in a global economy.

CHAPTER 2: CONTEXT AND BACKGROUND

9. The central principles governing the Internal Market, a market without obstacles to the free movement of goods, persons, services and capital, are set out in the EC Treaty. The right of establishment[4] ensures that nationals and companies of one Member State can freely move to another Member State in order to carry out activities as self-employed persons and to set up and manage undertakings. The freedom to provide services[5] ensures that nationals or companies of one Member State can provide their services in another Member State. Employed persons benefit from the provisions on the free movement of workers[6]. These principles of the right of establishment, free movement of services and the free movement of workers, are the three so-called "fundamental freedoms" central to the Internal Market and relevant to the Commission's proposed Directive on Services in the Internal Market[7] with which this report is concerned.

10. The principles of freedom of establishment and free movement of services have been clarified and developed over the years through the case law of the European Court of Justice. In particular, the Court has made clear that freedom to provide services applies not only where the person providing the services and the recipient are established in different Member States but also where the person providing the services offers those services in a Member State other than that in which he is established, wherever the recipients themselves may be established[8].

11. In addition, European Union legislation is already in place for an internal market in financial services, gas and electricity supply services, some transport services, telecommunications and broadcasting. Cross-border trade in services was further simplified by an agreement in the Council on 6 June 2005 of a directive on the Recognition of Professional Qualifications which establishes rules for those with certain professional qualifications to work in any other Member State.

12. However, despite progress in these specific service sectors and despite the basic principles set down in the original Treaty of Rome, the overall Internal Market for services is far from working well.

13. There are two main reasons why an internal market in services is considered important for the European Union. As services account for 54% of European Union Gross Value Added (GVA)[9], fully opening up the internal market for services is expected to make a considerable contribution the Lisbon goal of more economic growth and jobs in the European Union by 2010. The second reason for prioritising the development of an internal market in services is that the European Union service sector is much larger than the manufacturing sector and reducing the present barriers to an internal market in services will have a considerable positive effect on the cost and quality of

---

[4] Article 43 of the EC Treaty

[5] in Article 49 of the EC Treaty

[6] in Article 39 of the EC Treaty

[7] COM(2004)2

[8] Case C–198/89 *Commission v Greece* [1991] ECR I–727

[9] Gross Value Added (GVA) measures the contribution to the economy of each individual producer, industry or sector. Its relationship to Gross Domestic Product can be explained thus: GVA + taxes on products – subsidies on products = GDP.

services to consumers, whether these consumers are other service providers, manufacturers or private consumers.

14. However, despite these incentives, experience has shown that reducing barriers to service industries trading in any EU Member State cannot develop at its own pace through existing measures of EU legislation.

15. The Commission has said that "services are the engine of economic growth". This view is different from many traditional perspectives on services. Traditionally they have frequently been considered little more than low-paid activities such as office cleaning. In fact, services accounted for around 50% of GVA in the UK economy in 2002 (DTI evidence). This dominance of services in generating Gross Value Added is reflected in the EU as a whole where the figure of Gross Value Added is 54% of EU Gross Domestic Product. This is illustrated by Table 1 which shows a breakdown across service activity in the UK as well as in Poland, France and Germany. Although there are obvious broad differences between the economies of these countries—France has more agriculture than Germany or the UK and Germany has a much bigger manufacturing base than the other three countries—the dominance of service activities is evident in all four countries. It is notable that, with the exception of financial activities and real estate, the figures for Poland and the UK are broadly comparable.

TABLE 1

Gross value added at current basic prices, by industry, 2002

Industry	UK Percent	France Percent	Germany Percent	Poland Percent	EU25 Percent
Agriculture, fishing etc	1.0	2.6	1.1		2.1
Mining, extraction, quarrying etc	2.8				
Manufacturing	16.6	19.7	24.3		21.6
Electricity, gas water	1.6				
Construction	6.2	4.9	4.5		5.6
Wholesale, retail, hotel and restaurant	16.0	19.0	18.0	22.0	21.7
Transport and communication	8.2			7.8	
Financial activities, real estate etc	24.1	30.3	30.4	16.0	26.9
Public administration and defence, education	11.3			12.3	
Health and social work	7.0	23.6	21.7	4.0	22.1
Other social and professional services	5.2			4.5	
Services subtotal	71.8	72.9	70.1	66.6	70.7
Non-public services plus construction					54.2

Source: UK: Annual Abstract of Statistics, 2004.

EU25, France and Germany: International Statistical Yearbook, 2004:

Polish Source: Provided as evidence on our visit.
For EU25, France and Germany, Mining, Manufacturing and GEW are combined. Financial services is defined rather more broadly. The figure listed opposite health and social work roughly covers the last three categories.

Non-public services plus construction is defined as the sum of construction, wholesale and retail and financial activities, for the purposes of this table.

Note: Categories may not match exactly across countries.

16.   In the UK in 2002 services accounted for 32% of UK global exports and 23% of imports. The problem for the European Union as a whole, however, is that although 54 % of EU Gross Domestic Product derives from services, cross-border trade in services only amounts to 20% of intra-EU trade.

17.   In order to unlock the potential for more intra-EU trade in services, the Commission published in January 2004 its draft Directive on Services in the Internal Market[10]. The proposal aims to provide a legal framework that will eliminate obstacles to:

- the freedom for service providers to establish their business in any Member State;

- the free movement of services between Member States.

18.   The second objective, namely the free movement of services between Member States is the subject of our inquiry and Report. On this, the draft Directive provides for:

- The application of the Country of Origin principle which allows temporary provision of services in a "host" Member State on the basis of "home" Member State regulation;

- The rights of recipients to use services from businesses established in other Member States;

---

[10] COM(2004)2

- A mechanism to provide assistance to recipients who use a service provided by a business established in another Member State;

- In the case of posting of workers, an allocation of tasks between the Member State of origin and the Member State of destination.

19. There was widespread support among our witnesses as to the need for a Services Directive. Evelyne Gebhardt MEP[11], who is critical of the Commission proposal agreed: "it is important to have a Services Directive, because we have a good deal of protectionism in Member States and we do not really have an open market for services." (Q 430)

Services covered by the draft Directive

20. Article 2 of the Directive states that it shall apply to services supplied by providers established in a Member State. Article 4(1) states that "service" means "any self employed activity, as referred to in Article 50 of the Treaty, consisting in the provision of a service for consideration." The draft Directive says that the definition of "service" is based on the case-law of the European Court of Justice, according to which "services" mean any self-employed economic activity normally performed for remuneration which need not be paid by those for whom the service is performed. "The essential characteristic of remuneration lies in the fact that it constitutes consideration for the service in question, irrespective of how this consideration is financed"[12]. Under this interpretation, "services" includes those for which a fee is charged or which is free to the final recipient. As we discuss below, this definition is contested by some opponents of the draft Directive, especially by those who argue that the proposal poses a threat to the "European Social Model".

21. In more concrete terms, the Commission had in mind that "service" would cover a wide variety of ever-changing activities including:

- business services such as management consultancy, facilities management, including office maintenance and security; advertising; recruitment services;

- services provided both to businesses and to consumers, such as legal or fiscal advice; estate agencies; construction and architectural services; distributive trades; the organisation of trade fairs; car hire; tourist services including travel agencies and tourist guides; audio-visual services; and security services;

- consumer services, such as leisure services, sports centres and amusement parks; health and health care services; and household support services, such as help for the elderly;

- services which may require the proximity of provider and recipient;

- services which require travel by the recipient or the provider; and

- services which may be provided at a distance, including via the Internet.

---

[11] German MEP, member of the European Parliament's Committee on the Internal Market and Consumer Protection and that committee's rapporteur on the draft Services Directive.

[12] Proposal for a Directive of the European Parliament and of the Council on Services in the Internal Market SEC(2004)21

22.   The Report of May 2005 by the European Parliament Committee on the Internal Market and Consumer Protection[13] sets out a narrower definition of services saying that the Directive shall apply only to "commercial" services, only to services of a commercial nature [amendment 52 and justification]. This distinction is apparently made by the EP Committee in order to justify their argument that services of general economic interest should not be covered by this directive. We deal with this point below.

Do Services of General Interest fall within the scope of the draft Services Directive?

23.   The proposal states that "this Directive establishes general provisions facilitating exercise of the freedom of establishment for service providers and the free movement of services." As explained above, "services" is defined in the broad sense of the European Community Treaty and as consistently reiterated by the European Court of Justice, as those service activities normally provided for remuneration.

24.   This definition therefore includes what are often referred to as services of general economic interest but excludes services of general non-economic interest[14]. The latter cannot be traded easily across Member States. They include activities such as defence services, and those other services provided by the State in pursuit of its social, cultural, educational and legal obligations which do not usually involve remuneration, that is, they are not purchased for consideration from service providers. The extent to which services of general interest are or are not purchased by public authorities from remunerated service suppliers and provided to the final recipient free or substantially free of charge varies between Member States.

25.   When the Commission published a White Paper on Services of General Interest in May 2004[15], Member State governments raised concerns about the distinction between services of general economic interest and services of general non-economic interest and the role that the Commission should have in affecting Member State policies regarding the provision such services. As we concluded in our October 2004 report on this White Paper, [16] there are widely differing views among Member States about the nature of such services and the role they play in creating a specifically European model of society.

26.   Although services of general non-economic interest are exempted from the scope of this draft Directive, there are some public services (services of general economic interest) which have been outsourced to or purchased from businesses by the governments of some Member States and made available to recipients free or at a low cost. These would be affected by this proposed Directive. However, under the Commission proposal certain services of general economic interest are subject to derogations from the country of origin principle "in so far as this is justified by their specific nature", e.g. postal services, gas, electricity and water distribution. Critically, even in the

[13] *Draft Report of the European Parliament's Internal Market and Consumer Protection Committee on the Proposal for a directive of the European Parliament and of the Council on Services in the Internal Market.* Rapporteur: Evelyne Gebhardt (25 May 2005)

[14] Proposal for a Directive of the European Parliament and of the Council on Services in the Internal Market SEC(2004)21

[15] COM(2004)374

[16] *Services of General Interest*, 29th Report of Session 2003-04, HL Paper 178.

fields covered by the draft Directive, the proposal does not affect the freedom of Member States to define what they consider to be services of general interest and how they should function.

27. The European Parliament, in its May 2005 draft report on the draft Services Directive[17] considers the position of services of general interest. It proposes the explicit exclusion of all services of general interest from the scope of the Services Directive [e.g. Amendments 7 and 8]. The justification for given for this is that "given their role in promoting social and territorial cohesion, services of general economic interest should not be covered by this Directive but should be addressed by a specific framework directive". **There are important issues here but we disagree with such a blanket exclusion. This could be used as a means of circumventing competition. Where governments and public bodies in Member States do engage in services of general economic interest (purchase services from suppliers for remuneration to be made available to recipients for reduced or no charge) then in general we would expect such purchases to be transparent and open to competition. The supply of such services should be a market opportunity for businesses from any Member State unless there are over-riding and justifiable reasons of national interest.**

28. The distinction between services of general *non-economic* interest and services of general *economic* interest must rely on the question of whether the service is provided for remuneration. It is important that the draft Services Directive is unambiguous about the exclusion from its scope of services of general interest that are not for remuneration and that it confirms the freedom of Member States to define what they consider to be services of general interest, whether economic or non-economic services, and how they should function. Member States must retain sole competence over how their Governments decide to provide public services. We believe that the draft Directive recognises this and strikes that balance. The Government should seek to ensure that the final version of the Directive maintains that balance while ruling out a blanket derogation for all services of general economic interest.

Other Exclusions from the scope of the Directive

29. Stripping out public services, services amounting to a total of around 54% of EU Gross Value Added are amenable to cross-border trade. A number of other services have also been excluded from the scope of the draft Directive.

30. Financial services, electronic communications services and transport services (with the exception of cash-in-transit and the transport of mortal remains) are excluded from the scope of the draft Directive because they are covered by other EC legislation. Financial services are covered by the 42 legislative measures which make up the Financial Services Action Plan concluded in 2005 and electronic communications are covered by the 2002 EC Telecom Package. Tax is also excluded from the Directive as tax has a different legal base in the Treaties. Gas, electricity and water services are exempted from the application of the Country of Origin Principle, but fall within the scope of all the other provisions of the draft Directive.

---

[17] *Draft Report of the European Parliament's Internal Market and Consumer Protection Committee on the Proposal for a directive of the European Parliament and of the Council on Services in the Internal Market.* Rapporteur: Evelyne Gebhardt (25 May 2005)

A horizontal Directive

31. The list of services to be included and excluded illustrates the many forms that an internal market in services would cover and the ever-changing nature of the activities involved. To reflect this diversity of activity and the changing nature of services, the Commission's proposal is for a "horizontal directive". This means that the Directive would cover all types of services with the exception of services of general non-economic interest and the specific exclusions listed in paragraph 28 above. The alternative to a horizontal directive is sector by sector or "vertical" harmonisation. We consider this in more detail in chapter 4.

Simplification of Procedures

32. The Directive would require Member States to simplify the procedures and formalities relating to establishment of a service industry business. The proposed mechanism is for the establishment by the end of 2008 in each Member State of "single points of contact", where all formalities for offering services in another Member State can be dealt with. These single points of contact are to provide information on requirements on establishment, application materials and assistance among other matters. All forms that are required are to be accessible electronically from remote locations. Any authorisations agreed by the relevant authority should be public, objectively justified, non-discriminatory and non-discretionary. With the aim of enforcing the non-discriminatory nature of the exercise of service activities, a whole range of possible methods for discriminating indirectly are no longer allowed under the draft Directive.

33. Such simplification is a significant objective in enabling service firms to establish in other Member States more easily than hitherto, and it is clear that the simplification will require considerable effort by all Member States. Simplification is a priority if a functioning internal market in services is to be achieved.

34. In order to assist the free movement of services, i.e. provision of services on a temporary basis, the Directive seeks to establish mutual trust between Member States through provisions for the development of stronger mutual assistance between national authorities, developing measures of quality assurance such as voluntary certification of service activities and cooperation between the chambers of commerce and encouraging codes of conduct. We welcome these aims, although we note that some witnesses raised concerns about the practicality of such initiatives.

The Focus of our Inquiry

35. In drawing up the terms of our inquiry, it appeared to us that there was broad agreement on the aims of simplify process for establishment and for and of better cooperation through mutual assistance between relevant national authorities. We therefore decided to concentrate our attention on those aspects of the proposal where there was a broad range of views.

36. In particular our inquiry has concentrated on issues concerning the freedom for businesses and the self-employed to provide services in another Member State on a temporary basis (that is, the right to provide services without needing to be established in the Member State).

The Country of Origin Principle

37. The draft Directive allows for temporary service provision on the basis that the service provider complies with "the national provisions of their Member State of origin". In the words of the proposal, under this principle, "a service provider is subject only to the law of the country in which he is established and Member States may not restrict services from a provider established in another Member State." This is the Country of Origin Principle which we consider in detail in Chapter 5. This principle is particularly important for Small and Medium Sized Enterprises (SMEs). The proposal includes provision for a number of derogations which are either general or temporary or which may be applied on a case-by-case basis.

38. The measures which the Commission wishes to introduce with the draft Directive must be seen in the context of other European Union Directives, particularly the Posting of Workers Directive[18] and the Directive on the Mutual Recognition of Professional Qualifications[19]. The first relates to employment rights of employees working in a Member State other than their own and the second relates to agreed principles of mutual recognition of certain professional qualifications. We consider the relation of these to the draft Directive in more detail later.

Expected Benefits of an Internal Market in Services

39. It is difficult to say with any certainty what the full benefits of an internal market in services would be. The Commission cites a report it commissioned by the consultancy company Copenhagen Economics which suggests that the benefits would be substantial and would accrue (in different measure) to all Member States. This report concludes that total consumption in the European Union would increase by around 0.6%, or €37 billion. If trade in services were completely liberalised, an effective internal market for services would lead to prices falling in all service sectors, output rising with total value added increasing by around €33 billion leading to an increase in total employment of up to 600,000 jobs.

40. These predicted benefits are substantial and would contribute greatly to the Lisbon goal of more economic growth and jobs for the European Union by 2010. It is therefore important that agreement is found between the Council of Ministers and the European Parliament on the Commission's draft and a speedy programme of implementation is begun.

41. We make this report to the House for debate.

---

[18] Directive 96/71/EC

[19] COM (2002) 119 amended by COM (2004) 317 and agreed by Council in June 2005

CHAPTER 3: PROVISION OF SERVICES ON A TEMPORARY BASIS

42. In some Member States it is not possible to offer services other than on an "established" basis. Furthermore, the requirements for a service provider to become "established" in a Member State are different in each EU country. The Commission believes that this is one of the barriers to an effective internal market in services. The draft Directive on Services therefore distinguishes temporary provision of services in a host Member State from the provision of services on an established basis. Temporary provision of services in a host Member State according to the Services Directive would be permitted on the basis of the home country rules of the service provider.

43. Traditionally, there has been a significant emphasis on manufacturing and manufacturing jobs in the Member States of the European Union. In this context, services are commonly seen as quite separate businesses from those involved in manufacturing goods. In fact, the production and supply of many goods requires the supply of significant service inputs[20]. The production of a motor car for example, requires many service inputs such as design, marketing, technical analysis and sales, just as the supply of the car requires services such as finance, insurance and training. Increasing the competitiveness of the service sector should therefore help the competitiveness of the manufacturing sector.

44. The supply of some services can be subject to particular regulations pertaining to the country in which they are being supplied, or even to the region or locality of supply. In some cases it may be argued that these regulations exist as an indirect signal to consumers of the quality of the service (e.g. that the service provider has been trained to a particular standard). In other cases, the regulations serve primarily as a means of protecting those providing the services and shielding them from competition, for example the adoption of a standard fee, or a requirement that no competitor to a particular activity be allowed within a certain distance.

45. Any action taken to reduce these barriers necessarily involves a judgment by the policymaker that it is beneficial to switch the balance more towards the individual consumer and away from established provider interests. It allows more competition. But it may require greater vigilance on the part of consumers and communities to ensure that greater competition does not compromise the quality of the services provided.

46. The benefits to consumers from reduced restrictions on trade arise as a consequence of greater competition among suppliers, through reduction in barriers. As a result of greater competition, consumers, and some producers, benefit, and do so to a greater extent than the producers who suffer. There is a net gain,[21] because some consumption takes place that previously did not.

---

[20] To take an example, the Commission in its Impact Assessment on the Services Directive quotes a lift (elevator) manufacturer's estimate that soon only 8% of its labour force will be engaged in manufacturing with the remainder associated with providing related services.

[21] To see this, take the example of an airline that introduces a new low cost service in place of an existing higher cost service. The airline's profits (and many other elements, such as staff wages) are lower, but consumers benefit on their existing flights through lower fares and, in particular, some journeys are made that would not have been undertaken at the previous higher prices.

For these reasons the Commission brought forward its draft Services Directive in January 2004.

47. Since the EC Treaty already makes provision for a single market in services, one might ask why the Services Directive is necessary. The Commission's answer is that earlier elimination of various barriers has "been partly offset by the erection of new legal barriers or by the increasing impact of those barriers which were already there but whose effects became evident only gradually as trade between Member States developed." Moreover "one common feature of many ... is that they derive not from national legislation but from other forms of intervention and regulation whose impact on the internal market is becoming more and more relevant."[22] For example, authorisation procedures may involve bodies made up of competing operators already present in the area concerned. Authorisation may also involve excessive formalities and procedures, coupled with a lack of transparency. In some cases it involves authorities at several levels, regional and local as well as national. Authorisation requirements which would allow the provision of services across a whole country may require manifold applications to local bodies.

48. In other words, to an established local service provider, the provision of a particular service may seem quite straightforward, whilst a new operator coming from outside the area faces a jumble of requirements and little scope for redress to make these requirements easier to understand. The new operator faces no overt discrimination, but the *effect* is in opposition to the judgment of the European Court that "A Member State *cannot* make the provision of services in its territory subject to compliance with all the conditions required *for establishment* and thereby deprive of all practical effectiveness the provisions of the Treaty whose object is, precisely, to guarantee the freedom to provide services" (emphasis added)[23].

49. For those service providers that wish to establish in another Member State, the proposed Directive includes a number of provisions requiring the simplification of national rules of establishment to address such implicit discrimination. However, such rules of simplification would not fully address the provision of services on a temporary basis.

50. In the Services Directive, the Commission therefore has distinguished temporary provision of services from the provision of services in a host Member State on an established basis. This is because firms wishing to provide a service in another Member State may not wish, at least in the first instance, to establish there. For example, a firm may want to bid for a construction contract, but will not establish unless it wins the contract. Or it may establish only if, after working on that contract for some time, it decides to set up in business more permanently. An architect may journey to another state to supervise construction of a building for which he/she has won an open design competition. A firm may be very uncertain as to demand for its service in the other Member State, and therefore may go there on a temporary basis to test the market.

51. It is clear that there are many instances in which a legislative base for temporary provision of services would be beneficial. The ability for a service

22 Report from the Commission to the Council and the European Parliament on the State of the Internal Market in Services, COM (2002) 441.

23 Case C-43/93 *Raymond Vander Elst v Office des Migrations Internationales* [1994] ECR I – 3803, at para. 17.

provider to test the market of a host Member State on a temporary basis and without going through the regulatory hoops of establishing there is particularly important for Small and Medium sized Enterprises (SMEs). As SMEs are often seen as an important driving force of innovation and competitiveness, it is particularly apt that cross-border trade in services should be encouraged on a temporary basis as well as an established one.

52.   The draft Services Directive seeks to address this by applying the Country of Origin Principle which allows service providers to test the market of another Member State under the national provisions of their Member State of origin. We discuss this in greater detail in Chapter 5. The question that needs to be asked therefore is what does temporary operation, as opposed to establishment, mean?

The definition of "Establishment"

53.   In the draft Directive "establishment" is defined as it is in the EC Treaty as, "the actual pursuit of an economic activity through a fixed establishment of the provider for an indefinite period"[24]. A clear definition of "temporary" on the other hand is not readily available.

54.   "Temporary" would seem not to be a solely temporal concept, such as a period less than a particular number of weeks. "Temporary" has been "defined" in the case law of the European Court of Justice in the context of determining whether a business is established. The "temporary" nature of activities has to be determined not only by reference to the duration of the provision of the service but also to the "regularity, periodicity, or continuity". Further, the fact that the provision of services is temporary does not mean that the service provider may not have some form of infrastructure in the host Member State (e.g. an office or consulting rooms) if needed to perform the service in question[25].

55.   In their evidence session with us, Clifford Chance expanded on these necessary attributes: "you need to look at all the factoral circumstances surrounding the particular business concerned to decide whether this business is participating in the economic life of the host Member State and is therefore providing services on an indefinite basis". The European Court of Justice case law considers whether the service provider has a permanent infrastructure in the host Member State. For example in the case of a nursing home which has patients, the service provider requires the infrastructure of a building with carers who are on duty all the time. By its nature this is indefinite and the service would therefore be considered established. A travelling hairdresser who goes to a Member State once a week and maintains a salon in that Member State, on the other hand, need not be established, as the existence of a salon in which he or she works one or two days a week is not an indication of a permanent presence. (Q 526).

56.   Although testing whether a service activity has these attributes provides some guide, it is clear that it does not provide a straightforward answer to the question most important for a SME which is whether the business will be treated as established or not. This is of great importance because if the service the SME provides is considered by the local legal representative to be

---

[24] Article 43 of the EC Treaty

[25] Case C 55/94 *Gebhard* [1995] ECR I – 4165, at para. 27.

established, the business will have to comply with all the rules for establishment in the host Member State. If on the other hand, the service is considered temporary such regulatory burden does not apply and the SME's home country rules apply.

57. Such uncertainty could also offer opportunities for service providers operating in their own country to fight competition from temporary service providers from a different Member State.

58. The significance of this uncertainty is difficult to estimate precisely, although it is clear that this question is proportionately more significant for small firms, which might be ruined by the expenses of litigation should the basis of their operations in another Member State be challenged, than for larger concerns. Also, SMEs may well decide that it is not worth offering their services in a host Member State if they must be established. The uncertainty of no clear definition for "temporary" is a further barrier to intra-EU trade in services for some service providers.

59. This last point was taken up by the Federation of Small Business (FSB) who told us that they would like to see "a clear definitive set of guidelines" to determine "temporary" as at the moment "the legislation and the interpretation of the legislation is unclear and there are unclear sets of principles." (Q 138) The FSB witnesses suggested there could be "a grey black list or a grey list so that nothing is definitive, but you have a guide in principle so people have something to work towards" (Q 145). The FSB suggestion of a "grey black list" further indicates how difficult it is to achieve clarity in the definition of "temporary".

60. Despite this difficulty, establishing certainty about the meaning of "temporary" is particularly important if the Services Directive is going to be effective in encouraging SMEs to trade their services across EU borders. As the Minister, Douglas Alexander told us, "up to 90% of service providers are SMEs" (Q 483). To ensure there is a wider opportunity for services to be triggered across the European Union, the EU must ensure that SMEs are able to test the market in another Member State on a temporary basis, without having to fully commit to permanent establishment. "At the moment SMEs are often deterred from providing a service in other Member States because of lengthy and costly authorisation procedures" (Q 483).

61. SMEs in particular find the legal uncertainty created by the lack of a positive definition of temporary operation a major barrier to exploring entry to a market. We therefore urge the Government to push for greater clarity on the meaning of "temporary".

62. Some witnesses would prefer a positive definition of "temporary". On the other hand, it is possible that producing a clear definition of "temporary" could itself introduce inflexibilities in the marketplace. At the moment the position appears to place the onus on the relevant authorities to justify the need for a business to become "established" in a Member State. Producing a clear definition of "temporary" could result in a business being required to prove that its operations are "temporary" otherwise the presumption is that it will need to become "established" in the Member State. There is a fine balance to draw here if the objective is to secure maximum market flexibility. Those who are concerned about "temporary" provision of services under a country of origin principle may favour a restrictive definition of "temporary". If establishing a positive definition of "temporary" remains elusive, we

recommend a set of clear guidelines is established in order to ensure that freedom to provide services on a temporary basis is made more predictable and involves fewer obstacles.

CHAPTER 4: WHY A HORIZONTAL FRAMEWORK DIRECTIVE?

A Horizontal Directive as opposed to Sector by Sector Harmonisation

63. The two possible broad EC legislative approaches to achieving greater trade between Member States are for the Commission either to propose a series of sector-specific directives as it did for an internal market in goods, or to propose what is called a "horizontal framework Directive" which sets out broad framework principles which apply to all the areas within its scope. The Services Directive adopts the latter approach based on the principle of "mutual acceptance".

64. Evelyne Gebhardt, the MEP responsible for the European Parliament's draft report on the Services Directive, told us she would prefer to have more harmonisation through sector-specific legislation (Q 430). A number of our witnesses agreed with Ms Gebhardt that sector specific legislation would be preferable to a horizontal directive. However, as this chapter shows, on balance we believe that the weight of evidence is in favour of a horizontal approach as proposed by the Commission.

65. Harmonisation, that is to say, sector specific legislation that seeks to establish common standards for all Member States, can be contrasted with the principle of mutual acceptance. The difference between the two approaches can be illustrated in the following way: under the principle of mutual acceptance, all Member States may agree to recognise basic professional qualifications from other Member States allowing European Union professionals, subject possibly to some minimum adaptation requirement, to work in a Member State other than that in which they qualified. This is different from seeking to harmonise the professional qualifications of, say, doctors across all Member States. Experience has shown that the latter is a far more cumbersome and lengthy process and is often politically highly sensitive.

66. In seeking to achieve a more effective internal market in goods, the European Union and its Member States pursued a legislative process of sector-specific directives which laid down harmonised requirements for certain goods. This was because to establish an internal market in, for example, cars tyres it was essential that the precise rules covering for instance the permitted composite materials for a tyre, its width and grip must be the same throughout the European Union so that a car manufacturer in France can source its tyres from Italy without any problems. As the Labour MEP Philip Whitehead, Chairman of the European Parliament's Committee on the Internal Market and Consumer Protection told us, this process of harmonisation "took about ten years to produce an internal market in goods. That led to something like 250 or more sectoral proposals coming out". (Q 441) Harmonising national rules across a broad range of sectors is a complicated process which takes a long time to achieve.

67. Whereas harmonisation of rules may be necessary to establish an internal market for some goods, it is not necessary for an internal market in services. This is because there are a number of fundamental differences between goods and services. One difference between most manufactured goods and services is that standardisation in production allows goods to benefit easily from economies of scale. The provision of services, on the other hand, often involves an individual or idiosyncratic element—what would be an attractive

design for a building for one client will strike another as inappropriate. A second difference between goods and services it that it is possible to define precisely what form a manufactured good should have, whereas it is very difficult to define in advance the form and nature of every service. A third difference between goods and services is that goods are objects, whereas the essential element of a service is that in most cases it relies heavily on the person who provides it. It is not possible to define precisely what makes up, for example, the output of a plumber. Two architects with the same training may have entirely different types of projects at which they excel.

68. The Commission argues that although a sectoral approach has proved successful in removing barriers in financial services, as there are 83 non-financial service sectors, harmonisation of services would be too extensive and the same issues would have to be covered in many areas. The Commission points out that the workload involved in sector-specific legislation would be likely to involve a timescale stretching much beyond the Lisbon target date of 2010. The Commission therefore proposed a horizontal approach[26] applying across all service sectors. The Commission justifies a horizontal directive by saying that it "could provide legal certainty for service providers without imposing over-complex rules and provide for a system of administrative co-operation, the application of the country of origin principle, and where necessary harmonisation, in a single instrument."[27]

The European Parliament

69. The Commission's decision to propose a horizontal directive met with a mixed reception in the European Parliament. In February 2003, the European Parliament passed a resolution which "welcomed the proposals for a horizontal instrument to ensure free movement of services"[28] In contrast to the European Parliament's statement in 2003, the German Socialist MEP Evelyne Gebhardt represented the view of many MEPs in 2005 by telling us that although legislation is needed in this area it should be based on harmonisation of service sector by service sector (Q 441).

70. The Conservative Michael Harbour MEP (from the UK), on the other hand, supported the Commission's horizontal approach telling us that, "If we try to harmonise everything, we will wait forever" (Q 414). Mr Whitehead told us that "The Labour Group within the Socialist Group here, is aligned with the British Government view, namely that the passing of the Services Directive will be a major step forward in the establishment of the internal market ... That cannot be gainsaid; it is an important element" (Q 430).

Critics of a horizontal Directive

71. It is also proving difficult to find a consensus in the Council of Ministers on a horizontal services directive. Diverging views in the Council about the Services Directive were reflected in the meetings we had in Germany and Poland. During our inquiry, the sternest critics of the horizontal approach came from Germany. On our visit to Berlin, we were presented with the SPD Parliamentary Group's "Initial Evaluation of the Services Directive", which

---

[26] SEC(2004)21: Extended Impact Assessment of Proposal for a Directive on Services in the Internal Market, 13 January 2004.

[27] SEC(2004) 21, p. 28

[28] European Parliament Resolution, 13 February 2003 at http://www.europarl.eu.int

states "the large-scale abandonment of harmonisation is the Directive's major shortcoming in terms of achieving its intended goal of creating a competitive single market for services".

72. The opposition to a horizontal directive expressed by the German Socialists in Berlin and Evelyne Gebhardt in the European Parliament is shared by the UK Trades Union Congress (TUC). Although the TUC told us that it is not against the idea of a horizontal Directive in principle, it wishes to see a greater scope for derogations in favour of host country regulation. Amicus[29] went further, describing the draft directive as impractical and unworkable (Amicus written evidence).

73. A different view was presented to us by the CBI who commended the Commission for taking a framework approach to this proposal. In the past "business has seen an overload of the wrong sort of legislation" (Q 71) and "a tradition within the Commission to [produce] 25 draft directives answering every question known to man but leaving us without the will to do anything about it." (Q 60) The CBI believes that the directive "could make a positive contribution to making the EU work for business" (Q 71).

Conclusion

74. We believe that EC legislation to facilitate an Internal Market in services must rely on a horizontal approach and cannot be based on stringent harmonised rules. Hence we agree with the Commission's approach. If the EU is to achieve the (revised) Lisbon goal of greater economic growth with more and better jobs by 2010, a horizontal directive will be the only way of reaping the full benefits of an internal market in services.

75. We believe the most powerful argument for a horizontal framework directive on an internal market in services is the length of time it took to achieve the legislative basis for an internal market in goods. **We see a clear danger in the sector-by-sector harmonisation of regulations route that negotiations will become bogged down for many years.**

---

[29] The UK's largest manufacturing, technical and skilled persons' trade union .

CHAPTER 5: THE COUNTRY OF ORIGIN PRINCIPLE

76. The most controversial part of the Services Directive is the Country of Origin Principle. The Country of Origin Principle in the draft Directive relates only to operators providing cross border services on a temporary basis. Once a service provider becomes established in a Member State, the company must comply with all the rules of that country. Under the Country of Origin Principle a company which provides services in one country is automatically qualified to provide services in any other Member State on the basis of home-country regulation. Under Article 16 (1) of the draft Directive "Member States shall ensure that providers are subject only to the national provisions of their Member State of origin which fall within the coordinated field".

77. Article 16 (2) elaborates on the coordinated field. This shall cover "national provisions relating to access to and the exercise of a service activity, in particular those requirements governing the behaviour of the provider, the quality or content of the service, advertising, contracts and the provider's liability". Article 16 (4) says that Member States may not, for reasons falling in the coordinated field, restrict the freedom to provide services in the case of a provider established in another Member State, in particular by imposing a number of specified requirements. Articles 17, 18 and 19 provide for a large number of derogations from this general rule, derogations aimed at meeting many of the concerns that might arise. The controversy around the proposal appears to show that this has not assuaged its critics.

78. In EC law the fundamental freedoms of movement of goods and services have been given effect by the European Court of Justice striking down discriminatory provisions and other restrictions in national laws on the movement of goods and services, introducing the idea of mutual acceptance. This has caused the Commission to shift its focus away from the harmonisation of Member States' laws. The rationale for this shift was most clearly stated by the Commission in 1980: "Any product imported from another Member State must in principle be admitted to the territory of the importing Member State if it has been lawfully produced, that is, conforms to the rules and processes of manufacture that are customarily and traditionally accepted in the exporting country, and marketed in the territory of the latter"[30]. The Court has similarly taken an active role in striking down obstacles to the free movement of services. Only under very strict conditions will the Court accept exceptions to the rule of mutual acceptance. That is where the Treaty provides an express exception or where there are overriding reasons relating to the public interest.

79. The Commission argued in its submission to us that the Country of Origin Principle is not new. It was originally developed by the European Court of Justice to give effect to the free movement of goods in 1978. More recently it has been used in other legislation such as the TV without frontiers Directive[31] and the E-Commerce Directive[32], but the provision of it in the draft Services Directive to facilitate the free movement of services on a

---

[30] Communication from the Commission concerning the consequences of the judgment given by the Court of Justice on 20 February 1989 in case 120/78 ("Cassis de Dijon"). OJ C256

[31] 89/552/CEE

[32] 2000/31/CE

temporary basis is the most ambitious use of the principle by the Commission to date.

80.   Many of the concerns regarding the application of this principle for service provision in a host Member State on a temporary basis appear to be a suspicion of what "the coordinated field" might mean in practice. Some of the concerns are explicit, while others appear to be engendered by a general mistrust in the standards of regulation or of business performance in other Member States. On this latter point, the Commission told us " ...the starting point should be that Member States accept that, give or take a couple of exceptions, their legislative regimes are basically comparable and do not subject their citizens to unreasonable risks." We agree with them.

81.   The most significant explicit concerns relate to the effect which applying the Country of Origin Principle will have on the following:

    • Health and safety and environmental standards;

    • Employee rights;

    • Consumer Protection;

    • Problems arising from a web of contracts; and

    • How the government of a service provider's home country can or will supervise the operation of a supplier operating under Country of Origin Principle in another Member State.

82.   These issues have been raised by some to allege that the operation of the Country of Origin Principle will encourage a "race to the bottom". By this it is meant that it will precipitate a serious and unacceptable drop in standards in some Member States.

The European Parliament

83.   The German Socialist MEP Evelyne Gebhardt represented the view of many MEPs by telling us that although legislation is needed in the area of services the Country of Origin Principle is not a common EU principle and that "the present draft threatened employment rights, public healthcare and consumer rights (QQ 430-437). Ms Gebhardt has proposed that an amended services directive should be based on harmonisation and "mutual recognition" (Q 441). Ms Gebhardt's use of the term "mutual recognition" must be distinguished from "mutual acceptance" as she is effectively advocating an internal market in services achieved by means of sector specific legislation (Q 430).

The Council of Ministers

84.   It is also proving difficult to find a consensus in the Council of Ministers on the Country of Origin Principle. The optimism expressed by the Competitiveness Council in March 2004 that "in the services sector, which remains highly fragmented, more competition is required to improve efficiency, increase output and employment and benefit consumers"[33], was diluted by the Council of Ministers a year later in March 2005: "In order to promote growth and employment and to strengthen competitiveness, the internal market in services has to be fully operational while preserving the

---

[33] Presidency Conclusions, Brussels European Council 25 and 26 March 2004.

European social model. In the light of this ongoing debate which shows that the directive as it is currently drafted does not fully meet these requirements, all efforts should be taken in order to secure a broad consensus"[34].

85. Those in the Council and the European Parliament who are most critical of a horizontal approach, fear abandonment of what is often called the "European Social Model"[35]. This term is used in many ways and has a very broad interpretation. The German SPD in its Parliamentary Group's "Initial Evaluation of the Services Directive" argued that the draft directive overlooks wider aims such as employment rights, social protection, environmental standards and economic and social cohesion, which are anchored in the EC Treaty as basic principles. The document concludes that: "the Directive ignores the social dimension (of trade liberalisation)". It has been reported that a similar view is held by leading political figures in France.

86. However, the critics such as the SPD in Germany are challenged by those we spoke to on our visit to Poland. Witnesses told us that after the political act of accession in May 2004, full economic accession of the new Member States would have to follow and that the proposed draft Directive would facilitate this. They argued strongly that Polish suppliers must be allowed to compete economically on an equal basis with providers from the 15 Member States. Our Polish witnesses also questioned the suggestion that their systems of health and safety and regulation of service provision are inferior to those in the "15 Member States". For these reasons they also believe that mutual acceptance in service provision is a better principle than harmonisation.

87. The United Kingdom Government takes the Commission's view that as much of the essential legislation that protects citizens and consumers is already harmonised at European Union level, the Country of Origin Principle is a realistic legal basis for delivering free movement of services on a temporary basis.

Proponents of the Country of Origin Principle

88. The Federation of Small Business (FSB), the Management Consultancies Association, the Association of Building Engineers, the Confederation of British Industry, the Advertising Association, the Royal Institute for Chartered Surveyors and the Institute of Practitioners in Advertising agree with the United Kingdom Government and the Commission that the Country of Origin Principle is a realistic way of increasing trade in services between Member States.

89. Some of our witnesses went further and argued that the Directive would be of little use without the Country of Origin Principle. The Confederation of British Industry (CBI) saw the Country of Origin Principle as a "core component of the proposal" (CBI written evidence) and believed that "failure to achieve agreement on this element of the text can be seen as nothing less than a lack of confidence by Member States and their agents in the fundamental rationale of the European Union, namely that of trust between Member States fostering economic and social progress, and societal prosperity". The Management Consultancies Association agreed with the Confederation of British Industry telling us that they would be very

---

[34] Presidency Conclusions, Brussels Council, 22 and 23 March 2005.

[35] This concept is further explained and dealt with in Chapter 7: Will there be a race to the bottom?

concerned if this "essential underpinning of the draft Directive were to be weakened" (MCA written evidence).

90.   The Federation of Small Businesses (FSB) were strongly in favour of opening up an internal market in services and in reducing restrictive regulations. They pointed out the difficulties caused by harmonisation and argued that one benefit of a horizontal directive was that those businesses that chose only to operate in their own country were not affected by EC legislation. Harmonisation on the other hand, "would mean a change in every Member State and that means it affects businesses in every Member State" (Q 158).

91.   The example the FSB gave was that of a hairdresser. Hairdressers in Germany receive five years training before they can practice their trade independently. In the United Kingdom for example, hairdressers train for a shorter time. By adopting a system of mutual acceptance, a British hairdressing salon which does not wish to expand abroad is not affected by EU law. If the European Union were to harmonise the necessary qualifications of hairdressers across the EU, every hairdressing business would be affected by this decision, whether relevant to their particular situation or not. A path of harmonisation in services, therefore could lead to cross-border European Union trade becoming too burdensome for business. A system based on the Country of Origin Principle would give business more choice and the FSB therefore believes that for the small business community, mutual acceptance would be better.

92.   Some rules for mutual recognition are already in place in the area of services through sector-specific directives. For example, seven professions have agreed training requirements across the EU. This means that as long as they are qualified to work in their own country, doctors, dentists, nurses, midwives, pharmacists, vets and architects have the right to work in any foreign European Union Member State. These sectoral directives have now been superseded by a directive on the mutual recognition of professional qualifications which creates a single, consistent legal framework and extends the scope to all regulated professions[36].

Opponents of the Country of Origin Principle

93.   Others, such as the UK Trades Union Congress (TUC), other unions including Amicus and TGWU and also the RIBA were strongly opposed to the Country of Origin Principle.

94.   The fear expressed by the German Socialists in Berlin and Evelyne Gebhardt in the European Parliament is shared by the UK Trades Union Congress (TUC). The TUC told us that they recognise an internal market in services is an integral part of the European Union common market, but for it to work well markets need to be based on clear rules that promote high standards of trading conduct and acceptable minimum quality standards (Q 89). European Union minimum standards for health and safety, consumer protection and the role of regulators in particular would have to be established before the Country of Origin Principle can be effective as the fundamental principle underpinning the cross-border trade of services on a temporary basis (Q 103). As long as minimum standards of harmonisation

---

[36]   COM(2002)119 amended by COM(2004) 317 and agreed by Council in June 2005.

for these issues had not been established, they should remain subject to individual national standards (TUC, written evidence).

95. Amicus[37] went further, describing the draft directive as impractical and unworkable and even contended that if implemented it would threaten employment and social rights (Amicus written evidence).

96. The RIBA told us the Country of Origin Principle was unrealistic, discriminatory and confusing: "Unrealistic and inoperable—because of the difficulties that would arise in verifying qualifications and other credentials of service providers; discriminatory—because a recipient would, in the case of a problem with a provider, have to seek redress under the laws and in the language of a country that is not their own; and confusing—for consumers. RIBA was also concerned about a large team of workers on a construction project where members could come from more than one country." (Q 275)

97. The TUC told us the Country of Origin Rule should only be applied on a sectoral basis "on a time scale that allows proper discussion and agreement on harmonisation measures and appropriate derogations." It viewed the proposed timetable as very ambitious. (Q 130)

98. The Construction Confederation and others argued that particular activities need to be excluded (derogated) from the Country of Origin Principle. The Commission's draft excludes only electricity, gas and water distribution services and a number of very specific services such as postal services from the Country of Origin Principle.[38] In its written evidence, the Government notes, "there is widespread recognition that the derogations from the principle need further negotiation and the UK has stated its intention to seek changes to the Directive in its response to the (UK) public consultation".

99. The draft Directive also excludes the provisions of the Posted Workers Directive[39] from the Country of Origin Principle. This Directive stipulates that workers that are posted to a Member State other than their own, will be subject to the labour law of the country in which they are employed. Labour law concerning maximum work periods and minimum rest periods minimum paid annual holidays; minimum rates of pay; the conditions of hiring-out of workers and health, safety and hygiene at work will be governed by the Member State in which they are employed.

Health and Safety

100. The most common call from our witnesses for a derogation was health and safety. The Construction Confederation, the Construction Industry Council, the FSB, the General Dental Council, the General Osteopathic Council, the Health and Safety Commission, and the TGWU call for health and safety to be the responsibility of the host Member State.

101. At present EC law sets minimum standards for health and safety. As the Minister told us: "there is a EU framework directive on health and safety standards, plus a range of sectoral directives that impact on the issue of health and safety"(Q 486). This allows Member States to legislate at the EU level or higher if they wish to do so. It should be noted that the transitional

---

[37] The UK's largest manufacturing, technical and skilled persons' trade union .

[38] Art 17 of the draft Directive on Services in the Internal Market

[39] Directive 96/71/EC

arrangements granted in the field of health and safety to a number of the newly-acceded Member States expire on or before 1 January 2006. Therefore, by the time the Services Directive is likely to be in operation all Member States will have to enforce agreed European Union-wide minimum standards of health and safety.

102. A number of our witnesses argued that despite the European Union–wide application of these minimum European Union standards, health and safety matters should be excluded from the application of the Country of Origin Principle. They argue that because the United Kingdom has well developed health and safety regulation that goes further than the required European Union minimum, temporary service providers may not be as rigorous in the application of health and safety standards as domestic United Kingdom legislation requires. The UK Trades Union Congress (TUC) argues that "a full derogation for all health and safety requirements must be made absolutely explicit in the Directive itself."

103. If health and safety is to come under the Country of Origin Principle, the Trades Union Congress (TUC) argues that other sector-specific derogations are necessary on health and safety grounds. The TUC argued for derogations in the areas of "healthcare, care and social services, transport services, construction and environmental regulation".

104. The Trades Union Congress is not alone in calling for the construction sector to be excluded from the Country of Origin Principle on health and safety grounds. RIBA and the TGWU agree. It appears that they believe that the European Union *acquis* standards on health and safety are not high enough.

105. AURE (Alliance of UK Health Regulators on Europe), the General Dental Council and the General Osteopathic Council wish all healthcare *professions* to be exempted from the Country of Origin Principle, on the grounds that healthcare providers from outside the UK constitute a potential risk to patients.

106. We believe that the Country of Origin Principle is a realistic legal base for temporary service provision in any Member State.

107. We are not convinced that health and safety should be exempted from the Country of Origin Principle. We agree with the Government "that concerns in this area are not as justified as some of the commentary would suggest" (Q 495). EC legislation sets minimum standards acceptable to all 25 Member States, with which temporary service providers from all Member States must comply.

108. We are also not convinced by those in the European Parliament, the European Council or the Trade Unions who argue that the draft Directive threatens employment rights, public healthcare, consumer rights and health and safety. There are specific derogations included in the draft Directive which address these concerns (see chapter 7). We find the argument that the new Member States should be able to compete freely with the "the 15 Member States" a powerful one.

109. A horizontal Directive based on the Country of Origin Principle combines ease of access for service providers, without imposing over-complex rules. We accordingly wholly endorse this approach.

110. We acknowledge that UK legislation on health and safety sets a higher standard than that required by EC legislation, but we do not see many instances in which this could cause serious concern. We conclude this because all employees of service providers established in the UK are bound by UK legislation on health and safety. Those employees who have been posted to the UK from another Member State to provide services on a temporary basis also are subject to UK standards of Health and Safety as a result of the derogation of the Posted Workers Directive from the Country of Origin Principle.

111. For the same reason, we urge the Government to resist any attempt to exclude specific service sectors from the Country of Origin Principle.

112. We believe that the economic benefits from applying the Country of Origin Principle temporary service provision as set out in the Commission's draft Directive are greater than the threat to UK health and safety standards. In particular SMEs will benefit from the application of the Country of Origin Principle which will enable them to effectively test the water in another Member State on a temporary basis, without having to fully commit to permanent establishment. We agree with the Government that this could make a vital contribution to opening up fully the European market in this area.

CHAPTER 6: CONSUMER PROTECTION

113. Concern about the Country of Origin Principle also focussed on consumer protection.

114. In broad economic terms consumers fall into two categories, final consumers (businesses, individuals or households) and intermediate consumers (businesses). As Which? pointed out, the difficulty with purchase from a non-home Member State company is that redress in the case where something goes wrong may be complicated.

115. There are a number of possible complications which witnesses raised. The first is the possibility that the company cannot be traced for the purposes of redress related to consumer protection. This could be exacerbated if the service provider is from another country. A second concern raised by our witnesses was that the contract under which the temporary service was provided could be in law with which the consumer is unfamiliar. A third possible problem could be that the supplier is not aware of standards which apply in the Member State where the service is provided, so provision is made in good faith, but is inappropriate. The first of these points is an issue that needs to be addressed in the services Directive. The second and third we find unjustified.

116. Clifford Chance argued that with regard to individual consumers, "the concern about UK law not applying is largely misplaced" because the draft Directive includes a specific derogation from the Country of Origin Principle related to consumer contracts. Clifford Chance also told us that "if a foreign service provider is dealing with a consumer, it will always be the host country's consumer rules that apply" (Q 557).

117. Clifford Chance added: "the only practical difficulty would be if you sue in your own country and you get judgment in your own country, under the Brussels Convention you have to enforce it in the other Member State where the person is established". The lawyers contended that in that case "the Services Directive will help because it will require professional indemnity insurance for services, so ultimately there should be somebody to pick up the tab" (Q 584).

118. Which? agreed with Clifford Chance that there is no need for concern about a possible lowering of standards in consumer protection, but did point out that consumers prefer to buy services from local providers because "most consumers will be poorly placed to assess the consumer protection regimes of other Member States", Which? went on to say that surveys show that UK consumers are not yet confident about using services from other Member States (Which? written evidence).

119. Where services are purchased by a firm, then a different derogation to the Country of Origin Principle, (Article 17(20)) is applied, giving parties from any Member State, freedom to choose the law applicable to their contract. Here it is likely that, for example, a master contractor would insist on concluding contracts in a single law with which they were familiar.

120. Awareness of standards should not be an issue in cases where temporary provision of professional services is concerned. This is because the Services Directive derogates to the Directive on the Mutual Recognition of Professional Qualifications. This Directive was agreed at the beginning of

June 2005 and consolidates, simplifies and rationalises the rules on recognition by incorporating a number of existing Directives into one. The Mutual Recognition of Professional Qualification relates to doctors, nurses, dentists, veterinary surgeons, midwives, pharmacists and architects.

121. Mutual Recognition of Professional Qualifications applies to anyone wishing to pursue a regulated profession (by law or administrative provision), in a Member State other than that in which they obtained their professional qualifications. Where there is no exact correspondence between the qualification required in the Member State of origin and that in the host Member State, migrants will be required to complete an adaptation period or an aptitude test. Service providers who wish to work in the health sector of a host Member State are required to register with the competent professional organisation of the host Member State. In the UK such checks include service provision in the areas of child care, social care, veterinary and gas installation.

122. In the UK the question of standards in those services that do not fall under the Mutual Recognition of Professional Qualifications Directive should not be an issue of concern. This is because the UK does not have systems of national or local standards applying to all providers of services. For instance, a plumber in the UK can choose to register with the Council for Registered Gas Installers (CORGI), but CORGI registration is not a prerequisite for providing non-gas plumbing services in the UK. This is not the case in all Member States. In Germany for example, a hairdresser must have a master hairdressing qualification to practice his or her trade. In the UK anyone is free to set up as a hairdresser although the business will have to provide a good service at good value if it is to succeed.

123. We conclude that although consumers should, as with all purchases, exercise due caution in their choice of supplier, consumers are unlikely to be the victim of suppliers as a particular result of their operating under the Country of Origin Principle.

Professional Indemnity Insurance

124. We are persuaded that there are a number of issues regarding professional indemnity insurance that need to be addressed in the draft Directive. These relate both to the market for such insurance and to ascertaining that a supplier has it. Indeed, somewhat surprisingly, the Association of British Insurers (written evidence) questions whether insurance should be insisted upon at all.

125. The professional indemnity insurance brokers Griffiths and Armour Professional Risks told us that: "there will need to be statutory limits on liability for those particular risks to ensure that all the liability arising is covered within the cover of the PII policy[40] of the service provider. This is to be applauded but it has to be recognised that such a cap is not the custom and practice of purchasers in the various Member States."

126. As we understand it, insurance requirements (often statutory), for practicing various professional activities differ significantly across Member States. Insurers are well able to provide insurance in their own country, but may be unfamiliar with the risks faced in other States and perhaps unwilling to

---

[40] PII = professional indemnity insurance.

provide cover. To some extent, we can expect the insurance market to develop naturally in order to respond to this need, just as Lloyds of London became used to insuring a wide variety of risks in various places. Indeed, insurance is also a service that one may envisage being traded across borders (although as a financial service, is itself excluded from the draft Directive).

127. This issue is taken up by the Federation of Small Business and the RIBA, in written evidence, that extra costs and difficulties may ensue. We have not had opportunity to test this issue in detailed questioning of witnesses, except in the case of Clifford Chance, who "do not think we have had any difficulty in securing cover for practising in those different jurisdictions." (Q 558).

128. On the question of finding out whether a supplier has appropriate insurance, the following passage from Clifford Chance is relevant: "One good thing which the Services Directive would do is this provision about professional indemnity insurance under Article 27. This is where the services provided pose a particular risk to the health and safety of the recipient or a financial risk to the recipient and in that situation the Member State shall ensure that the service provider is covered by professional indemnity insurance or some other equivalent. I am not quite sure how a Member State is going to be able to ensure all cross border service providers are actually covered but that is what the Directive says." (Q 590).

129. We also welcome this. In our opinion, there are two essential requirements. First (to the extent this is not true already), all Member States need to have in place some minimum set of regulations on professional indemnity insurance that inspires confidence. Second, Member States should not require of a supplier operating temporarily inside its borders a *separate* insurance pertaining to that Member State, if the supplier can demonstrate that its insurance *satisfies the requirements* of that Member State.

130. Consumer protection by extension relates also to third party effects. This is the province of Private International Law and is an important issue. Suppose a contractor in the United Kingdom engages a self-employed plumber from another Member State to work on a contract. Whilst engaged in the task, the plumber drops a tool from some height which lands on a passer-by, causing injury. On this point, Article 17 (23) excludes "the non-contractual liability of a provider in the case of an accident involving a person and occurring as a consequence of the service provider's activities in the Member State to which he has moved temporarily", from the Country of Origin Principle. In other words, in this case the answer is clear: the passer-by can pursue the self-employed plumber under United Kingdom law, subject to any changes that might be introduced by Rome II.

131. More generally, the position is not entirely clear, as the DTI notes in its supplementary written evidence on the link between the Services Directive, Rome I and Rome II sets out. There is, as currently drafted, some difference on private international law between the SD and Rome II. Rome II "provides a general rule that the law of the country in which the damage arises or is likely to arise shall apply. This differs from the proposed Services Directive, which aims to use the country of origin principle to determine the applicable law in all cases of non-contractual liability, except in cases involving accidents caused by services providers that temporarily provide a service in another Member State (Article 17(23))." (DTI supplementary written evidence).

132. We conclude that there are several issues arising in respect of insurance for temporary operation that need some clarification, but we do not believe any of these will prove insuperable.

CHAPTER 7: WILL THERE BE A "RACE TO THE BOTTOM"?

133. "In its current form the draft Services Directive is impractical, dangerous and certainly unworkable and is an invitation for abuse and manipulation and threatens to undermine the European Social Model". This is the evaluation that Amicus gave us in written evidence to this inquiry.

134. The view held by Amicus sums up widespread concern that has made the draft Services Directive a hotly debated subject in Brussels and in Member States. It is difficult to define clearly what is meant by the "European Social Model". The term is used by many with different meanings. As the Minister, Mr Douglas Alexander told us: "one of the points that emerges when discussions take place on the European Social Model is that it is more often discussed than defined" (Q 486).

135. Jacques Delors, the former Commission President speaking before the French referendum on the EU Constitutional Treaty used the term in the following way: "there is a European Social Model in the sense that we refuse the triumphant individualism of some and the excessive oppression of society in others". He went on to say "But we have a Scandinavian model, a Blairist model, a German model, and the French state model. Each one has its own system which guards its diversity."[41] This illustrates the vague definition of the term. Most often it appears to relate to a relatively liberal market economy with strong social norms embedded within it. Most Europeans could sign up to the broad concept. It is the balance and relationship between the liberal market economy and the extent and means of achieving social objectives that brings differences of judgement.

136. Interestingly, the first three proposed amendments to the draft Directive proposed by the European Parliament Committee Report of May 2005 all refer to "preserving" or "upholding the European social model" without defining that term or in what ways the draft Directive impacts upon it. Discussions on the draft Directive have become caught up in wider political debates to the detriment of the belief in an open, single market in the European Union.

137. It is clear from this that the draft Directive has exposed grave concerns, that often reach well beyond its scope, about the state of the European Union and its future as a Union of 25 Member States. The concern most often expressed, is that if the new Member States can compete on an equal economic basis without applying the often higher social security norms of the "15", they will undermine further the foundations of the welfare state as it exists in most of the "15". The critics of the draft Directive, like Amicus, argue that the principles of Country of Origin and of Mutual Acceptance will mean that the lowest level of pay and social protection will become the norm.

138. This chapter analyses these concerns and concludes that they have been exaggerated.

Employment Rights

139. To analyse and dispel the concern that the Services Directive will cause a "race to the bottom", it is necessary first to consider the relationship between

---

[41] Reported in the Financial Times, 25 May 2005.

the draft Directive and the application of the Posting of Workers Directive which was agreed in 1996. For, as will be shown, the Services Directive establishes a complex relationship between it and the Posting of Workers Directive. It is possible that it is the application of the Posting of Workers Directive, rather than the Services Directive, which is the true target of much of the criticism.

140. The Posting of Workers Directive[42] requires that if a worker is posted temporarily to another Member State (the host Member State) by his or her employer, the terms of that employment will be the minimum terms and conditions in the host Member State. The purpose of this Directive is that any foreign EU worker is bound by the employment laws where the work is carried out, even if the employment conditions in his/her own country are less stringent. The DTI defines a posted worker as: "one who, for a limited period, carries out his work in the territory of a European Community Member State other than the State in which he normally works."[43]

141. The draft Services Directive derogates to the Posting of Workers Directive in respect of the Country of Origin Principle under Article 17 (5). That is to say, the draft Directive is only relevant for services provided temporarily by those who are not employed by others, i.e. self employed persons. We return to this matter later.

142. Since the Posting of Workers Directive covers employment rights such as statutory minimum rates of pay, maximum hours of work, health and safety, non-discrimination and other well established employment rights, posted workers automatically benefit from host country conditions for the time that they work in the host Member State.[44] Workers from a different Member State working in the UK would therefore be bound by the UK rate of minimum wage, European law on working time[45] and UK non-discrimination law.

143. The only way therefore that workers from a different Member State would be able to undercut host country workers is if it were customary for employment to be provided on more generous terms than the legal minimum. In the United Kingdom, there are some examples of such collective agreements that offer better employment conditions than the minimum required and which are not legally binding agreements.

144. In those Member States where some of the above employment measures are not in place some undercutting of the host market is more likely. Our witnesses in Germany provided us with an example: Germany has no legally binding national minimum wage, instead minimum rates of payment are agreed collectively across sectors. Thus it becomes more likely that a workforce posted to Germany which is not subject to the national collective agreement that exists for German workers, is able to undercut the German workforce by being cheaper by the hour. However, this is not a legitimate criticism of the Services Directive, but rather of the Posting of Workers

---

[42] Directive 96/71/EC

[43] www.dti.gov.uk/er/directive.htm

[44] It may be that an unscrupulous employer would seek not to provide even the statutory provision, but such an employer would be proceeding illegally in any case.

[45] The European Working Time Directive, 93/104/EC which stipulates a maximum week of 48 hours on average calculated over six months.

Directive which fails to address the particularity of the German system of establishing employment rights.

145. In its written evidence, the Transport and General Workers Union (TGWU) raises a number of other employment rights relating to such matters as unfair dismissal, redundancy, trade union related protections as well as others, that it asserts would be undermined by the Services Directive. As the preceding paragraphs illustrate, these rights are not threatened by the Services Directive. Moreover, as we have seen with "offshore" call centres, service providers can move such activities around the globe with or without the Services Directive and may well continue to do so if they feel employment costs in the EU become too high. It is important to bear in mind the main aim of the Services Directive which is to make the EU more competitive. As Mr Joyce of the Architects' Council told us, "a number of the efficiencies that could be delivered to this sector would give the European construction sector an edge in a global marketplace and in the context of WTO—I do not wish to complicate the debate, but if we are more competitive, we get more contracts" (Q 233).

146. We do not believe the TGWU's concern is justified. The Services Directive would not change the present situation for posted workers in the UK or any other Member State where statutory minimum employment standards are set. Just as now, under the Directive there would be some workers employed with collective agreements above the statutory minimum and others who were not and were therefore cheaper to employ.

147. As we have already mentioned, the Services Directive and the position of self-employed persons is complex and must be further analysed. Self employed persons working for consumers directly are subject to the derogation from Country of Origin Principle in Article 17 (21). This means that they provide services under UK law in the UK. It is therefore only those who take on self-employed businesses providing a service for a business customer in a different Member State that they come under the aegis of the Country of Origin Principle. In this situation the Services Directive stipulates that the parties can then choose the law applicable to their contract. **We are aware that the Government wishes to raise points of detail on the current draft of the Services Directive in this particular area, but we are hopeful that a satisfactory compromise can be reached by the Government on this particular matter.**

Environmental Standards

148. It is argued that a race for the bottom can take on other forms such as environmental standards. However, we see no grounds for concern in this area, since these are covered by an extensive body of EU legislation, the Acquis Communitaire, with which all Member States must comply.

Web of Contracts

149. Another concern that was raised during our inquiry was that of a web of contracts. In the construction industry, particular projects often may involve a number of groups of workers which are each covered by their own contract. It is clear that costly difficulties may arise if the law of a number of Member States can be invoked in relation to particular parts of a big construction contract. Therefore, from the limited evidence that we received on this point, we would assume that the lead contractor would choose the law applicable

and that this law would cover the entire series of contracts that make up the construction project.

Quality Assurance

150. During our inquiry we were confronted with an attitude of natural patriotism from many of our witnesses who appeared to view other countries' service providers with some suspicion. On the face of it, this tendency could be mistaken for a belief that other Member States could not offer the same quality service as a national provider, but when probed it often came down to uncertainty due to different national approaches to the regulation of services and who may provide them. Each Member State has a different historical tradition and preserves aspects of that in relation to the legal framework relating to service provision. The main difference between Member States which we discerned was between approaches to quality assurance.

151. In general the UK Government takes a relaxed or consumer-focussed approach to the issue of quality assurance. Except in the professions and special cases such as gasfitters, the UK Government are content to allow consumers to determine quality. So for instance, in the United Kingdom it is not necessary to have a relevant qualification to set up in business as a hairdresser. The UK's approach to quality assurance in this case would be that if in fact the hairdresser knows little of hairdressing, it is likely that their haircuts will be of poor quality and the salon is unlikely to prosper.

152. By contrast in Germany, a hairdresser must, in order to call themselves a Friseur (hairdresser), have had an extensive training. Therefore, it is relatively unlikely that a poor haircut will be sold, but the price may be higher (this effect may apply particularly in professions where training requirements severely restrict entry). There is of course no necessary link between the higher price and better quality of the haircut, and the UK Government are content to let the consumer decide which hairdresser to patronise. The Institute for Chartered Surveyors made a similar point with regard to the service provision of architects: "A more liberalised market such as already exists in the UK and Ireland will not lead to a lowering of standards or put the public interest at risk. It is clear, for example, that buildings in the UK and Ireland are no less safe than those designed, constructed and maintained elsewhere in the EU." (RICS)

153. Mr Bretz of Clifford Chance reinforced this point: "Once you have a free trade area such as the European Union and you have case law of the European Court of Justice that provides for the free movement of services, it is inevitable for an unregulated service to be provided on the basis of country of origin and therefore there will be a trade-off between the price and the quality of the service" (Q 565). He then went on to say: "The whole concept underlying the free movement of unregulated services is that you will increase welfare ultimately by allowing ... more service providers to provide services at different price levels. There may be variations in quality".

154. We believe the trade-off as Mr Bretz describes it above is clear. Under the draft Services Directive, the consumer will be allowed more choice and entry in the market is made easier, which is likely to drive the cost of services down.

155. We understand that some Member States are concerned that an internal market in services may require changes to certain local, regional, or national

systems of service providers, but it may prove an inevitable concession to consumer pressure for change towards greater choice. It must not be assumed that a cheaper service can be equated with an inferior service. Just as with goods, the Which? Best Buy is not necessarily the most expensive.

156. As we argued in Chapter 4, it must be recognised that professionals also employ arguments about quality to limit others from entering into their professional activity. This is understandable since they have spent time and effort training for the activity and desire a return on that training. Therefore we must be alert to the difference between genuine concerns about quality and concerns about the economic interests of particular groups.

157. There is a clear difference between disallowing those who are not adequately trained from engaging in a particular activity and disallowing all those who do not possess a particular title from engaging in that activity. This was a point made to us forcibly by the Chartered Surveyors who told us that a RICS building surveyor in the UK and Ireland can design buildings, whereas in many other Member States this would need to be done by a professional qualified as an architect. A further example illustrating this difference is that in Greece 80% of roads are built by appropriately qualified surveyors, whereas in most other Member States a road builder would be expected to be qualified as a civil engineer (Q 246).

158. The Chartered Surveyors went on to say that in a number of EU countries professionally qualified and highly experienced RICS valuers are unable to provide their valuation services for bank lending, insurance and financial reporting because these activities are reserved for those who hold the title of architect. Removing such monopolies will bring greater competition in the professions and so lead to better choice and value for clients, as well as a more efficient internal market. **We agree that such obstacles to an internal market in services do little to help purchasers and removing them will lead to the EU becoming more competitive.**

"Brass Plating"

159. A final concern about a mechanism by which there might be a "race for the bottom" is if companies decided to move to a regime with the least onerous controls and with the least effective surveillance in order then to operate under the Country of Origin Principle in Member States with more restrictive regulatory systems.

160. The Government response to this question was that much of the legislation that protects European Union citizens either as employees or as consumers is already harmonised at some level within the European Union. Consequently, service providers will be bound by this legislation regardless of which Member State they are established in. Those Member States who have recently joined the European Union are committed to implementing all current European Union legislation. The Government went on to argue that all Member States have an interest in maintaining high standards of domestic legislation to protect their own consumers and workers. For these reasons there is little or no prospect of a movement to reduce standards amongst Member States, all of which must meet at least the standards required by the Acquis Communitaire.

161. The draft directive safeguards against the possibility of businesses opening a "letterbox", "post-box" or "brass plate" in a Member State where some aspects of the regulatory environment were perceived as advantageous as an "established" base from which then to operate on a temporary basis in other Member States under the directive. The Directive makes it clear that it will not be sufficient for a business to register a "post box" in one Member State to qualify as established there. Businesses must be carrying out genuine economic activity in the Member State in question.

162. One extreme form of this would be brass-plating whereby companies abuse the fundamental freedoms in the EC Treaty and therefore look at the practicality of introducing a provision on the "evasion of home country legislation". According to the Government such a provision would stop service providers from setting up in another Member State with the primary objective of offering services back to their home Member State thereby avoiding home Member State legislation. This proposal is based on a similar provision included in the E-commerce Directive agreed in 2001.

163. Subject to this provision proposed by the UK Government, we accept their reassurance on this issue.

164. It must be remembered also that the country of origin basis of business operations does not apply to more permanent, established operations in a country. The Country of Origin Principle is largely to the benefit of small, self employed businesses looking to explore and break into new markets. Larger businesses will, as before, operate substantially on an established basis. For them, it is the sections of the directive dealing with simplification of establishment and creating a level playing field for all established businesses with a Member State that will benefit them.

165. In summary, our arguments reject the contention that the draft Services Directive would lead to a race to the bottom. In particular, we do not accept the implicit argument of many critics of the draft Directive that competition in service provision on the basis of temporary operation under the Country of Origin Principle inevitably undermines the "European Social Model", or indeed the way of life of any particular Member State.

CHAPTER 8: CONFIDENCE BUILDING MEASURES AND SURVEILLANCE

166. Clearly, for some people, or in some circumstances, choosing a supplier who comes from another Member State will be a matter of concern. Just as with any new choice, for example choosing a new domestic electricity supplier in the circumstance where you have never previously had that choice (or never exercised it), consumers may be wary. A few scare stories in the press may be enough to dissuade others from trying out new suppliers in this way. The same may well operate for businesses also (as in the famous adage "No one ever got fired for choosing IBM"). Unnecessary caution could stifle the growth in cross-border supply of services.

167. It should also be borne in mind that no-one will be forced to buy services from a business established in another Member State but providing its services on a temporary basis in another Member State. It will be a matter of consumer choice for the consumer. Such service providers will inevitably have to work harder to persuade customers that it offers a good quality, reliable service and value for money. Critics of the draft Directive sometimes appear to give neither consumers or service providers too much credit for rational behaviour and enterprise.

168. Problems might arise in the area of poor work, or inadequate safety procedures or even simple lack of knowledge. What does the draft Directive propose in order to address such problems?

169. Article 26 deals with information provision to service recipients. Member States are charged with making information available on name, address, registration and authorisation particulars, professional titles, VAT registration, etc. The information may be supplied by the provider, or through other means. The Member State is also required to ensure that some details, such as service features, price, etc are also supplied. Articles 27 and 28 relate to professional insurance, guarantees and after-sales guarantees. Where particular risks to health or safety arise, Member States are required to ensure that providers are covered by professional indemnity insurance.

170. As regards quality, "Member States shall, ... take accompanying measures to encourage providers to take action on a voluntary basis in order to ensure the quality of service provision ..." (Article 31). Member States are also enjoined to give each other mutual assistance in respect of points of contact, speedy supply of requested information, confirmation that a supplier is established and exercising its activities in a lawful manner, etc. (Article 35). In particular it should be noted that Member States are responsible for supervising their suppliers who are operating temporarily in another Member State under the Country of Origin Principle.

171. Nevertheless, significant concerns remain. In evidence, whilst some welcomed the idea of "single points of contact", several were concerned that the proposal would become an additional tier of bureaucracy, complicating the administrative procedures. There was significant concern that there would be no, or inadequate, supervision of enterprises operating in another Member State on a temporary basis, and further that this would have an impact upon high quality suppliers who would be tarred with the brush of "cowboy" operators.

172. We put these concerns to the Minister. We asked "how you currently think the Mutual Assistance Framework would work". The Minister's response emphasised the preliminary nature of the Commission's thinking on this subject, along with the need to ensure that any solution did not lead to more bureaucracy. He also pointed to the SOLVIT tool[46], something raised by others, in particular Mr Harbour (Q 424) in discussion. The Minister asserted that "the information necessary [for provision of Mutual Assistance by the UK] largely exists within the Government or regulatory sphere ..." (DTI supplementary written evidence).

173. We further enquired as to how the UK Government would know whether and when a UK-established business is undertaking "temporary" activities in another Member State. The evidence that we received on this point was not sufficiently specific to allow us to understand fully how the UK Government planned to address this issue (DTI supplementary written evidence).

174. The United Kingdom may be less prepared in this area than other Member States, by nature of the general business surveillance regime. In Member States where there is considerable regulation of service activity and providers, regulatory authorities are likely to have a clear picture of the set of providers and some further information about, or at least indicators of, their competency. In such Member States, the problem may be more the consolidation and simplification of this information where it is requested in different ways across various levels of bureaucracy (central, local, etc), so as to comply with the "single point of contact" requirement.

175. In the United Kingdom, for better or worse, a less regulated regime operates. No Governmental body (we believe) keeps a list of hairdressers or plumbers, for example[47]. If this is so, a response coming from another Member State as to a particular operator engaging in hairdressing there on a temporary basis may find limited information is forthcoming from the Single Point of Contact or from a mutual assistance provision (the DTI?) in the UK. Much depends upon how these matters are organised and much will need to be done to support UK SMEs seeking to export their services within the EU. **We are doubtful that the changes the United Kingdom may need to make in registering or providing information on service businesses that wish to trade in other Member States on a temporary basis has been fully grasped.**

176. More generally, it is clear to us that the mechanism of Mutual Assistance at present lacks an incentive structure on Member States that would make it work effectively and swiftly. If the Service Directive is to have an impact, it is necessary that greater attention is paid to these important issues of confidence-building.

177. In this respect, we welcome the concern of the Committee on the Internal Market and Consumer Protection of the European Market (e.g. Recital 38) to ensure that adequate supervision of service providers is effected. However, we are at the same time anxious to avoid issues of over-regulation and of possible bias against providers from another Member State. Therefore, it is not clear to us that their proposed solution of supervision by the country of destination is necessarily the best approach.

---

[46] http://europa.eu.int/solvit/site/index_en.htm

[47] Of course, CORGI has a list of plumbers authorised to do gas-fitting. But there are many non-CORGI providers of plumbing services.

178. More generally, we view this area as one of the rather under-explored aspects of the draft Directive.

CHAPTER 9: SUMMARY AND RECOMMENDATIONS

179. The draft Directive has met with strong expressions of support but also of concern, even opposition. On balance we regard the draft Services Directive as a bold attempt on the part of the Commission to make a reality of a freely accessible single market in services. We believe that many of the concerns and criticisms are not well founded. Some are based on a misunderstanding of the draft directive; some are based on concerns about the impact of change and freer markets upon established interests.

180. We recognise that the draft Directive has come under discussion at a time when agreement on the benefits of a single market has been overshadowed by relatively high levels of unemployment in some Member States, by the additional pressures for economic restructuring as 10 new Member States joined the European Union and by the discussions on the European Union Constitutional Treaty. These circumstances and associated pressures appear to us to have strengthened voices resisting change and increased market flexibility and competition. **We believe that these circumstances make it all the more important for the European Union to be bold and resolute in its embrace of the single market. Creating a competitive, single market in services offers significant benefits of choice, price and innovation for consumers and business users of service industries. Competition and innovation brings change, with winners and losers, but the experience of the single market in goods demonstrates the overall benefits that can be achieved.**

A horizontal framework Directive

181. We agree with the Commission that these matters should be pursued through a horizontal framework directive based upon the country of origin approach rather than a detailed vertical, service industry by service industry sector approach. The Commission told us in their oral evidence that they could not harmonise across a large number of service sectors, "It would be time consuming and would probably be impossible. Also we believe that it would not be desirable... Notions like subsidiarity, over-regulation and over-harmonisation have become much more important" (Q 443).

182. We believe the most powerful argument for a horizontal framework directive on an internal market in services is the length of time it took to achieve the legislative basis for an internal market in goods. **We see a clear danger in the sector-by-sector harmonisation of regulations route that negotiations will become bogged down for many years.**

183. We believe that EC legislation to facilitate an Internal Market in services must rely on a horizontal approach and cannot be based on stringent, sector-by-sector harmonised rules. Hence we agree with the Commission's approach. If the European Union is to achieve the (revised) Lisbon goal of greater economic growth with more and better jobs by 2010, a horizontal directive will be the only way of reaping the full benefits of an internal market in services.

Freedom to provide services

184. Commitment to the process can be stalled in more than one way. It can be done by blocking moves such as the draft Directive. But equally, stalling can

be effected by agreeing with the principles then hedging them around with so much bureaucracy and red tape that they become unworkable. **We believe that if the harmonisation approach were accepted, the whole process would grind to an expensive halt. We also take the view that mutual recognition rather than mutual acceptance should be viewed with suspicion as being not sufficiently flexible.**

185. There is controversy about the concept of freedom for a business to provide services, in effect on a temporary basis, in a Member State other than its own rather than as a business established in a second or more Member States. The Commission and others saw this as an important, indeed vital, element in increasing market opportunity for SME service providers, widening choice for consumers and strengthening the pressures of competition in services industries across the European Union. We agree with them.

186. The freedom to provide services on a temporary basis throughout the European Union, exists now and has been upheld in rulings by the European Court of Justice. Some proposals, including those within the latest European Parliament[48] Committee Report, appear to us likely to reduce the freedom to provide services on a temporary basis and to increase the complexities involved in such business activities. **Nothing should be done through this Directive, as eventually amended and agreed, that diminishes in any way the existing legal freedom to provide services. Rather, the aim should be to simplify and strengthen that freedom.**

187. There is a degree of doubt about the meaning of "temporary" business operations as opposed to those based upon "establishment" within a Member State. Small and Medium-sized Enterprises in particular find the legal uncertainty created by the lack of a positive definition of temporary operation a major barrier to exploring entry to a market.

Country of Origin Principle

188. Some witnesses would prefer a positive definition of "temporary". On the other hand, it is possible that producing a clear definition of "temporary" could itself introduce inflexibilities in the marketplace. At the moment the position appears to place the onus on the relevant authorities to justify the need for a business to become "established" in a Member State. Producing a clear definition of "temporary" could result in a business being required to prove that its operations are "temporary" otherwise the presumption is that it will need to become "established" in the Member State. There is a fine balance to draw here if the objective is to secure maximum market flexibility. **If establishing a positive definition of "temporary" remains elusive, we recommend a set of clear guidelines is established in order to ensure that freedom to provide services on a temporary basis is made more predictable and involves fewer obstacles.**

189. The freedom to provide services on a temporary business basis is linked in the draft directive, rightly in our view, with the proposal that such operations should be on the basis of the Country of Origin Principle. Larger companies can often afford to devote substantial resources to exploring new markets and can face the costs of more permanent, established operations in other

---

[48] *Draft Report of the European Parliament's Internal Market and Consumer Protection Committee on the Proposal for a directive of the European Parliament and of the Council on Services in the Internal Market.* Rapporteur: Evelyne Gebhardt (25 May 2005)

Member States than simply their local or their national markets. **The Country of Origin Principle is, in our view, an essential part of enabling SME service providers to break into the markets of other Member States. We agree that the option of temporary operations is especially important for SMEs that need to be convinced that they can start offering their services on a broader scale.**

190. A horizontal Directive based on the Country of Origin Principle combines ease of access for service providers, without imposing over-complex rules. We accordingly wholly endorse this approach.

191. We believe that the Country of Origin Principle is a realistic legal base for temporary service provision in any Member State. The Commission told us, "the starting point should be that Member States accept that, give or take a couple of exceptions, their legislative regimes are basically comparable and do not subject their citizens to unreasonable risks. Full harmonisation prior to free movement is therefore not required." (Q 434). We agree with this judgement and believe that some concerns about the country of origin principle are based on a suspicion, often vaguely expressed, of the standards that apply to business operations in other Member States.

192. Some of those doubts stem, we believe, from a basic opposition to the very notion of business operating on a temporary basis in a Member State other than their own. The most recent report of the European Parliament Committee[49] appears to suggest that service businesses should be able to operate on either a temporary or established basis in other Member States but the practical effect of their proposals comes very near to requiring all business to operate on the equivalent of an established basis.

193. Some express opposition to the Country of Origin Principle because there is a degree of confusion, as the Commission admitted to us "as to exactly what is the law applicable to certain situations covered by the directive" (Q 442). When do the laws and regulations of the "host" Member State apply and what does that mean for SMEs operating in other Member States and for users of their services in those "host" countries? When do those of the "country of origin" apply and how do SMEs and users of their services know this? What are the practical implications for consumer rights and consumer protection, employee's rights and conditions, and for health and safety at work and in relation to service delivery?

194. Our enquiry spent some time examining these issues. We found that many concerns can be answered. In other cases there remains doubt.

195. Many issues that were raised appeared to us to stem from attitudes of protectionism rather than a concern that the market mechanism should work well across Member States. Still other concerns referred to a threat to "the European social model". Interestingly, the first three proposed amendments to the directive proposed by the European Parliament Committee Report of May 2005 all refer to "preserving" or "upholding the European social model" without defining that term or explaining in what ways the draft directive impacts upon it. Discussions on the directive have become caught

---

[49] *Draft Report of the European Parliament's Internal Market and Consumer Protection Committee on the Proposal for a directive of the European Parliament and of the Council on Services in the Internal Market.* Rapporteur: Evelyne Gebhardt (25 May 2005)

up in wider political debates to the detriment of the belief in an open, single market in the European Union.

Health and safety issues

196. We are not convinced by those in the European Parliament, the Council of Ministers or the Trade Unions who argue that the Directive threatens employment rights, public healthcare, consumer rights and health and safety. There are specific derogations included in the directive which address these concerns (see Chapter 7). We find the argument that the new Member States should be able to compete freely with the "15 Member States" a powerful one.

197. Perhaps the concern that gathered most support related to health and safety where businesses are operating under the freedom to provide services. We remain in some doubt on the validity of this concern. Trade unions and the UK Health and Safety Executive expressed concerns on this. Many of these concerns are met by the Posting of Workers Directive. The only outstanding area is the operations of self-employed service businesses under the Country of Origin Principle.

198. We acknowledge that legislation on health and safety in the United Kingdom and a number of other Member States sets a higher standard than that required by European Union legislation (under the aquis communitaire), but we do not see many instances in which this could cause serious concern. **We conclude this because all employees of established service providers in the United Kingdom, for example, are bound by United Kingdom legislation on health and safety. Those employees who have been posted to the United Kingdom from another Member State to provide services on a temporary basis also are subject to United Kingdom standards of Health and Safety as a result of the derogation of the Posted Workers Directive from the Country of Origin Principle.**

199. For the same reason, we urge the Government to resist any attempt to exclude specific service sectors from the Country of Origin Principle.

200. We are not convinced that health and safety should be exempted from the Country of Origin Principle. We agree with the Government "that concerns in this area are not as justified as some of the commentary would suggest" (Q 495). European Union legislation sets minimum standards with which temporary service providers from all Member States must comply. **If the Government were to seek derogation from the directive for all health and safety issues they should make clear on what basis they do so. Does the Government believe that there are important loopholes in the Directive and that Health and Safety is not adequately covered? We found little evidence of the latter during our inquiry.**

201. We believe that the economic benefits from applying the Country of Origin Principle to temporary service provision as set out in the Commission's draft Directive are greater than the threat to United Kingdom health and safety standards. In particular SMEs will benefit from the application of the Country of Origin Principle which will enable them to test the market effectively in another Member State on a temporary basis, without having to commit fully to permanent establishment. We agree with the Government that this could make a vital contribution to full opening up of the European Union market in this area.

"Social dumping"?

202. The Posting of Workers Directive largely deals with the fears expressed either of "social dumping" or of "a race to the bottom". We think there are safeguards built into the draft Directive and the Posting of Workers Directive that significantly reduce these concerns as far as employed workers are concerned. **The Services Directive would not change the present situation for posted workers in the UK or any other Member State where statutory minimum employment standards are set. Just as now, under the services directive there would be some workers employed with collective agreements above the statutory minimum and others who were not and were therefore cheaper to employ.** The Commission told us that there was a need to make clear that the directive could not lead "to a situation where companies can bring their labour force from a cheaper country and create a sort of unfair competition ... for instance on a building site" (Q 447). **We do not believe, however, that it is for the directive to get involved in issues of labour-employer collective bargaining relations or in matters such as minimum wage legislation. These are matters for individual Member States and their institutions.**

203. The draft directive safeguards against the possibility of businesses opening a "letterbox", "post-box" or "brass plate" in a Member State where some aspects of the regulatory environment were perceived as advantageous as an "established" base from which then to operate on a temporary basis in other Member States under the directive. In any case, it must be remembered that the country of origin basis of business operations does not apply to more permanent, established operations in a country. The Country of Origin Principle is largely to the benefit of small, self employed businesses looking to explore and break into new markets. Larger businesses will, as before, operate substantially on an established basis. It is the sections of the directive dealing with simplification of establishment and creating a level playing field for all established businesses with a Member States that will benefit them.

Consumer protection

204. In our view, consumer protection for individuals and households is properly covered by derogation from the directive. Consumers will be covered by the law as of their own Member State. Business users of services will be able to choose the legal base for contracts. That appears to us to be satisfactory. Even so, it must be recognised that individual consumers might find it more difficult to enforce their rights, should they seek redress for some reason, if the service business is established in a Member State other than that of the consumer. This is a matter that needs to be considered further by the Commission.

205. We conclude that although consumers should, as with all purchases, exercise due caution in their choice of supplier, consumers are unlikely to be the victim of suppliers as a particular result of their operating under the Country of Origin Principle.

206. There was significant concern that there would be no, or inadequate, supervision of enterprises operating in another Member State on a temporary basis, and further that this would have an impact upon high quality suppliers who would be tarred with the brush of "cowboy" operators. The mutual assistance framework proposed in the draft Directive is important in

establishing and maintaining trust and confidence in cross border provision of services. **We are doubtful that the changes the United Kingdom may need to make in registering or providing information on service businesses that wish to trade in other Member States on a temporary basis has been fully grasped. More generally, it is clear to us that the mechanism of Mutual Assistance at present lacks an incentive structure on Member States that would make it work effectively and swiftly. If the draft Services Directive is to have an impact, it is necessary that greater attention is paid to these important issues of confidence-building.**

Services of general interest

207. The European Parliament, in its May 2005 draft report on the Services Directive considers the position of services of general interest. It proposes the explicit exclusion of all services of general interest from the scope of the Services Directive (e.g. Amendments 7 and 8). The justification for this is that "given their role in promoting social and territorial cohesion, services of general economic interest should not be covered by this Directive but should be addressed by a specific framework directive". There are important issues here but we disagree with such a blanket exclusion. This could be used as a means of circumventing competition. Services of general economic interest are those services purchased from a supplier by governments or public bodies to be made available to recipients for reduced or no charge. Where governments and public bodies engage in such services, then in general we would expect these purchases to be transparent and open to competition. The supply of such services should be a market opportunity for businesses from any Member State unless there are over-riding and justifiable reasons of national interest.

208. The distinction between services of general *non-economic* interest and services of general *economic* interest must rely on the question of whether the service is provided for remuneration. It is important that the draft services directive is unambiguous about the exclusion from its scope of services of general interest that are not for remuneration and that it confirms the freedom of Member States to define what they consider to be services of general interest, whether economic or non-economic services, and how they should function. **Member States must retain sole competence over how their governments decide to provide public services. We believe that the draft Directive recognises this and strikes that balance. The Government should seek to ensure that the final version of the directive maintains that balance while ruling out a blanket derogation for all services of general economic interest.**

APPENDIX 1: SUB-COMMITTEE B (INTERNAL MARKET)

The Members of the Sub-Committee were:

Baroness Cohen of Pimlico
Baroness Eccles of Moulton
Lord Fearn
Lord Fyfe of Fairfield
Lord Geddes
Lord Haskel
Lord Roper
Lord Shutt of Greetland
Lord St John of Bletso
Lord Swinfen
Lord Walpole
Lord Woolmer of Leeds (Chairman)

Professor Michael Waterson was appointed as Specialist Adviser for the inquiry

Declarations of Interests:

Baroness Cohen of Pimlico
Non-executive Director, LSE plc (London Stock Exchange)
Non-executive Chairman, BPP Holdings plc
Non-executive Director, MCG Plc
Hon. Fellow, St. Edmunds College, Cambridge

Lord Geddes
Director, Chromecastle Ltd
Director, Photo Corporation (UK) Ltd
Director, Portman Settled Estates Ltd
Director, Trinity College London
Member, Trinity College of Music
Trustee, Portman Trusts

Lord St John of Bletso
Consultant to Merrill Lynch (Europe), 1992–
Director, Regal Petroleum plc 2003–
Chairman of Spiritel PLC (Telecom Managed Services provider)
Consultant to Globix Europe
Chairman of the Governing Board of Certification International
Director of Estates and General plc
Trustee, Oxford Philomusica
Trustee, Life Neurological Trust
Trustee, Tusk
Trustee, Tikkun
Chairman of the Trustees, Citizens on Line

Lord Woolmer of Leeds
Partner, Anderson McGraw
Partner, Halton Gill Associates
Chairman, East Leeds Initiative Ltd
Director and Member of the Council of Foundation for Management Education

APPENDIX 2: CALL FOR EVIDENCE

1. Sub-Committee B (Internal Market) of the House of Lords Select Committee on the European Union is undertaking an inquiry into issues raised by the European Commission's Proposal for a Directive on Services in the Internal Market (6174/04).

2. The Directive aims to make it easier for service providers to establish in other Member States and to increase the free movement in services across the European Union. In particular, the Commission proposes to:

- Eliminate obstacles to freedom of establishment;

- Abolish barriers to the free movement of services; and

- Establish mutual trust in services provided between Member States.

3. The Directive's definition of Services is broad and its ramifications are considerable. While considering some wider issues, the inquiry will have a particular focus on the Country of Origin Principle. We welcome evidence from all service industries but we particularly welcome evidence from firms in business services and in construction and related services.

4. The Sub-Committee seeks evidence in particular in the following areas:

A. The current state of the Single Market in services.

- Are there significant barriers to firms seeking to offer their services in other Member States of the European Union? If so, what are the most important of those barriers? What measures are needed to overcome those barriers? Does the Commission's proposed Directive adequately address those issues?

B. The Country of Origin Principle

- Is the principle that a company registered to provide services in one country is automatically qualified to provide those services in any community country on the basis of home country regulation a reasonable and/or realistic starting point? What significant benefits to businesses and consumers are likely to occur as a result of the adoption of the Country of Origin Principle? Is the Principle workable in practice?

- Will the application of the Country of Origin Principle move business in favour of firms based in Member States with the least stringent regulatory regimes? What issues does this raise for businesses and consumers? How might those issues be resolved?

- The application of the Principle relies on the development of an extensive mutual assistance framework, whereby Member States cooperate in supervising enterprises based in their country in respect of their operations in other countries. Is this a workable framework?

- What other significant concerns are there regarding the practical implementation of the Country of Origin Principle and how might these be addressed?

- Assuming efficient operation of the Country of Origin Principle, what significant barriers to trading in other Member States are likely to remain, so far as firms in the relevant business sectors are concerned?

C. The future

- Do you expect the implementation of the Commission's proposed Directive to have a significant impact upon trade in the services sector within the European Union? In which services industries do you expect the least and the largest movement towards a European Union single market in the next five to ten years?

APPENDIX 3: LIST OF WITNESSES

The following witnesses gave evidence. Those marked ★ gave oral evidence.

★   The Advertising Association

        Alliance of UK Health Regulators on Europe

        Amicus

        Association of British Insurers

        Association of Building Engineers

★   Clifford Chance, London

★   Confederation of British Industry

        Construction Federation

★   Construction Industry Council

★   European Commission

★   Members of the European Parliament

★   Federation of Small Businesses

        General Dental Council

        General Osteopathic Council

        Griffiths & Armour Professional Risks

        Health and Safety Commission

        Institute of Practitioners in Advertising

★   Management Consultancies Association

★   Royal Institute of British Architects

★   The Royal Institution of Chartered Surveyors

★   Department of Trade and Industry (DTI)

★   Trades Union Congress

        Transport and General Workers Union

★   Union of Industrial and Employers Confederations of Europe (UNICE)

★   Professor John Van Reenen

        Which?

Minutes of Evidence

TAKEN BEFORE THE SELECT COMMITTEE ON THE EUROPEAN UNION
(SUB-COMMITTEE B)

MONDAY 28 FEBRUARY 2005

Present	Cohen of Pimlico, B	Swinfen, L
	Fearn, L	Walpole, L
	Geddes, L	Woolmer of Leeds, L
	Haskel, L	(Chairman)

Examination of Witness

Witness: PROFESSOR JOHN VAN REENEN, Director, Centre for Economic Performance, London School of Economics, examined.

Q1 Chairman: Good afternoon, Professor Van Reenen.

Professor Van Reenen: Good afternoon, my Lord Chairman.

Q2 Chairman: May I thank you for coming at short notice. We have a range of questions which are starters really. There may be other things that flow from your responses that people will want to follow up. We have around 40 minutes in total. It would help, therefore, if in your customary way you could be fairly brief in your responses so that we have a chance to follow up and so on. Is there anything you would like to say by way of introduction?

Professor Van Reenen: Yes. I would like to make a short introductory statement. Thank you for inviting me to give evidence. I have to warn you, however, that I will speak very much as a generalist, not an applied economist, in response to your questions. I am not an expert on the Directive by any means, nor am I legally trained. I hope you will forgive my ignorance on the intricacies of the Services Directive, but I will do as much as I can to help you in terms of a general economist and to give my views on the questions you ask.

Chairman: Thank you.

Q3 Lord Fearn: Consultants have suggested significant gains in productivity and employment as a result of the actions proposed by the Services Directive. How likely do you think these are? What are the preconditions for achieving them?

Professor Van Reenen: I had a brief look at the Copenhagen Economics Report. I do not think that the precise figure of £36 billion or so is the one to focus upon. The important thing is to think about what the mechanisms are, which the report talks about in terms of what the likely effects of the Services Directive will be. My sense is that the mechanisms as described in the report are actually quite plausible and I think overall the Services Directive will give significant benefits, although the precise amounts are going to be open to some discussion. What are the mechanisms which the report sets out which are likely to happen? There are two elements to it. The first element is essentially the cost of simplification. The Services Directive is an attempt to make it easier for a company which is based in one Member State to sell in another Member State or indeed to set up another company in another Member State and it proposes a variety of quite sensible things in order to enable that to happen. If that is successful two things follow from that. Firstly, by simplification of either setting up a foreign direct investment or setting up an ability to sell to another Member State this will reduce costs. The reduction in costs is an economic saving which will reduce waste and increase efficiency, so that is good. The second thing—and this is also something that is often not realised—is that by the variability of firms to set up in other countries that will increase the degree of competitive intensity facing firms in the other country in which there are some entrants. Increased competition is probably the most important thing. Increasing competition should reduce the amount of profit margins or price cost margins which firms are able to earn because it increases competition. This has the effect of reducing prices, which is good for consumers, and this will have other positive effects. The forces of competitive intensity should increase the incentives on managers to work harder, to reduce slack and become more efficient, so there may also be an increased degree of sufficiency or maybe even innovation. Those things are not discussed very much in the report. My sense is that this report may underestimate to some extent some of the advantages of product market competition. Through those mechanisms those benefits are likely to flow.

Q4 Lord Fearn: How will that affect employment?

Professor Van Reenen: Overall what we expect to happen when product market competition increases is that in the long run employment should increase. By reducing prices and increasing the degree of competition facing firms this should mean, again in the long run, higher rates of employment. There will be some costs as well. It is not necessarily the case that every industry will gain employment. As competition increases some firms will lose employment and other firms will gain, but overall by increasing competition there should be an increase in aggregate employment.

Q5 *Chairman:* In many service industries Small and Medium Sized Business Enterprises (SMEs) predominate. Is it true that having more SMEs will increase competition? In this country surely the kind of services in which SMEs proliferate are very competitive anyway? Try telling an SME in the fast-food business or someone in the hairdressing business and so on that there is no competition; it simply is not true. Is this not exaggerated? This is talking as if they are big companies and huge enterprises. That is not what we are talking about, are we?
Professor Van Reenen: There is a mixture. It is true to say that some parts of the service sector is dominated by small outlets, for instance, your proverbial hotdog seller on Charing Cross Road, but in many other parts of the retail industry it is dominated by quite large firms. The supermarket sector, for example, is dominated by quite large firms, and accountancy and legal services are dominated by quite large firms. I think there is a mixture of different sectors here. When I think about SMEs my sense is that the larger firms are in a much better position because they have big departments which enable them to sell things across countries or serve foreign outlets. I think it is the medium-sized firms which actually face bigger regulatory costs when they are thinking of setting up an outlet in another country or selling to another country, because they have not got the same resources to invest in finding out all the different regulatory schemes and so they cannot do what you need to do in order to sell to a new country. I think that for the small and medium-sized firms this may create an opportunity for them to be able to invest in other countries or to sell to other countries.

Q6 *Lord Haskel:* We are told that the simplification of the regulatory procedure will reduce costs and that will encourage firms to be more competitive because of the increased competition, but do you not think that the market here in Britain is pretty competitive as it is? We are told that we have the least regulated regime. Do you not think our firms are as competitive as they are going to be? Why should being able to operate in Europe increase their competitiveness and make them more efficient?

Professor Van Reenen: You are right to say that we have relatively high degrees of competition in the UK in many respects and for that reason there may be less of an effect on us than there is in many other countries. However, I would add two provisos to that. Firstly, there are sectors of the economy where competition could be increased above where it currently is.

Q7 *Lord Haskel:* Give us an example.
Professor Van Reenen: I do not know to what extent this Directive will fundamentally change this, but it is often quite hard for new stores and retail outlets to open up because of planning restrictions, so there may be opportunities there. It is certainly true to say of the large retail banks that I sometimes wonder whether there is sufficient competition in order to enable them to deal with some of their customers.

Q8 *Lord Haskel:* But this excludes financial services.
Professor Van Reenen: Exactly. The proviso is that I do not know to what extent this particular Directive will change that. The second proviso I would make is that the UK is quite a service intensive economy compared to other countries, it is bigger in the UK than in other countries and that creates an opportunity for many UK firms to be able to sell into other countries or set up in other countries which they currently might find it quite hard to do because of the restrictions on British service sector firms that operate in those countries. It may be quite a big opportunity for us to be able to get into other countries with our service sector firms. We buy a lot of service sector products from other countries as well. To the extent that we use a lot of them, that may help reduce costs for us as well. I do not disagree with the main point but I would add these provisos.

Q9 *Lord Geddes:* Professor, we are in the very early days of this inquiry so forgive me if some of my questions sound naive in the extreme, but I just want to do a bit of probing. The object of the draft Directive is to lower barriers. Is that a fair statement?
Professor Van Reenen: Yes.

Q10 *Lord Geddes:* What are the big barriers that exist at the moment that need lowering?
Professor Van Reenen: If I think of a firm trying to take a decision on whether to export to another country, what are the barriers to doing that? There is one set of barriers which you could broadly call cultural or informational barriers, which are things like the fact that if I want to sell something to another country I need to find my clients to whom to sell my services, I need to know the language, so I need to overcome all of those barriers of uncertainty which can be very high. The Directive will not directly change those because those are fundamental economic problems

which have to be overcome, but they are a reason why, if you are a firm in your home country, you have some home advantage and that enables you to have some degree of protection and enables you to have greater market powers than you otherwise would, and this is why we want to try and to reduce those and to increase competition as much as possible. The second set of things is regulatory barriers. Those are to do with the problems of being able to deal with the local regulations in the foreign country you are going to which may be quite different from what you are used to in your own country. You have to learn what those regulations are, you have to make sure you are complying with them, but you will have lawyers and other advisers to do that. That type of learning procedure, the procedure of going through the barriers to learn those and overcome those, can in some circumstances be quite significant barriers. I do not know enough about the particular details of the sector to tell you precisely what those are, but those are the general principles.

Q11 *Lord Geddes:* As an economist, do you think the Directive includes the right recommendations, answers, whatever word you would like to use, to overcome those barriers or do you think there are some that are missing?
Professor Van Reenen: I do not think you will overcome those first set of fundamental barriers; those are still going to be there.

Q12 *Lord Geddes:* The regulatory ones?
Professor Van Reenen: It seems to me that it is going for the right type of thing. I like the idea, for example, that part of the Directive is to try and have a single point of contact. If you want to be able to sell into a country and you want to meet the regulatory barriers, there is a single point you can go to instead of having to deal with multiple agencies. I talk to firms and they say that the biggest problem is not being able to deal with one department, it is dealing with six or seven departments. Having a single point of contact will help tremendously. Having it done as an electronic procedure will also be a big advantage. I think the Country of Origin Principle—this idea that so long as, so far as I understand it, you have satisfied your local Member State's regulatory conditions then you can deal with other countries— should be a tremendous advantage as well. It does seem to me that it is going in the right direction in terms of regulation.

Q13 *Lord Geddes:* Is there anything missing? Have you identified holes in the draft Directive?
Professor Van Reenen: I have not, no, but I am sure there are some.

Q14 *Lord Haskel:* I wonder whether we are not making a mistake here by not looking at this from the point of view of the consumer. You have explained to us how regulation is a barrier to firms going into business in another country, but would you not agree that what is a barrier to the company providing the service is in fact a protection to the consumer? I think many consumers probably rather like the regulations because it gives them some sort of protection from the firm from whom they are receiving the service. Do you not think that there is a balance to be achieved here, rather than saying, as you are, that because regulation comes down we are going to cut costs and things are going to be much better because of that?
Professor Van Reenen: I would turn that question on its head because I think the benefits of reducing barriers to entry are fundamentally benefits to consumers. If you are a consumer purchasing services from a local firm you are paying a higher price for that service than you would do if you had other firms coming in and competing with that local firm, and through the process of competition you will get a better quality of service and a better price for that service than you would have done. If you are facing a monopolist you are going to get a worse price than you would if you were facing two or three firms competing to give you that service. The reduction in the barriers will benefit the consumers more than the producers. The local producers will be very happy to keep high barriers because it prevents competition coming in from other countries.

Q15 *Lord Haskel:* That is all very fair when we are talking about products, but here we are talking about services, and I am just trying to explore this again from the point of view of the consumer. I get the impression that many consumers perhaps are happy that some of these regulations which the supplier looks at as a barrier are in fact there for their protection. The Financial Services Authority we look upon as protecting our interests, but the banks look upon it as getting in the way of them becoming more efficient. Do you not think that there is a certain element of that here but it is magnified as far as services for the consumer are concerned?
Professor Van Reenen: Which particular regulations are you concerned with that you think would make consumers feel they were being undermined from this?

Q16 *Lord Haskel:* I thought we were asking the questions!
Professor Van Reenen: That is why I was interested in precisely which regulations you are worried about. Clearly there may be some regulations which a particular group of consumers think are absolutely necessary in their country and that this will be undermined to some extent if there is another

company selling the same service as them, but the consumer has a choice. The consumer does not have to purchase the service from this alternative provider if he or she does not want to. It always seems to me that the consumer would benefit from greater choice from other people who could offer them a service rather than being stuck with just the one choice from the local provider. It may well be the case that some consumers are worried about that, but you would want to take it on a case-by-case basis. That is why I wondered if there were particular areas that you were concerned about. Maybe one of your Lordships would like to give an example.

Q17 *Chairman:* Let me give you one. Imagine you are a German consumer and you are buying the services of a plumber or electrician secure in the knowledge that in order to practice plumbing or electricianing in Germany you have got to be very well qualified, having been through school and college for years, and somebody turns up from England with no qualifications at all and says, "I am a plumber in London. I can practice as a plumber in London and I am going to set up as a plumber in Berlin." Do you not think the consumer feels the German system has certain beneficial regulations of who can act as a plumber or as an electrician that they can feel reassured by, or would you take the view that the customer should beware? In other words, if you want to buy a service from somebody who is not necessarily qualified in Germany that is for you to choose.
Professor Van Reenen: That is my attitude. If some dodgy plumber turns up from Southall—

Q18 *Chairman:* I was not suggesting they were dodgy plumbers.
Professor Van Reenen: Let us say a perceived dodgy plumber turns up on my brother-in-law's doorstep in Berlin and offers his or her services, it is *caveat emptor*, it is up to the buyer to decide. The buyer is perfectly able to say they would much rather have their highly qualified, German, very expensive local plumber to do the service.
Chairman: I shall put that point of view when we are in Berlin.

Q19 *Lord Swinfen:* Would it not be extremely difficult for someone from country A to break into the market in country B because the population in country B know that the operator there knows what people want, knows the market locally and knows where to get all the bits and pieces to put it together quickly and efficiently rather than someone breaking in from another country completely, particularly when talking about small and medium-sized enterprises?

Professor Van Reenen: Absolutely. I was asked earlier about the barriers to entry into a new market. Those are exactly the barriers that you have just described, that it is hard to go to a new country when you have not got an existing set of clients or suppliers, but if on top of that you have all the regulatory barriers then that is an additional difficulty. To the extent this Directive could reduce some of those barriers, at least it helps the process of entry even if it does not do so completely.

Q20 *Lord Swinfen:* Do you think this Directive is going to be much used and of much real use?
Professor Van Reenen: I think that is probably the toughest question. I think the biggest risk—going back to the first question that if these numbers and analyses in the Copenhagen Economics principle are correct—is that it may be very difficult in practice to make them work. It may be the case that this goes down on the statute book, but putting it into practice is much harder than we think because of all these other barriers, maybe because of resistance from other Member States. The biggest risk from my perspective is that this will not work, although it is a good idea, but it may be hard to make it work in practice. In goods there have been some local successes. It should also be a possibility for services, but it is going to be a long, long process.

Q21 *Lord Haskel:* We have had a conversation about barriers. Let us assume we have overcome the barriers and we are now going to start doing business in other countries as service providers. What are the main mechanisms by which some types of services will benefit more from this competition than others? We have discussed the Copenhagen Economics conclusion. Do you agree that the benefits are greater in the area of professional services? I presume that means lawyers and people like that.
Professor Van Reenen: It is back to first principles. Where are they going to have the most effect? They are going to have the most effect where the existing regulatory barriers are very high. My understanding is that those barriers are pretty high in professional services, legal and accounting, so by that token they should have quite a big effect. They will also have a big effect when there is a big difference between the regulatory barriers facing local service providers compared to foreign service providers. So when that difference is big then there will also be a larger effect. I do not know enough about institutions to say precisely whether those are big or small, but those are the two general principles.

Q22 *Lord Haskel:* Do you think that argues for trying to introduce this a bit at a time? For instance, those professions where there are big barriers, where it is going to be more difficult, maybe we need a bit more time there. For instance, I understand that architects do a lot of business in different European countries and the barriers do not seem to be so great. Architects could probably get on with this fairly quickly. There are other professions, like accountancy, where there are obviously big barriers because of the different rules and laws governing accountants. Do you think that this argues for introducing different professions rather than just going for the big bang and doing the lot in one go?

Professor Van Reenen: The incremental approach seems to have some common sense behind it, but political fiscal reality means that there is already a very slow process behind this. It has taken a long time even to get to this stage. If we started saying okay, we are going to have this on a fast track and this other element on the slow track, my suspicion is that this will make the process even slower than it otherwise would have been. At least if this gets put forward it is not going to take a long time to make the exchanges against very entrenched professional interests or positions of many other Member States. Going for at least getting this Directive put through is still going to take a long time and it is still going to happen very incrementally. My personal sense is to go for it now and then do as much as you can as fast as you can because it is going to be very slow no matter what happens.

Q23 *Baroness Cohen of Pimlico:* Every Committee of this sort has to remember the great question "What's in it for me?" or, in this case, for the United Kingdom. The Copenhagen analysis suggests the United Kingdom is going to be a particular beneficiary. I have been trying to think about this and I cannot see why. We have got very strong professional services, but then that is where the barriers are quite difficult to overcome. How do you see that? What are the mechanisms that give rise to us apparently doing better than anybody else?

Professor Van Reenen: I wish I could give you a good answer to that, but I am afraid I also found it difficult to understand exactly how Copenhagen Economics came to find Britain was larger than some of the other countries. You might want to question some of the other witnesses or the authors of the reports and find out why. I would speculate that Britain is one of the largest countries and it is very service based and so by its size it is likely to have larger benefits. Secondly, it is the case that we have a large service sector and we also consume a lot of services. By that token we could benefit either as consumers from consuming more of those services if the price goes down or as producers of those services and service providers, accountants and so on, might benefit from moving it to other countries. Those are my speculations. As one of the earlier questioners said, our barriers are relatively slow and so by that token it is not obvious why we

should benefit so much. That is a speculative answer to those questions.

Q24 *Lord Walpole:* I find it very difficult to understand the basic fact, which must be correct, that if we have gone as far as trading without tax—you know what I mean, we are in Europe for good—it must be right to go in for services, must it not, or am I wrong there?

Professor Van Reenen: It must be right to go into the Services Directive or into services in general?

Q25 *Lord Walpole:* No. Services must be treated in the same way as goods must, must they not?

Professor Van Reenen: Yes. My starting point would be that if we have free trade in Europe in goods, why not services? There is no economic reason why we should not have that.

Q26 *Lord Walpole:* Whether this is the right way or not, I do not know. Will the application of the Country of Origin Principle favour firms in Member States with the least stringent regulatory regimes? What are the issues it raises for business and consumers, and how might these issues be resolved?

Professor Van Reenen: I noticed that this was one of the elements which raised lots of responses in the DTI's consultation.

Q27 *Lord Walpole:* It seems to be the most controversial thing that has come up so far.

Professor Van Reenen: In terms of the economics, I think there is an incentive. If you are allowed to sell anywhere in Europe so long as you meet the regulatory requirements of your host country then there will be an incentive for firms to set up activities in the Member State with the lowest regulatory burden. So I think there is an incentive there as exists at the moment for goods. Companies will look for Member States which have a low regulatory burden, less red tape and they will have an incentive to move their activities towards there. This always remind me of the debate on globalization, where people say that globalization has also this effect of giving incentives to companies to move wherever the lowest tax or least regulated area is. The corollary from the left is that this is a terrible thing because it will mean the erosion of the tax base and the structure of the welfare state; and the corollary from the right is they agree with the analysis but this is a jolly good thing because there will be pressure on governments to reduce regulation and reduce taxation. I think both of those perspectives are exaggerated. Although there is an incentive to do that, and there is an incentive here, the question is how quantitatively large is that really going to be. My sense is that we should not over-exaggerate this incentive because when companies make decisions about where to sell or where to set up service provision there are a whole host of other factors which are much more important than the level of regulation which exists in different Member States, things like access to skilled labour forces, access to good supplies of clients and suppliers. My sense is that those things are much more important than the precise differences or the degree of regulation. If you think about the globalization debate, it is exactly the same. If you look at taxes as a proportion of GDP, they have gone up consistently over the last 30 years rather than fallen. Although that incentive does exist, I do not think it is so large as to cause huge amounts of relocation activity in my opinion.

Q28 *Lord Walpole:* If you were selling your services as an economic adviser what country would you go to?
Professor Van Reenen: I would stay in this country, of course. Where else? A better question would be if I was French and I was trying to maximise my revenue which country would I go to. I have the home buyer's incentive as well as the incentive to go to the place which has the lowest regulatory burden. Maybe Luxembourg has a low regulatory burden, I do not know. Britain is pretty low.

Q29 *Lord Geddes:* What would your answer be if you were French?
Professor Van Reenen: That is a rather philosophical question, my Lord.

Q30 *Lord Geddes:* You posed the question.
Professor Van Reenen: I suppose if I was a true home economist and all I cared about was maximising my narrow wealth then I suppose Britain would be the best country to set up in. In reality, there are lots of other benefits of living in France, good food and wine and a convivial atmosphere et cetera.
Chairman: We are not talking here about a company setting up in country A with lower regulation to sell services into country B with higher regulation because that can be done now with call centres in India and so on. We are talking here about a company set up in country A with low regulation taking some operations and operating in country B but being subject to less stringent regulation because they are less stringent back in country A. So we are not here talking about you and anyone else going into India to sell services from there, it is going into India to establish a base to say, "This is where I am based. I satisfy the regulations here. I am now going to go back into country B". It is not the call centre scenario, is it? I am simply saying that for the record. The response in the Commission's papers and so on is that businesses will not simply be able to go to a country with limited regulation and put up a brass nameplate and say "This is where we are now based". They will have to demonstrate that they operate in that country

for, as it were, *bona fide* operations in the country, so they are based there. There is no reason why you should not be up to scratch on that. It is a rather more complicated issue we are talking about.

Q31 *Lord Swinfen:* Professor Van Reenen, assuming for the moment the efficient operation of the Country of Origin Principle, what significant barriers will still remain to trading in other Member States?
Professor Van Reenen: I suppose there will be the ones which I discussed earlier on in response to some of your earlier questions perhaps. Let us go through the barriers. One is exchange rates, of course, if you are in Britain and not in the euro-zone, which is the exchange rate risk.

Q32 *Lord Swinfen:* But that will not apply to most of the euro-zone, will it?
Professor Van Reenen: No, but it will for Britain and those countries not in the euro. The other important things will be getting knowledge about the local people that you are selling to. You are selling a service and you want to tailor the service you are selling to the people who you are selling it to. That might be harder if you are coming from a foreign country and have less knowledge about the people that you are selling it to, what they need, what their desires are and so on. There are also barriers of language and culture in terms of selling to other countries. Did I answer your question properly? You seem to be looking for something else.

Q33 *Lord Swinfen:* I am not looking for anything in particular. I want your views. Far be it from me to put words into your mouth. That is a reasonable answer so far.
Professor Van Reenen: Exporting to a foreign country is always difficult and export of services is particularly difficult because if you are selling a physical object it is easier to know what you are buying, whereas if you are selling a service it is more difficult to know what the quality of that service is until you have experienced that service. If you want to get legal advice from somebody, it is very difficult to know before you have had some experience about the quality of the person giving that advice. A lot of services are "experienced goods", to use the jargon. You need to experience them before you know whether they are useful.

Q34 *Lord Swinfen:* Legal advice is rather special, is it not, for the simple reason that despite the European Union the laws are different in every country?
Professor Van Reenen: Yes.

Q35 *Lord Swinfen:* You are bringing up a special case.

Professor Van Reenen: Getting a haircut would be another case. If you went to the hairdresser, you would want to get your hair cut at the same place more than once before you went back later on. Any service has some element of wanting to experience the thing which is being provided before you go back to purchase it again. You might want to try out service goods a few times before you trust them, which makes people more cautious about using the services of somebody they do not know, especially if that company is based in a foreign country.

Q36 *Chairman:* That is not always true, is it? It does depend almost factually on what is the pattern of purchase. Some purchases of goods and services are not very often in a lifetime; others are and you learn by experience and the force of competition varies a bit.
Professor Van Reenen: These things vary tremendously.

Q37 *Chairman:* The average person might only use the services of an estate agent two or three times in their lives with big gaps between. If you use a service that is pretty poor, you cannot apply the learning principle for a long time, so it does vary, does it not?
Professor Van Reenen: Absolutely. That is why for those types of services it is quite useful also to have other consumer agencies to aggregate that information and publish reports on the quality of the service.

Q38 *Chairman:* Is there anything further you think we should have asked you but have not?
Professor Van Reenen: No. You did not ask me many detailed questions about the Copenhagen economics report. There are a lot of useful things in there to look at. You have to take all of these things with a pinch of salt. A lot of the precise numbers are very difficult to be sure about but it is not a bad place to start.

Q39 *Chairman:* We have been asking a number of oral witnesses questions about this and in all the other evidence we have had many comments along the lines of, "We like the general principle but we want a derogation for this. We do not want that being covered. We want this being covered. We want it by sectors. We do not want it horizontal. We want it slowly rather than quickly. We want more health and safety issues left out and we do not want general, mutual agreement and mutual trust. We want harmonisation of standards", a bit like manufacturing goods, and so on. Does this report seek in any way to qualify the expected benefits to the extent that these various limitations upon a pure single market might apply? I can see an economist saying, "Let us imagine there is a nice, theoretical market; what would the outcome be?" but the real world is not like that.
Professor Van Reenen: Of course not. I do not think they are particularly sophisticated at looking at every single nuance. The main thing they look at is the overall fall of barriers and they say, "Okay, let us divide that into the barriers falling and also equalise them between the foreign and the home producers." There is death by a thousand cuts so if you allow so many derogations here and compromises there you end up with such a mish-mash of a Directive that it loses a lot of its power. Maybe this is my terrible economist training but I would much prefer a clean sweep and a level playing field.

Q40 *Chairman:* You are the Milton Freedman of modern micro-economics.
Professor Van Reenen: Keynes also in that respect.
Chairman: Thank you so much. You have been vigorous and forthright and that is very much appreciated.

Memorandum by Confederation of British Industry (CBI)

1. The CBI is the national body which represents the views of the UK-based business community to the Government and to other authorities in the UK, Europe and elsewhere. It is the UK's leading business organisation, speaking for some 240,000 businesses that together employ around a third of the private sector workforce. The CBI is an independent, non-party political organisation funded entirely by its members in industry and commerce.

2. We welcome the opportunity to contribute to the Committee's research into the Commission's proposal, and would like to acknowledge the inquiry as being both timely and a valuable means by which to allow Parliamentarians and business to discuss this necessary piece of European legislation.

RATIONALE FOR THE CBI'S SUPPORT OF THE PROPOSAL FOR A DIRECTIVE ON THE PROVISION OF SERVICES IN THE INTERNAL MARKET

3. The 2004 "Kok report" visibly demonstrated the failings in the EU's economic performance, *vis-à-vis* the standard comparitors of the US and Japan. More worryingly, however, the EU is now being seriously challenged by the improved and dynamic economies of China and India.

4. The 2005 half-term review of the Lisbon Agenda is likely to show that there is common agreement across the Member States and between the EU's institutions[1] that the Union must find a means to invigorate its component economies, as well as finding a means by which to encourage new and innovative generators of future economic growth.

5. British business feels that as part of the wider package of proposals recommended in the Kok report, and which will hopefully be supported by the Spring summit, the Commission proposal for a Directive on Services in the Internal Market will assist in the achievement of the Lisbon goals.

We believe that the proposed Directive will:

— reduce burdens for companies already operating across Member States' borders, resulting in savings that can be then invested in research and development—helping to realise the Lisbon goal of achieving a 3 per cent GDP investment rate in such activities[2].

— remove barriers for companies that provide temporary services across Member States' borders, promoting both expansion of existing companies' activities as well as enabling new entrants into markets—helping to realise the Lisbon goal of achieving an employment level of 70 per cent across the EU.

General Analysis of the Proposal

6. As with all "draft" legislative texts, work remains to ensure a satisfactory removal of ambiguities, a focusing of ambit to ensure necessary exclusions are covered, and a tightening of the placement of the text within the wider framework of the Community *Acquis*.

7. We believe that the core component of the proposal, the "Country of Origin Principle" (Article 16), is sound and in keeping with the spirit of the Treaty and the four fundamental freedoms.[3] Further, we believe that in achieving its successful operation, the proposed Directive will add demonstrably to levels of economic activity by service providers operating across intra-EU borders.

8. Furthermore, we believe that, when combined with the secondary element of the Proposal, the removal of discriminatory regulations (Article 14), and the requirement to evaluate any remaining and new regulations in the light of their compliance with non-discrimination requirements (Article 15), "Country of Origin Principle" will assist in the simplification and reduction of administrative burdens for EU business. In this approach, the Proposal echoes the commitments made in 2004 by the four Presidencies of the Republic of Ireland, the Netherlands, Luxembourg and the United Kingdom.[4] It also fits well with the ongoing the SLIM[5] programme of regulatory simplification.

The CBI believes that failure to achieve agreement on this element of the text can be seen as nothing less than a lack of confidence by Member States and their agents in the fundamental rationale of the European Union, namely that of trust between Member States fostering economic and social progress, and societal prosperity.

9. Finally, we believe that the creation of "Single Points of Contact" (Article 6) will greatly assist businesses across the EU in accessing information and fulfilling their obligations in a timely and simple manner. Achievement of this obligation can only add benefit to the EU's commitment to reducing and simplifying regulation.

10. There are two caveats; over-riding concerns that must be borne in mind during the political debates that will surely engulf this Proposal during the forthcoming negotiations:

— the first is that the resulting Directive must not increase the regulatory or financial burdens experienced by a company wishing to operate solely within its home state;

— the second is that any increased regulatory or financial burdens imposed by the resulting Directive on companies operating across intra-EU borders, are both justifiable and proportionate to the resulting benefits achieved by both business and the wider EU economy.

---

[1] *See* the recently published EESC report, "Priorities of the single market 2005–2010" (INT/249).

[2] *See* 2004 report of the CPB Netherlands Bureau for Economic Policy Analysis, "A quantitative assessment of the EU proposals for the Internal Market in Services".

[3] Freedom of movement of goods, services, persons and capital.

[4] *See*, "'A Joint Initiative on Regulatory Reform"—An initiative of the Irish, Dutch, Luxembourg and UK Presidencies of the European Union (2004).

[5] The SLIM Initiative, "Simpler Legislation in the Internal Market" was launched by the EU Commission in May 1996 with the objective of identifying ways in which Single Market legislation could be simplified.

RESPONSES TO KEY CRITICISMS OF THE COMMISSION TEXT

11. Posted workers.

The CBI is in accord with the report of rapporteur of the Internal Market and Consumer Protection Committee regarding this point; we feel that there is a potential for confusion in the operation of the Directive on Services in its interaction with the Directive on the Posting of Workers (96/71/EC). To this end we support the Proposal to clarify the situation by deferring to the said Directive in the matter of posted workers. This position is in line with the position adopted by UNICE in its position paper of the 26.07.03.[6]

12. Services of General Interest (SGI's).

The CBI is aware that this issue remains an area of great contention between and within the Member States of the EU. Whilst acknowledging that resolution on a legislative and regulatory framework could generate much needed new and increased economic activity, the CBI recognises that much more work is necessary before a solution acceptable to all of the interested stake-holders is likely to be reached.

With that in consideration, and given that the ambit of the proposed Directive on Services does not include those areas of public service provision that are contentious, or allow Member States to retain differentiation in national practice between the Member States where there are different societal settlements, the CBI believes that it is neither necessary nor desirable that the Services Directive proposal be detained pending agreement on SGIs.

13. International Private Law.

We are aware that during recent debates in Council regarding a Proposal for a Regulation on the Law applicable to non-contractual obligations,[7] "Rome II", the proposal for a special exception for internal market matters from the general principle of Country of Destination was deleted.

Given the proved importance of services to the EU's economy, and our concomitant belief in the necessity of this Proposal, notably via the use of the "Country of Origin Principle for the single market in services" future growth, it is essential that other Community Instruments do not undermine its operation. On this basis we would argue strongly that any agreement on Rome II should be reached without prejudice to internal market legislation.

Both the Member States and the EU must give a clear commitment to the establishment and functioning of an internal market in services, a commitment that necessarily requires clarity and consistency in the application of the regulations applying to cross-border services.

SPECIFIC CBI CONCERNS ON THE TEXT

The following paragraphs contain specific comments on key articles of the text and are aimed at improving or finessing the text in order that the resulting Directive may more effectively achieve its stated aims and objectives.

14. Member State Commitment.

The operation of the proposed Directive cannot be achieved without Member States' commitment to the operation of the single market. Many of the barriers identified by the Commission are illegal under the existing Treaties and as such are subject to infringement proceedings.

15. Scope.

Whilst accepting that reference to the Treaties and European Court of Justice case law provides an adequate base for the Proposal, we would caution that the lack of a clear and unambiguous definition within the text is likely to cause confusion. Therefore, for reasons of clarity, we would recommend that Article 4 (Definitions) contain a clear definition of which services will be subject to the Directive's remit.

More specifically, the Proposal must be amended so that it clearly and explicitly states that a service provider operating solely in one Member State is not subject to its requirements. As it currently stands, the text is ambiguous on this point. It must be a fundamental objective of the Directive that a service provider must not be obliged to provide services Inter-Member State.

---

[6] Provisions relating to posting of workers contribution of the employment working group on the interface with the Posting of Workers Directive.

[7] COM (2003) 427 final.

16. Definitions.

A number of terms contained within the text are either imprecise or lack a definitive definition, eg "easily accessible" (Article 7—Right to information); "arbitrary and discretionary" (Article 10—Conditions for the granting of authorisation); and "reasonable period" (Article 13—Authorisation Procedures).

Such vagueness may lead to complications in application at the Member State level and obfuscation when Member States are fulfilling their reporting requirements; neither of which will be helpful in the creation of a fully functioning and competitive single market.

With reference to the terms "overriding reason" and "public interest", the Directive should refer to European Court of Justice Case Law.

17. Legislative Overlap.

For the Directive to function as intended, further work must be undertaken to ensure that there is no unnecessary or conflicting overlap between its requirements and those of other Community instruments, eg Rome I & II, the E-Commerce Directive (2000/31/EC) and the Posting of Workers Directive.

18. Assessment.

The provisions of Article 15 (Requirements to be evaluated) will necessitate a valuable and urgent review of individual Member States' provisions, which act as impediments to the provision of Inter-Member State services. However, we are concerned that some of the provisions are identified as needing merely evaluation, eg the requirement for a minimum number of employees and bans on more than one establishment. We would argue that where they are enforced in a discriminatory fashion these provisions are necessarily contra to the Treaties, and as such should be listed in the Directive under Article 14 (Prohibited requirements).

19. Enforcement.

The operation of the Directive will depend upon mutual recognition and respect between Member States concerning their regulatory regimes. The successful achievement of this can only be secured by effective enforcement, achieved via the collaboration of each Member State's enforcement authorities, and where necessary and suitable, an adequate level of harmonisation. We would refer to the recently approved Consumer Protection Enforcement Regulation (COM 2003/443) as a model for how this might be successfully developed.

20. Derogations.

We are aware that the UK Treasury has raised concerns regarding the impact of the Directive on its ability to raise tax. The CBI holds firm to the principle of tax sovereignty and would not support any element of the Proposal that would render this principle invalid.

In addition, we understand that the UK Health and Safety Executive has raised serious concerns in respect of the implications of the proposed Directive for the adequate observance and maintenance of health and safety standards. The CBI would not wish to see any companies being subject to unfair competition from service providers operating at lower standards of health and safety, nor having the health and safety of their employees being compromised by such practices. We therefore feel that this issue must be explored further, and any problems identified must be satisfactorily resolved before the Directive is agreed.

19 January 2005

Examination of Witnesses

Witnesses: Mr John Cridland, Deputy Director General, and **Mr Mark Platt**, Senior Policy Adviser, EU Affairs, Confederation of British Industry, examined.

Q41 *Chairman:* Good afternoon, Mr Cridland and Mr Platt. Is there anything you would like to say by way of introduction before we go into questions?
Mr Cridland: I am happy to go straight into questions.

Q42 *Lord Haskel:* What are the significant barriers to firms seeking to offer their services in other Members of the European Union? Perhaps you could give us some examples. We are a bit thin on the

ground for examples. Do you think that the proposed Directive adequately addresses the problems of firms wanting to offer their services in other European Union countries?
Mr Cridland: We, too, are thin on examples so I am not going to pretend that I can answer your question in the way I would wish. The story of this whole draft Directive has been that it has been a concept in search of examples. I should stress we are very supportive of the principle. It makes very good sense. The business

28 February 2005   Mr John Cridland and Mr Mark Platt

community is persuaded that there is a case to be answered in terms of effectively completing the single market in this important area, but I cannot say that the CBI has been receiving a wide number of specific examples of regulatory barriers that need addressing. We are, as everyone else is, reliant on what the European Commission has offered us.

Q43 Lord Haskel: What we have been told is that the barriers are to do with regulation. I wonder whether you could tell us which regulations your members are concerned about and whether they are significant barriers.

Mr Cridland: The principal concern of businesses would be about jumping through administrative hoops in gaining authorisations for activity, whether it is selling services from a home base, a new market entry or seeking to establish a new business. To give a practical example of that, as it happens, I spent Thursday and Friday meeting with the Czech government in Prague. One of their major priorities at the moment as a result of lobbying from the CBI, the British Chamber in Prague and a number of other foreign business organisations is a new commercial registry, to make it much easier for businesses to establish themselves and get the authorisations. This is not untypical of the experience of a number of accession states, that they still have a tradition of pages and pages of authorisation and a very non-user friendly approach to business establishment. If you say to business, "Which are the regulations?" it would principally be in that area: authorisation to undertake economic activity.

Q44 Lord Haskel: Is it administration that you are more concerned about rather than the rules and regulations about practising, quality, standards, qualifications and all that sort of thing?

Mr Cridland: They are all pertinent points but I think the issue of procedural authorisation would be at the front of people's minds and the other issues would perhaps follow.

Q45 Baroness Cohen of Pimlico: Will the Country of Origin Principle fix that particular problem, because if you can set yourself up on a temporary or permanent basis presumably you do not really have to go through any of the hoops, if that is accepted as a principle, if that solves the particular ill which is the one that seems to be worrying businesses?

Mr Cridland: Indeed. Conceptually, it certainly does. The CBI is very strongly supportive of the Country of Origin Proposal, so supportive that we believe without it the proposal makes little sense.

Q46 Chairman: There is a distinction between temporary provision of services in a Member State and provision when one is established. Does the Country of Origin Principle only apply to a service business when it is operating on a temporary basis? In other words, once it is established, can it no longer fall back on the Country of Origin Principle because it is now established and it now has another country with which it is doing business? Can you clarify that for me?

Mr Platt: The idea of the Country of Origin Principle is that companies, for example, can test the water but once they decide to establish in another Member State they must apply and follow the regulations in that Member State. This would provide them with a means to see if it is worthwhile to do so with some degree of legal certainty and clarity.

The Committee suspended from 5.30 pm to 5.36 pm for a Division in the House

Q47 Lord Swinfen: Will the application of the Country of Origin Principle move businesses in favour of firms based in Member States with the least stringent regulatory regimes? What issues does this raise for business and how do you overcome them?

Mr Cridland: Clearly, we are dependent for an effective market on effective regulation and one of businesses' biggest concerns, particularly in the area of consumer policy, is uneven enforcement of regulation. We have sympathy with the concern but it is a concern that can be overcome over a period of years by effective implementation of the *acquis communitaire*. We need to balance and parallel this particular initiative with continuing efforts to make sure that, particularly in accession states, their regulatory regimes are up to the standard to which we would adhere. I do not think you will see as much forum shopping as the sceptics of this Proposal anticipate. In practice, there is a steady move towards improved standards in accession countries in particular and, in essence, we know that this Proposal is seeking to build cross-border trade because, in the services area, cross-border trade has been relatively modest. Therefore, I do not think there is a huge appetite from the business community to chase those parts of the European Union where they believe regulatory standards may be lower.

Q48 Lord Swinfen: There is a suggestion—or at any rate a number of people think—that some states enforce their regulations more vigorously than others. Do you see this changing in any way?

Mr Cridland: I have found by experience it is usually the Member State you are in that thinks it tends to apply its regulation more rigorously than others. Over time, we are seeing a steady, market-led harmonisation of these issues but it does take time. If I cast back to my experiences last week in the Czech Republic, if we had been having this discussion three or four years ago, issues of the quality of the Czech legal infrastructure, issues to do with corruption for example, would have been far more prominent. It is remarkable how much progress is being made quite quickly, but it will take time. It will only result in full harmonisation when we have an equally level playing field in GDP. The extent to which these countries remain under-resourced to provide some of the protection that this Directive relies on should not be under-estimated.

Q49 Lord Swinfen: Do you want to give a guesstimate as to how long?
Mr Cridland: It would be no more than a guesstimate. What has encouraged the business community about this Directive is that it has adopted a framework approach. The drafters of this Directive, and certainly people in the European Commission, recognise that this is a long-term gain and it will take at least a decade to see the sort of market that they are working towards.

Q50 Lord Geddes: You have twice mentioned accession states and I think we are all very grateful you have, particularly with your recent experience. In your answer just now, you also talked about scepticism. Can you tell us whether there is a difference in the contacts you have round the EU? Do you feel a difference between the attitude to this draft Directive in the accession states to, let us say, the 15 or even going further back to the seven and, if so, can you be a little more specific? Where is the scepticism? Why is it there?
Mr Cridland: The key issues of scepticism relate to different interest groups rather than different countries. Clearly, there is a degree of variation in national government attitudes to the draft Directive but I have certainly found a great deal of support in eastern Europe for the Services Directive because they want the opportunity to trade in a fully effective single market. When I refer to scepticism, I am conscious that the proposed Directive has not been well received by our colleagues in the trade union movement. In a number of non-governmental organisations, particularly those speaking for the consumer, there have been concerns. It has not been well received in parts of the European Parliament. The group that believe this Directive is a threat are those who believe it is a threat to standards of protection, either for the worker or for the consumer. I think many of these concerns are misguided but they are innocently misguided. We are all suffering from a Proposal which is quite embryonic in form, what we need is much more exemplification. Many of the concerns of the sceptical group can be satisfied by more illustration and explanation.

Q51 Lord Geddes: You slightly swept aside any form of national scepticism.

Mr Cridland: I did say that there were different attitudes between Member State governments. I just said I did not think that was the primary area of scepticism.

Q52 Lord Geddes: Where are the "thumbs up" and where are the "thumbs down"?
Mr Platt: Mostly the thumbs up are from anglocentric viewing countries, which many of the new Member States are. Sir Digby Jones was in the Czech Republic two weeks ago at a conference about the internal market and the Czech junior minister for trade and industry was very keen on promoting this as being a Directive that would help Czech business growth. The Member States that have difficulty are the Member States that have concerns about protecting the way in which their economies and social structures run. France and Germany, for example. In France, it has become confused as being a political issue over and above an economic issue, with Mr Chirac using this as a means to try and win his Constitutional Treaty vote. In Germany, it is a specific issue around the Posting Workers Directive, specifically in the construction sector. We fought a long and hard battle to get that Directive. As a consequence, our concern is that this Directive will cross over in a way that will undermine that Directive. The Scandinavian countries are generally a "thumbs up". Everyone has a concern that this Directive is ambitious. It is a framework and horizontal Directive. There has not been anything quite as ambitious as this for some time. Many countries have looked at it first and thought that the breadth of the Directive is too great, but looking down at it, it breaks down into more easy parts. Those countries that are comfortable with accepting competition as a generator for economic growth are happy with that.

Q53 Lord Haskel: You mentioned consumer policy: my concern is that the consumer is being forgotten in this whole debate because enforcement of regulation, although seen as a burden by some businesses, is seen as some sort of protection by the consumer. In view of the fact that you have been travelling around, I wonder if you could tell us how consumers are driving this enforcement of regulation so that this scheme can go through, because without some enforcement of regulation, presumably consumers would not put up with it?
Mr Cridland: The European consumer voice is strong and active. You have a Pillar operating at Brussels level which is as effective in its own way as the trade union movement is in protecting the interests of workers. You will find that as this debate goes forward on this draft Directive the consumer lobby becomes more and more involved in ensuring that there is no reduction in the level of protection. A

number of consumer representatives that we have talked to have recognised that there are real benefits to the individual consumer if we can get this Proposal right. Consumers benefit from effective competition. The extent to which Member States are protecting home state businesses from the full force of competition by arbitrary and artificial rules of procedure which make market access more difficult for businesses from one of the other 24 Member States is inimical to the interests of the consumer. Clearly, if the debate continues with the consumer lobby believing that that benefit is outweighed by a reduction in regulatory protection, the Directive will continue to have problems. Therefore, it is very important that some of those concerns are addressed head on. In the debate that we have had so far on the draft Directive, for example, health and safety has been raised a number of times. It is another example of a concern that needs to be flushed out and fleshed out. I do not see anything in this Directive which should be a threat to health and safety. It should not be beyond the wit of man and woman that we can ensure that health and safety is in no way threatened by this proposal. We have invited any organisations that have health and safety concerns to make us aware of them because reputable businesses would not in any way want to trade on poor health and safety standards. We do not see anything in the Directive that should of itself lead to less consumer protection on safety.

Q54 *Chairman:* Is consumer protection another area of derogation from the Country of Origin Principle?
Mr Platt: I am afraid I do not know that specifically.
Chairman: It would be useful if you could let us know what the CBI's understanding of it is because, if it is not, I do not see how Mr Cridland can give reassurance to consumers. If the Country of Origin Principle applies, there will be different standards of consumer protection. If there is a derogation so that it is the rules of the country of operation that apply, that answers the consumer protection concern. I do not think one needs a long answer. It is a question of fact: is it a derogation issue or not? According to reports we have had from *The Financial Times*, Mr Barroso told *The Financial Times* yesterday that he saw the risk that the law could allow social dumping.
Baroness Cohen of Pimlico: What is social dumping?
Chairman: A dash for the bottom and all that argument. There is a real concern here.

Q55 *Lord Geddes:* On the removal of barriers for those working other than in their own country on a temporary basis, how temporary is temporary?
Mr Platt: The text does not give a definition and we feel that there should be a push to try and give a strict definition of what "temporary" constitutes. For us, temporary is as opposed to established. A company

may wish to test the water in a new market to find out if it could be successful so it could provide that service for a limited time but with the ambition of eventually becoming established. It is an issue on which we have not had communication from members to give us an idea about what they would consider to be temporary. It is an area that still needs more work.

Q56 *Lord Geddes:* Are you trying to find out?
Mr Platt: Yes. We are consulting with our members. I have another meeting with our stakeholder group in two weeks' time. The difficulty for many of our members, be they big or small, is because this text is so detailed and deep, getting to grips with what it will mean for their individual operations is quite difficult and the ramifications for their businesses and the way in which their businesses operate. I would hazard a guess that different sectors and different kinds of business will each view temporary in a different way. It is easy to provide a temporary planning service but a temporary counselling service would perhaps take longer and be more detailed.
Lord Geddes: It will vary between the type and size of the business. Lord Chairman, are we permitted within the Committee structure to ask the CBI whether they can let us know, even on a preliminary basis, what their members think on this subject?
Chairman: It would be helpful. We would anticipate drafting the report by the middle of, or late, May so anything that got to us by, dare I say, 6 or 7 May would be helpful. This is an important issue and much of the concerns raised are about this temporary issue and the country of origin. There is a nexus here. Getting to the bottom of that and what reassurances can or cannot be given is quite important.
Lord Swinfen: What would be the position of a major construction firm undertaking a contract for a major development that was known would take, say, three years to complete? Being a one-off, would that be temporary?

Q57 *Chairman:* In construction there would be 50 subcontractors, some of whom are temporary and some of whom are established, so help us through that.
Mr Platt: Hypothetically, if there was a one-off, that could perhaps fit within the constraints of temporary, but if it is part of an ongoing process of bidding by a company in that Member State then it probably would not. That would be my considered view. However, that is not based on any reference to documentation or to legal text.

Q58 *Lord Swinfen:* You might have a different opinion if it was something like a power station that took 10 years to build?

Mr Platt: More than likely, if you were to build a power station, you would have to be established somewhere in the Member State. You would have to have some kind of fixed base to be able to administer these things. This also connects with the debates going on in the European Union around public procurement and public private partnerships, which are also touched on by this Directive, although indirectly.

Mr Cridland: The problem in giving you the answer you deserve on a question of that kind is that the Directive does not help us.

Q59 *Lord Swinfen:* Perhaps we should ask the Commission.

Mr Cridland: Indeed. Business has found this Directive particularly difficult to grapple with. The more we have sought examples from them as to how it might impact on them and what business opportunities or business challenges might result, the more they say, "We cannot get a clear picture of what the Commission has in mind. There is a high level concept and we have a lot of support for that but there is so little here that is painted in with all the colours." On this issue of temporary and how it relates to the country of origin, we have been through the text several times. I do not think the answer lies in the text and therefore business struggles to conclude what would be possible.

Q60 *Chairman:* The Commission in their documentation say they started this in about 2000 or earlier and spent two years in consultation and then carefully discussed it further. How has a Directive got to a point over critical issues such as what is temporary? You say that if the Country of Origin Principle does not apply, by which I take you to mean if the ability to operate temporarily is not applied, that strikes at the very heart of the Directive. Do you think it is satisfactory for the Commission to have got us all in the position in early 2005, after over four years of discussion, where uncertainty exists about critical elements in the Directive? How has that happened?

Mr Cridland: There are two answers to that, one of which is a little bit of support for the Commission's position, the other of which is not. The Commission is to be commended for taking a framework approach to this proposal. The tradition within the Commission would have been to have given us 25 draft Directives answering every question known to man but leaving us without the will to do anything about it. After the financial services liberalisation action plan which fell precisely into that trap, where many of our financial services businesses feel that the goal of liberalising financial services has been lost in a rush to deliver 42 maximum harmonisation measures, there is a breath of fresh air here. The

Commission has been bold and come up with something which is deliberately embryonic in order to try to change the nature of the debate and not get bogged down in an endless battle of detail. We support them in that regard because the CBI's view of European legislation is that it should provide a framework and should not take away from houses like this House the role of detailed regulation relevant to the national level. To that extent, I think they have done a good job. Where I think we have every sympathy with your point is that we made it very clear at the time of the Green Paper from the European Commission, much earlier in this exercise, that business was having tremendous difficulty grappling with what the European Commission was offering us. Many of the points we have been debating we made two or three years ago, in the early stages of that process. The European Commission could have helped itself if it had exemplified some of these issues more clearly in its proposal. It is interesting discussing with the new Commission who are left, as President Barroso was only a few days ago, having to deal with some of the concerns and criticisms that have been raised. It is for the Commission to speak but certainly in discussions I have had with them there is a degree of regret that they did not produce a Proposal which answered some of the very obvious concerns that other interest groups would raise.

Q61 *Baroness Cohen of Pimlico:* My only experience of exporting services is that I chair a company which trains accountants in most parts of central Europe and in the EU. I know about setting up and regulation there. I am hard pressed to invent many more businesses that might want to do that. Is there a list of the sort of people for whom these are burning issues? I cannot imagine they are burning issues, for instance, for hairdressers or restaurants. What sort of people are you talking to? I have a slight feeling of wrestling a ghost here.

Mr Platt: There is not a definitive list. The pitch of this Directive works in two ways. We have looked at this in terms of small enterprises who perhaps wish just to go across the border to provide something, a delivery service or something of that nature, which is just across the border, say, from Italy to Austria, but where the regulations about doing that are so strict that it is difficult or impossible to do. On the larger company side of things, it is possible the second bit of the Directive, which is about the reduction of regulation and requirements, would facilitate them or assist them in reducing their costs.

Q62 *Baroness Cohen of Pimlico:* They are already there and they would just reduce costs?

Mr Platt: Yes. It is not about them being prevented; it is about the costs they have to absorb. For example, retailers who are forced to go and buy another chain to get established in a Member State. The way the regulatory system works, you have to have a home base and all these things which add extra costs of establishing in that country. There is no definitive list but those are the two thrusts that we would see.

Q63 *Baroness Cohen of Pimlico:* In paragraph 10 of your evidence you say that the Directive must not increase the regulatory or financial burdens on a company wishing to operate solely within its home state. You want the Directive amended so that it makes clear that a service provider operating solely in one Member State is not subject to its requirements. Is this the same point just made in two different ways?
Mr Platt: Yes. We have had protestation from some member associations representing people who repair washing machines. The washing machines may be sold by a company in one Member State and used in another. They do not want to be forced to go and repair it if it is not in their business model. They simply wanted to make sure that the Directive was explicit that no one can be forced to provide a service, which the text does not necessarily read as saying. It is more of a concern.

Q64 *Baroness Cohen of Pimlico:* If you repair agas in this country you do not have to do it in Germany?
Mr Platt: Yes.
Chairman: Why should you?

Q65 *Baroness Cohen of Pimlico:* I do not think the Directive says that.
Mr Platt: No. It was more that the federation would raise the concern.

Q66 *Baroness Cohen of Pimlico:* Is it paranoia?
Mr Platt: Possibly, but because it is not explicit in the text there was a concern that it may be something to which they would be subjected. It is something on which we are seeking further clarification.
Mr Cridland: Business may be chasing its own ghosts but it is a further indication of how difficult this is to grapple with that some companies are concerned that an impression might be left with consumers that they should provide a service across national boundaries, rather than that they can and may.
Baroness Cohen of Pimlico: That is interesting.

Q67 *Chairman:* The Financial Services Authority and you have made the same point in similar terms. Somebody somewhere might accidentally see what the other was saying. That sounds as if it is almost certainly an unjustified concern. Somebody says, "This regulation is going to affect us and we are doing

nothing different at all" and the answer is, it almost certainly does not, but you need to check it out.
Mr Cridland: Indeed. We will seek clarification.
Mr Platt: I think the concern is the law of unintended consequences.

Q68 *Chairman:* That is an easy thing to say but it is our job to ascertain whether it is a valid concern. From what you have just told me as the CBI, you have not convinced me there is a problem there and I do not think you are yet convinced.
Mr Cridland: There is nothing in the Directive that supports the concern.

Q69 *Lord Fearn:* The application of the Principle relies on the development of an extensive mutual assistance framework. Member States cooperate in supervising enterprises based in their country in respect of their operations in other countries. Is this a workable framework? From what you say so far, the programme seems too ambitious.
Mr Platt: It is ambitious but not too ambitious. We would refer to SOLVIT (European Commission's on-line internal market problem solving network[1]), which is already in existence, which is used by individual Member States to manage the internal market for goods, as being a model which could be used for the Services Directive and mutual collaboration between Member States to ensure that regulations are followed and that companies operate within requirements.

Q70 *Lord Fearn:* You used the phrase "not well received by the trade union movement". Is there true opposition coming from the trade unions?
Mr Cridland: Yes, I think there is, largely based on a misunderstanding of the implementations. A number of the trade union concerns have been that they believe the proposed Directive would override the protection afforded to workers under the Posting of Workers' Directive. We do not believe that need be the case and we are certainly supporting our trade union colleagues in the argument that the Directive should make clear that, in relation to posting of workers, the Posting of Workers' Directive should have primacy. To the extent to which their concerns are legitimate, it is not made explicit in the draft Directive, although you could argue that it is implicit, that posting of workers would be the primary protection. That would go a long way to assuaging their particular concern, although they do have other concerns.

Q71 *Lord Fearn:* That is one reason. What is your main reason when opposition comes to the CBI?

---

[1] For further information on SOLVIT see http://europa.eu.int/ solvit/site/about/index—en.htm

Mr Cridland: I do not think there is much opposition to this Directive in the British business community. I think the British business community is strongly supportive of the principle but scratching its head on the practical application. There have been very few CBI member companies or sectors who would not wish to see this proceeded with. It comes at a key moment. Over the last two years, it would be our judgment that business in Britain has become more frustrated with the practical effectiveness of the European Union because of a significant tendency to over-regulate. I have given one example in relation to financial services. I guess the other *bête noire* of the British business community at the moment would be the potential regulation of manufacturing industry through the REACG proposals on chemicals upstream and downstream. Business has seen an overload of the wrong sort of regulation. There is therefore an appetite to make this work because this is one of the most high profile examples, if we can get it right, of where the European Union would be making a positive contribution to making the European Union work for business. If we can do that, I think it will shape the nature of the business community's reaction to the European Union at a very important moment when we are asking British business what it thinks, for example, about the Constitutional Treaty. When we talk to CBI member companies about an issue as esoteric as that, their response is, "Show me what is working. Show me where the European Union is delivering a more effective single market." In principle, we are supportive but what does it actually mean?

Q72 *Lord Fearn:* I presume you are in negotiation or you give advice to the Government?
Mr Cridland: Indeed.

Q73 *Lord Fearn:* Those sorts of things have been said?
Mr Cridland: Yes indeed. We have discussed this dossier regularly with Ministers, most recently in the context of the priorities of the UK Presidency.

Q74 *Chairman:* The question Lord Fearn asked was about the mutual assistance framework. Has the UK Government or the Commission had any discussions with you or with industry about how the mutual assistance framework would work? Is it a workable framework? Is it a workable idea?
Mr Platt: In that it is an aspiration for Member States to cooperate to make the single market work, it is an idea that we would like to see made manifest. The SOLVIT programme is still relatively new and starting to work properly but we do think that provides a blueprint. I do not think we see a difficulty with Member States cooperating to ensure that the single market works well. We have not had direct

communication with the Commission about what we think the best proposal would be, for example, over the single points of contact.

Q75 *Chairman:* This is a very important part of the package. Here we are in February 2005, several years after the journey started, with a desire for this to make an impact on the Lisbon agenda by 2010, implemented by 2007, and the discussions have hardly started on that issue.
Mr Platt: In the DTI's consultation document, there was reference to how this would operate and we did put forward some ideas about using the existing structures within the DTI's ambit. There have been discussions. This is very much at a Member State level rather than at Commission level. The Commission are not seeking to impose a model but the reference to SOLVIT provides a good example of where there is corroboration and collaboration and it is working reasonably well.

Q76 *Chairman:* Could you write to us on question 6(a)? It is asking what are the most significant areas of unnecessary or conflicting overlap between this Directive and other European Community instruments. We are all concerned, as you are, about whether there is overlap. Is there unnecessary conflict and so on? If you could kindly do us a note on that, that would be very helpful. What is the potential for confusion, in your view, in the operation of the Services Directive and its interaction with the Directive on Posting of Workers? In your evidence, you said that is one example. What is the potential for confusion between those two Directives?
Mr Cridland: I can only reiterate what I have just said: that implicit in the current draft and the Article that refers to Posting of Workers is that Posting of Workers would have primacy. The unions need to see this explicitly derogated and we are supportive of the unions in that regard if it helps to avoid concerns and would enable the trade union movement to see the benefits of this Proposal.

Q77 *Lord Walpole:* How significant are the potential health and safety issues arising from the operation of the Services Directive? What can be done to meet the concerns in this area? You did half answer the question.
Mr Cridland: I am not sure there is a lot more we can add helpfully on that point because we are a little bemused by the concerns that have been raised. There is nothing explicitly in here that gives us cause for concern. It is not something member companies have registered with the CBI, but if those who do have health and safety concerns could be more explicit about what worries them, we would want to see that issue addressed. We have no wish to weaken the framework of health and safety protection in any

way. We would want there to be a level playing field in that regard.

Q78 Chairman: A company operating temporarily on the Country of Origin Principle would have to meet the country's standards on health and safety in which it was operating. There would be derogation on health and safety matters, would there, under the Country of Origin Principle?
Mr Platt: The way the Directive stands at the moment, if you are using the Country of Origin Principle, you take your health and safety standards with you.[2]

Q79 Chairman: That is what the unions are precisely concerned about.
Mr Platt: All the Member States have signed up to the *acquis* and the *acquis* contains within it the debated health and safety requirements. You may disagree that that is the maximum or minimum required but that is the minimum which they have all signed. On that basis, what some of the critics are implying is that some Member States are not meeting those requirements. We feel that health and safety across the EU is of a standard that is acceptable to the EU and to EU Member States. Some Member States operate in slightly different ways but there is a baseline of operation.

Q80 Chairman: In this country, if a business from outside this country operated on a temporary basis under the Country of Origin Principle, it would not be bound by the full health and safety requirements of this country?
Mr Cridland: Indeed.

Q81 Chairman: As I understand it, that is what some of the trade unions are concerned about. I am simply trying to establish your understanding. Your understanding is that the Country of Origin Principle would apply to health and safety—that is, for companies operating on a temporary basis, not yet established?
Mr Cridland: Indeed. The problem though is that if we allow extensive derogation from the Country of Origin Principle without evidence that their concern is borne out in reality we wreck the Principle and it is a slippery slope. We supported in principle the Directive on Unfair Commercial Practices. At the very last stage in European developments, the Country of Origin Principle was lost so we now have

an extra level of regulation with no net benefit for the business community. We cannot support this Directive if the Country of Origin Principle is effectively gutted. If the unions demonstrate that there are actual, practical concerns, we would want to meet those in whatever way was necessary but they cannot simply assert the concept, in our judgment, because that leads to the Country of Origin Principle being holed below the water line.

Q82 Chairman: You said the Country of Origin Principle is central to this Directive and if it is lost you could not support it.
Mr Cridland: We would not support this Directive without that.

Q83 Chairman: Is that because the temporary provision of services is the critical objective and the way to achieve that is through the Country of Origin Principle? Is it because you want the temporary provision of services as an important feature of entering markets and the Country of Origin Principle is a way of achieving that?
Mr Platt: Yes. It also gets on to the European statute recognition of the Country of Origin Principle for usage in other forms of legislation later.

Q84 Chairman: That is extremely important to the Committee. Is the temporary provision of services, prior to becoming established, in your view, itself at the heart of this Directive or not important?
Mr Cridland: I think our answer to both your questions is yes: it is important in its own regard and it has ramifications for further measures to make the single market effective.

Q85 Chairman: It does mean that from our point of view pursuing the question of what is meant by temporary is important.
Mr Cridland: Yes.

Q86 Chairman: And also exploring whether or not the Country of Origin Principle itself in this Directive is central to achieving temporary operation. You have said one of your reasons for supporting the Country of Origin Principle is because it would establish an important principle hopefully elsewhere, as I understood it.
Mr Cridland: Indeed.

Q87 Chairman: Is there anything you want to add before we finish?
Mr Cridland: I have nothing more to add, my Lord.
Chairman: Could I say how much we appreciate you coming along today? I have certainly found it very helpful.

---

[2] On subsequent study of the Posting of Workers Directive, we find that the Directive does indeed afford a posted worker the health and safety protection available in the state of posting.

Supplementary evidence from the Confederation of British Industry (CBI)

NOTES ON THE APPLICATION OF COUNTRY OF ORIGIN PRINCIPLE IN THE SERVICES DIRECTIVE

1. What is the relevance of "temporary" to the operation of the proposed Directive?

The reference to "temporary" is a negative inference from the explicit definition of "establishment" given in the text: the definition is vague as a consequence.

The Proposal's definition of establishment—Article 4.5—when taken together with the Country of Origin Principle (COOP)—Article 16—is designed to allow a service provider from one (origin) Member State to offer a service in a second (host) Member State, without having to fulfil any obligations in that Member State that have been met by virtue of the provider's establishment in its country of origin and are not covered by any derogation from the COOP—Article 17 (full derogations), Article 18 (transitional derogations), Article 19 (case-by-case derogations).

The basis for the definition of establishment is taken from European Court of Justice (ECJ) case law on the freedom to provide services, specifically two cases:

(a) *Gebhard* (date unknown).

(b) *Schnitzer*—11 December 2003.

The ECJ's rulings "create" a definition for the temporary provision of services, such that it must be determined following consideration of the following key factors:

(c) the duration of the provision of the service;

(d) the regularity of its provision, ie its periodicity or continuity.

NB: Chapter 2 (Freedom of Establishment) applies only to situations where a provider is established in the Member State in which it operates. Chapter 3 (COOP) applies only to situations where an operator provides cross-border services, ie remaining within the Member State in which it is established but travelling to another Member State to provide a service but without establishing (in line with the conditions allowed under COOP, ie ability to operate a depot or distribution centre) in the second Member State.

The UK Government's official negotiating line (shared by some other Member States) is to seek a tighter definition of "established", in order that the definition of "temporary" will be, by direct comparison, more easily and clearly defined.

2. What is the relationship between COOP and consumer protection?

Consumer protection is partially derogated from COOP, namely under:

(a) Article 17.16, which provides for derogations on the basis of public security, public health or the protection of the environment, and;

(b) Article 17.21, which provides for derogations in respect of contracts for the provision of services that are not completely harmonised at Community level.

Further to these derogations, Chapter 4 (Quality of Services) provides for the harmonisation of information and guarantee requirements provided to consumers.

3. Further information.

(a) The Posting of Workers Directive enshrines health and safety, in so far as it relates to the management and operation of posted workers in a host state; at present the operation and primacy of this Directive when considered against the proposal is unclear.

(b) It should be noted that the Posting of Workers Directive carries a health and safety element (Article 3.e), which requires the posted worker be subject to the health and safety requirements of the Member State of posting.

(c) Regarding health and safety matters in so far as they concern the safety of third parties, these are covered by a general derogation from the COOP, contained in Article 17.23.

(d) The relationship between the proposed Directive and Private International Law (Rome I and Rome II) remains of concern.

    The current Council Rome II text would create legal disparities between different Member States in the operation of the Services Directive, the key issue being that certain rules are not always dealt with in the same branch of law in all Member States. A good example is given by the application of competition rules, where some Member States enforce competition as a matter of private law and others as public law. This would militate against seeking a wholesale "carve out" of Rome II.

April 2005

WEDNESDAY 2 MARCH 2005

Present   Cohen of Pimlico, B   St John of Bletso, L
                 Eccles of Moulton, B   Swinfen, L
                 Geddes, L   Walpole, L
                 Haskel, L   Woolmer of Leeds, L (Chairman)

Examination of Witnesses

Witnesses: MR OWEN TUDOR, Head, European International Relations Unit, Ms JANET WILLIAMSON, Economic and Social Affairs Department, and Ms HANNAH REED, Equality and Employment Rights Department, Trades Union Congress, examined

[NOTE: The Trades Union Congress submitted detailed written evidence in May 2004 to the Department of Trade and Industry as part of that Department's consultations on the draft Services Directive. This was made available to the Committee but is not printed in this Report]

Q88 Chairman: Good afternoon. It is extremely, kind of you to come at relatively short notice. We do appreciate it. Thank you also for your written evidence, which, as you will see, we have read, and that was helpful too. I wonder if there is anything you would like to say by way of introduction? Certainly you should introduce yourself and your colleagues for the record—that would be most helpful—and, if you have any introductory remark, please make it.
Ms Williamson: Thank you very much. I am Janet Williamson, I am a Policy Officer in the Economic and Social Affairs Department at the TUC and I have policy responsibility for the Services Directive. This is Hannah Reed from the Equality and Employment Rights Department, Senior Policy Officer, and Owen Tudor, Head of the European International Affairs Department.

Q89 Chairman: Is there anything any of you want to say by way of introductory remarks?
Ms Williamson: Yes, thank you, if I may. I suppose our overall position, in a nutshell, is that we do support the completion of the internal market so long as this goes hand in hand with the expansion of the European social model. Therefore, we can support the aims of the Directive, which are to create a genuine internal market in services. The issue as far as we are concerned is how this should be done. We support the principle that service providers should be able to establish themselves in other Member States and be treated on a non-discriminatory basis there, and we can support also the provisions aiming to simplify the administrative functions that relate to establishment. What we cannot support are the current proposals on the Country of Origin Principle as put forward in the current draft. We are aware that there are discussions and negotiations going on in Brussels, but, obviously, we have to base our position on the proposals that are currently on the table. We believe that introducing the Country of Origin Principle on a horizontal basis without commensurate harmonisation measures is a very broad and essentially an untried measure, and we believe that the balance of risks and benefits of such a broad and untried measure make this an undesirable step at this time. We would prefer to see a country of origin rule applied on a sectoral basis, on the basis of an agreed floor of minimum standards.

Q90 Chairman: Thank you very much. I think that probably neatly summarises the gist of your paper too.
Ms Williamson: It does.

Q91 Chairman: My first question you have really answered in part, which is, effectively, is the objective correct even if improvements need to be achieved as to how to do it? I think I am right in saying that you have just said that you could not support the Country of Origin Principle as it is currently formulated?
Ms Williamson: That is right.

Q92 Chairman: Implying that it might be possible to make changes that would still enable the Country of Origin Principle to be a part of the Directive, which I took to be the case? You went on to talk about a horizontal as opposed to a mutual recognition principle. Is that right? The Country of Origin Principle in itself is not a show stopper for you if it can be achieved in certain ways. Have I got that right?
Ms Williamson: We could support the Country of Origin Principle if it went hand in hand with harmonisation measures. I do not think that is practical to achieve on a horizontal basis. Therefore, in a sense, the way that the Country of Origin Principle is conceptualised in this Directive is problematic for us, but our position on the Country of Origin Principle, in general, is we could support it if applied on a sectoral basis and if it went hand in hand with harmonisation measures that would, in effect, set some sort of level playing field that would operate across Europe in terms of the rules with which service providers would be complying.

Chairman: As you know, a number of questions are going to pursue those points, and so let us not go into too much detail now. The questions will bring this out. If we do not come to this, let us know.

Q93 *Lord Haskel:* I wonder if you could amplify what you mean by "sectoral basis"? Do you mean industry by industry, or market sector by market sector, or market segment by market segment? Could you say what you actually mean by that?

Ms Williamson: What we are saying is that the Country of Origin Principle has been applied to date on a sectoral basis, for example, in the television sector and financial services. The Directives which have brought that about have included a whole run of harmonisation measures that apply to that sector, so that across the sector everybody knows what the rules are that apply to the service providers, and all service providers and all market participants can have clarity about that so that it operates on a level playing field. We can understand the case for the Country of Origin Principle being applied on that basis. It is obviously a big step to go from that to the proposals in the current draft of the Services Directive.

Q94 *Baroness Eccles of Moulton:* In your preamble, and the discussion that has already taken place, you place a great deal of emphasis on harmonisation rules governing quality, content and, in particular, safety standards of services; and you have said that the country of origin rule is best applied on a sectoral basis and that harmonisation measures of the rules would need to be agreed for each service sector before the implementation of the Country of Origin Principle and, by implication, before the concept of temporary service business operations could take effect under the Directive. I think that is a fair summary of what has been said so far. You have also touched upon why you think the concept of sector specific harmonisation is better than the concept of mutual recognition for service industries, but is there anything further on that particular point that you could tell us?

Ms Williamson: On the specific point about harmonisation versus mutual recognition?

Q95 *Chairman:* The mutual recognition issue, yes.

Ms Williamson: We believe that mutual recognition works only if there is a degree of equivalence between the regulatory requirements of different Member States which are sufficient to build the trust and confidence of all market participants, and I think at the time when mutual recognition was established for trade in goods, that was generally agreed to be the case. But it is not clear that that is the case for services at this time and there are all kinds of differences in terms of licensing systems, authorisation systems,

and so on, across the board. That is why we would advocate a very cautious approach in this area, and why we do not think that the equivalence principle, which is the basis of mutual recognition, can be applied. Also harmonisation or an agreed floor of minimum standards, as I have said already, would establish a level playing field, whereas without that the Country of Origin Principle does have the potential to create up to 25 different regulatory systems operating at any one time in one Member State, which can create a large degree of complexity and uncertainty.

Q96 *Baroness Eccles of Moulton:* I suppose that complexity and uncertainty can apply even if you are proceeding along a sectorial basis, if you define each and every service sector and get agreement across 25 Member States on harmonisation rules governing quality and content of services. Is that practical and how could this approval be applied to diverse, changing, inflexible services, for example, ranging from hairdressing to marketing to management consultancy? Is not either route going to be inflexible and complex?

Ms Williamson: I repeat that we would support a cautious approach. The sectoral approach is the basis on which the Country of Origin Principle has been applied with relative success, according to some people, to date. We think it is a very big step to go from that to the very broad measures which are being proposed in the Directive. A more practical and manageable approach could be to start with the service sectors which are most likely to be traded across borders and to address those sectors hand in hand with harmonisation measures and then to take stock, learn from that experience and go on from there. We do not feel that the experience to date of the Country of Origin Principle can warrant this very large jump from doing it on a sectoral basis with harmonisation to doing it on a non-sectoral basis, and, crucially, without harmonisation.

Q97 *Baroness Eccles of Moulton:* That all sounds very sensible, but no doubt you have seen the written evidence from Federation of Small Businesses. Maybe you have or have not, but it says that if mutual recognition is replaced by sector specific harmonisation rules this will be hugely damaging and there will be little point in adopting the Directive at all. Can you see where they are coming from and why that is their fear of going down that particular route?

Ms Reed: We certainly recognise that the small business sector is more likely to benefit from the proposed Services Directive than maybe larger businesses would. Certainly if larger businesses are seeking to expand into operating in other countries, their current practice would be to merge with other companies or to take over other companies. They are less likely to wish to go and establish in another county in order to set up operations. In contrast, often SMEs (Small and Medium Sized Enterprises) do not have the economic power to take over other companies or to merge with other companies. Therefore there would be clearer benefits for the small business sector from the current proposals in the Services Directive. However, our view is that the conclusion of the Federation of Small Businesses may be ill-founded at the present time. Our suspicion is that the rules on mutual recognition may not be as flexible as might have been suspected and could lead to a large degree of uncertainty for businesses. Our expectation would be that the European Court of Justice, for example, when seeking to determine whether there was mutual recognition, would apply certain minimum standards. However, if the mutual recognition approach were adopted, the Court would be deciding those standards on a case by case basis which provides businesses with much less certainty than, we believe, the harmonisation approach would. No small business wants to embark upon trading in another country if there is a risk of legal challenge or uncertainty for the premise on which they are operating. I think it may be worth drawing to the Committee's attention that UEAPME, which is the European Federation for Small Businesses and is one of the leading social partners in Europe for the small business sector, has stated that it would prefer a Country of Origin Principle combined with harmonisation. They recognise the benefits of the right of establishment for simplification, the right of establishment that the current draft of the Directive might bring. However, they have concerns that there would be a conflict between the Country of Origin Principle and the host country principle, they are arguing for a minimum level of harmonisation on establishment. We believe that approach would be the best approach. It is likely to provide companies with greater certainly and is less likely to lead to extensive litigation. We were all very conscious, for example, that when the rules on the free movement of goods were first established within the European Union, it resulted in hundreds if not thousands of cases, having to be heard by the European Court of Justice on these issues. Nobody wishes to see the Services Directive leading to the same level of litigation, particularly where we are talking about the small businesses sector being the primary beneficiary of this Directive.

Q98 *Baroness Eccles of Moulton:* Do you think there is a possibility that they could be reassured about that argument?
Ms Reed: We would be happy to engage in that debate. That is certainly the case that we are putting forward, and we welcome the fact that other small business federations within Europe recognise that

debate and are arguing that before the Commission and the Council.

Q99 *Chairman:* You have obviously thought about this. Which sector of services do you think could be an early participant in your cautious and general approach to these matters?
Ms Williamson: We are not advocating any particular sectors for our approach, we are simply saying that this is the basis on which we could conceptualise it going forward. The obvious candidates would be sectors where it is expected there would be most potential growth in intra-EU trade in a sector. That would seem to be where to start—look at where the greatest expansion in trade could be achieved—start there and go on from that point.

Q100 *Chairman:* Your critèrion would not be which the easiest sector to obtain harmonisation; it would be which sector is most likely to lead to growth?
Mr Tudor: I think probably which sector is currently the biggest, which is the one where those cross-border issues are most pressing. I think that is part of our generally pragmatic approach to these issues. We look at the areas where the biggest problems exist at the moment and try and deal with them first, rather than go for a global solution that affects people who may not be that much obstructed by the sector, but I think it is partly for those sectors themselves to decide where they need that to happen, which, again, if you move to a sectoral approach, they can come through and say, "We have got big problems. Deal with us first please."

Q101 *Chairman:* Can I put it another way to you? Given that your view appears to be based on concerns of one approach and it would be better to have another approach and, being the TUC, I am sure your views are based on concrete cases, as it were, as opposed to theoretical propositions; which service sectors do you think would not be desirable to go for early on? You must have some concerns. You cannot be saying this because it is a theoretical proposition. You must have some fears, concerns, about some sectors.
Ms Reed: We may want to identify, at least at the outset, one sector where there is already consideration within Europe for a sector specific Directive, which is the Agency Worker Directive. The agency sector is perhaps distinctive from most other service sectors in that it relates to the actual provision of labour as opposed to the provision of a direct service; but our approach will be that the Temporary Agency Worker Directive, which is in draft form and being debated before the Social Affairs Council, offers a better model approach to this issue because it sets out a framework for the removal of restrictions on the use of temporary agency workers, but does so

in combination with the introduction of minimum standards, in this case minimum standards relating to employment protections for agency workers, including equal treatment on pay and other conditions. We believe that model is obviously more sensitive to the needs of the sector, and also identifies what the risks of that sector are, in any given circumstances. It is a clear example where we are already pressing the European Union to adopt sector specific legislation which would enable the liberalisation of that sector but would bring with it certain minimum rules of harmonisation.

Q102 Chairman: Let me just finish my own question, because this is central to your views. What characteristics, what aspects of services do you want to harmonise? When you say "harmonise the sector", what do you want to harmonise?
Ms Williamson: If we are seeking to expand trade in services, then we want to harmonise the conditions under which that would be done. The starting point for us saying we want to harmonise is the assumption that the aim is to promote expanded trade in services throughout the EU. We are not saying we want to harmonise for the sake of it, we are not saying our aim is harmonisation in a vacuum, we are saying it should be a condition of expanding trade, especially if the Country of Origin Principle is going to be applied.
Ms Reed: We do recognise there is currently a proliferation of different rules in relation to establishment across the EU, and, therefore, the Services Directive offers a way for bringing a common approach to the rules regarding how businesses may establish in other counties, but in terms of—

Q103 Chairman: That is not the point. We are not talking about "establish", we are talking about temporary operations in the Country of Origin Principle where you are saying it should be based on harmonisation. What I am asking you to clarify when we come to consider our report is, what do you want to harmonise? We want to try and understand what it is. Is it the terms on which a service is offered for sale? Is it the qualities, characteristics, of a service? I am trying to understand what it is. Is it the conditions of employment with the service, which is quite a different issue? I am seeking generally to help the Committee. What are we trying to harmonise?
Ms Williamson: We are seeking to harmonise the conditions under which the service is provided, offered, produced—if that is an appropriate word for the service—and traded, traded with the consumer, the way that it relates to the regulator. I think, in a sense, we are talking about harmonisation across the board to the extent that a service provision, a service is regulated. We are saying there should be a degree at

least of harmonisation across the Member States to enable a level playing field in the context of expanded trade. If one sector is much more highly regulated than another sector for reasons of safety or whatever, then it would obviously require a larger degree of harmonisation applied in that particular case.

Q104 Lord Geddes: I would like to press on with this. Pursuing what the Lord Chairman was asking some moments ago, just to repeat by way of a question, the TUC is in favour as a generality, of sector specific harmonisation. Is that correct?
Ms Williamson: We can support that, yes.

Q105 Lord Geddes: Mr Tudor said, and I must say I thought it was a very positive statement, that the TUC wished to be, and the word he used was, "pragmatic". Holding on to those two points; your evidence, for which we are extremely grateful, specifically said that you wanted all transport services excluded from the Country of Origin Principle, health care as a whole, social services, the construction industry, and you want clearly defined public services or services of general interest to be ring-fenced. Going back to the Lord Chairman's question, your written evidence leads me to think that those are the areas where you would like sector specific harmonisation. If by definition you want, to repeat, transport services, etcetera, etcetera, to be excluded from the Country of Origin Principle, by definition you must want them included in the sector specific harmonisation, must you not?
Ms Williamson: We would have to look at the proposals being put forward for that sector specific harmonisation in each case.

Q106 Lord Geddes: I am sorry, why then do you want them excluded? I cannot follow this.
Mr Tudor: There is a third category. You can deal with things through the Country of Origin Principle or you can deal with things through harmonisation. There is a third category, which is that, at the moment, they might not be appropriate to be dealt with in either category. We are saying that we think there are certain things which are not appropriate to the Country of Origin Principle, the sectors that you mention. It may well be that those sectors were keen to pursue the idea of harmonisation, but it may not be the case. We are simply saying that those are not appropriate to deal with through the Country of Origin Principle; there are some sectors which would want to proceed to harmonisation.

Q107 Lord Geddes: Can I finish my own question, because it seems we have gone so far down the track? What areas of business services, therefore, do you regard as suitable for encouraging by means of the Country of Origin Principle, which, I note, has the wonderful acronym of COOP. Anyway, that is a facetious comment for which I apologise. What areas do you think would be suitable? Any?

Ms Williamson: Potentially, the other areas that were suggested. I think we have answered this as far as we can go. We have suggested a criterion whereby sectors could be selected. We could accept there could be other criteria, which the Chairman has suggested. We are not coming here to strongly advocate that any one sector should go forward. That is not the basis of our position.

Q108 *Lord Geddes:* Can I ask one more question then? I think I know the answer, but I would like to have it on the record. Is your concern in this respect with regard to the import of services under the Country of Origin Principle, ie, whomever they may be, businesses from it does not matter what EU country it is, one of the other 24, coming into the UK on a temporary basis? Because, of course, once a company is established, then the rules of that country in which they are established apply; so we are only talking of the Country of Origin Principle on a temporary basis. Are your fears import or export?

Ms Williamson: Potentially both. It could be either. It could be either depending on whether a lowering of standards was the net result.

Mr Tudor: Can I make clear that our evidence on this, and our views on this, are influenced by our existence as part of the European Trade Union movement; one person's import is another person's export, so in that sense, our view on what is appropriate in this case is conditioned by concerns among our Swedish affiliates, concerns among our Polish affiliates, and so on, so it is not easy to decide about imports, exports. If you were looking at it as an external issue in terms of the European Union, it would probably be easier to say that we would be worried there about imports, but since we are talking about a single market, our view is that there is not much difference between an import and an export because we import someone else's export.

Lord Geddes: That is a valuable comment, Mr Tudor, if I may say so, but you are looking at it from a pan-European view point and not from a United Kingdom view point.

Q109 *Lord Swinfen:* Purely for my own clarification, by "harmonisation" do you mean the standardisation of regulations and law affecting the service?

Ms Williamson: Not necessarily standardisation, an agreed form of minimum standards, and obviously Member States could decide to go above that, so, no, not uniformity necessarily, a minimum standard.

Lord St John of Bletso: I think consistency is what you want to be talking about. Certainly one of the biggest impediments to any business, both small and

large, is uncertainty. I understand what you say on that. I think it is absolutely right.

Q110 *Chairman:* You mentioned financial services. Are you suggesting that the financial services action plan, all the Directives and the vast amount of comitology regulations that are going to come out of that, are good models for harmonisation of each and every sector of services? Have you thought about that at the TUC? That is a serious question. Some people would say that would be a nightmare for Brussels if you applied that approach, if that is what you mean by sector harmonisation?

Ms Williamson: I do not think we can comment in detailed terms.

Q111 *Chairman:* You did quote it. You said, for example, financial service has been that sort of good example of a sectoral approach which has been done?

Ms Williamson: Yes, we noted that to date harmonisation has taken place on a sectoral basis and gave that as one of three or so examples where it has happened. I do not think I can comment in detail without more consultation with our affiliates who have been more directly affected, but my impression of what their experience has been is, in one word, somewhat mixed. I think it is worth noting that financial services regulation is very, very complex on a national basis, and so in a sense one would expect that harmonisation would be complex and lengthy, and if that is necessary to increase trade, and the aim is to increase trade, and it is an area where it is extremely important that the interests of consumers are protected, then sometimes harmonisation will be complex.

Baroness Eccles of Moulton: Before we move on could I ask one very quick question?

Chairman: Of course, it is your question!

Q112 *Baroness Eccles of Moulton:* I might have misunderstood something Mr Tudor said some time ago. I thought he made a distinction between harmonisation and the Country of Origin Principle; I just wanted to be clear whether harmonisation is seen as a precursor to the Country of Origin Principle working, or whether harmonisation was one route to achieving a single market function for services applied, and the Country of Origin Principle was a distinctive route down which it could be monitored. I might be in a complete muddle about this, but I just wanted to be clear about the relationship between harmonisation and Country of Origin Principle, whether they were two separate routes or whether one was a precursor of the other?

Ms Williamson: I think we are saying that harmonisation should be a precursor for the Country of Origin Principle. That does not necessarily rule out harmonisation *per se* with a different agenda, if you like.

Baroness Eccles of Moulton: Thank you. That is what I wanted to know.

Chairman: Clearly, if everything was harmonised, the Country of Origin Principle would be irrelevant. I hear your words. One effectively means the other is redundant really.

Q113 Lord Swinfen: I want to move on to a slightly different subject. The draft Directive, as you know, makes a distinction between the temporary provision of services in other Member States and more permanent establishment of a business. How would you wish to define these terms in a way that is both meaningful and also does not give rise to unintended consequences?

Ms Williamson: Clarity on the definition of establishment is important, because whether a service provider is established or not affects whether their service provision is subject to the Country of Origin Principle or not. That is why we put a lot of store on the definition. An example of why this has been important is that to date the Department of Trade and Industry has not been able to tell us whether the definition of establishment, as currently drafted, would exclude the care sector from the Country of Origin Principle or not. Our concern with the current wording is that the requirement of economic establishment over an indefinite period could allow, or give rise to, service providers using temporary renting and temporary contracts to, if you like, circumvent conditions of establishment and therefore use their home country rules. So far we have not received reassurance that the current wording does not give rise to those risks. We understand that most Member States do agree that there is more clarity needed on the definition of establishment, indeed work is taking place on that, but the current definitions are based on European case law and, without seeking to become experts in this complex area, we are not seeking to suggest specific amendments which themselves could give rise to unintended consequences, but to suggest areas within the wording that we believe need to be addressed in the round.

Q114 Lord Swinfen: Would you put a time limit on it? For instance, if you have got a contractor who contracts to build a power station in another state, it is obviously going to take several years, but if you are, for instance, a hairdresser you can go over and get the job done in half an hour. When does temporary stop being temporary and become permanent, I think is the question I am really asking?

Ms Reed: We have concerns about any time limited concept, and we would prefer establishment to be based on the nature of the establishment, the nature

which the business has based itself in another country, not least because, as our response indicates, we do have some concerns about the operation of the Country of Origin Principle and particularly how it could be used to undermine standards. Our concern is if there was a clear time limit specified, businesses might use that to circumvent higher standards within the host country and would ensure that their operations only existed for a limited period of time which was shorter than the period of time specified within the Directive. Therefore we would wish to avoid any time limit definition. Indeed, the latest guidance from the Commission on the Directive indicates that they also take the view that a time limit approach should not be adopted.

Chairman: I think we will probably return to that question later, so I would rather pursue it then.

Q115 Lord St John of Bletso: We have perhaps already exhausted the country of origin issue quite early on! My question revolves around it as well. In your evidence you said the TUC is very concerned about the implications of the country of origin rule for health and safety standards, and, of course, this applies right across, other Member States all face the same problems. You also go on to say that it is absolutely essential that health and safety requirements are specifically listed as derogations from the rule. What has been the response of the Department of Trade and Industry to these concerns and your proposed solution and what has been the response from the Commission?

Ms Williamson: We are engaged in on-going discussions with Department of Trade and Industry on this and on many other things. They are sympathetic to our concerns on health and safety, and their negotiating position does include a commitment to uphold UK standards of health and safety in all circumstances, so we are pleased that is their negotiating position. What we have not seen yet are proposals as to how this might be achieved, and clearly we would want to see any proposals on the table for protecting health and safety and comment on those when they are put forward.

Q116 Lord St John of Bletso: What about the Commission?

Mr Tudor: Everybody tells us that it is all going to be all right, but, as you know, the Commission has not responded formally. It is doing it at the moment through a series of articles in the *Financial Times*, which, though it may be generally a paper of record, I do not think anybody would claim that you can actually put your house on it. The Commission has not responded formally to any of these things, as I understand it, even in the working groups of the Council it has not circulated revised texts or anything like that, so we wait and see. Everyone says it is going to be okay. We will see what it comes up with.

Q117 *Lord St John of Bletso:* Wait and see, I suppose?
Mr Tudor: I did not want to use that phrase!

Q118 *Chairman:* If I understood the evidence of the CBI a few days ago to us—and I have not seen the written transcript of that, so could I qualify my remarks that I may have misunderstood them—I believe I understood them to say that they fully supported the TUC's position on health and safety, but when asked if that applied to the temporary provision of services they said, "Oh no, they are clearly talking about when businesses are established." I think that is what they said. I think I will probably be writing to them to clarify that is their view. Would you make any distinction between health and safety standards or businesses operating on a temporary basis from an established basis?
Ms Williamson: No, absolutely not. I think there is quite a strong consensus across Europe on this issue.

Q119 *Chairman:* I am simply trying to get it for the record; that is all.
Mr Tudor: It might also be worth checking out the Health and Safety Commission's view on that, because obviously the CBI and the TUC are both engaged with perhaps a tripartite institution.
Chairman: We have had written evidence from them.

Q120 *Lord Swinfen:* Can I ask a question on that? The health and safety standards tend to vary from one country to another. Which country should apply?
Ms Williamson: Those of the host country, those where the service is provided.

Q121 *Lord Swinfen:* Even if they are lower that the standards of the country from which the people doing the job come?
Ms Williamson: We would obviously wish to see the highest possible health and safety standards applying in all circumstances, but, yes, it would have to be those that apply in that country.
Ms Reed: There is no rule of law that says if you go beyond what the minimum legal requirement is, that that—

Q122 *Lord Swinfen:* I appreciate that, but the problem comes if an accident occurs. It is not until then that the law gets tested?
Ms Reed: Therefore the test would be: is the company complying with the health and safety rules of the host country?
Lord Swinfen: Thank you. That is just what I wanted.

Q123 *Chairman:* Is there anything further that you want to say on the question of health and safety in relation to the Directive? There may not be, but if there is now is the time to tell us.
Ms Williamson: I think our evidence makes it clear that we see it as absolutely essential that the UK's standards of health and safety are upheld in all circumstances, and there are lots of issues relating to the enforcement of health and safety, and so on, which are unworkable in the current draft. I think that is also made clearly in our written evidence, and the Health and Safety Commission's evidence, I am sure, goes into these points as well. I dare say it has been well understood and well covered.

Q124 *Lord Walpole:* I think this is the last question on the Country of Origin Principle to do with labour law. Your view is that the labour law should be exempted from the Country of Origin Principle. You also take the view that posted workers should be totally excluded from the terms of the Directive. What response have you had to your concerns and views from the Department of Trade and Industry and presumably the Commission by reading the *Financial Times*?
Ms Reed: In terms of the response from the Commission, I think our previous answer to the previous question in terms of the Commission stands. The TUC is continuing to have on-going discussions with the Department of Trade and Industry, particularly in relation to the implementation within the UK of the existing Posted Workers Directive and our concerns in relation to that. Our wider views on why we believe that the issue of labour rule should be excluded from the Country of Origin Principle, and therefore why there is no need for the provisions in the Directive in relation to posted workers, is based on the premise that the Posted Workers Directive itself only offers very limited employment rights protection to any individuals on a temporary assignment. As I am sure members of the Committee are aware, those rights in the UK context would only cover the rights of the national minimum wage, working time regulations, some health and safety rights, limited rights for agency workers and some maternity related rights and rights for young workers. All EU Member States recognise within their employment laws that workers should be entitled to a higher standard of employment protection. Certainly within the UK we guarantee individuals rights to unfair dismissal protection, rights to redundancy, a wider range of family friendly rights including, for example, rights to paternity leave and the right to request to work flexibly. Those clearly are not covered by the Posted Workers Directive and therefore would not be guaranteed under the Country of Origin Principle with the Services Directive. Our view is that any individual

worker who is employed in another country should be entitled to the basic employment rights of that host country, and therefore we take the view that labour law should be excluded from the country of original principle. May I also mention briefly one other point in relation to this, if that is appropriate, which is our particular concerns in relation to the enforcement of employment right and labour law under the current drafting of the Services Directive. As we understand it, if individuals are temporarily assigned to another country and covered by the country of origin rule, they would be required to enforce their employment rights again through the enforcement authorities of their home country as opposed to that of the host country. We believe that is unrealistic and would basically mean that a minimum labour standard would not be complied with. Our view is that they should have the right to make complaints to the enforcement authorities of the host country where they are working.

Q125 *Lord Walpole:* I think you did say that in your evidence, did you not?
Ms Reed: Yes.
Lord Walpole: Thank you.

Q126 *Chairman:* Again to help us, could you begin to make this proposition concrete? Give us an example of a business sector service where posted workers are fairly commonly occurring, it is a common occurrence, and explain in relation to this country if a worker was a posted worker working elsewhere in Europe what your concern might be and, in reverse, if a worker posted in the UK from another Member State would those same concerns exist?
Ms Reed: One issue in terms of UK workers who would be posted abroad and would be working abroad under the terms of the Country of Origin Principle, is that those individual workers may not have rights, for example, to trade union representation which they would otherwise have within that host country. Therefore if they felt they had particular employment law problem, they would not necessarily have a legal right to access the trade union and to have their rights to representation, which is obviously a clear concern for the TUC. I think there are also some concerns from other trade union federations and in the TUC that under the Country of Origin Principle rules and minimum terms which are set out in international level and sectoral level collective agreements, which are legally binding in those countries, the terms would not apply to posted workers who were working within those countries. Within the UK our affiliates have often reported to us concerns of enforcing employment rights for individuals who are being posted to the UK to work in the construction sector; and in particular, in some of the worst examples, where individuals are

being recruited by agencies. Those individuals sometimes do not even receive the national minimum wage. That is in breach of UK law. The difficulties of enforcing those rights are such at the present time that individuals are losing out on the basic protections that they are entitled to in law.

Q127 *Lord Walpole:* They are not even being paid the national minimum wage?
Ms Reed: Yes, in some instances they may not be being paid the national minimum wage, partly because there is a practice at the current time by agencies to make deductions from agency workers' pay packets to cover the costs of equipment, to cover the costs of transport and the costs of accommodation. UK law says that all workers must be entitled at least to the national minimum wage, and therefore any deductions which take the person's pay package below the national minimum wage would be unlawful. However, certainly in recent weeks we have had a number of cases reported to us where that is happening. The difficulty for the individual concerned, often because of their language barrier, is that they do not know how to enforce those rights. Were the Services Directive to be implemented, and particularly the rules in relation to enforcement of posted workers' rights where the home country would have the responsibility for enforcing those rights, we believe that many particularly vulnerable workers, but also workers generally, would lose out on their legal entitlements.

Q128 *Lord Walpole:* The law on gang masters has literally gone through in the last day or two, which must help quite a bit or not?
Ms Reed: We certainly very much welcome the legislation on gang masters.

Q129 *Lord Walpole:* So do I.
Ms Reed: We also very much welcome assurances given by the United Kingdom Government that they will seek derogations from the Services Directive to ensure that the current gang masters legislation is protected. We welcome that and we support that initiative.

Q130 *Lord Haskel:* I hear what you say about workers and gang masters, and we have heard your concerns and your caution. We have also discussed the problems of harmonisation. I wonder whether, in practical terms, the impact of this proposed Directive on employees, that is people who are working in these companies, will be of increased flexibility in starting up new service businesses in other Member States on a temporary basis. Is this not going to be fairly small? With the result for the employees of more employment opportunities? Is not your attitude perhaps belying that opportunity?

Mr Tudor: I should say that I know it does not sound like this sometimes, but the TUC is actually in favour of completing the internal market. We know that means liberalising services. We do think that completing the internal market, generally speaking, is something that promotes jobs and increases the number of jobs. We are a free trade organisation. We believe in that because it encourages increased employment. The difference, I think, and the point where we part company slightly with some of the terms of the Directive, or break with the terms of the Directive, is that what we want to see is the growth of quality jobs—the old phrase "good jobs at decent wages"—and what we are concerned about is to make sure that we get the completion of the internal market on a basis which makes sure that the jobs that are created are good ones. We think that in many sectors that is best achieved by the harmonisation process sector by sector, rather than by adopting the somewhat blunderbuss approach the Country of Origin Principle has set out in this Directive. I want, if it is possible, to nuance the position we have got. We are generally in favour because it creates extra jobs of completing the internal market. What we are concerned about is the terms on which those jobs are created because we think that conditions what sorts of jobs those are, and I am not sure we are necessarily in favour of creating lots of badly paid jobs and in particular of creating a knock-on effect on the jobs that already exist as a result of doing that.

Q131 *Lord Haskel:* Do you really think that what you are trying to do is practical? Surely in a huge market like the significant single market in Europe, if the market becomes wealthier, if the single market achieves its purpose, we all rise up on the tide. We are all in this together and to try and say you are in favour of quality jobs rather than jobs which are low paid, do you really think it is practical to try and influence the market in that way?
Mr Tudor: Yes.
Lord Haskel: You are a brave man!

Q132 *Chairman:* I do not follow that—
Mr Tudor: The answer is, yes.
Chairman: —fascinating though it would be. We could go on all afternoon, but sadly we have already overrun our time. I apologise for that. Can I say how helpful we have found your evidence and how grateful we are that you have spared the time to spend that time with us. Thank you very much indeed.

Memorandum by Federation of Small Businesses

1. INTRODUCTION

1.1 The Federation of Small Businesses (FSB) is the United Kingdom's (UK) leading non-party political lobbying group for small businesses existing to promote and protect the interests of all who own and/or manage their own businesses. With over 185,000 members the FSB is the largest organisation representing small and medium sized businesses in the UK. We welcome the opportunity to contribute to the Committee's Inquiry into the European Commission's proposal on the Services Directive and believe that this is both a valuable and timely investigation.

1.2 FSB members frequently find that European Union (EU) laws are not implemented evenly throughout the EU and there are discrepancies between Member States. One consequence is that this makes it extremely difficult for UK small businesses to enter new EU markets. This runs contrary to assertions that EU laws are meant to create an area where businesses could operate in an Internal Market with one set of rules. This was recently recognised by the High Level Group chaired by Wim Kok when it conducted its review of the Lisbon Agenda. Its report noted that: "in too many cases, implementing legislation is not in line with the original directive or is excessively complex". The FSB believes that in order to have a successful Internal Market, solutions must be found for this problem.

1.3 In this way, FSB members would welcome moves that are designed to reduce the red tape differential and facilitate trade in services within the EU. Therefore, we believe that the proposed Directive on Services in the Internal Market (Directive) could potentially benefit small businesses as it has been promoted as enabling businesses to go into other Member States under simplified rules for both establishing a new company in another Member State and providing temporary services. There are, however, two caveats that must be considered during the legislative scrutiny of this Directive. First, the resulting Directive must not increase the regulatory or financial burdens experienced by a company wishing to operate solely within its home state. Secondly, any increased regulatory or financial burdens imposed by the resulting Directive on companies operating across intra-EU borders, must be both justifiable and proportionate to the resulting benefits achieved by both business and the wider EU economy. The FSB believes that an Impact Assessment should be conducted in order to answer these questions.

2. ONE-STOP SHOPS AND THE FREEDOM OF ESTABLISHMENT

2.1 FSB members would welcome moves that are designed to reduce red tape and facilitate trade in services within the EU. In this way the FSB welcomes moves to create one-stop shops where a small business can go to meet all the administrative requirements of establishing a company in another Member State. This will make it easier for a small business to establish in another country.

3. WHEN DOES A TEMPORARY SERVICE PROVIDER BECOME AN ESTABLISHED SERVICE PROVIDER?

3.1 The FSB is concerned that the Directive does not resolve the issue of when a temporary provider of services becomes an established provider of services. EU case law on this matter is unclear. In some instances a business providing services once every six months will be classed as an established business. In this way, it would be difficult for a small business to find out whether it must register with the national authorities in the Member State where it provides services, as required by Article 6, or whether it is governed by the Country of Origin Principle as outlined in Article 16. Therefore, the FSB believes that this Directive should be revised in order to create a clear set of guidelines outlining what is considered to be "temporary provision of services" and what is "an established presence". If this is not clarified a small business might fall foul of the law and genuinely believe that it is a temporary service provider whilst the national authorities, in the Member State where he is providing a service, may consider that it is established business and penalise the small business for a genuine mistake. It is the FSB's view that this policy decision should not be left to the European Court of Justice (ECJ). The average small business would never be in a position to challenge an erroneous decision of the national authority in the Courts.

4. THE COUNTRY OF ORIGIN PRINCIPLE

4.1 Article 49 of the EU Treaty, as interpreted by the ECJ, already gives a business the right to provide a service temporarily in another Member State. It is the FSB's view that Article 16 of the proposed Directive merely confirms the current position. Therefore, the FSB supports the use of the Country of Origin Principle, which promotes mutual recognition, in this Directive. This is because it allows free trade for those businesses that wish to engage in EU cross-border trade without imposing further regulatory obligations on businesses that choose to trade exclusively in their home country.

4.2 Mutual recognition is meant to facilitate the creation of the Internal Market by making it unnecessary to harmonise all regulatory rules when national laws are based on the equivalent objectives.[1] The concept of mutual recognition was developed by the ECJ in the Cassis de Dijon ruling.[2] Mutual recognition has not been fully applied within the European Union and for a long time it has been necessary to establish a clear set of principles so that it operates and is enforced effectively.[3] Article 49 of the European Treaty also has derogations akin to those in this Directive and a national Member State can prevent a business from selling a service for "imperative reasons relating to the public interest and where the restrictive effect was not more severe than necessary to achieve the objective pursued".[4] This involves demonstrating that the concern underlying the host country's rules, which represent the barrier to providing services, were not adequately addressed by the regulatory system of the service provider's state of establishment.

4.3 The FSB also believes that national health and safety laws should not be undermined. It is the FSB's view that UK health and safety laws should be retained to protect UK small businesses from being undercut by foreign firms who do not have such stringent health and safety requirements in their own Member States. Foreign firms providing construction services in the UK should be subject to the same health and safety regime as UK businesses. It is the FSB's view that this is not a restriction to trade and the retention of UK health and safety laws can be justified by "imperative reasons relating to the public interest".[5] At present there is a perception that small businesses in the UK will be undercut by foreign companies entering the market as these new market entrants will not meet UK health and safety standards. Therefore, the proposed Directive should

---

[1] According to the interpretation by the ECJ, mutual recognition should apply to foreign regulations having equivalent objectives or effects to the regulations applying in the importing Country.

[2] The principle of mutual recognition was developed in Cassis de Dijon. The ECJ held that, in principle, a Member State must allow a product lawfully produced and marketed in another Member State into its own market, unless a prohibition of this product is justified by mandatory requirements, such as Health and Safety protection. The principle was extended to services in *Van Binsbergen v Bestuur vand de Bedrijfsverniging voor de Metaalnijverheid.*

[3] *See Unfinished Business Making Europe's Single Market a reality.* A report by Accenture and Chatham House, 2004.

[4] *EU Law,* Stephen Weatherill and Paul Beaumont, Third edition 1999.

[5] This is the test outlined in the ECJ case law on the subject of free movement of services. *See Sager v Dennemeyer,* Case C-76/90 [1991] ECR I-4221.

expressly state in what circumstances the Country of Origin Principle will not apply and in particular clarify the situation as it relates to health and safety. The general derogation to the Country of Origin Principle in Article 17 (17) "Specific requirements of the Member State to which the provider moves, that are linked to the particular characteristics of the place where the service is provided and with which compliance is indispensable for reasons of public policy or public security or for the protection of public health or the environment" is too vague and this wording needs to be more explicit. Indeed this has been widely argued by the Health and Safety Commission (HSC).[6]

4.4 The focus should be on removing trade barriers that discriminate against business entering markets. Therefore, this Directive should have this as its main aim. Some small businesses entering new EU markets, especially in the trade sector (electricians, builders, plumbers etc) encounter difficulties because of compulsory memberships of trade guilds. They find that if they want to practice their trade in other EU Member States, they have to join the local trade guild in the country where they would like to supply their services. This Directive will hopefully remove this type of discriminatory barrier.

4.5 The European Parliament currently appears to oppose the use of the Country of Origin Principle in the Directive in favour of sector specific harmonisation Directives. Indeed this was one of the conclusions of the rapporteur, Evelyn Gebhardt's, recent report.[7] Sector specific legislation causes problems for small businesses which do not trade across EU borders in that they are required to implement standards and regulations while they receive none of the benefits of engaging in cross-border business activities. Therefore, the FSB favours the retention of the Country of Origin Principle in this Directive.

5. Contract Law and Private Law

5.1 The FSB feels that both business customers and consumers expect to buy products under their own national law. If this were not the case FSB members fear that the potential customer will opt for a national supplier of services as opposed to one operating across borders. Conversely, FSB members would be reluctant to deal with a French or German company in the UK under the national contract law of the Member State where that company originates. The FSB supports the parties to a contract right to negotiate their own terms including the choice of applicable law. The FSB is concerned that these issues of private international law are not adequately addressed by the Directive in its current form.

6. Information Requirements and a Potential Transferral of Red Tape

6.1 Article 22 passes a requirement on Member States to ensure that the recipient receives information on consumer protection, how to obtain redress in the event of a dispute. The FSB is concerned that the Member State will ensure this happens by placing the burden on the service provider to provide this information.

6.2 The provisions that relate to the quality of service are a clear example of creating extra red tape for a business. Rather than cutting red tape when a business provides services in another Member State, as the Directive claims to do, it might result in a transferral of red tape from the host country to the home country. This would defeat one of the initial assumptions that this Directive was intended to remove the red tape that is associated with cross-border trade.

6.3 Article 27 will require service providers to take out professional indemnity insurance which goes beyond current UK insurance requirements. Already small businesses experience problems when obtaining employers' liability insurance.

6.4 Article 28 equally imposes a requirement on Member States to "ensure that providers supply a recipient, at his request, with information or otherwise of an after-sales guarantee"; this requirement should not be interpreted in a way to place extra burdens on businesses that are not already standard business practices. Indeed not all services can be guaranteed. For instance Training and Consultancy on "Change Management" cannot be guaranteed because once the service provider has left the company it is not certain that the company in question will implement the methodologies and training effectively.

6.5 Article 31 requires Member States to ensure that service providers have their services certified or assessed by independent bodies. It further requires Member States to introduce labels and quality marks to the assessed service. This would appear to be extra bureaucracy. Moreover, there is no detail as to which bodies will have

---

[6] See *Draft Directive on Services in the Internal Market* HSC Response to the DTI Consultation, July 2004.
[7] 21 December 2004 WORKING DOCUMENT on the proposal for a Directive of the European Parliament and of the Council on Services in the Internal Market (COM)2004 0002 of 13 January 2004 Committee on the Internal Market and Consumer Protection, Rapporteur: Evelyne Gebhardt.

responsibility for assessing the quality of services and indeed how assessments/certification will be conducted. The FSB would not support this type of move as it envisages that this would be impossible to implement or police. Is it in fact possible to categorise all trades and services so that each has an overarching "independent" assessing body without incurring huge financial costs?

6.6 Some FSB members are also concerned how these information requirements will affect businesses that advertise and sell on the Internet. There is a fear that as soon as a business advertises its services on the internet it will be categorised as an "international trader". Will the provisions of this Directive affect them even if their services are destined for the home market only? This point needs to be clarified and costed.

7. SIMILAR PROPOSALS

7.1 It is unclear how this Directive will relate to other proposals. For instance will the Directive enable small businesses to employ the same marketing strategies cross-border? This would be extremely beneficial to small businesses, however, the Unfair Commercial Practices Directive was looking at this and recent manoeuvres in the European Parliament indicate that the Country of Origin Principle will not apply to this Directive. Therefore, it is unclear to what extent a small business can conduct business as it would in its home state. In its current form the Directive is not creating legal certainty and there is much to be resolved.

8. CONCLUSION

8.1 At the time of writing, it would appear that the European Union is re-evaluating the Services Directive and that the concept of mutual recognition will be abandoned in favour of sector specific harmonisation. This would be highly damaging. Mutual recognition is important for small businesses, in that those who choose to can easily operate in other EU Member States and those that do not are not forced to adapt to new legislation. The free movement of services is a fundamental right of the European Treaty and at present the European institutions are failing to deliver it. It is necessary to put in place the mechanisms to allow small businesses to provide services across EU borders albeit with exemptions for health and safety and public policy. The Directive, in its current form, suggests that the EU will not cut the red tape that prevents small businesses taking advantage of the Internal Market. If mutual recognition is defeated there would be little point in adopting the Directive at all.

17 February 2005

Examination of Witnesses

Witnesses: Ms TINA SOMMER, Chairman International Affairs, MR STEPHEN ALAMBRITIS, Head of Press and Parliamentary Affairs, and Ms ELIZABETH START, Policy Development Officer, European Affairs, The Federation of Small Businesses, examined

Q133 *Chairman:* Good afternoon. I am sorry we have kept you waiting. We have allowed about 45 minutes for the evidence, so we will aim to finish about five o'clock. First of all, many thanks indeed for sending in your written evidence and for coming today to meet with us. Are you Mr Alambritis?
Mr Alambritis: Yes.

Q134 *Chairman:* Would you like to introduce yourself and your colleagues? If there are any introductory remarks you feel you want to make, please do, and then we will go into questions.
Mr Alambritis: Thank you, my Lord Chairman. I am Stephen Alambritis, Head of Press and Parliamentary Affairs to the Federation of Small Businesses. On my left is Tina Sommer. She is our International Affairs Chairman within the FSB, but, more importantly, she is an entrepreneur with a service business in the UK in Wales, 20 miles north of

Cardiff. Tina also has business interests in a non-automated parts company in Latvia, which is relevant to both service and other aspects. To my right is Elizabeth Start. Elizabeth is the FSB's Policy Development Officer on European and trade matters. I wanted to make a short statement with regard to both the FSB and the backdrop against which we feel this Directive is very important not only to our members but to the generality of small businesses in the UK. FSB has 185,000 members. Together they employ 1.25 million people and turnover £10 billion. We have a presence in Brussels as well in terms of our lobbying. With regard to the generality of businesses, small businesses employ 56 per cent of the private sector work force in the UK and account for 50 per cent of the gross national product, so a very important sector. Within the FSB's membership 25, 5 per cent are in the service sector, which is why this Directive is important to us. Our understanding is, both within the UK and within the European Union, 70 per cent of businesses are in the service sector and their GDP is 70 per cent and the service sector employs 70 per cent of the employment. There are two ways businesses can increase their turnover: going to new markets, going to new products. I believe the Services Directive is important in terms of new markets, added markets, and the increase in the European Union of some 350 million customers with the additional 10 new Member States taking it to 450 million customers; and that is why it is crucial that we engage small businesses so they can gain access, especially in services, to as many customers as possible within the internal market. That closes my opening statement.

Chairman: Thank you. Lord Haskel.

Q135 *Lord Haskel:* Thank you, Lord Chairman. I notice in your submission, you are generally in favour of this. You speak about barriers and you mention regulation. Could you tell us what are the significant barriers to small businesses seeking to offer their services in other Member States of the European Union? Could you tell us what they are, could you tell us what are the most important and do you think that the Directive addresses these barriers?

Mr Alambritis: Can I ask Tina, as a real entrepreneur, to have a stab at that initially.

Ms Sommer: Yes, there are barriers. I think that has been studied quite extensively by the Commission and also by the United Kingdom Government. It is anything between just about under 100 identified barriers, but that also varies, of course, by the industry you are in, whatever kind of industry you are there for. The main barrier we believe is anything to do with licensing requirements, authorisation you may need in another country, also to find out what you actually need to set up a business in another country. It is not only a language problem, it is also to know where to go, who to ask, and if you are not really settled in a country yet, you do not have very good contacts, it is quite a chore to do that, so the proposed first or one stop contact line is a very good idea. As a small business person, the question is: how do you go about setting up a business abroad? There are actually some steps you do in that. First, you export, and whether that is goods and services does not really matter because it is the safest way of doing this. You do not establish yourself totally; you just export a service via the Internet, which has become very popular now. The next step you can take to avoid potential barriers is to find a joint venture partner who is local in that host country, who knows the regulation and can help you. That is one way of getting around these barriers at present. If we had a first point of contact, you would not necessarily have to do that and that would be a benefit. These barriers

are definitely there and they need to be overcome and then they can have a new start.

Q136 *Lord Haskel:* You spoke very much in terms of setting up a business. You told us about the problems of getting authorisation, but this Directive speaks about temporarily going into business, putting your toe in the water, and you mentioned the use of the Internet. Do you think this Directive helps and encourages firms to do precisely that, to temporarily go into a market so you can begin to feel your way without making too much of a commitment? Because I think that is what it tries to do.

Ms Sommer: This is where the principle of country of origin comes in, which I believe is quite a contentious subject. For temporary set-up abroad, that probably would happen if your own law applies: if I am a British company and I want to go into Italy, Germany or wherever, of course I know my own law best and if that applies to whatever I do in my host country then that would potentially help. What the ramifications are for the companies in my country is another question of course, but from an export point of view, that would probably help.

Q137 *Lord St John of Bletso:* If I can just ask a supplementary. It is very interesting what you say about the constraints and the lack of having an interface. We have here London First and Business Link, which are hugely helpful for foreign companies operating in London. To what degree does the FSB promote links which we have here with links in other Member States? You mention joint ventures; certainly you could appreciate joint ventures with larger companies, but for many SMEs they are not large enough and they do not have the brand recognition in order to get into joint ventures, so often when they are establishing themselves in the service sector it is organic growth rather than through joint ventures. My question is, what assistance do you promote for UK-based SMEs operating in other Member States and how closely do business links operate with similar agencies in other Member States?

Mr Alambritis: The FSB provides good links between UK businesses and businesses within the Member States through our affiliation and membership of the European Small Business Alliance, where like-minded business organisations in most of the Member States also meet and discuss issues regularly. The FSB works very closely also with United Kingdom trade partners within the Department of Trade and Industry. We also inform our members about Euro information centres, information they can garner. We think Business Links would be better placed to help United Kingdom businesses get into the internal market when the Business Links come under the remit of the RDAs (Regional Development

Agencies), so local advice for local businesses. The RDAs are competing with each other, hopefully without duplicating monies and so on, to push their region and their region's businesses into the internal market. We believe that giving the Business Link contract to the RDAs will immensely improve that. We have some concerns about exhibitions and the cost of those.

Chairman: Can I just ease you away from this line of question and answer because it takes us quite a way away from the inquiry, although it is an extremely interesting area. It is immaterial to the purpose of this inquiry, but we will come back to some of the things you have said.

Q138 *Lord Walpole:* You say in your written evidence, in paragraph 3.1: ". . . the Directive does not resolve the issue of when a temporary provider of services becomes an established provider of services". You also say the Directive should make it clear with a set of guidelines outlining what is a "temporary provision of services" and "an established presence". Have you thought of such guidelines?
Ms Start: I will do a little bit of background, if I may. We are referring to the Article 4 definitions, which defines establishment and there is definitely a lack of a definition for temporary in those definitions. In terms of guidelines, we have not come up with an exclusive list ourselves. We have talked about them and thought about the situation, when does a temporary work service provider become established? Some of the considerations we have thought through have been: if you are going into a country more than 10 or 20 times, is that becoming more established, more permanent? Alternatively, you could look at it in terms of qualification for tax purposes or the number of days you are out of the UK, those sorts of considerations. I think the case law of the European Court of Justice has got some ideas on this; obviously we are not legal experts, so we would like to see those principles being taken by legal drafters to provide a clear definitive set of guidelines. Here I am saying it is difficult for us to find out what the criteria are, for a small business that is going to be even more difficult, therefore we feel a guideline about "when temporary" could be based upon the guidelines of the European Court of Justice.

Q139 *Chairman:* You require clarity on what is meant by temporary and what is meant by established—temporary in a sense is non-established—that is important in your view, is that right?
Ms Start: Yes, it is important in our view because this affects the application of the Country of Origin Principle. Therefore, if you do not know when you are considered a temporary or when you are considered established, you are not going to be

certain of when the Country of Origin Principle affects you or when you have to apply to the host state.

Q140 *Chairman:* Is not the problem that what might reasonably be regarded as temporary in one service industry could be quite different from another? Let me put this conundrum to you: how can you define or set out some guidelines that are meaningful for all sections or sectors if, in fact, it differs by sector? The conundrum is—we will be coming to this when we talk about harmonisation or not—that once you try to define a service sector, you are into a real problem, you are into rigidity. How can you define forever more what a service sector is, and if you cannot define a service sector, how can you have a different meaning to temporary by different sectors, so there is a conundrum. How can you define something by another criterion which many people think you cannot define anyway?
Ms Sommer: It is a major problem because every industry in the service sector is different. If you look at the Internet, it becomes even more difficult because that may not be temporary or established because you cannot say how often something is ordered or whether you provide a service via the Internet.

Q141 *Chairman:* Can I check on that because I do not use it? I understood that provision of service by the Internet is not covered by this Directive.
Ms Sommer: I am not clear on this.

Q142 *Chairman:* The Directive does not cover provision of services on the Internet, as I understand it. Is that your understanding? This is an important issue. Can we leave provision of service on the Internet aside for the minute because I do not think that it is covered. This is dealing with a service provider physically in a country providing a service.
Ms Sommer: It is still difficult because it depends on the industry sector. I would not know how to address that.
Mr Alambritis: One way forward, which we could look at, is by talking to the Trade Association Forum, of which we are members, which is based in the CBI. It carries a classification for all trades and sectors and tries to group them in terms of their trade association aspect. Lord Heseltine attempted, when he was President of the Board of Trade, to get everyone rationalised, so he met less people coming through the door than he would have rather liked. It is a huge conundrum, but the Trade Association Forum could be a way through. They have the authority to have a list of services and who qualifies for service.

Q143 *Chairman:* I will come back to this later, but I will leave it at this point: do you think you can define, meaningfully, a service sector?

Mr Alambritis: You can define, meaningfully, a service sector by talking to the Trade Association Forum and also by bringing in specialised lawyers and councils.

Q144 *Chairman:* Across all 25 Member States?

Mr Alambritis: It would be very, very difficult.

Chairman: We will come back to that when we do harmonisation because it lies at the heart of the harmonisation issue.

Q145 *Lord Geddes:* A very brief supplementary: if one achieves that idyllic state—which you say would be very, very difficult, it was said in earlier evidence—it would then have to be proven, if you like, by a judgment from the European Court of Justices. You have got two steps to this, and you have already said the first one is unbelievably difficult and the second one will take quite a length of time. What about the finances of that, from your point of view?

Ms Start: We referred to the European Court of Justice route in our evidence. What we are referring to is the fact that the European Court of Justice is often required to take policy decisions because of the gaps within the way the legislation has worked, partly because you have not got these definitions of what is temporary and the Courts have to make those policy decisions themselves. The legislation and the interpretation of the legislation is unclear, and there are unclear sets of principles. Therefore, as the FSB sees it, we need to clarify this and try to work towards the definition. Ultimately, you will have to have that interpreted, but once you have got clearer guidelines, that will focus the minds of the judges so they do not come up and have to take the policy decision. You could have a grey black list or a grey list so that nothing is definitive, but you need a guide in principle so at least people have something to work towards. At the moment we have not got anything to work towards.

Q146 *Lord Swinfen:* In your written evidence, at the end of paragraph 1.3, you say an impact assessment should be conducted on the effects of the Directive on regulatory or financial burdens on companies wishing to operate solely within their home state and also on companies operating across intra-European Union borders. Are the Regulatory Impact Assessments, so far published by the Commission and the Department of Trade and Industry, defective in this regard and, if so, how?

Ms Start: We have seen *The State of the Internal Market*, which is the first report from the Commission. The Department of Trade and Industry then carried out an Extended Impact Assessment; the

majority of those studies were focusing on the costs and benefits of cross-border operations. To the best of my knowledge, they have not undertaken a cost study purely on companies having to adapt to this legislation or the alternative sector specific legislation who are solely operating in their local markets. Recently I spoke with the Department of Trade and Industry on this point and they have been looking at commissioning other studies. Again, to the best of my understanding, that work will be purely looking at the costs and benefits of this Directive in relation to crossing borders. They are not addressing the issue of companies operating solely in the UK.

Q147 *Lord Swinfen:* Do you think it would cost companies operating solely in the UK, or in their own home state, more or less?

Ms Start: To date, the indication of the way EU legislation operates is that in EU regulation, and adapting to a new regulation, produces costs for a small business. We have done studies to show that small businesses have to spend five times as much to comply with EU regulation than other large companies and, therefore, the trend would be to suggest, yes, it would increase costs based on our previous experience of EU regulation. We have not carried out our own cost benefit analysis purely because we do not have sufficient resources at this stage. We would envisage also that if you do not go with the Country of Origin Principle, and you are looking to more sector specific legislation as an alternative, that would increase costs because you are having more and more regulations which will apply at home, so it would cost more if they went for sector specific.

Mr Alambritis: One of the ideas we have, with regard to both United Kingdom legislation, regulations and Directives from the European Union, is for Post-Implementation Regulatory Impact Assessments—PIRIAS as we call them—and we feel that is a useful way to revisit a Regulatory Impact Assessment. It is not that you will undo all the legislation, but it will iron out glitches and allow Member States' governments to see how they can help feed their information services to address any blips in what the RIA originally said before it was implemented and post-implementation. That is one route we have suggested to the Cabinet Office.

Q148 *Chairman:* We need to be clear on this issue because your written evidence appears to say something slightly different from what Ms Start said then. In your written evidence you said that there were two caveats to your support for the Directive: one was the Directive must not increase burdens on companies who only wish to operate within their own state; the other was that increased regulatory burdens on current businesses that do want to cross borders must not be too high. You believe that Impact Assessments should be conducted to answer these questions; are you saying, in both cases, that the existing Impact Assessments have not been adequately carried out? That is important to us as a Scrutiny Committee. As I understood your written comment then, it was that on the first one your answer is yes, they were inadequate and they did not consider the case of businesses that are not wishing to go cross-border and in the second case, the Impact Assessments did consider their case, is that right?

Ms Start: I am sorry if there has been a misunderstanding about the point. We would say the Impact Assessments are all inadequate, at this stage, regardless of whether they are referring to cross-border or home states.

Q149 *Chairman:* In what way?

Ms Start: They have not done sufficient costs, they have not done the surveys of businesses and it has all been based on speculation. We have not been asked to provide details of our members to anybody to ask about how much it is going to cost the UK business, therefore the businesses have not been asked about the Impact Assessments and it has not been undertaken, as of yet. The Department of Trade and Industry are currently going to start something afresh, but obviously we cannot comment on something which has not been finalised.

Chairman: I am afraid we are going to have to adjourn to vote, but we will come back on this important issue. It is a most important issue because the Regulatory Impact Assessments are supposed to be a very important part of ensuring the Directive does reasonably and properly address a proportion of the relevant issues.

The Committee suspended from 16.34 pm to 16.46 pm for a Division in the House.

Q150 *Lord Haskel:* I just want to probe this matter of our regulations affecting a business which is not going to subject themselves to this regulation. If I have got a service business and I am not going to go out and do business outside the UK, you are saying regulations about doing business outside the UK are going to be a cost to that business. Can you explain why? Is it because it means businesses from other European countries will come and impact on my business here or is it that regulations generally are a cost for businesses? I wonder if you can explain that a little and then we could understand your dissatisfaction about the Regulatory Impact Assessment better.

Ms Start: At the moment EU legislation is being passed quite significantly and there are always new regulations coming out of Brussels. It is being passed on the rationale that these are meant to complete the internal market so all companies can operate within the EU, and the reasoning and objectives behind the legislation are to finish the internal market. When these are adopted within the UK and are applied into UK legislation, these regulations will then impact on small businesses operating in their local market. It is a cost to them to adapt to new procedures, and new requirements of authorisation standards, to be in compliance with those regulations and that is where we see the costs. Things which are meant to further the objective of the internal market, and making money through the internal market, also affect businesses that just stay and operate at home, but they have add-on costs.

Q151 *Baroness Cohen of Pimlico:* What add-on costs? If I am a service business, for example, I am a hairdresser and I am not planning to launch out on a chain of hairdressers in any other country, what additional costs will accrue to me as a result of the Services Directive?

Ms Start: From the Services Directive, I cannot answer that, I am not a hairdresser, I am afraid.

Lord Haskel: Any service or business. I am not going to expose myself to the needs of those regulations.

Q152 *Baroness Cohen of Pimlico:* I am not going to go overseas.

Ms Start: It depends on how this Directive is interpreted into UK law. A lot of what I am saying is based on theories, I am not certain, and I am basing it a lot on experience of other pieces of legislation which have impacted on UK businesses with the aim of completing the internal market.

Q153 *Chairman:* This piece of proposed legislation, as currently framed, appears on the face of it to have no additional costs burden or otherwise, on businesses which do not wish to operate outside the UK—as currently framed—I use my words with care. If—and we are going to come to it later—one went to a harmonisation approach, then clearly, in my view, in fact, it will come to that. As a Committee, we are anxious to understand the difference between—how might I put it gently—rhetoric and fact. When we asked the CBI this in oral evidence they said that faced by the question, they could not think of any costs that this Directive would bring. You represent small businesses, so it is very important we understand what you believe to be the case. I would invite you, if you say there are costs, to submit to us in writing practical examples of what they would be because that would influence this Committee.

Mr Alambritis: We will send a note to the Committee. It could be that the totality of regulations, the need to be up to speed with what regulations are coming through, the advice from one's trade association, from one's law people, all that has to be fed through and given to the business whether they are going to be in that area or not. We will send a note to the Committee because we feel the totality of EU legislation could impinge in terms of keeping up with the legislation, so ticking it off, does not apply to me, but you still need to have read it or looked at it.

Q154 Chairman: On the question about the Regulatory Impact Assessments, you say the Department of Trade and Industry are going to undertake additional work on the impact of this proposed Directive on businesses that do cross-border business. They are not going to do a further study on businesses that do not cross borders?
Ms Start: That was my understanding from the conversation I had with the Department of Trade and Industry.
Chairman: That is extremely helpful. We will pursue that.

Q155 Lord Geddes: In your evidence at paragraph 4.1—and indeed you exemplified this in reply to Lord Haskel's opening question—clearly and not surprisingly you came down on—if I can put it this way—the pro-Country of Origin Principle. Then in 4.3, you say there is a perception in the UK that small businesses will be undercut by foreign companies entering the market as these new entrants will not meet United Kingdom health and safety standards. In fact, you effectively ask for a derogation on that particular subject. Do you have any firm evidence to date that this perception has substance?
Ms Start: The evidence for this perception was based on the Health and Safety Commission and having meetings with them and their response to the Department of Trade and Industry consultation. They were very concerned that health and safety was not protected by this Directive. We feel that whilst you should have mutual recognition, you also have to retain certain protections for workers, self-employed and small businessmen who operate on sites. That is where we came from; it is based on the health and safety.
Ms Sommer: I had a conversation with a representative of the Commission in Brussels on this particular issue. I was told the health and safety legislation is exempt, it is one of the many exemptions. I was assured that health and safety is not affected and the Health and Safety Commission in the UK has been assured about that as well. I asked, "Where exactly is it?" and we went through the phrasing. This is where, as a business person, I have a problem because the way this is phrased is a little bit open to interpretation depending on how you read it and it is not entirely clear. I think that problem has been dealt with because it will mainly affect the construction industry. As far as I know, Impact Assessments, particularly for that industry,

with regards to health and safety, have not been done because everybody is now assuming it is not affected. When Directives come out, the way in which they are written are a little bit open to interpretation. That means that in the end, however it is interpreted in each Member State, there may be problems arising because there are different interpretations and then you might possibly have to wait for a judgment by the European Court of Justice. From a business point of view, I am only talking as a business person now, this creates a degree of uncertainty and that really is terrible. We cannot live with uncertainty because, first of all, as a small business person, if I was treated unfairly or I felt I was treated unfairly in another Member State because I interpreted something differently, I would have absolutely no means to take another Member State to the European Court of Justice, I would not have the finances or the time to do that. Even if the Commission does it, to make sure it is all equally implemented, I would not be able to wait for it. I would say, yes, there are derogations there, and I have been assured verbally it is not a problem, but it creates uncertainty.

Q156 Lord Geddes: You would like Article 17(17) to be much more specific?
Ms Sommer: I think it should be more specific because even the Health and Safety Commission and the Commission thought it was not right.

Q157 Lord Geddes: Do you still take this view, bearing in mind—and we have had a long discussion already about how temporary is temporary, let us just take that as read for the moment—that there can only be a problem in this respect in the temporary situation. Once a company is established, then it is bound by the laws of that country from a health and safety point of view, and every other point of view for that matter, but are you still concerned?
Ms Sommer: I am not because I was assured, but it is only the word of one person. I am not in the construction industry, it does not affect me personally, but I could well imagine that somebody who is in the construction industry in the United Kingdom now may be concerned about a temporary service provider coming in who may follow the health and safety instructions of their own country, which may be a lot less—we are fairly accurate and fairly stringent here, for good reasons—and that may cost that company less, therefore they could quote a better price for the same job. I can see the concern there.
Chairman: The Health and Safety Commission submitted powerful written evidence on this point and certainly we will be raising this in the Commission when we meet them the week after next.

Q158 *Baroness Eccles of Moulton:* I think we are moving on to the Country of Origin Principle here. In your evidence you expressed dismay that where the Service Directive is being evaluated—this is in your conclusion—the concept of mutual recognition is being abandoned in favour of sector specific harmonisation. I think it is possible to gather from your evidence, under the Country of Origin Principle, that provided mutual recognition is the basis, then you would support the Country of Origin Principle. I think what would help us a lot would be if you could explain how you see the differences between the two approaches and why it is so damaging if the Directive moves from one basis to the other and whether this could be an exaggeration.

Ms Sommer: This is a very difficult question and I think you will appreciate that. First of all, we have the concept of mutual recognition and the way I understand that, which is really just my opinion, is if you have mutual recognition of qualifications, for instance, you do not have a change within the Member State, as such, you are basically comparing that qualification with a similar one in another country and you agree the terms where these two should be compatible and can be acknowledged. For instance, I did a university degree on the side and last year I finished it. I tried to find out what that degree means in Germany, what is the equivalent, but nobody in the United Kingdom could tell me that and in Germany they could not tell me either. There is an interest that we have mutual recognition of any kind of qualification, whatever it is, and that means there is no change in the Member State. If you have harmonisation, that is a completely different ball game, in my eyes, in that, first of all, 25 countries have to agree a certain standard which they all aim for and then each Member State has to get to that standard, either come down or go up, which I think is very difficult to achieve. That would mean a change in every Member State and that means it affects the businesses in every Member State. That is where we are coming from; to say mutual recognition does not mean a change for the company in the UK who does not really want to go abroad, they just carry on as before. For the ones who do want to go abroad, they can agree, they know what they have to do to have that mutual recognition. If they have not got that qualification which gets them there, they can do it, but at least it is only affecting those who actually want to get involved in this. I think long-term for the small business community it is better.

Q159 *Baroness Eccles of Moulton:* What if there is a small business that wants to operate in six different countries? Then the mutual recognition has to be compatible across all six countries, which surely means there would have to be some quite substantial changes in some of them in order to be able to achieve

some form of mutual recognition. Is that not beginning to approach a form of harmonisation?

Ms Sommer: That is my personal view, I do not know how the rest of our members think. If I want to deal in six countries, that is my decision as a business. I have a qualification in the UK and I see how that matches in Italy, France, Germany, wherever I what to go and it is my responsibility to make sure I have this. Provided these recognitions are there, I can find out what they are and I can aspire to that, whatever it is. That is a business decision, I do not think it needs 25 countries to come up with the same standard.

Q160 *Baroness Eccles of Moulton:* How would the Country of Origin Principle and harmonisation then apply?

Ms Sommer: The Country of Origin Principle only comes in for temporary services. I think mutual recognition should happen in any case, it is not dependent on the Country of Origin Principle. It will make life a lot easier, not just for business people, but also for people who want to move around and work in different countries. That is much more preferable, in my view, to harmonisation, there is no doubt about it.

Q161 *Chairman:* In your view, moving to harmonisation would—as in your written evidence— be highly damaging and there would be little point in adopting the Directive at all. That is very strong language which is used in your written evidence. Do you stand by that now you are before us?

Ms Sommer: I think harmonisation will be very, very damaging.

Q162 *Chairman:* Why?

Ms Sommer: Because everybody has to change. We are all human beings; I am a German national, I live here in the UK; Germans have a different viewpoint on certain industries and certain attitudes to those that we have here or in Italy. To find total harmonisation in service industries, and agree on it, is almost impossible, I cannot imagine it.

Q163 *Chairman:* You use the example of degrees and qualifications, which I have to say I think we can all understand and, indeed, there is a Directive on professional qualifications and so on. Can you give us an example of a service industry where harmonisation is less easy to be clear about? Qualifications are not an industry thing, in general it is person-specific thing.

Ms Sommer: I have to be a little bit careful because I only know a little bit about it, hairdressers were mentioned: my sister happens to be a hairdresser in Germany and I know how their qualification system works because she had to go through it. There is a degree where you have to have two or three years' apprenticeship and then there is a masters degree, which takes five years. It is very old fashioned guild thinking how to work yourself up, and it is quite difficult to achieve. A hairdresser—my sister—is very, very proud of this qualification. They have to study hard and it costs a lot of money to get it. I do not know exactly how it is in the UK, but I have never heard anything like that.

Q164 *Chairman:* Explain how this relates to harmonisation versus mutual recognition?
Ms Sommer: If you now have harmonisation and you say, "Okay, the Germans win", they say, "This is the standard we want", then a hairdresser in the UK will have to go through the same process and possibly the cost attached to it, plus having all the systems in place to make this happen. If it is mutual recognition and if in the UK there is a certain test, or whatever it is, that person in the UK knows it is as good as the one who has a masters in Germany without having to go through the entire loop. It would cost a lot less and it would be much more time saving.
Mr Alambritis: I think you need to note the principle of public law status, ie in Germany, France or Holland, businesses have to qualify first before they start to trade, whereas here, we have a very laissez-faire approach in starting a business; from day one, for instance, as a hairdresser, you can open up on your own training with your own resources.
Chairman: There are several questions arising from this and it is a very important issue, but Lord St John wants to come in.

Q165 *Lord St John of Bletso:* No, I was just looking to qualify what you were saying. It is quite clear you are saying that you are not in favour of harmonisation, you are in favour of co-ordination?
Ms Sommer: Mutual recognition.

Q166 *Lord St John of Bletso:* Mutual recognition which encompasses co-ordination. We had this sort of issue about tax as well, whether one was in favour of tax harmonisation or co-ordination.
Ms Sommer: Tax is a different issue.
Lord St John of Bletso: I was just trying to qualify that.

Q167 *Chairman:* We understand that one might think a German national might regard mutual recognition as dumbing down.
Ms Sommer: No.

Q168 *Chairman:* People regularly express the danger of the phrase, the race for the bottom. We understand there is quite a lot of opposition to the Country of Origin Principle and to harmonisation in Germany.
Mr Alambritis: The hairdressing industry in the UK is the envy of the remainder of the Member States.

Q169 *Chairman:* I did not mean hairdressing *per se*, I meant the general question of the guild approach to trade services and so on, in the UK is a much more pragmatic approach. My question is this, we were told in oral evidence before you came in, that the European organisation of small businesses, in its support for the Country of Origin Principle, supports harmonisation not mutual recognition.
Ms Sommer: Which organisation is that please?

Q170 *Chairman:* The European Small Business Alliance.
Ms Sommer: If you ask 10 small business people, you will get 10 different answers, I am afraid.

Q171 *Chairman:* I apologise, but frankly as a Select Committee we cannot quite take that view. You are telling us in Britain small businesses are saying that the harmonisation principle is the end of the world, it almost destroys the purpose of the Directive. The Pan-European body of small businesses, we were told by the TUC before you came in—
Ms Sommer: We are not a member of that organisation, so I cannot speak for them.
Ms Start: We are a member of ESBA. I think perhaps you are referring to the Union Européenne de l'Artisanat et des Petites et Moyennes Entreprises, which is known also as UEAPME. It has a different position to us.

Q172 *Chairman:* As far as you know, why do they have a different position?
Mr Alambritis: Because their membership is public law status led.

Q173 *Chairman:* It is helpful for us to understand that because you will appreciate it is confusing to us as a Committee.
Mr Alambritis: Their membership is public law status led which means a lot of their members have what is called "statutory chambers", where before you can begin to trade you have to join the guild to do the training to set up in business. Whereas the organisation we are part of, the European Small Business Alliance, supports the voluntary approach to both business representation and setting up in business in your own free way and, hopefully, making it by convincing your customers that you are the best business, not through a certificate or a plaque, but through your own business skills.
Baroness Eccles of Moulton: Chairman, would it be worth knowing which represents the largest number of small businesses in Europe?

Q174 *Chairman:* Which countries?
Mr Alambritis: We can send you a note.
Baroness Eccles of Moulton: That would be helpful just to get a feel for the weight of opinion.

Chairman: That would be very useful indeed. If I may say, that is a most helpful part of our proceedings today. Is there anything further on that issue?

Q175 *Baroness Eccles of Moulton:* Presumably you represent small businesses which produce goods as well as services, how has the harmonisation single market approach to the industries producing goods fared in small businesses?

Ms Start: The approach for goods is a mutual recognition approach based on the principle in the Cassis de Dijon, where if one good is produced in compliance with the legal requirements of one Member State then its equivalent objective should be recognised in any Member State and be able to sell it throughout. Again, there have been some common standards in health and safety and quality of products which have come out of the EU. Therefore, the goods have benefited from the mutual recognition approach.

Chairman: I would like to push on, but I would like to come back, if the Committee would bear with me, on the harmonisation issue because we have heard two such different approaches today where the European Parliament and the Commission are totally at odds, as I understand it. We are meeting both the European Parliamentarians and the Commission when we are in Brussels the week after next, including the German rapporteur, and the Chair of the Committee, to look at these matters.

Q176 *Lord St John of Bletso:* You mentioned that your members often find the EU laws are not implemented evenly throughout the EU. It is right at the beginning of your submission (paragraph 1.2), that there are discrepancies between Member States. In your evidence, in paragraph 5.1, the whole *locus standi* contract law and private law, it says the FSB supports the parties to a contract, the right to negotiate their own terms, again the choice of applicable law and that the FSB is concerned that issues of private international law are not adequately addressed by the Directive in its current form. In what respect are they not adequately addressed by the Directive? That is my first question. Going on from there, how should the draft Directive be changed in your view and can individual consumers or small business buyers of services realistically negotiate their own terms with the service providers including their choice of applicable law?

Ms Start: The only reference in the Directive, at the moment, about contract law is Article 16, and it states that Member States may not impose the requirement to use the host country law. For instance, a country like France cannot force a British company, who is going in temporarily, to use French contract law if the parties agree and that is how it is stated at the moment. There has been a lot of debate,

especially in the working document from Evelyn Gephardt to which we have referred, which talks about the implications of Rome I and Rome II, whether it should be incorporated and whether businesses should have taken away the right to choose their right to elect what type of contract law. Basically, we are just firming our position that we believe in the freedom of contract and if we are affected we would try to promote the view that businesses should be able to choose their contract. Tina has some more to add from her own experience of using contract law.

Ms Sommer: As a business, obviously I want the choice. If I have a contract with another partner or customer in another country, it is business to business, you agree the terms and a business should be capable of doing that. As far as consumers are concerned, I would not like to comment, we are a business organisation so maybe you should talk to a consumer organisation. If it is business to consumer, it is a different ball game again because you already have Directives that are looking after the interests of consumers, consumer protection laws, and they are in place and every business has to respect that. This has all been covered already and I do not see where the Directive comes in here.

Q177 *Lord St John of Bletso:* Business to business is normally covered by the contract in itself, it is normally a *locus standi* clause.

Ms Sommer: That is right and that is why we are keen to keep it that way.

Q178 *Lord St John of Bletso:* You support the *status quo*?

Ms Sommer: Yes.

Chairman: There is a vote. We lost 10 minutes from the previous session and we are going to lose a few more now. I would like to deal with that last topic, so for those of you who can come back, it would be very helpful. We have to adjourn.

The Committee suspended from 17.11 pm to 17.22 pm for a Division in the House.

Q179 *Lord Haskel:* Going back to the Country of Origin Principle, the application of this Principle relies on the development of an extensive Mutual Assistance Framework whereby Member States co-operate in supervising enterprises based in their country and in respect of their operations in other countries, whether it is people doing business from overseas here or people from this country going to other European countries. How workable do you think this framework is and is it practical?

Ms Sommer: I cannot answer that question and you are asking me to speculate, I do not know. From a business point of view, I find it very difficult to imagine that they can handle this because in the end it will require—and I am thinking business again—human resources to do this. Does that mean they will have to have more civil servants to be able to set all of this up? I do not know. I cannot answer for the Member States' administrations whether they are able to handle this. When I spoke to that person in the Commission they said to me, roughly, "The Directive is geared more towards the Member States to make it easy and facilitate inter-state trading for business". My first impression of the Directive was, this is fantastic, for a change it is the States who get the regulations and the legislation to put something in place, like the first point of contact, which will make my life a lot easier. If the Commission and all agree, they will do that, that will be fine, it will help. Whether they can do it or not, I cannot tell you. I find it difficult to imagine right now, but I would be speculating. I am sorry, this may not be very helpful, but I cannot answer for the administration of Germany, Latvia or Hungary, I just do not know. I would say it is a horrendous challenge and I am a firm believer that the implementation of Directives varies to such a degree in various countries—and there are statistics available proving that—that this one will be a major one. I said to that person, "How are you going to make sure this is implemented, it is such a crucial Directive for small businesses?" "Oh, we have 25 people looking after that and they will sort it all out" and I said "Good luck to you, that is one per state".

Q180 Chairman: The Department of Trade and Industry in this country has not consulted you on how such a system might work if it was brought into operation? That is a question not a fact.
Mr Alambritis: Normally they do, they have not yet, but they normally come to us with transposition questions about how to transpose Directives into UK law. Normally we get consulted on that, but they have not yet on this one.

Q181 Chairman: So far, we have got to the point where the draft Directive has been published, there has been a lot of consultation and if there had been agreements in principle—and clearly there are disagreements, so there is a long way to go—this Directive could have been in place in a few months' time, which was originally hoped, and it would have been in place, as I understand it, without anybody sitting down in this country to say, "Is it workable?"
Ms Start: The Department of Trade and Industry had meetings about this Directive, but they have been mainly focused on negotiations, how things are happening with their negotiations, what their lines are and how they are approaching their relationships with France and Germany. As yet, we have not got into those technical details.

Q182 Chairman: How would it work actually?
Ms Start: Probably, we are not the best people to say how it would work. There is a slight fear that they would make it work by imposing the requirements upon businesses, because if you look at some of the further articles in the Directive, they have got some information requirements and which Member States must ensure that this information is provided. There could be a risk that would be interpreted in the home state, "When you are going abroad you have got to give all of these policies and all of this information out and tell your customers about our laws", so there is a potential fear that they might get around the problem by making small businesses do it. As yet, we have not had in-depth conversations.

Q183 Chairman: Ms Sommer, you said in answer to an earlier question that there is an enormous variation between Member States and the way this Directive is put forward and that it puts a great onus on individual Member States to take any necessary implemented action, which has a virtue because of the flexibility and responsiveness if a Member State wants flexibility and responsiveness. Of course that may mean Member States differ in how flexible and responsible they want to be.
Ms Sommer: It is a Directive, it is not a regulation. A Directive means the Member States decide how they get to a particular end; it is the end that counts, so a Directive gives a lot of room and that is probably partially the problem. I am not for regulation either, but it gives room for manoeuvre.

Q184 Chairman: This is the way I want to finish off on this point, harmonisation and back again to mutual recognition. The critics of harmonisation say that would be the most expensive way to do it, it would take a long time to get agreement on a whole range of qualitative elements to services by sector and that would be a very lengthy expensive process. Every business in a particular sector would have to meet harmonised standards of various kinds and it would take a long time. Those supporting mutual recognition say this will enable it to be introduced much more speedily. From what you have told us, that speedy implementation could be a bit of an illusion because whenever we have asked you, I think you have said to implement it would be a nightmare and you could not understand how it could be done. So the apparent speed from flexibility in Member States could be one where the slow snail might ultimately win the day. Where harmonisation is concerned it might take longer but it would be more certain. What do you feel about that argument? I do not know if you have followed that? The critics of harmonisation say it is a very lengthy process and it will take a long time. Today the TUC said: "We would have to do it sector by sector" and they quoted the Financial Services Action Plan. The critics say that will take forever. Do you think the Country of Origin Principle with the Member States' Mutual Assistance Framework with mutual recognition rather than harmonisation in practice will be a more flexible and speedier route to creating single market services? Is it a superior approach? Ultimately the question is how do we get a single market? Is it through harmonisation by sector by sector by sector or is it by the country of origin, mutual recognition, mutual assistance? It is a choice.

Ms Sommer: For my business, I will go for country of origin, mutual recognition; there is no doubt about it. Simply because there is one Member State with another, only two and they sort it out. With harmonisation you have to talk to 25 Member States in one go for one sector and then again 25 Member States in one go.

Mr Alambritis: Mutual recognition is the more entrepreneurial approach. Harmonisation would be torturous and may lose businesses on the way.

Q185 *Chairman:* I asked the question so that your view on this is on the record and clearly views differ. That is very helpful. Are there any further questions? Can I say how extremely helpful you have all been and it is very much appreciated. We have had two excellent sessions today. I would like to thank you on behalf of the Committee for your attendance and your contribution.

Mr Alambritis: That was Elizabeth's first attempt at written evidence.

Q186 *Chairman:* Ms Start, you did very well. You had to help us with the tough questions and I thought you handled it very well indeed.

Ms Start: Thank you very much.

Supplementary written evidence by Federation of Small Businesses (FSB)

QUESTION 153: CHAIRMAN AND MR ALAMBRITIS, ON THE MATTER OF POSSIBLE COSTS OF THE PROPOSED LEGISLATION

The FSB has been unable to quantify the exact costs of this regulation. We are able, however, to draw conclusions from recent FSB reports on the costs of regulation in general. Please find enclosed copies of *Lifting the Barriers to Growth in UK Small Businesses, The FSB Biennial Membership Survey 2004* and a recent report for the FSB by Professor R Baldwin of the London School of Economics, *Better Regulation is it Better for Business 2004?* (*not printed*).

QUESTIONS 173–174: CHAIRMAN, BARONESS ECCLES OF MOULTON AND MR ALAMBRITIS: ON THE QUESTION OF WHICH TRADE ORGANISATION REPRESENTS THE LARGEST NUMBER OF SMALL BUSINESSES IN EUROPE

In the European Union there are several organisations representing business: Union of Industrial and Employers' Confederations of Europe (UNICE), European Association of Craft, Small and Medium-sized Enterprises (UEAPME), Eurocommerce, Eurochambres (the Association of European Chambers of Commerce and Industry), ESBA (European Small Business Alliance).

UNICE represents more than 20 million small, medium and large companies. It has been active in European affairs since 1958. Its members are 38 central industrial and employers federations from 23 countries.

UEAPME is the employer's organisation representing the interests, at European level, of crafts, trades and small and medium-sized enterprises (SMEs) in the whole of Europe. As the European SME umbrella organisation, UEAPME incorporates 78 member organisations consisting of national cross-sectorial SME federations, European branch federations and other associate members, which support the SME family. Across the whole of Europe, UEAPME represents over 11 million enterprises with nearly 50 million employees.

Eurocommerce was established in 1993 and represents the retail, wholesale and international trade sectors in Europe. Its membership of over 100 includes commerce federations in 29 European countries, European and national associations representing specific branches of commerce and individual companies.

Eurochambres represents 43 national associations of Chambers of Commerce and Industry, a European network of 2,000 regional and local Chambers with over 18 million member enterprises in Europe.

ESBA represents member organisations from 22 European countries. It is the only organisation in Europe to focus its representation on (fully) independent small business organisation needs (vs. statutory or compulsory membership groups). ESBA currently represents almost 2 million small business entrepreneurs and represents them through targeted EU advocacy activities. ESBA also works towards the development of strong independent lobby and benefits groups in European countries. ESBA is a member of WASME, the World Association of Small and Medium-sized Enterprises.

A European Court of Justice decision, Case T-135/96 held that UNICE represented the interests of small businesses and excluded UEAPME from the formal negotiations and consultations on social law as outlined in Articles 138–139. Therefore, on the basis of this decision UNICE is the only organisation considered to represent small businesses. This does not, however represent the reality of the situation and the above organisations are recognised by the Commission as representing small business interest. In this way they all have regular dealings with the Commission and European Parliament.

May 2005

MONDAY 7 MARCH 2005

Present	Eccles of Moulton, B	St John of Bletso, L
	Fearn, L	Swinfen, L
	Geddes, L	Walpole, L
	Haskel, L	Woolmer of Leeds, L (Chairman)
	Shutt of Greetland, L	

Written memorandum by the Construction Industry Council

1. This evidence is submitted by the Construction Industry Council (CIC), which is the representative body for the professional institutions, specialist trade associations and research organisations in the construction industry. A list of members is attached. Some members are also submitting their own evidence, which highlight issues from their own particular discipline. This evidence deals with factors which affect CIC members collectively.

2. The current state of the Single Market in services: The CIC welcomes moves to eliminate the barriers to the free movement of services by removing national regulations which act as obstacles to cross-border establishment and the provision of services. At present, there are barriers which hamper CIC members from working in some other Member States. Moreover, the CIC would not want any amendments to the proposals to take away from the intention to enable service providers to work freely across borders. However, some of the provisions put forward are complicated, uncertain and will create a fresh layer of bureaucracy, which is of concern.

3. The Country of Origin Principle: there is particular concern in the construction industry that there are aspects—we emphasise aspects—of this principle that are likely to be impracticable in the context of the built environment. Concern is concentrated on issues of health and safety, but it goes wider than that. It also covers advice given and design undertaken, as well as construction work on site. We do not feel that the derogations contained in Articles 17(17) or 17(20) go far enough. To be workable, to protect standards and to create a level playing field, there needs to be more certainty.

4. Article 16(1) is very wide. "National provisions" covers not only qualifications and requirements such as being a member of a certain body (ie something a service provider needs before it can gain access to work in another Member State) but also "requirements governing . . . the quality or content of the service . . . contracts and the provider's liability" (ie things relating to the exercise of the service). The two aspects are fundamentally different.

5. In our evidence, we concentrate on the problems that would arise in the construction industry (in relation the built environment in its widest sense) if service providers visiting another Member State could operate on the basis of the requirements that relate to the built environment of their country of origin, rather than local requirements.

6. It is not clear what "the coordinated field" (particularly the "exercise") means. "Member States shall ensure that providers are subject only to the national provisions of their Member States of origin which fall within the coordinated field [any requirement applicable to access to service activities or to the exercise. thereof]".) We agree that national provisions should apply to the access to service activities, but suggest there is a problem with the exercise moose activities (in so far as this means that a visiting service provider would not have to apply local law and regulations).

7. We note from the Report on the responses to the public consultation and the Government response to the public consultation, that attention has been drawn to health and safety aspects of construction. However, it goes wider than application of the Construction (Design and Management) Regulations, for example. Work in the built environment is governed by numerous regulations covering planning, environmental issues building regulations, asbestos, disability, discrimination etc. Different Member States might interpret in different ways whether particular regulations relate to public policy, security or health or the environment (Article 17(17)) which would cause chaos unless the local legislation and bye laws applied.

8. There are particular characteristics of the construction industry: the end product is a development or structure which becomes a permanent part of the built environment—whether it be a power station or block of flats. The interests that have to be taken into account include those with a legal interest in the construction, end users, the public and the Member State.

9. Secondly, invariably there are many different service providers working on construction projects—from inception to completion and on-going maintenance. Often, on even small and medium size projects, there are many different parties working together, resulting in a network of contracts and collateral contracts. There will be advisers of various kinds, consultants involved in designing and advising on all aspects of the construction and contractors and subcontractors. If one or more of these parties come from different Member Sates, able to apply the requirements that apply in their country of origin, the determination of roles and responsibilities would be a nightmare.

10. Although a number of requirements in relation to construction result from European Directives, the fact is that these are interpreted in very different ways in different Member States. Other requirements result from the policy of Member States themselves—which may or may not be said to be "directly linked to the particular characteristics of the place".

11. We understand that it is intended that the problem is accommodated by the derogation in Article 17(17). However, this is not clear enough, or wide enough (and this seems to be accepted). CIC understands that it was intended that this provision exempt health and safety and planning aspects of construction from the rules—but that otherwise construction would be included. This distinction would lead to great uncertainty; the line between aspects of the design process which were "indispensable for reasons of public policy or public security or for the protection of public health or the environment" and other aspects would in practice be impossible to draw. Design work and advice given, and the construction process itself, are similarly inseparable in practice. Design and construction are seamless; design is carried out during construction as well as before work begins on site—often by the same service provider. It must be clear that in all Member States, for all work in relation to the built environment, and in v relation to all advice, design and work on site, local provisions will apply.

12. Recital (43) also refers to specific requirements linked to the particular characteristics of the place, and gives "requirements relating to the safety of building sites" as an example. We hope we have shown however, that the derogations needs to go much wider than that.

13. If there was any doubt about whether a service provider was subject to the requirements of their country of origin or the Member State in whose country the development was situated, at what stage would that be determined? Before or after the development was completed? There would be no point in doing so afterwards; there is a clear need for certainty so that everyone can understand their contractual obligations, and what standards should be applied to the construction.

14. Moreover, in the UK, the sanctions for breach of the Construction (Design and Management) (CDM) Regulations and other health and safety legislation are criminal ones. Currently a service provider from another Member State working in the UK would be subject to the criminal law of the UK. Is it proposed that the provider would still have to comply with the UK CDM Regulations to avoid being criminally liable? The answer does not seem to have been thought through. We do not know whether this is intended to be caught by the derogation in Article 17(23) referring to "the non-contractual liability of a provider in the case of an accident . . . "—however, a criminal offence may have been committed under the Health and Safety at Work Act in the absence of an accident. The criminal sanction must remain as an incentive to ensure compliance with health and safety legislation.

15. Article 16 paragraph 2 refers to "the provider's liability". In the context of the " myriad of contracts and collateral contracts that is characteristic of construction projects, this would create uncertainty and unfairness. Clients may not appreciate that they are contracting with a service provider governed by the liability laws of another Member State. There should not be "traps for the unwary" and it should not be necessary for clients to obtain legal advice in order to understand the implications of contracting with a service provider from another Member State. (For example, the laws of the country of origin might limit the service provider's liability to their fee; the client engaging the service provider would be unlikely to know this, and indeed would be surprised to find that this was the default provision—in the absence of agreement to the contrary (see the paragraphs 15 and 16 below).) Unfairness can also be caused to other service providers working on the same project (see paragraph 16 and the reference to joint and several liability).

16. It is not clear how far the derogation from the general principle in Article 17(20) will assist. In the clarification of questions frequently asked (in the Report on the response to the public consultation) it is said that the effect of Article 17(20) is to provide that then Country of Origin Principle will not apply if the contracting parties choose to apply the law of another country. However, in the United Kingdom, a lawyers' understanding of the phrase "the freedom of the parties to choose the a law applicable to their contract" is

that the parties can decide that the law of a particular jurisdiction applies. If it is intended to mean that the parties are free to contract on any terms they wish (subject of course to the law of the jurisdiction they choose), this should be made clear.

17. Even if the wording is clarified, there are a number of problems. The operation of the derogation would be too haphazard. First, if there is no written contract there is likely to be disagreement as to the terms of the agreement (there should be clear evidence that the parties have chosen "the law applicable to their ' contract"). All too often there are arguments about whether there is a written contract and if so on what terms—the Law Reports are full of such cases. Secondly, it is dependant on the terms of the contract. Thirdly, it could cause problems if some of the parties do choose that local law applies, and others do not. (For example application of the Civil Liability (Contribution) Act 1978 and "joint and several liability" could create unfairness by a party finding that they are unable to obtain a contribution from a party also causative of the damage, because of the different law applying to them). Any legislation must have a clear application even if the parties have not signed a written contract, since it is common in the construction industry for contracts not to be in place.

18. The mutual assistance framework: we find it particularly difficult to understand how Article 16(2) would work in practice. We suspect that in many cases there would be no supervision of services provided in other Member States, which would threaten standards, and we suspect that the Member States least likely to supervise enterprises operating in other countries would be those with less stringent regulatory regimes. The administrative burden on Member States would be considerable.

Graham Watts
Chief Executive

February 2005

CIC MEMBERSHIP AT JANUARY 2005

FULL MEMBERSHIP

ABE	Association of Building Engineers
ACA	Association of Consultant Architects
ACE	Association for Consultancy and Engineering
APM	Association for Project Management
APS	Association for Project Safety
BIAT	British Institute of Architectural Technologists
BIFM	British Institute of Facilities Management
BRE	Building Research Establishment
BSRIA	Building Services Research and Information Association
CEBE	Centre for Education in the Built Environment
CIBSE	Chartered Institution of Building Services Engineers
CIOB	Chartered Institute of Building
CIRIA	Construction Industry Research and Information Association
DSA	District Surveyors Association
GF	Ground Forum
ICE	Institution of Civil Engineers
ICES	Institution of Civil Engineering Surveyors
ICWGB	Institute of Clerks of Works of Great Britain
IHIE	Institute of Highways Incorporated Engineers
IHT	Institution of Highways & Transportation
IMBM	Institute of Maintenance and Building Management
IPHE	Institute of Plumbing & Heating Engineering
IStructE	Institution of Structural Engineers
LI	Landscape Institute
HBCt	National House-Building Council
RIBA	Royal Institute of British Architects
RICS	Royal Institution of Chartered Surveyors
RTPI	Royal Town Planning Institute
SCI	Steel Construction Institute
TSA	The Survey Association

ASSOCIATE MEMBERSHIP

ACAI	Association of Consultant Approved Inspectors
ACostE	Association of Cost Engineers
ACED	Association of Civil Engineering Departments
ACBS	Association of Consultant Building Surveyors
BACH	British Association of Construction Heads
CHoBE	Council of Heads of the Built Environment
CHSG	Construction Health & Safety Group
CIMCIG	Chartered Institute of Marketing Construction Industry Group
CICA	Construction Industry Computing Association
COTAC	Conference on Training in Architectural Conservation
CQSA	Consultant Quantity Surveyors Association
FoB	Faculty of Building
FPS	Federation of Property Societies
ICM	Institute of Construction Management
RSME	Royal School of Military Engineering
SCHOSA	Standing Conference of Heads of Schools of Architecture
SCL	Society of Construction Law
SPONGE	(a network of young construction professionals focusing especially on sustainability)
TAG	Local Government Technical Advisers Group
TeCSA	Technology and Construction Solicitors' Association
TRADA	Timber Research And Development Association

Examination of Witnesses

Witnesses: Ms GILLIAN BIRKBY, former Chairman, Health and Safety Panel of the Construction Industry Council, MR ADRIAN JOYCE, Senior Adviser to the Architects' Council of Europe, and Ms FRANCES PATERSON, LLB, Chairman of the Liability Panel of the Construction Industry Council, examined.

Q187 *Chairman:* Good afternoon. Ms Paterson. I do apologise for the delay. I usually invite people to make introductory remarks, but I wonder if we might waive that and get on to questions. I am sure you can weave anything into your answers.

Ms Paterson: Yes, my Lord Chairman. We would just like to thank you very much for inviting us to give evidence. It is an honour and a privilege to be here. You can see that we have concerns and we hope we are able to help you understand what they are.

Q188 *Chairman:* Indeed, and I should thank you for your written evidence. It was to the point and helpful. Have you have had some initial thoughts on the terms of reference of our inquiry?

Ms Paterson: Yes.

Q189 *Lord Fearn:* In paragraph 2 of your written evidence you say that there are barriers which hamper CIC members from working in some other Member States. Can you give us some examples of such barriers? Secondly, would the draft Services Directive take away those barriers?

Mr Joyce: There are barriers, and we have identified at least two: one that relates to the uneven treatment of professional indemnity insurance within our sector across the European Union and the lack of clarity in the proposal on whether or not it will be obligatory for service providers in the construction sector. A

second barrier that is significant, certainly for access to other countries for, say, UK architects, are the authorisation procedures in some Member States. They do exist today, and the removal of those barriers would be very helpful. We do feel that, if implemented, there would be benefits for the construction sector, but the professional indemnity insurance issue would remain an ambiguous issue because of its double treatment within the text of the current proposal.

Q190 *Lord Fearn:* You mentioned authorisation. What do you mean by that?

Mr Joyce: I mean by that that if a person is properly registered and qualified in this country and wishes to move to another country in the European Union such as Spain or Greece to exercise their profession, there are a number of regulatory requirements in those countries, such as membership of a professional body, such as licensing to practise, that are real barriers to access in that country.

Q191 *Lord Fearn:* You can only think of two examples?

Mr Joyce: I am not saying that I have the full range of examples but I have heard of particular cases in those two countries.

Q192 *Lord Geddes:* You mentioned just now in that very interesting answer the problem of professional indemnity insurance. What is your answer to the problem? You say it is too complicated, there is a conflict—these are my words, not yours.

Ms Birkby: The issue is that if the professional indemnity insurance which is taken out in this country is recognised in the other Member States, that would deal with the issue rather than having to take out yet another set of professional indemnity insurance, which is going to be more expensive, more onerous and more complicated. That is the sort of answer that we are looking towards.

Q193 *Lord Geddes:* You do not think that is covered under the draft Directive at the moment? That is your problem, is it?

Ms Birkby: Yes, I think that is right.

Mr Joyce: In fact, my Lord, the Directive has that as an aspiration. We would be concerned about the workability of that provision in the Services Directive text at the moment. The aspiration is that you cannot as a Member State put a requirement to an incoming professional, if I can use that phrase, to take out a policy in that country; you must allow it to be a policy in that person's home country. So that is the aspiration; we are saying it is not workable.

Q194 *Lord Geddes:* You have suddenly thrown me with that very last phrase: it is not workable. Why not?

Mr Joyce: Because of the disparities that exist between Member States in their local regulations as to what is required in terms of cover.

Q195 *Lord Geddes:* So the Country of Origin Principle—which is, I think, what we are talking about here—you say would not work as far as professional indemnity insurance is concerned. You would not be happy with an incomer travelling with his or her own professional indemnity insurance into this country. Is that your problem or is it the other way round?

Mr Joyce: No, it is the other way round. We would support the idea that you can supply or provide your services in another country using the professional indemnity insurance you have purchased in this country.

Q196 *Lord Geddes:* That is what I thought you were going to say, but are you saying that the Directive is not strong enough in this respect? It is not sufficiently specific?

Mr Joyce: What I am worried about is that it is covered in two different places in two different ways in the Directive. Article 16(2) is the first place it is mentioned and Article 27 is the second, and there is a lack of clarity as to whether or not it would be obligatory for it to be implemented under the provisions of the text as it stands.

Lord Geddes: That is very helpful. Thank you.

Q197 *Chairman:* Are you referring to the Country of Origin Principle as being obligatory?

Mr Joyce: Professional indemnity insurance being obligatory.

Chairman: I have to say you have certainly lost me.

Q198 *Lord Haskel:* In spite of what you say, in spite of these problems, we have had a Spanish architect designing a building in the City, we have had an Italian architect doing the Tate Modern; how come these things are working despite the difficulties, as you say, regarding professional indemnity insurance, authorisation and other things?

Ms Paterson: The answer may be that barriers do not exist to working in this country, but there are barriers when our architects want to work in other Member States.

Q199 *Lord Swinfen:* Are you saying that a United Kingdom architect wishing to work in other European states is unable to get professional indemnity insurance in this country that will cover him in the other Member States? That is what it sounds to me as though you are saying.

Ms Paterson: There may be more of a problem in meeting the insurance requirements of the other Member State. It may be that his insurers here are happy to cover him if he works in France, but in France he will be required to have a particular sort of insurance, which will be different.

Q200 *Lord Swinfen:* But the insurance industry is very flexible and will insure almost anything, at a price, if you ask them to do so.

Ms Paterson: I am not sure I would agree with that.

Lord Swinfen: I did say almost anything.

Q201 *Chairman:* You are saying you would have to take out one form of insurance here, another form of insurance in France, a different one in Germany. It could be a different one in 25 Member States?

Ms Paterson: Yes.

Chairman: One of the burdens of this whole inquiry and, of course, the Directive, is to say under some circumstances, is it really sensible or necessary to have 25 different ways of doing things that you have got to do if you want to operate in another country? We will come back to that.

Q202 *Lord Walpole:* I am not totally sure whether my question should not be under the Country of Origin Principle. One of the things I did notice from your submission, which I thought was a very good one, was that you are also worried about legal problems being barriers, are you not?

Ms Paterson: Yes, the service provider's liability.

Q203 *Lord Walpole:* That sort of thing, and also health and safety, presumably, but that is more a Country of Origin Principle problem, is it not?

Ms Paterson: Yes, that is right.

Q204 *Lord Walpole:* But you have other legal problems?

Ms Paterson: One of the problems with the Country of Origin Principle...

Q205 *Lord Walpole:* We are on barriers. If it is the Country of Origin Principle we will deal with that later.

Ms Paterson: The point we made in our evidence was in relation to the Country of Origin Principle.

Q206 *Lord Swinfen:* We understand that the Country of Origin Principle relates only to businesses operating in a non-home Member State on a temporary basis, and that if the business becomes legally established in that other Member State, the Country of Origin Principle would not apply to its operation. Is that also your understanding of the draft Directive?

Ms Paterson: Yes, it is. The Directive differentiates between freedom of establishment and the free movement of services. Once you are established in a Member State, if you do any work in that Member State, that is your country of origin.

Q207 *Lord Swinfen:* How in the construction industry would you define "temporary", particularly bearing in mind that some construction contracts can go on for years?

Ms Birkby: That is right. What we have done is that we have made a distinction to say it is either an establishment or, if it is not an establishment, it is a temporary operation. So if a consultant, say, is working abroad, he is either established there or working on a temporary basis—and there is no hole between those; it is either one or the other. If you look at Article 4(5), that defines what establishment is. We are not entirely sure that we understand what that means, whether it actually means that you have got to become, say, a foreign entity, like a foreign company or a foreign partnership, or whether it means something short of that but you actually set up a permanent office. But the fact is that temporary operation we understand to mean an operation which can go on for years, because some of these projects are extremely lengthy, but quite often in those circumstances the consultant may be working out of part of the site office, the site hut, if you like, which is on the site itself, and can be doing that for several

years, and that would still be on a temporary basis. I suppose I am saying, because it is project-specific, if it is just for one particular project that he is there, even if he is there for 13, 15, 20 years, it is temporary, because it is just for that project. That ties in with things like the Mobile Sites Directive, which looks at temporary sites and it considers construction operations as being temporary sites, whereas if you were in a foreign country for a group of projects or for a project and you are trying to develop other business there, then you may set up an office and you may look at yourself as having some more permanent establishment there for general business.

Q208 *Lord Walpole:* Would you say that in order to prove that he was only operating temporarily he would also have to be covering projects in his home country?

Ms Birkby: He may be working full-time in the foreign country if it is a large project. The organisation may be doing other projects in the country. There is a wide variety, because if you think of small architects or an engineer who has maybe two or three partners, they may all be working almost full-time on a particular project but they still will be going back to their home base, if you like, ultimately, when that project finishes. They will usually keep a skeleton office, if not a proper office, back at the home Member State.

Q209 *Lord Walpole:* Do businesses in your industry currently provide services in other Member States within the apparent intention of the draft Directive?

Ms Birkby: On a temporary basis, yes, they do. I have a couple of examples. We believe, though we have not investigated this totally, that Norman Foster, when he was building the Reichstag in Berlin, operated out of this country—he certainly has a very large office here—rather than setting up a permanent base in Berlin. Another example, which I know more about, is of a client of mine who was a project manager for an IT installation, fitting out some offices in Hamburg. The architect was also English, the client was English, who was opening his office in Hamburg to provide website design, that kind of thing. So they were all working in Hamburg to set this office up, to fit it out and so on, but they were doing that on a temporary basis because they were going to be coming back, where they would still have their home base; they went out to Hamburg, as and when required, to carry out those services.

Chairman: I fear there is a Division. When we return, it would be useful if you could just explain the difference between cross-border provision of services and temporary provision of services in the way you have just described, because, I must confess, you almost began to talk about cross-border provision to me.

The Committee suspended from 5.28 pm to 5.33 pm for a Division in the House

Q210 Lord Walpole: You raise concerns about a number of aspects of the Country of Origin Principle that you believe are likely to be impractical in the context of the built environment. We will turn to those shortly. However, you agree that the Country of Origin Principle should apply to the access to service activities but that there is a problem with the exercise of those activities in another Member State. Can you explain this distinction more fully, with some practical examples?
Ms Paterson: Yes, my Lord. One way to illustrate the difference, it seems to us, between access and exercise is this. "Access" is about whether you can go on the tender list, whether you can be considered to be appointed for a project. "Exercise" is about having won the tender, how you then undertake the project. Looking at Article 16(3), Article 16(3)(a), (b), (c), (d) lists a number of examples of barriers to access such as "an obligation on the provider to have an establishment in their territory"; I will not read them but they are examples of barriers to access. Then (e) talks about the exercise. Also, if you look at Article 16(1), paragraph 2, it talks about the exercise being "the behaviour of the provider, the quality or content of the service, advertising, contracts and the provider's liability." That is about how you do the job once you have won it.

Q211 Lord Walpole: Do you think the distinction between rules governing access to provide service and the exercise of service provision are adequately reflected in the draft Directive?
Ms Paterson: As far as we can see, the distinction is not made at all.

Q212 Lord Walpole: If I could just quickly ask a supplementary, this was under, I believe, the legal thing about health and safety, where you say in some countries it is a criminal offence and in some countries it is not. There must be a problem here, must there not?
Ms Birkby: There is a huge problem in relation to health and safety. Do you want me to talk about health and safety? There are quite a few things I need to say about that. The question abut health and safety is that if you have people working on a building site who are subject to different laws and different restrictions, it will become unworkable, for various reasons. One is that if some of the workmen see that some of them can smoke and others cannot, some of them are allowed to drink alcohol and others cannot, it will cause more tensions than are perhaps necessary. The whole question of the application of the CDM (Construction (Design and Management)) Regulations, which are the main Regulations

governing the activity on site—although they are the implementation of the Mobile Sites Directive and therefore across Europe they should work the same—there is an example somebody has given me of some German contractors who were installing in this case high-speed printing presses, so it was quite complex, technical equipment, and first of all their senior managers denied all knowledge of the Mobile Sites Directive.

Q213 Chairman: Where were they doing this work?
Ms Birkby: They were doing it in England. First of all they denied all knowledge. They were told to go and look at it and they came back and said, "Yes, we have heard of the Mobile Sites Directive," which, of course, applies across Europe, "but we don't really go with it very much. We don't actually apply it particularly." It was explained to them that this is how it works on an English site, this is what you have to comply with, and it was the no smoking and the no alcohol and the protective equipment which is required, which is not just hard hats but boots and various other things. They accepted that they had to do that because it was on an English site, but the workmen themselves found difficulties in actually complying, because they were used to being able to smoke, and they found that difficult. That was interesting to me because, first of all, we are talking about Germany, which has very high standards, and in my experience very high standards of safety and concern for safety and so on, but it is also a country that has been familiar with the Mobile Sites Directive since about 1992. It was brought into force in 1995 in this country. So they have had a long time, and this example was only a couple of years ago, so they had had six or eight years in which to become familiar. The implementation of something like that, which emanates from an EU Directive, is obviously patchy or different.

Q214 Chairman: So we do not get bogged down in the detail of this, what conclusion do you draw from that in terms of the Country of Origin Principle in this Directive?
Ms Birkby: I think it is extremely unhappy as far as health and safety is concerned. I do not think it will work.

Q215 Chairman: Do you think there should be derogation of health and safety issues?
Ms Birkby: I do, but it is actually a little more complicated than that because health and safety is not just for the workers on site but it is also for the designers. The designers are under an obligation to design so that things can be installed safely: HSE (Health and Safety Executive) has spent years in trying to persuade designers that they must integrate health and safety with their other considerations,

aesthetics, money and so on, so they are trying very hard. So you cannot say of a design "This bit is for health and safety purposes and this bit is for other purposes."

Q216 *Chairman:* So as far as you are concerned, in what I keep calling the construction services business but I think you call the built environment business, the Origin of Country Principle, in significant areas to do with health and safety, both for employers and through to the design process, cannot practically work on a country of origin basis?
Ms Birkby: Yes. I am very firmly of the view. I understand the HSE also firmly supports that.

Q217 *Lord Haskel:* You have told us of your concerns about the Country of Origin Principle and how impractical you think it is. How do you think these concerns can be met? Can they be met by derogations or are there other alternatives such as harmonisation, or must the principle be dropped entirely to meet these concerns?
Ms Paterson: My Lord, our suggestion is that if you deleted reference to the exercise, if you restricted the Country of Origin Principle to the access to services, so that there was a level playing field when it came to whether you could be included on the tender list or be considered, or enter the competition, for example, but that if you got the job, you then had to comply with all the requirements of the host country, that would solve the problems, we suggest.

Q218 *Lord Haskel:* Are you suggesting that people should go on the list of bidders, as it were, only if they are then committed to carrying out the requirements of the country where the job is going to be done?
Ms Paterson: Yes.

Q219 *Lord Haskel:* Will this not cause problems for small companies, companies just starting out? Would this not give preference to people who are already well established?
Ms Paterson: I would suggest, my Lord, you have to balance that against the problems in relation to the built environment if they were able to go and work on the basis of their home requirements. One of the characteristics of the built environment is that you leave something permanent in the Member State, so this is not just an exercise which affects the parties, the client and the service provider, or all the people working on the building site or all the people engaged on the project. It will concern the owners of the building, the funders of the building, the occupiers, visitors who come to the building, the passers-by and the Member State itself, because whether you have built a dam or a block of flats, we are talking about something which is very permanent.

Lord Geddes: This may be appallingly over-simplistic but that last bit of evidence got my mind racing. I spent most of my business career in the shipping industry, and when I first started everybody said, "Of course, this industry is unique" and I quickly realised it was not unique at all; it was just slightly different and our assets moved around the world whereas other people's assets stayed put. The bit of the construction industry that is unusual seems to me that it goes on for a very long time, project by project, and we had good evidence from Ms Birkby just now. Is the answer then to not redefine the word "temporary" but to give it a different meaning? From the evidence that Ms Paterson has just given us, you would say country of origin is fine to get on the bidding list. Thereafter, obey the laws of the host country. So temporary in that context could just mean to get you on to the bidding list and after that you become established; it is not temporary at all. Is that over-simplistic?
Chairman: That appears to be what you are saying.
Lord Geddes: That is what I thought I heard.

Q220 *Chairman:* So the idea of "temporary" as a concept is of no value to the built environment industry at all, I take your evidence to be.
Ms Paterson: Because if you adopt the amendment we are proposing you would have the same rule as you do for freedom of establishment.

Q221 *Lord Geddes:* Once you are established, I do not think anyone is arguing that the draft Directive certainly is saying you obey the rules of the host country.
Ms Birkby: As long as establishment does not also include some of the barriers we are talking about here, that you have got to qualify, you have to be a member of the local Chamber of Commerce, that kind of thing. That is not relevant. I am wondering if, as a concept, yes, I can see what you are saying. That sounds really quite interesting and quite attractive, as long as it did not then have all this baggage attached to it. It may be that perhaps "temporary" is being used in too wide a sense, and that what we are trying to achieve is that the exercise by the provider in the other Member State should comply with that, but everything else which leads up to that, which is the Chamber of Commerce type issues, should not. If the words can be phrased so that that is what is included and that is what is excluded, so that it achieves what you have just said, I think that is fine, but I would personally like to look very hard at the drafting of that particular concept to see that that in fact did achieve that purpose.

Q222 *Chairman:* Clearly, in some industries—but that is not your concern—some businesses, some areas of business, the concept of tendering to be able to do something is irrelevant. If you want to set up a retail outlet or do many entrepreneurial activities, you are not in a tendering process, so naturally, your evidence is really relating to the construction industry or the built environment industry.

Ms Paterson: Yes.

Q223 *Chairman:* You cannot envisage anybody wanting to set up in another country on a temporary, try it and see basis, "Can I break into this market?", other than by tendering for contracts. You feel that the industry you represent, all aspects of it, will be happy that as long as you can tender from your home base, there is no need for anything else between that and meeting all the rules of establishment. You cannot pick and choose that. There is no need for this concept of temporary provision of services.

Ms Birkby: I am not sure that I have fully understood what you mean by "temporary." The construction industry is very wide and very complex and there is an enormous variety. Not all jobs are tendered. Some are done on a negotiated basis. You could have an architect, an engineer, somebody going into a foreign country saying, "Let's see if I can get some business here," but mostly people, I think, because that is a tricky thing to do, would do it on the back of a job they had already got, probably on a tendering basis, but maybe they knew somebody, had contacts, that kind of thing. Then when they have achieved it, they have a foothold, a base, and from that they would build out.

Q224 *Lord Swinfen:* What happens with a large firm that has a lot of business and a lot of projects in its home country? At the moment we have only been talking about one temporary project in another country. What happens if they want to indulge in a number? Does that then make them established in the second country? How often can you be temporary? How many times? Can you be temporary on more than one occasion at the same time, so to speak, in the host country?

Ms Paterson: My Lord, I think we have said that is a question of looking at the definition of "establishment". I think we have said it may not be clear, and I am sure there will be situations where it is difficult to determine whether there is establishment or if someone is there on a temporary basis, which again suggests that a difference between complying with your home rules or the host rules is not a good idea.

Ms Birkby: Can I also just say that I am not sure that we are actually talking quite the same language, because you are talking about whether you can be established in more than one country . . .

Lord Swinfen: No, I was not saying that. What I was saying is, if you have a number of temporary projects in the host country, does that then establish you? I think we have to ask the Commission this.

Q225 *Chairman:* In your view, "temporary" could mean operating over 10 years on a contract.

Ms Birkby: Yes.

Q226 *Chairman:* Lord Swinfen was saying if you are involved in two different contracts in a country, and your business was operating on two 10-year contracts, is that still compatible with the notion of "temporary"? I have to say I find that stretching the rules of the game a long way.

Ms Birkby: It may be that the words that are used by the Commissioners and the reality of the construction, which is immensely complex, are not actually matching here. That is my feeling.

Q227 *Chairman:* Can I just ask you one fundamental question? The Commission undertook an Impact Assessment, looked in depth, said they carried out lots of inquiries, lots of consultation. Her Majesty's Government and the Department of Trade and Industry (DTI) have similarly held consultations. Were you consulted? Were your concerns and your views expressed to the Commission's Impact Assessment people and the DTI?

Ms Paterson: Do you mean the consultation that took place in the summer?

Q228 *Chairman:* That is the DTI, but the Commission also undertook a Regulatory Impact Assessment, and they apparently surveyed thousands and thousands of businesses and consulted widely in considering the impact. You are being forcible in drawing to the attention of the Sub-Committee the peculiarities of the built environment industry and the difficulty of complying. I am enquiring whether those issues were drawn to the attention of the Commission. The discussion has been going on for years. I am wondering how the Commission has got to the present state with these considerations not being clear and understood and accepted.

Mr Joyce: My Lord Chairman, certainly those consultations have taken place. We are concerned that there was inadequate preparation for this Directive and we would judge that Commissioner McCreevy's words of last week are a *de facto* admission of that fact, that in essence this was rushed through the Commission's services to get it into the process quickly, and we do have concerns that a more extended Impact Assessment is necessary for this particular Directive, for our sector and other sectors.

Chairman: That is helpful.

Q229 *Lord St John of Bletso:* My question relates to the issue of the Mutual Assistance Framework. In your evidence you said you found it difficult to understand how Article 16(2) would work in practice and you suspect that there would be in many cases no supervision of services provided in other Member States, which would threaten standards. Can you elaborate on these concerns? It is always very useful in your evidence that you give practical cases of where this applies.

Ms Birkby: I was talking to some HSE inspectors about this concept, and they were delighted at the prospect of popping over to Portugal or France to inspect a building site where there were UK workers, but, on a more serious note, they felt there would be serious problems with that. HSE, as you probably know, is totally overstretched in terms of the number of sites which it is required to cover. One of the ways in which they achieve their purpose is not just to visit sites on an *ad hoc* basis but to do what they call a blitz. They will do a blitz on working at height, for instance, and during one particular week they will go and visit as many sites as they can and they will look at issues relating to working at height. They can do that in England because it is fairly confined. It is a small-ish area and they can just do that, but if you are looking at the whole of Europe and you are talking about providing mutual assistance, which is supervision—this is what we are talking about, HSE supervising—there is no realistic way in which they can possibly supervise the work of UK contractors on sites abroad. It just is not going to happen. If we are talking about the mutual assistance in general, taking it away from an example, it seems to me that either it is going to be ineffective, in which case it is not going to achieve anything, or it is going to be incredibly expensive, and expensive to the benefit of other Member States—and I am not going to try and be chauvinist about this but I can see that unless there is a benefit, a reciprocal benefit to the UK so that overseas workers here are equally supervised, there is no benefit but there is possibly a great expense for the UK. There is a difference in terms of implementation, in terms of attitude throughout the 25 states. That is part of the concern that we have about it.

Q230 *Lord St John of Bletso:* In which ways do you think these concerns can be met, or do you just feel that the Mutual Assistance Framework in the construction industry is totally ineffective; it cannot work?

Ms Birkby: I find great difficulty in seeing how it can work. If we went back to our idea of saying that the exercise is omitted from the Country of Origin Principle, then I can see that what that will mean is that, if anybody is working on a site in this country,

they are subject to the health and safety legislation of this country, and therefore the sort of rules that apply now will apply and the sites will have the level of supervision that they have now, and that will also, of course, make it much easier for people like the main contractor, who is trying, in health and safety terms, to control everybody on that site, if he can say to them all "You've got to comply with the UK rules" rather than them saying "The rules in our country are different." You can see that it is a very difficult thing to control and to deal with.

Q231 *Lord St John of Bletso:* It is perhaps a bit of an *obiter dicta*, but is it not perhaps one solution that contractors across Europe should be accredited to certain standards of uniformity?

Ms Birkby: Yes, that is a little way down the line but certainly, if there can be a way of convergence so that there is perhaps the same interpretation of a basic EU Directive like the Mobile Sites Directive, that would be excellent. That would be a real way forward if that could be achieved, but this Directive is not the mechanism, I think, for doing that.

Q232 *Lord Geddes:* I fear I may be clutching at the proverbial straw here but are there any aspects of the draft Services Directive which in your opinion improve the prospects of a single market in your industry across the European Union?

Ms Paterson: Yes, my Lord, we think there are. If there is a level playing field when it comes to access to services, that would be of great benefit to the professionals in this country.

Q233 *Lord Geddes:* That is what you were saying before, the tendering/bidding process. Is that what you mean?

Ms Paterson: In quotes: "It is the ability to go and work in another Member State or to accept a commission in other Member States", yes.

Mr Joyce: Additionally, Lord Geddes, there are other aspects under Chapter IV on quality, and that is the quality of service provision at the exercise stage, which could have great benefits for the industry as a whole and for society at large, because, for example, adopting quality assessment methods for service providers that underwrites a good delivery to the consumer and gives protection to the consumer and his or her interests would be a great benefit. Under the convergence programmes of Chapter VI of the Directive—one example, the European codes of conduct in to which national codes would then merge or align themselves—could underwrite, again, consumer protection and really give a competitive edge to the European construction sector. When it also then goes from Europe abroad into the global market—and we should not miss this point in our evidence to you—a number of the efficiencies that could be delivered to this sector would give the European construction sector an edge in a global marketplace and in the context of WTO—I do not wish to complicate the debate, but if we are more competitive, we get more contracts.

Q234 *Lord Geddes:* Could I ask the question in reverse: clearly, from the evidence you have given us, both written and oral, you do not like the Country of Origin Principle, other than to get to the bidding stage, and you particularly do not like it under the health and safety side, but leaving those two extremely important parts of the Directive on one side, other than those two, would you give the Directive a nod or are there other bits that stick?
Ms Birkby: There are quite a few other areas.

Q235 *Lord Geddes:* Basically, what I am trying to get at is, on the whole, is it that you like the draft Directive but you hate the Country of Origin Principle, particularly on health and safety, or do you hate the draft Directive but you can cherry-pick one or two bits out of it that you could live with?
Ms Paterson: There are a lot of complications in the Directive. The DTI heralded it when they consulted as getting rid of red tape, very graphically, and reading it, it seemed to create a lot of new red tape, even if it got rid of some old red tape. That is not the main thrust of our evidence, but there may be other aspects which others would concentrate on more than we have done, where there are complications. Mutual recognition is one example, but I think there may be others. We are concerned about the insurance provisions in Article 27.
Chairman: I am conscious of the hour. We have kept you a long time already. I wonder if you could write to us about that. It is important that we do know what you wanted to say. As you appreciate, written evidence is as important as oral evidence, and we will take note of that and reflect upon it in coming to our views.

Q236 *Lord St John of Bletso:* When you write to us, could you mention how you see the construction industry becoming more competitive—I think those were the words that you used. You mentioned about professional insurance cover particularly. It would be very interesting to us to understand, in the light of the draft Directive, as to where you see there being scope

for the construction industry being more competitive.
Ms Birkby: I will do that. Thank you.
Chairman: One last question, which is an enormous topic, but I fear I may then say again to you to write further, otherwise I am going to lose my next witnesses.

Q237 *Baroness Eccles of Moulton:* It is a question on the difference between the two approaches, harmonisation and mutual recognition, and whether you have a view on which would be the most effective way of achieving a single market in the construction service.
Ms Paterson: Shall we restrict our answer to that to our written evidence?

Q238 *Chairman:* Can you just give us two sentences, and then write to us.
Mr Joyce: In two sentences, my Lord Chairman, our view would be that the harmonisation route is significantly less desirable than the mutual recognition route, and that has been borne out by the experience with goods. In 20 years of work at the European level they (the European Union Commission) have not succeeded in harmonising trade in goods and they are now going for mutual recognition in goods as well.

Q239 *Chairman:* That confirms my view that it was worth you summarising, because it is extremely important that we have that view put in writing to us. We are meeting with the Commission a week on Tuesday, and with others in Europe, and also elsewhere. To have it by next Wednesday or Thursday would be enormously helpful to us. Is that possible?
Ms Birkby: Yes.

Q240 *Chairman:* I apologise for that, but this issue of harmonisation versus mutual recognition is an important issue, as you know. If we could have your views in writing, that would be jolly useful.
Ms Birkby: Can I just clarify the timing? You say you are meeting with the Commission a week on Tuesday.
Chairman: A week tomorrow, so by Thursday of this week. It is only three days but if we are to read it and absorb it and allow it to have an effect on our line of questioning, it would be very helpful. Could I say to all of you how patient you have been and extremely valuable it has been. We are very grateful to you.

Supplementary written evidence by the Construction Industry Council (CIC)

1. This further evidence is submitted following the oral hearing on 7th March 2005.

2. Our main concerns about the Country of Origin Principle are:

— Different in implementation: Even where legislation emanates from an EU Directive (eg the Mobile Sites Directive) implementation is so different in the various Member States that the Country of Origin Principle is not workable. Everyone must work to the same health and safety rules on a construction site to achieve safe working conditions.

— Breach of health and safety legislation: This attracts criminal liability in the UK. It will be divisive if workers from other countries are not subject to the same sanctions.

— Cutting edge construction: Cutting edge construction, following the Egan Report, is based on the use of integrated teams, from the designers through to contractors and subcontractors. If these entities are not all working under the same legislative regime, this integration will be difficult to achieve.

— Integrated design: The Health and Safety Executive has for several years encouraged designers to integrate health and safety issues into their design, when considering other factors such as cost, aesthetics and environmental impact. Indeed, a health and safety coordinator (or planning supervisor as he or she is currently known in the UK) has to be appointed by the client at the outset, so that these issues are considered as soon as work on design begins. It is not therefore feasible to exclude health and safety issues without at the same time excluding the whole design process.

— Interlocking contracts: Whether working as part of an integrated team or not, construction contracts interlock, eg the contractor will pass on his liabilities to the subcontractors and they in turn will pass them down to sub-sub-contractors and suppliers. The client for a project will want to see that responsibility for design and workmanship is taken on by the various entities. If the buntry of Country of Origin Principle applies, they will need to investigate the rights and obligations arising under one or more foreign jurisdictions. The assistance mechanism in Articles 22 and 26 will not be satisfactory, unless it gives the client the right to sue a Member State if inaccurate or misleading advice is given on the relevant law applicable to the contracts with the overseas entities.

— Joint liability: Consultants and contractors rely on the law on joint liability if they are sued (see paragraph 17 of our earlier evidence). If the Country of Origin Principle applies, they will need to spend time and money in investigating whether overseas entities have, for instance, a cap on their liability which makes UK consultants and contractors more exposed to a claim in excess of their proportionate liability.

— Quality of services: Paragraph 37 of the preamble talks about a "wide choice of high quality services" but the reverse effect may occur, and the UK market may be flooded with low quality services. If the Country of Origin Principle applies, there is an incentive for unscrupulous entities to set up an establishment in a country which has less regulation or is more lax in enforcing the law, and then selling their services throughout the rest of the EU. This could make it more difficult for clients to recognise what quality of service they are being offered, so as to choose the service which is appropriate to their particular needs.

— Compliance of design: Our understanding of the Country of Origin Principle is that overseas designers will be subject to the design standards of their Member State. This could result in unpleasant surprises for clients, who need structures which meet UK design standards. An example is the standards required for new buildings to satisfy disability discrimination legislation, which are not the same throughout the EU.

— Contracts: it is a feature of the construction industry that often contracts are of agreed and signed until well into the construction process, if at all. It is not therefore sufficient to rely on contractual provisions, as these may be either unclear or non-existent.

3. Scope for construction consultants to become more competitive: The proposed Directive contains, in Chapters IV and VI, a number of provisions that relate to the quality of services. The aspects raised, such as quality charters, settlement of disputes and codes of conduct, could be used by construction consultants to improve their business performance, their standing in the eyes of clients and therefore their competitiveness.

For the construction sector as a whole, an innovative approach is needed to ensure that these quality aspects are implemented as the sector is very fragmented and is principally made up of SMEs (Small Business Enterprises). The prize for such implementation will be increased competitiveness for the sector as a whole and therefore for European business in the global marketplace. Equally, it is important that standards are maintained in all Member States, to avoid services being provided at low cost, but to an unacceptable standard.

4. Harmonisation/mutual recognition: For services in the construction sector there is no doubt that mutual recognition is the favoured way of treating cross-border provision of services. In the field of cross-border movement of goods, the EU has been trying for over 20 years to harmonise provisions—without success. The treatment of services is far more complex and mutual recognition is the only approach that has a chance of being successful. The CIC believes that there is merit in pursuing a convergence approach that would, over time, deliver an approximation of laws so as to simplify the provision of services across borders. In doing this it would be useful to group certain categories of services together and then seek to achieve convergence and approximation on a sector-by-sector basis. One result of this would be to deliver greater efficiencies for each sector in turn, thus increasing their competitiveness and that of the EU as a whole.

5. Barriers to the free movement of services: In our oral evidence, we referred two types of barriers. The first is problems with authorisation schemes such as the variance in interpretation and implementation of procedures, onerous requirements on the submission of statements and declarations in relation to matters such as criminal records, financial status etc. These procedures represent a real bureaucratic barrier for service providers. The second relates to professional indemnity (PI) insurance. Some Member States require that PI insurance be provided by companies established in that Member State. However, it is not generally possible for service providers to purchase insurance from insurance companies established in other Member States—thus a barrier is created.

6. PI insurance and Article 27: Article 27 requires Member States to implement PI insurance provisions so that there is adequate insurance for health and safety and unspecified financial risk rising from the performance of the services. CIC is in favour of the objectives of Article 27 which, if implemented, would mean that service providers would be certain that competitors are carrying the same overheads. However, at present there are no systems in place allowing Member States to implement the proposed Directive and to do so would require additional legislation regarding the registration of all service providers to a common standard. Moreover, the current immense diversity of national requirements means that the provisions of Article 27 certainly cannot be put into operation until there is a significant convergence of policy wordings in the 25 member countries. There would be big hurdles to be overcome before this could be achieved and there is no guarantee that the insurance market would provide the necessary PI insurance cover at reasonably commercial rates, if at all.

7. Points of clarification:

— "Access"/"exercise": in giving evidence we illustrated the difference between access and exercise by describing characteristics which enable a service provider to go on a tender list as being matters of access, and matters of exercise being those governing how the provider does the job once he has won the tender. We did not of course intend to restrict consideration to projects which go out to tender— matters of access can equally well determine whether a provider is in a position to accept an offer to undertake a project which has not been the subject of a tendering procedure.

— "Established"/"temporary": We believe that it is important that the definition of these terms is clear as possible. A problem could occur as a result of the Country of Origin Principle: say a provider designs a building in another Member State, and there are defects in the building as a result of which the client sues the provider. Because of different laws relating to liability, the argument between the parties could become one about whether the provider was temporarily working in the host Member State, or was established there—rather than about the real issues. This just burdens the parties with uncertainty, and extra legal costs.

Frances Paterson
Chairman, Liability Panel

March 2005

Written memorandum by the Royal Institution of Chartered Surveyors (RICS)

CURRENT STATE OF THE SINGLE MARKET IN SERVICES

Barriers to service providers

RICS and its members, as professional property and construction service providers who frequently work across national borders, welcome the Commission's comprehensive and non-sectoral approach to creating a true internal market in services in the draft Directive. Our members are increasingly active in large and small-scale projects outside of their country of origin, and we welcome any attempt to remove the persistent barriers that exist to achieving true mobility in business service provision within the property sector. We actively support the Commission's objectives to create a genuine internal market for service providers, and the benefits that would flow from such an initiative, particularly in realising the goals set for the EU by the Lisbon Agenda.

In their current practice, our members report difficulties with the VAT legislation (reclaim and return), different fiscal regulations, differences in national law, resistance to work with foreign service providers, even if the local language is spoken, recognition of the professional title of "surveyor", a lack of understanding of the profession of "building surveying", as the title is not recognised in the EU, resulting national requirements to have a local qualification, the different structure of the construction/property industry in other countries, the difficulty to obtain information on tenders, currency exchange rates (UK), problems in marketing, language, cultural differences, lack of personal contact and lack of local knowledge.

THE COUNTRY OF ORIGIN PRINCIPLE

We very much welcome the horizontal, non-sectoral approach advocated in the draft Directive. The framework created by the Directive should be equally applicable to all sectors of the service industry and we will work hard to ensure the benefits of a horizontal approach are recognised amongst our members, and other organisations within the services sector. We stress that any attempt to incrementally alter the horizontal approach towards sector specific opt-outs or special provisions would be a retrograde step and we encourage the institutions to strongly resist calls for such developments. The benefits of a broad horizontal approach would be quickly lost if a sector specific focus were allowed to develop.

We consider the inclusion of chartered surveyors and the property professions under the terms of the draft Directive as being of vital importance. Many of our members are frustrated by regulatory barriers that exist to working cross-border. Yet the benefits of facilitating cross-border working amongst professionals, particularly those involved in highly complex, internationally important property, construction, transport and regeneration projects are of huge value, socially, economically and practically. In addition to restraining the economic activity of a large number of service providers, current barriers also reduce the possibilities for innovation, exchanging best-practice, the transfer of skills, prevents the maximisation of both quality and value to the consumer, and they do nothing to encourage greater efficiency of service or more ethical behaviour.

Member State co-operation in a mutual assistance framework

If the Country of Origin Principle is to work, then there is a need for effective administrative co-operation between Member State authorities, in order to ensure effective supervision. However, excessive burdens must be avoided, and many steps have already been taken to facilitate administrative co-operation, eg by way of promoting e-Government services.

Supervision could also be made easier by introducing harmonised European forms for attestations and certificates, EU-wide databases containing information on service providers, which would enable authorities to have better control.

The solution cannot be to limit freedom of service provision by red tape in order to spare national authorities the effort of collaborating effectively. A study presented by EFBH in Scheveningen says there are on average five telephone contacts per year, which shows that even more than new technology, a change in attitude by national administrations is needed. The Services proposal has the potential of setting a political signal to stimulate that change.

Other significant concerns

Article 27: Professional insurance

RICS supports the proposal to include a requirement for professional indemnity insurance or other appropriate cover in the scope of the Directive. (For clarity, the term "professional indemnity insurance" should be used throughout.) Our main concern in the context of professional indemnity insurance, however, is the practical availability of effective insurance cross-border. Further focus must be placed upon the European insurance market and providers of insurance to ensure appropriate and cost-effective insurance options are in place. This will be a necessary requirement for the Directive to have the liberalising effect envisaged by the Commission and supported by RICS.

Any shortcoming in the provision of cross-border professional indemnity insurance may turn out to be a major obstacle to achieving the proposal's objectives, as insurance at prohibitive cost will effectively discourage service providers from operating cross-border, simply because it would not be profitable. Where professional indemnity insurance is not available, a service provider would only have the choice between continuing to provide services in breach of the Directive, or cease trading entirely. In this case, an over-ambitious proposal would have the contrary effect to what it envisages, as it would discourage cross-border service provision rather that boost its economic potential.

Articles 16–19: Country of Origin Principle and derogations

RICS supports the proposed Country of Origin approach which would avoid duplication of authorisation and supervisory procedures. However, clarification is needed concerning the scope of certain derogations.

We are unclear with Article 17 (8) as to which particular element of the proposal on recognition of professional qualifications is being referred to. RICS would like to avoid a wholesale exclusion from the Services Directive for the regulated professions. In its recently published Communication on Competition in Professional Services the Commission urges national legislators and professional bodies to revise and amend some of their restrictive rules and practices. This Directive must reflect these moves towards greater liberalisation. If the Services Directive is to deliver increased flows of cross-border service providers, they must have access to their preferred regulated professionals who are equally allowed to operate, with their clients, on a cross-border basis.

Barriers likely to remain assuming efficient operation of the Country of Origin Principle

Articles 9–15: Authorisations and Prohibited requirements

RICS welcomes the objective to remove unnecessary authorisation schemes and discriminatory requirements. We would like to see the "name and shame" approach to identifying both existing and new barriers within the Internal Market for Services vigorously applied and maintained as an on-going initiative.

Article 15 (2d) requires Member States to evaluate the necessity of requirements which reserve access to a service activity to particular providers by virtue of the specific nature of the activity. However, it excludes those concerning professional qualifications. We would like to see this exclusion removed—professional services should be explicitly included. Reserving certain service activities to professionals with a specific professional title causes problems in terms of free provision of services: a professional qualified to perform a specific function in one Member State may have a different professional designation from a person in another Member State qualified to carry out the same function.

For example, an RICS building surveyor in the UK and Ireland can design buildings, whereas in many other Member States the same function would need to be carried out by a professional qualified as an architect. In Greece 80 per cent of roads are built by appropriately qualified surveyors, whereas in most other Member States a road builder would be expected to be qualified as a civil engineer. In a number of EU countries professionally qualified and highly experienced RICS valuers are unable to provide their services for bank lending, insurance, financial reporting or other purposes, for example, because these activities are reserved to those who hold the title of architect. These restrictions are unnecessary, are a major obstacle to the free provision of services, and are unjustified.

A more liberalised market such as already exists in the UK and Ireland will not lead to a lowering of standards or put the public interest at risk. It is clear, for example, that buildings in the UK and Ireland are no less safe than those designed, constructed and maintained elsewhere in the EU. In addition, removing these effective monopolies will bring greater competition in the professions and so lead to better choice and value for clients, as well as a more efficient internal market.

Article 30: Multidisciplinary activities

Multi-disciplinary partnerships are a common and essential way of working within property and construction projects and our members have vast experience in how these can operate to the benefit of the service providers and their clients, whether in the public or private sectors. RICS does not believe the excessive use of national restrictions regarding multi-disciplinary working provides any true guarantee of consumer protection, quality assurance or ethical behaviour. Proper international accreditation, stringent application of clear codes of professional ethics and guidance on best practice are all effective, non-regulatory alternatives which do not prevent barriers to cross-border working.

Continued and excessive national regulation would also run contrary to the promotion (by the EU, national governments and professional bodies) of multi-disciplinary working amongst professionals, the free flow and exchange of skills and best practice, and may also hinder the potential of public–private partnerships.

Article 39: Codes of Conduct

We whole-heartedly support the need for a comprehensive European code of conduct for professionals. This is something RICS already produces for all its members (see www.rics.org/downloads/static/rules_conduct_2004.pdf).

We oppose paragraph 4 of Article 39, as it is drafted in the Commission's proposal, and as reinforced by the Presidency text of 10 January 2005, as it provides that Member States shall take accompanying measures to encourage professional bodies to implement Community codes at national level.

Codes at European level represent, by definition, a compromise reached by all Member States, which results, as a rule, in a compromise solution. We believe that professional bodies should not be deprived of the possibility to raise standards and compete on quality by having more ambitious codes. Encouraging the adoption of Community codes discourages development towards higher standards.

Such a solution would prevent the development of high quality codes and consumer protection. In cases where considerable investment efforts have established a brand, and consumer goodwill has been built up due to positive experience with that brand, ie by establishing an effective system of consumer redress, these efforts would turn out to be sunk cost could they retrospectively be annulled by putting a European level code in place replacing them and laying down lower protection standards.

14 February 2005

Written memorandum by Royal Institute of British Architects (RIBA)

A. THE CURRENT STATE OF THE SINGLE MARKET FOR SERVICES

ARE THERE SIGNIFICANT BARRIERS TO FIRMS SEEKING TO OFFER THEIR SERVICES IN OTHER MEMBER STATE OF THE EU? IF SO, WHAT ARE THE MOST IMPORTANT OF THOSE BARRIERS? WHAT MEASURES ARE NEEDED TO OVERCOME THOSE BARRIERS? DOES THE COMMISSION'S PROPOSED DIRECTIVE ADEQUATELY ADDRESS THOSE ISSUES?

1. Mobility & regulation—the architectural profession is already one of the most mobile of the liberal professions in Europe terms of cross-border provision of services. For the last 20 years, the Architects' Directive has provided for mutual recognition of diplomas and its provisions have been retained in the proposed new Directive on the Recognition of Professional Qualifications.

2. The fact that architectural services are extensively regulated in many Member States has not hindered circulation within the internal market, so regulation is not, of itself, a barrier to cross-border trade. On the contrary, the architectural profession is regulated in the general interest and for consumer protection reasons. Regulations underpin the quality of services provided by the profession and do not interfere with the provision of architectural services across borders.

3. Uneven playing field: while the barriers may be few for architects, there are a number of factors that contribute to the distortion of competition and the creation of an uneven playing field in relation to service provision eg the different liability regimes that prevail in the EU.

4. It is not clear whether the draft Directive will recommend the introduction of a mandatory requirement for Professional Indemnity Insurance for all providers of professional services. However, it must be said that there are many factors relating to this issue that represent real difficulties for service providers, notably different periods of liability (leading to different overheads) and the near-monopoly enjoyed by re-insurers. Note, an EU study, in the early 1990s, sought to put the case for harmonising liability regimes. Though much information was gathered, it was ultimately abandoned, and thought too difficult to achieve.

5. Article 6—single points of contact already exist in many Member States for the architectural profession. However, their role in relation to the proposed "contact points" in the draft Qualifications Directive needs clarification. They could play an important role in making available information on service providers (cf. Article 26) and we believe that professional institutes/registration bodies also have a role to play in this area (see para 7 below)

6. Article 15—requirements to be evaluated—it would have been more useful if this exercise had been carried out before the Directive was drafted. A detailed impact assessment requires to be undertaken before seeking further views.

7. Role of professional organisations—in addition to acting as points of contact and assisting with the provision of information on service providers, there is much more that professional organisations can do to help deliver the various "quality of service" and "convergence" measures outlined in the Directive, and this, in line with the principles of co-regulation and self-regulation set out in the "European Parliament, Council and Commission Inter-Institutional Agreement on Better Law-making—2003/C321/01)."

Such measures could include the development of:

— a professional card and/or the creation of a central, independently administered register at EU level to record cross-border activity and professional misconduct;

— a EU Code of Conduct;

— a EU Quality Charter; and

— collation of historical data for cost information systems.

B. COUNTRY OF ORIGIN PRINCIPLE

IS THE PRINCIPLE THAT A COMPANY REGISTERED TO PROVIDE SERVICES IN ONE COUNTRY IS AUTOMATICALLY QUALIFIED TO PROVIDE THOSE SERVICES IN ANY COMMUNITY COUNTRY ON THE BASIS OF HOME COUNTRY REGULATION A REASONABLE AND/OR REALISTIC STARTING POINT? WHAT SIGNIFICANT BENEFITS TO BUSINESSES AND CONSUMERS ARE LIKELY TO OCCUR AS A RESULT OF THE ADOPTION OF THE COUNTRY OF ORIGIN PRINCIPLE? IS THE PRINCIPLE WORKABLE IN PRACTICE?

8. Unrealistic and inoperable—because of the difficulties that would arise in verifying qualifications and other credentials of service providers.

9. Discriminatory—because a recipient would, in the case of a problem with a provider, have to seek recourse under the laws and in the language of a country that is not their own.

10. Confusing—for consumers, and all the more complex in the context of the wider construction team where members could come from more than one country.

11. While the Directive provides that supervisory competence would lie with the country of origin, one wonders whether the country where the provider is established has any interest at all in supervising service activity outside its territory.

WILL THE APPLICATION OF THE COUNTRY OF ORIGIN PRINCIPLE MOVE BUSINESS IN FAVOUR OF FIRMS BASED IN MEMBER STATES WITH THE LEAST STRINGENT REGULATORY REGIMES? WHAT ISSUES DOES THIS RAISE FOR BUSINESS AND CONSUMERS? HOW MIGHT THOSE ISSUES BE RESOLVED?

12. This will give an incentive to service providers to establish themselves only where there are lower standards of protection. Member States could undercut each other in their minimum standards (a sort of "race to the bottom"). The Directive should not lead to a lowering of quality standards or evasion of individual countries' regulations, which would endanger social entitlements and consumers' rights.

13. The proposal to introduce the Country of Origin Principle is premature and can only function in a market that is significantly harmonised, without which, the effect of applying the principle will induce Member States into a form of regulatory competition where the objective will be to become the least regulated country—and therefore the most attractive for establishment by service providers.

THE APPLICATION OF THE PRINCIPLE RELIES ON THE DEVELOPMENT OF AN EXTENSIVE MUTUAL ASSISTANCE FRAMEWORK, WHEREBY MEMBER STATES CO-OPERATE IN SUPERVISING ENTERPRISES BASED IN THEIR COUNTRY IN RESPECT OF THEIR OPERATIONS IN OTHER COUNTRIES. IS THIS A WORKABLE FRAMEWORK?

14. In the case of architects, the mutual assistance framework exists in the form of a network of designated competent authorities (registration bodies, professional associations or—where neither exists—a Government department). However, the only way they can keep track of those operating in their jurisdiction is by requiring visiting service providers to register—thereby, binding them to national Codes of Conduct and other requirements (rather than home country rules). This ensures that cross-border practice takes place in a regulated and supervised manner.

WHAT OTHER SIGNIFICANT CONCERNS ARE THERE REGARDING THE PRACTICAL IMPLEMENTATION OF THE COUNTRY OF ORIGIN PRINCIPLE AND HOW MIGHT THESE BE ADDRESSED?

15. Derogation: Article 17 provides for a derogation for professions covered by the draft Directive on Recognition of Professional Qualifications. While confirmation has been sought, and obtained, that this derogation will apply to architects, yet further clarification is required regarding the specific nature of the derogation ie whether it is of a transitional or permanent nature.

16. In adopting a common position on the Qualifications Directive, on 18 May 2004, which included provision for "pro forma" registration for first time cross-border service providers, the Council confirmed, in the context of Member States' supervisory competence, that supervision of cross-border service should be carried out in the country in which the service is provided. This is in complete contradiction to the Commission's approach in the Services Directive.

17. The Country of Origin principle also runs contrary to other EU Directives eg:

— the Directive on Unfair Business Practices (on 20 April 2004, the Parliament rejected the inclusion of Country of Origin Principle in Article 4 of the proposal, as the Commission had intended, and this was endorsed by the Council on 15 November 2004);

— the Directive on the Posting of Workers, which states that the labour law of the host country shall apply; and

— the Directive on the Award of Public Contracts which states that national rules on working conditions, safety issues and regional and tariff agreements must be observed.

18. Moreover, the Country of Origin principle is contrary to international law:

— although the Rome Convention (Rome I) provides that the law of the country where the worker normally works should be applied if the worker does not regularly work in a particular country, Rome I also provides that either the law of the country where the employer is established or, under certain conditions, the host country principle will continue to apply; and

— the Rome II draft Directive (COM[2003]0427) states that the applicable law is the law of the country in which the damage occurs.

19. Finally, one is left to query the legal basis of the draft Directive, given its incompatibility with other EU Directives. The Country of Origin Principle consolidates differences rather than reducing them, because every service provider brings their own legal system.

20. This is particularly problematic with regard to the various members of the construction team, and we believe that the whole of the Construction Industry should be included in the article 17 derogation.

21. The Community has a mandate only to facilitate the free movement of services, not to make it more difficult, and on this basis, Article 16(1) alone would probably infringe primary Community law. There is also a need to check whether this is compatible with the proportionality principle of the Treaty (Article 5(3) ECT).

ASSUMING EFFICIENT OPERATION OF THE COUNTRY OF ORIGIN PRINCIPLE, WHAT SIGNIFICANT BARRIERS TO TRADING IN OTHER MEMBER STATES ARE LIKELY TO REMAIN, SO FAR AS FIRMS IN THE RELEVANT BUSINESS SECTORS ARE CONCERNED?

22. We do not "assume the efficient operation of the Country of Origin Principle" cf. section on Uneven Playing Field (Para 3) and the Role of Professional Organisations (Para 7).

C. THE FUTURE

DO YOU EXPECT THE IMPLEMENTATION OF THE COMMISSION'S PROPOSED DIRECTIVE TO HAVE A SIGNIFICANT IMPACT UPON TRADE IN THE SERVICES SECTOR WITHIN THE EUROPEAN UNION? IN WHICH SERVICES INDUSTRIES DO YOU EXPECT THE LEAST AND THE LARGEST MOVEMENT TOWARDS A EUROPEAN UNION SINGLE MARKET IN THE NEXT FIVE TO 10 YEARS?

23. We are generally supportive of the objectives set down in the so-called Lisbon Agenda and Gothenburg Declaration, and we acknowledge the reasons for which the Commission has made the proposal for a Directive on Services.

24. However, we are concerned that there is significant flaw in the approach. It appears after successfully dealing with the free circulation of goods across borders, the Commission is trying to deal with services in the same manner. This is simply not possible, and a significant shift in the Commission's understanding of services is required.

25. While the draft Directive defines Services as "any self-employed economic activity, as referred to in Article 50 of the Treaty, consisting in the provision of a service for consideration", and also (Article 4(13) "a professional activity or group of . . . activities, access to which or pursuit of which, . . . is conditional . . . upon possession of specific professional qualifications, pursuant to laws, regulation and administrative provisions", it is worth noting that a far more accurate definition exists (and is more appropriate to the architectural profession), as used by the European Court of Justice in its decision upon the *Adam* case (C-267/99):

> ". . . liberal professions . . . are activities which, *inter alia*, are of a marked intellectual character, require high-level qualifications and are usually subject to clear and strict professional regulation. In the exercise of such an activity, the personal element is of special importance and such exercise always involves a large measure of independence in the accomplishment of professional activities".

26. The RIBA urges the Commission, in all its deliberations, to take due account of the specific nature of certain categories of services, particularly architectural services, which impact directly on the quality of life of EU citizens. The assessment of the quality of such services cannot rely solely on the economic reasoning that currently underpins the provisions of the text presented by the Commission to the Council and the European Parliament.

Ian Pritchard
Director, Policy & International Relations
11 February 2005

Examination of Witnesses

Witnesses: Ms GILLIAN CHARLESWORTH, Head of Regulation Policy, Professional Regulation and Consumer Protection; Ms KERSTIN FISCHER, Regulation Policy Officer, Public Affairs, the Royal Institution of Chartered Surveyors; MR AARON EVANS, Vice President, Membership; Ms LEONIE MILLINER, acting Executive Director, Professional Services; and MR STEVEN HARDING, Head of Public Affairs, Royal Institute of British Architects, *examined.*

Chairman: Good afternoon. I gather Mr Evans has to leave early. We will understand that, and I apologise again that there has been a quite exceptional delay. Lord Haskel also has to leave early.

Q241 *Lord Shutt of Greetland:* Do you think that the distinction between temporary status as a service provider in another Member State, as opposed to established business status, is of any value in seeking a framework within which to establish the development of a single market in your services within the European Union, or does such a single market already effectively exist?

Mr Evans: We believe that a single market for architectural services already exists, and has been working successfully for the past 20 years. We had some examples earlier on: you referred to Italian and Spanish architects working here, and British architects are working abroad successfully, and as that already exists, the distinction between temporary and established businesses we do not feel is critical. I would not say it is valueless but I would say it is not critical in this context. We have had an explanation of how difficult it is to make that distinction and we do not feel it contributes anything.

Q242 *Lord Shutt of Greetland:* So we are going through this exercise really for no real benefit?

Mr Evans: I would not put it as strongly as that, my Lord, but certainly I feel that if you are asking if we believe that this single market exists for professional services, I think it is quite well established. That is the opinion of the RIBA.

Ms Milliner: We have had the benefit for the last 20 years of an Architects Directive, which has provided for the cross-border recognition of architectural skill, and that has been retained in the new proposed Directive on professional qualifications. From our perspective, this Directive reinforces that Directive in its provisions but does not necessarily advance it.

Q243 *Lord Geddes:* Does the same answer apply for the RICS?

Ms Fischer: On behalf of RICS, I think the situation presents itself slightly differently. We cover a vast variety of sectors. We represent Chartered Surveyors worldwide in 120 countries, and just to pick two examples, the services we provide range from valuation to extraction of minerals from the seabed, and these issues are regulated quite differently in different Member States, so that we would see great benefit in creating this, because in our view a single market for services throughout the European Union does not yet exist for the services that we are covering. In that context, we find the distinction between services provided on a temporary basis—and here I am referring to the definition by the European Court of Justice, as opposed to establishment—quite helpful because it provides legal certainty for our members on the basis of established jurisprudence by the European Court of Justice.

Q244 *Lord Geddes:* That last point is fascinating because we have probed and probed this. In your opinion, what is the ECJ judgment? What is their definition of "temporary"?

Ms Fischer: There are several judgments, for instance, the Insurance Services case and the *Gebhard* case, where the criterion for differentiating between the two is the nature of the economic activity, that is to say, whether there is a permanent base in a Member State, and in *Gebhard* it has been mentioned that the criterion of "temporary" is not necessarily not given just because a service provider provides himself with

the necessary infrastructure in one Member State. The criterion is a real and continuous link with the economy of one Member State, and that will have to be evaluated on a case-by-case basis, and we think it will serve the legal certainty of our members very well to be able to rely on the Court's body of jurisprudence that has been established so far.

Q245 *Chairman:* Some witnesses before us, including the body that claims to represent a substantial number of SMEs (Small and Medium Sized Enterprises) in this country, say that simply relying on a series of European Court of Justice judgments leaves far too much uncertainty for many small businesses and so on. That may obviously be something that businesses that are less professionally long established in international operations might find a little difficult. In your case, it has given you enough certainty for you to operate.

Ms Fischer: Indeed, my Lord Chairman, you are absolutely right in stating that. We believe that on top of that body of jurisprudence that already exists, we need the Services Directive because the jurisprudence established so far is simply not enough in order to create a satisfactory single market for services.

Chairman: We will have some lawyers before us in two weeks' time and that is something we will certainly go into with them.

Q246 *Lord Swinfen:* The profession of architects is recognised worldwide, but am I not right in thinking—because at one time I was a Chartered Surveyor but I am not now—that Chartered Surveyors are really only recognised as a profession in the old British Commonwealth and the Republic of Ireland?

Ms Fischer: Thank you for giving me the opportunity to reply to that, because this is one of our main concerns within the Services Proposal. There is a provision, notably Article 15, that interlinks the services proposal with the Directive on recognition of professional qualifications and, as you have said, we encounter problems because the reservation of the title of architect, for instance, in the UK is not linked to an equivalent reservation of the function, which leads to the result that for Chartered Surveyors there is not such a competitive problem in the UK as in other Member States, because in other Member States you also encounter the reservation of the title, but you do have a reservation of the function, so that, for instance, our members in France would not be able to submit planning documents to the local authority simply because they do not bear the right title for doing so.

Q247 *Lord Geddes:* We observed that you were sitting at the back for the previous evidence, so you know that we are pushing quite hard against the difficult door of the Country of Origin Principle. It may be these answers are quite different between chartered surveyors and architects. We will ask the architects first since Mr Evans has to go soon. In the architectural profession, would the adoption of the Country of Origin Principle be helpful, damaging or quite irrelevant? You have almost answered it.

Mr Evans: Yes, indeed, and I think you have had a very detailed exposition from our previous colleagues about why we also think it would be damaging. We think it would be contrary to other attributes which are upheld in other EU Directives, such as the local distinctiveness, local character of place and cultural diversity. We think it runs contrary to that. It would also be contrary, we think, to consumer protection, because redress would have to be taken in the country of origin and not in the host country where that difficulty arises. We see difficulties in seeking redress in the country of origin as opposed to the host country. On that basis alone, we feel it is damaging.

Q248 *Lord Geddes:* What about the Chartered Surveyors?

Ms Fischer: We see the Country of Origin Principle as very helpful in the context of service provision. The most important point is, again, that it would provide legal certainty to our members. The Country of Origin Principle has faced a lot of criticism, notably by asking what worth there is in having the Country of Origin Principle if there are already 23 derogations within Article 17 of the Proposal. But even if there are multiple exceptions, that leads to legal certainty for our members, because, as a rule, they follow a very specific sort of service provision. If you take the example of extraction of minerals from the seabed, it will be possible for our members to go through the list of derogations in Article 17 of the Proposal and find out easily whether they are covered by these, and by default they will fall under the Country of Origin Principle. So we find that this grants them legal certainty. Also, this will make it simpler to handle risk management, because it will be easier to define and to quantify the cases where enterprises or SMEs will have to comply with sets of different national laws, whereas now they are exposed to possibly 25 different sets of national laws that they will have to comply with.

Q249 *Chairman:* Can I come back to surveyors. Would the Country of Origin Principle be damaging if it only applied to bidding for contracts, the line of argument from the architects we heard from? Previous witnesses said the relevance of the Country of Origin Principle is that it enabled businesses to bid for contracts, but once they got a contract, they were quite happy to work within a host country regime. Is that your position?

Ms Milliner: Yes, it is.

Q250 *Chairman:* The surveyors' position is they would prefer to see the Country of Origin Principle apply both to the access to and provision/exercise, of services[1]?

Ms Fischer: My Lord Chairman, we see the Country of Origin Principle, as currently drafted, very positively. I do not think we would oppose limiting it to the access to service provision but we will have to reserve our position on that. Modifying the Country of Origin Principle, in the sense of just reducing it to access to the activity, is something we might consider discussing, but we do not have any opposition to the Principle as it is currently drafted.

Lord Swinfen: I wonder if it would be helpful to know what kinds of chartered surveyors there are because there are general surveyors, quantity surveyors, hydrographic surveyors and a number of different kinds of surveyors which are covered, in the other countries to some extent, by other professions.

Q251 *Chairman:* When you give answers, if the distinction is helpful between the different types of surveyors, can you include that in your answers but, separately, if you can send a note to the clerk explaining chartered surveyors for the record for our report, that would be useful. I do not think we have got time today to give us a useful explanation, but use it if it is helpful.

Ms Fischer: Thank you very much, my Lord Chairman.

Q252 *Chairman:* Can I note that Mr Evans has had to leave. We have a new representative. Can you introduce yourself for the record?

Mr Harding: I am Steven Harding and I am Head of Public Affairs at the RIBA.

Chairman: I noticed you have been keeping a close eye on us.

Q253 *Baroness Eccles of Moulton:* We are moving on to mutual recognition and harmonisation. Are they relevant to your services, are they important to the development of a single market in the EU or not and if so, which?

Ms Milliner: As we have already stated, the market for architectural services is very well established based on the principle of mutual recognition. We think this is a sound principle on which to proceed. We fully support the comments of earlier witnesses to do with the problems associated with harmonisation.

[1] cf. Q 210

Baroness Eccles of Moulton: That seems pretty much in a nutshell and quite conclusive.

Q254 *Lord Swinfen:* Does that apply to surveyors also?
Ms Fischer: We see mutual recognition as very helpful too, in particular as there are currently moves in the European Parliament to revert rather to a harmonisation approach which we believe will very much prolong developments. In view of the Lisbon Agenda, we believe it would be quite important, at this stage, to follow a mutual recognition approach. I would like to note that these two approaches are not necessarily exclusive, you can have a long-term objective of having harmonisation of national laws. At the same time, in the meantime, you can follow the mutual recognition approach to bridge the gap, as it were.

Q255 *Baroness Eccles of Moulton:* Which implies that in the long-term you would prefer harmonisation?
Ms Fischer: We would not exclude a harmonisation approach in the long run, however, we feel it is very much necessary to focus now on what is practicable and achievable to create a single market in services. We believe this will not be possible without following the mutual recognition approach now, which we see as the other side of the coin of the Country of Origin Principle.

Q256 *Lord Geddes:* Just picking up that point: surely if mutual recognition is established and—maybe to half quote your words—the harmonisation route is going to take forever and a day because we have got to get 25 countries, at the moment, and more coming, all to agree the same thing, by the time they have got to that agreement, will not the mutual recognition route have prevailed?
Ms Fischer: In an ideal world when we have achieved a level of harmonisation, which is so complete that Member States' laws hardly differ anymore, even do not differ anymore at all from each other, then mutual recognition and harmonisation will eventually coincide and it will be the same thing. We are not quite there yet. We believe, coming from a real world perspective, we will have to work very hard on mutual recognition, which is necessary as a counterpart of the Country of Origin Principle because if enterprises work on the basis of their Member States' law, then this set of rules will have to be recognised by other Member States for this structure to work. The Country of Origin Principle is not possible and not workable without mutual recognition.

Q257 *Lord Walpole:* If the Country of Origin Principle were to be implemented, the draft Directive proposes Member States co-operation in a Mutual Assistance Framework. Is that potentially helpful or unnecessary in your service area? Would it work in practice?
Ms Milliner: Under the Directive, architectural services are derogated and therefore the Country of Origin Principle would not apply. Therefore, answering those parts of your question, from our perspective, is highly theoretical. We can give you a view, but it is not relevant from our perspective.

Q258 *Lord Walpole:* It is more for the surveyors' sector.
Ms Fischer: We are very much in favour, as far as mutual assistance is concerned, of the Council's approach in Recital 38 of the current Council text of the Services proposal. In the context of Article 16, paragraph two, on Home Country Control, the Council proposes that checks and controls are carried out in the country of destination by the host country authorities, but that the ultimate responsibility for carrying out those checks remains with the country of origin. We believe this approach reunites the best of the two worlds because having the ultimate responsibility with the country of destination would lead to the protectionist approach which we face already and which the Services proposal wants to tackle. In our view, that would not be a solution. However, the Home Country Control has faced criticism because, very justifiably, it has been said that the country of origin cannot effectively carry out controls on site. We believe the Council's approach, in Recital 38 of the document, is a very good compromise and we support that very much. Also, in view of the fact that there are other EU Directives, notably the Directive on Recognition of Professional Qualifications, which rely heavily on mutual assistance in Article 8 of that Directive, we believe it would be a very good approach to effectively have a synergism of the structures, which are already there, to use them for other contexts and to have effective networking and e-government structures. I believe the UK has been quite a pioneer in that field with the e-envoy and we very much support that approach. We do not believe this will be necessarily a very expensive thing to do. We would like to draw your attention to the Net Impact 2004 study of European public sectors. There have been several benefits announced by the study, notably to make public administration more effective by both improving relationships with citizens and being more cost effective and, also, by having a networking of virtual organisations. That will mean the structures set up within the Framework of Recognition of Professional Qualifications, that is to say competent

bodies and co-ordinators, could forward their information by means of standardised forms to the competent bodies which would be established by the Services Proposal, so that there would not necessarily be enhanced cost involved in such mutual assistance. **Lord Walpole:** I think that was a very nice full answer.

Q259 *Chairman:* You are not as bothered as some witnesses about the possibility of using the principle of mutual assistance and so on? In summary, you think that is potentially a helpful thing, it need not be too bureaucratic and burdensome and it is workable? *Ms Fischer:* Yes, my Lord Chairman.

Q260 *Lord Swinfen:* My question is in the RICS's paper. You say you welcome any attempt to remove the persistent barriers which exist in achieving durability in the business sector supervision within the property sector. Then you outlined all the issues of VAT legislation, different fiscal regulations, differences in national law, cultural differences, differences in obtaining information on tenders, and the list went on and on. My question is, what are the most significant changes you would like to see in the draft Directive—I do stress the draft Directive, particularly after all the kerfuffle we have seen in the papers in the last week—as it now stands? *Ms Fischer:* I believe that is a question for the RICS. We believe the most important obstacles our members face are both the differences in national laws as well as the issue of recognition of the professional title of surveyor. This is where one of our main points comes into the discussion: Article 15, paragraph 2d and Article 17, paragraph eight. We would very much favour deleting paragraph eight of Article 17, which contains a derogation for everything which concerns the Recognition of Professional Qualifications Directive. Also, we would like to see a deletion in Article 15, paragraph 2d, of the reference to professional qualifications.

Q261 *Chairman:* That is very helpful. The Committee is extremely impressed with your detailed grasp. Clearly you do not work for the Commission. I wonder if you can put that in layman's language for us without all the numbers and so on. This is very helpful for the record. Can you tell us what that means? What is it that you want to be taken out and put in and what is the effect of it? *Ms Fischer:* The problem is that the Services Proposal effectively tries to achieve coherence between different legislative instruments. Article 17 contains all the derogations from the Country of Origin Principle. It says that everything which covers matters regulated by the proposed Directive on Recognition of Professional Qualifications will not

fall under the Country of Origin Principle because the proposed Directive, the outcome of which is not yet quite sure, seems to point to a country of destination principle. However, we believe that even if this Article 17, paragraph eight is kept as it is, there will not be a necessity for such a parallel in Article 15, paragraph 2d, because Article 15, paragraph 2d is contained in a different chapter, it relates to establishment, whereas, Article 17 relates to service provision.

Q262 *Chairman:* Why do you not want it in? Why do you not want the derogation? *Ms Fischer:* We do not want the derogation because effectively it would give to Member States the possibility to keep up barriers which are even disproportionate within the field of professional qualifications without even being obliged to report them to the Commission as provided for in Article 4.1.

Q263 *Chairman:* In summary, Member States do use apparent professional qualifications in your area as a barrier? *Ms Fischer:* Indeed.

Q264 *Chairman:* But not in the architects' case? *Ms Fischer:* Exactly.

Q265 *Chairman:* Here we have got a situation where some services have it one way and some another, if that is fair? In your case, professional surveyors use the barrier and in the architects' case, if sufficient agreement is reached, then it helps create a single market. In your case, it is stopping a single market? *Ms Fischer:* Indeed. *Ms Milliner:* If we were to make one significant change to the Directive, it would strengthen 17(8), which is this derogation to do with the draft Directive on Recognition of Professional Qualifications.

Q266 *Chairman:* You want to strengthen it? *Ms Milliner:* Yes, such that it includes—and this may well solve problems posed by the RICS—and embraces all construction industry professions.

Q267 *Chairman:* Let me put this to you, and we will learn more when we go to some of our Member States: very often professionals like to have qualifications recognised and so on, because effectively it does in itself become a barrier to other people. I can well understand you wanting to keep up some barriers and not others. Is not the reality that in some countries you have got people going through all kinds of hoops to get all kinds of qualifications? That is the qualifications of the producers gets confused with the product and it becomes a barrier to free competition in the marketplace. Effectively you say you cannot produce the product unless you are qualified as a producer. I will be frank about it: is this not German approach versus British approach?

Ms Milliner: In the case of architectural services and the architectural profession, we have a very clearly defined set of professional boundaries which demarcate what an architect can do in the production of their requirement.

Q268 *Chairman:* As I understand it, you want to extend it throughout the construction service industry?

Ms Milliner: It may well be helpful to lay that suggestion on the table in order that colleagues from the RICS have a similarly advantageous position to those enjoyed by members of the RIBA, the registered architects, throughout the European Union.

Q269 *Chairman:* It could be called harmonisation. Would you have that approach for every single service throughout the construction industry? Would you suggest then that the English in Britain, anybody in the UK who is a plumber or whatever, should have the same four qualifications as a German tradesman?

Ms Milliner: If I may, my Lord Chairman, I would like to respond to that question in writing. We had originally conceived of our suggestion operating at the professional level, not necessarily embracing the craft at trade level.

Q270 *Chairman:* Why? What is the distinction?

Ms Milliner: That is something I think we need go away and give more consideration to it. We will write to you.

Q271 *Lord Swinfen:* Where architects are recognised—their qualifications are recognised throughout the European Union—do they need a licence to practise in different Member States? For instance, I know if you are a lawyer or a doctor, you need to have a licence to practise in certain areas.

Ms Milliner: My understanding is that if as an architect you are registered in a Member State, you have a right to practise and offer architectural services in that Member State with no further regulatory hoops to go through.

Q272 *Lord Swinfen:* Can you have a licence to practise automatically in any other Member State?

Ms Milliner: As long as you are registered in that Member State under the Directive, which is a simple process to do.

Q273 *Lord Swinfen:* Which state do you mean by "that Member State"?

Ms Milliner: For example, an architect who is registered in the United Kingdom with the Architects Registration Board of the United Kingdom can very simply register with the equivalent competent authority in Germany or France, but that registration process is simple.

Q274 *Lord Swinfen:* You need a licence in other Member States?

Ms Milliner: That is right.

Q275 *Lord Shutt of Greetland:* Like you, my Lord Chairman, I am trying to get this to the practicalities. Bearing in mind the people we have had today, it seems to me that one of the features we have got in the real life is something called building regulations. I am trying to understand what is being said. When you talk about mutual recognition or harmonisation, how realistic is it that anybody can say: "I am an architect and I am available to go into business in 25 Member States of the European Union" and somehow just pick up what the building regulations are in all these States? It seems to me they could well be very different, I do not know, but I suspect they are and there are all sorts of different principles involved. How realistic is all this? Is what you are saying, "if they really want to do it, they have got to find out about these things and they have got to put that in the bag", because harmonising all of these things is just impossible? Is that what you are really saying to us?

Ms Milliner: Yes. There are two aspects to my reply. Firstly, that the supervision of cross-border services is carried out in the country in which that service is provided. For a German educated architect who is registered in Germany, who comes to live and work in the UK and is registered in the UK, then the supervision of that architect's work in the UK is the responsibility of the Architects Registration Board in the UK. We know—and there are specific examples—of European architects who register in the UK and are advised by us and by the Architects Registration Board to undertake a short course, there are plenty of them available in the UK, to enable them to get up to speed with the UK building regulations, planning regulations, health and safety regulations, et cetera. Across the European Union each professional statutory body has its own code of conduct which would make it mandatory to ensure professionally qualified architects do not undertake work which they are not sufficiently competent to undertake. There is a professional obligation on those individuals to ensure that they are aware of and suitably skilled in the local regulatory climate in which they are practising.

Ms Charlesworth: My Lord Chairman, I would like to apologise as Kerstin Fischer has had to go and catch the last Eurostar back to Brussels.

Q276 *Chairman:* I thought I should at least give you the chance to make sure we knew you were here for the record.

Ms Charlesworth: As you realise, she had all the detail.

Q277 *Chairman:* For the record, would you like to tell us who you are?

Ms Charlesworth: I am Gillian Charlesworth, and I am Head of the RICS Regulation Policy.

Q278 *Chairman:* Can I thank all of you for putting on an excellent tandem ride showing that you can ride a bicycle even if you are trying to go in different directions on occasions. It has been very helpful to us. If there is anything further you wish to respond, you can send it to us in writing.

Ms Milliner: There is one item which we will write to you on. Thank you very much for giving us the opportunity to come today.

Chairman: Thank you very much. It has been very kind of you.

Supplementary written evidence by The Royal Institution of Chartered Surveyors (RICS)

RICS POSITION

RICS welcomes the opportunity to comment on the European Commission's draft Directive on Services in the Internal Market. The proposal affects the greatest part of our members, providing services and expert advice on all aspects of land, property, construction and the associated environmental issues.

RICS is the world's leading professional body for property professionalism, regulating and representing over 110,000 individually qualified chartered surveyor members in 120 countries worldwide.

An independent, not-for-profit organisation, RICS acts objectively and in the public interest, providing authoritative advice on issues affecting business and society worldwide. Chartered surveyors are bound by rules of conduct on matters such as client confidentiality and conflict of interest.

KEY ISSUES

RICS specifically welcomes:

— the requirement to identify and subsequently remove national regulations which act as barriers to cross-border establishment and provision of services;

— the application of the Country of Origin Principle;

— the possibility of alternative methods of regulation, including self regulation and codes of conduct; and

— the advantages of single points of contact to help reduce and simplify the administrative burdens, particularly for SMEs.

It is important that the Commission takes a comprehensive approach to reform of the environment in which professional services operate.

We would therefore welcome clarification of the following:

— the scope of the Directive;

— compatibility with and complementarity of other proposed Directives, particularly the draft Directive on Recognition of Professional Qualifications;

— the scope of the Country of Origin Principle, particularly with regard to rules on recognition of professional qualifications;

— the impact on health and safety in the construction sector; and

— the availability and practicalities of cross-border professional indemnity insurance.

GENERAL COMMENTS

RICS and its members, as professional property and construction service providers who frequently work across national borders, welcome the Commission's comprehensive and non-sectoral approach to creating a true Internal Market in Services in the draft Directive. Our members are increasingly active in working on large and small-scale projects outside of their country of origin, both within the EU and beyond, and we welcome any attempt to remove the persistent barriers that exist to achieving true mobility in business service provision within the property sector. The fact that these obstacles remain more than 10 years after the launch of the Internal Market shows clearly that relying on existing legislation and on European Court of Justice jurisprudence has not been sufficient.

We actively support the Commission's objectives to create a genuine internal market for service providers, and the benefits that would flow from such an initiative, particularly in realising the goals set for the EU by the Lisbon Agenda. We also support the far-reaching approach in this draft Directive, which combines the Country of Origin Principle, targeted harmonisation, mutual assistance between national authorities and other non-legislative activity.

We stress that any attempt to incrementally alter the horizontal approach towards sector specific opt-outs or special provisions would be a retrograde step and we encourage the institutions to strongly resist calls for such developments. The benefits of a broad horizontal approach would be quickly lost if a sector specific focus were allowed to develop.

We consider the inclusion of chartered surveyors and the property professions under the terms of the draft Directive as being of vital importance. Many of our members are frustrated by regulatory barriers that exist to working cross-border. Yet the benefits of facilitating cross-border working amongst professionals, particularly those involved in highly complex, internationally important property, construction, transport and regeneration projects are of huge value, socially, economically and practically. In addition to restraining the economic activity of a large number of service providers, current barriers also reduce the possibilities for innovation, exchanging best-practice, the transfer of skills, prevents the maximisation of both quality and value to the consumer, and they do nothing to encourage greater efficiency of service or more ethical behaviour.

The publication of this draft Directive, the proposal covering Recognition of Professional Qualifications, the Communication on Competition in Professional Services, the creation of the Forum for Business Related Services, and efforts to promote further standardisation of services, are all important steps towards creating a real and functioning internal market. None should be treated in isolation. It is vitally important that the focus and main thrust of each of these initiatives remains over the course of the consultation period, future legislative process and implementation.

SPECIFIC COMMENTS

Article 2: Scope

We very much welcome the horizontal, non-sectoral approach advocated in the draft Directive. The framework created by the Directive should be equally applicable to all sectors of the service industry and we will work hard to ensure the benefits of a horizontal approach are recognised amongst our members, and other organisations within the services sector.

It is unclear, for instance, whether product-related services relevant in the building industry, such as installation, maintenance or repair, are within the scope.

We also have a doubt over services of general interest, such as social housing. The Explanatory Memorandum states that activities performed by the state as part of its cultural, educational, judicial and social functions are not covered where there is no element of remuneration, but Article 2 does not mention this. According to the Presidency text, the criterion for deciding whether a service is covered by the Directive is whether it serves a general interest, in which case it would be excluded from the scope, or a general economic interest, in which case it would be covered by the proposal. According to the Presidency, Member States may define which services they consider to be of economic interest. We would very much appreciate legal certainty in this regard, as currently, services such as social housing, which are marked by growing activity in the private sector, would be covered by the proposal in one state, but not in another.

As far as health services are concerned, we would not be opposed in general to excluding them from the scope of the proposal.

Article 6: Single points of contact

We very much support application of the "single point of contact" principle. However, we stress that implementation at the national level, and the subsequent delegation of functions to non-governmental regulating bodies to undertake monitoring and information exchange, must also apply the principles of transparency, simplicity and clarity. RICS already undertakes this role for the chartered surveying profession worldwide and welcomes the opportunity to explore how this may be achieved for the property and construction professions more broadly.

Articles 9–15: Authorisations and Prohibited requirements

RICS welcomes the objective to remove unnecessary authorisation schemes and discriminatory requirements. We would like to see the "name and shame" approach to identifying both existing and new barriers within the internal market for services vigorously applied and maintained as an on-going initiative.

Article 15 (2d) requires Member States to evaluate the necessity of requirements which reserve access to a service activity to particular providers by virtue of the specific nature of the activity. However, it excludes those concerning professional qualifications. We would like to see this exclusion removed—professional services should be explicitly included. Reserving certain service activities to professionals with a specific professional title causes problems in terms of free provision of services: a professional qualified to perform a specific function in one Member State may have a different professional designation from a person in another Member State qualified to carry out the same function.

For example, an RICS building surveyor in the UK and Ireland can design buildings, whereas in many other Member States the same function would need to be carried out by a professional qualified as an architect. In Greece 80 per cent of roads are built by appropriately qualified surveyors, whereas in most other Member States a road builder would be expected to be qualified as a civil engineer.

In a number of EU countries professionally qualified and highly experienced RICS valuers are unable to provide their services for bank lending, insurance, financial reporting or other purposes, for example, because these activities are reserved to those who hold the title of architect. These restrictions are unnecessary, are a major obstacle to the free provision of services, and are unjustified.

A more liberalised market such as already exists in the UK and Ireland will not lead to a lowering of standards or put the public interest at risk. It is clear, for example, that buildings in the UK and Ireland are no less safe than those designed, constructed and maintained elsewhere in the EU. In addition, removing these effective monopolies will bring greater competition in the professions and so lead to better choice and value for clients, as well as a more efficient internal market.

We are therefore also very concerned that *Article 9 (1b)*, which would allow restrictions relating to the public interest, should not be used to justify restrictive practices in some countries, when there is no evidence of harm to the public interest in countries which do not operate these restrictions.

Articles 16–19: Country of origin principle and derogations

RICS fully supports the proposed country of origin approach which would avoid duplication of authorisation and supervisory procedures.

Concerning the exercise of control (*Art. 16 paragraph 2*), the presidency text of 10 January 2005 clarifies, in recital 38, that the responsibility of the authorities of the country of origin for supervision of the service provider does not imply that the authorities of the Member State of origin must carry out the checks and controls in the country of destination themselves. Such measures will be taken by the authorities of the Member State of destination, pursuant to the mutual assistance obligations and the partnership between national authorities.

Much is to be gained in this regard by making effective use of e-Government services, which the Commission makes use of already, and by introducing harmonised European forms for attestations and certifications, as well as EU-wide databases containing information on established service providers.

As regards the derogation for professional qualifications, we are unclear with Article 17 (8) as to which particular element of the proposal on recognition of professional qualifications is being referred to. As stated above, RICS would like to avoid a wholesale exclusion from the Services Directive for the regulated professions.

In its recently published Communication on Competition in Professional Services the Commission urges national legislators and professional bodies to revise and amend some of their restrictive rules and practices. This Directive must reflect these moves towards greater liberalisation. If the Services Directive is to deliver increased flows of cross-border service providers, they must have access to their preferred regulated professionals who are equally allowed to operate, with their clients, on a cross-border basis.

We would ask the Institutions to be vigilant that any further derogations added under Article 17 during the negotiations are non-discriminatory, fully justified and regularly assessed to check that they are not being used to undermine the main objective of the Directive. We are particularly concerned by misuse of the term "in the public interest" and the umbrella "the safety of services" (as above).

We have no objection in principle to the requirement for service providers to continue to have to respect the law of the destination country in terms of minimum wages and other working conditions, in compliance with Directive 96/71/EC.

We would not be opposed either, to the derogation in Article 17 (17) in so far as it is used for ensuring the safety of building sites. As highlighted above, however, the non-discriminatory application of such rules needs to be ensured.

Article 24: Specific provisions on the posting of workers

RICS and its members support the Commission's approach to remove barriers to service provision in the context of the posting of workers. Any authorisation or declaration requirements, requirements to be established in a Member State, or to hold and keep employment documents on the territory, would reintroduce the very obstacles the proposal seeks to remove.

As regards safety and health of workers, as well as coherence with Directive 96/71/EC on the posting of workers, the proposal contains several provisions to address concerns in this regard. Article 24 (1) (b) makes sure Member States may still ask for declarations in the context of the posting of workers, and Article 24 (2) ensures that the Member State of origin assists the Member State of posting in complying with the Directive on the posting of workers, by way of an own initiative obligation to communicate information on the work and employment conditions.

This balanced approach allows for improving the monitoring of compliance with employment and working conditions under Directive 96/71/EC, at the same time as abolishing disproportionate administrative procedures.

Under the current proposal, workers are granted double protection. They benefit both from the labour law of the national law applicable to the employment contract, as well as from the health and safety standards of the national law of the country of actual service provision, according to the Directive on the Posting of Workers. We believe that this additional protection provides an efficient safeguard against potential abuse.

Article 27: Professional insurance

RICS supports the proposal to include a requirement for professional indemnity insurance or other appropriate cover in the scope of the Directive. For clarity, the term "professional indemnity insurance" should be used throughout.

Our main concern in the context of professional indemnity insurance is the practical availability of effective insurance cross-border. Further focus must be placed upon the European insurance market and providers of insurance to ensure appropriate and cost-effective insurance options are in place. This will be a necessary requirement for the Directive to have the liberalising effect envisaged by the Commission and supported by RICS.

Any shortcoming in the provision of cross-border professional indemnity insurance may turn out to be a major obstacle to achieving the proposal's objectives, as insurance at prohibitive cost will effectively discourage service providers from operating cross-border, simply because it would not be profitable.

Where professional indemnity insurance is not available, Member States are left to the choice of letting service provision continue, in breach of the Directive, or forbid service providers not carrying insurance to cease trading entirely. In this case, an over-ambitious proposal would have an effect contrary to that envisaged by it, as it would discourage cross-border service provision rather that boost its economic potential. Article 27 should reflect the possibility, in practice, to obtain efficient professional indemnity insurance, and its availability at competitive cost.

Moreover, we believe it should be clarified which services are covered by Article 27(1) of the proposal.

As regards Article 27(2), we believe that there is too much detail in the proposal as drafted. In requiring Member States to ensure that information is supplied to the service recipient on respective insurance or guarantees, the proposal regulates down to extensive detail. We believe that sufficient protection is provided to consumers if the sum insured and the type of insurance is disclosed to them. It should be left to the discretion of Member States to add additional information requirements.

Article 27(5): We question how equivalence is going to be achieved given the current position—large discrepancies between the amounts, types and coverage of professional indemnity policies in different Member States. Would the list envisaged in (5) be of generic insurance products or of specific schemes in each Member State?

Article 29: *Commercial communications by the regulated professions*

RICS welcomes the objective of removing restrictions on commercial communications.

Article 30: *Multidisciplinary activities*

We would like to highlight the need for the Directive, and the ongoing monitoring of its implementation, to ensure only minimal and justifiable restrictions are maintained by Member States regarding multi-disciplinary partnerships. Again, we do not see a need to make an exclusion for the regulated professions. The flexibility implicit in the current wording of the Directive could allow Member States to continue to apply unnecessary and anti-competitive restrictions.

Multi-disciplinary partnerships are a common and essential way of working within property and construction projects and our members have vast experience in how these can operate to the benefit of the service providers and their clients, whether in the public or private sectors. RICS does not believe the excessive use of national restrictions regarding multi-disciplinary working provides any true guarantee of consumer protection, quality assurance or ethical behaviour. Proper international accreditation, stringent application of clear codes of professional ethics and guidance on best practice are all effective, non-regulatory alternatives which do not prevent barriers to cross-border working.

Continued and excessive national regulation would also run contrary to the promotion (by the EU, national governments and professional bodies) of multi-disciplinary working amongst professionals, the free flow and exchange of skills and best practice, and may also hinder the potential of public–private partnerships.

Article 39: *Codes of Conduct*

We whole-heartedly support the need for a comprehensive European code of conduct for professionals. This is something RICS already produces for all its members (see www.rics.org/downloads/static/rules_conduct_2004.pdf). We would welcome the opportunity to explore the benefits and difficulties we have experienced ourselves, and look at ways in which our own Code could be improved in the light of this current initiative.

In this regard, we would oppose paragraph 4 of Article 39, as it is drafted in the Commission's proposal, and as reinforced by the Presidency text of 10 January 2005. According to the latter, Member States shall take accompanying measures to encourage professional bodies to implement Community codes at national level.

Codes at European level represent, by definition, a compromise reached by all Member States, which results, as a rule, in a compromise solution. We believe that professional bodies should not be deprived of the possibility to raise standards and compete on quality by having more ambitious codes. Encouraging the adoption of Community codes discourages development towards higher standards.

Such a solution would prevent the development of high quality codes and consumer protection. In cases where considerable investment efforts have established a brand, and consumer goodwill has been built up due to positive experience with that brand, ie by establishing an effective system of consumer redress, these efforts would turn out to be sunk cost could they retrospectively be annulled by putting a European level code in place replacing them and laying down lower protection standards.

Therefore, paragraph 4 should either be deleted, or redrafted to lay down minimum harmonisation, in order to ensure that professional bodies can compete on quality standards by laying down higher levels of protection in national codes.

CONCLUDING REMARKS

We have a number of examples of existing barriers drawn from the international experience of our members. These include different fiscal regulations, VAT legislation (reclaim and return), differences in national law, lack of recognition of the title of "surveyor" in the EU, resulting lack of understanding of the profession of "building surveying" and national requirements to have a local qualification, resistance to work with foreign service providers, even if the local language is spoken, different structure of the construction/property industry in other countries, difficulty to obtain information on tenders, problems in marketing, currency exchange rates (UK), language, cultural differences, and lack of personal contact.

While some markets in the EU are already comparatively liberalised, the key test of the success of the Services Directive will be in its implementation across the 25 Member States. Removal of the obstacles mentioned above will require willingness and commitment. It is essential that the Commission closely monitors implementation and progress, and brings pressure to bear on Member States to make the provisions of the Directive a reality on the ground.

THE PROFESSION OF "CHARTERED SURVEYOR"

There are various routes to RICS membership. Most people become a professional member of RICS (MRICS) by gaining an RICS approved academic surveying qualification. This must be followed by the Assessment of Professional Competence (APC), a minimum of two years of experience and a formal interview by a panel of assessors. The APC is intended to ensure that only those who have an acceptable level of competence, in carrying out the work of a professionally qualified surveyor on behalf of clients or an employer, are admitted to professional membership.

RICS also has a technical member qualification (TechRICS) for those with appropriate academic and/or vocational qualifications. Applicants are required to have completed a minimum two years post qualification experience and assessment and to attend an interview (the Assessment of Technical Competence).

As the profession is extremely diverse, many surveyors, like doctors or lawyers, specialise in one or more fields. RICS has grouped these 160 or so fields into 16 "faculties". Plus, there are seven market focused forums made up of members and non-members. These faculties are:

Arts and antiques
Valuation, buying and selling, auctioning and managing antiques and fine arts.

Building surveying

Management and maintenance, design, insurance assessments, condition surveys, statutory approvals and defect diagnosis.

Commercial property

Property management, landlord and tenant representation, investment and finance appraisal, dispute resolution.

Construction

Development and construction commercial management, estimating, project cost and schedule controls, risk and contract management.

Dispute resolution

Resolving property disputes, dispute avoidance, arbitration, adjudication, mediation and expert witness services.

Environment

Managing and assessing the impact of property and land use on the environment; sustainability, contamination, regeneration and land management.

Facilities management

Building management and operations, performance-oriented procurement, life-cycle and service management

Geomatics

Collection, analysis, interpretation of spatial information, land and hydrographical surveying, mapping and positioning, boundaries and data management.

Machinery and business assets

Management, valuation and sale of business assets, and plant and machinery, depreciation advice, insurance, rating and tax.

Management consultancy

Business property solutions, management and practice, strategic advice, corporate and personal insolvency, and turnaround management.

Minerals and waste management

Minerals extraction planning, valuation and rating. Waste management, landfill and landfill tax, valuation, and licensing.

Planning and development

Property valuation, easements, transport and infrastructure, marine and inland water resource management.

Project management

Planning and implementing development projects, team creation and management, implementing procedures and efficient handover of the finished project.

Residential

Investment and development of public and private residential properties; brokerage, valuation, negotiations and asset management.

Rural

Managing and valuing rural land, agriculture, forestry and woodland, farm management, appraisal, access and easement negotiations and environmental assessment.

Valuation

Appraisal of land, property and business for sale, letting or investment; measurement, performance assessment, funding strategies and expert witness services.

7 March 2005

Services of an MRICS

Property Brokerage

— Commercial Leasing of Buildings
— Commercial Sales of Buildings
— Investment Sales of Buildings
— Joint Venture Sales
— Sale/Leaseback

Advisory & Valuation

— Property Valuations
— Portfolio Valuations
— Financial Analysis (DCF)
— Due Diligence/Underwriting
— Lease versus Buy analysis
— Reality Tax Consulting

Specialized Properties

— Corporate Real Estate Strategy
— Public Sector Property
— Health Sector Property
— Academic Establishments

Landlord & Tenant

— Property Management
— Lease Renewal Negotiations
— Landlord and Tenant Issues

Construction

— Strategic Construction Consulting
— Construction Management
— Economics
— Planning
— Contract & Materials Procurement
— Management of Contracts
— Health and Safety for Construction

Facilities Management

— Property Management
— Business Support
— Strategic Planning
— Business Re-location
— Outsourcing
— Utilities

Project Management

— Contract Negotiation
— Contractor Liaison
— Cost Consulting
— Tenant Build Out

Building Surveying

— Building Conservation
— Building Insurance Assessment
— Building Regulation & Control
— Construction Design
— Dilapidations
— Energy Efficiency and Right of Light

Geomatics

— Land & Hydrographic Surveying
— Engineering Surveys
— Land & Marine Information Management
— Monitoring of Structures
— Cartography
— Global & Local Navigation Systems

Other

— Assessment of Land Use Requirements
— Planning Processes
— Minerals Dispute Resolution
— Ground Engineering
— Mineral Valuation & Taxation
— Compulsory Purchase & Compensation

16 March 2005

Supplementary written evidence by Royal Insititute of British Architects (RIBA)

The Royal Institute of British Architects was privileged to give oral evidence to your Committee on Monday 7 March. I am writing further to your request for clarification on the RIBA's views about the extent of the construction industry derogation to the Country of Origin Principle in Article 17 of the draft Directive.

The proposed derogation currently covers those professions which will fall under the proposed Directive on Professional Recognition of Qualifications. This includes, on the one hand, those professions with sectoral Directives (such as health professionals, lawyers and architects) and those governed by the General System (surveyors, engineers etc).

7 March 2005

We believe that the derogation should apply to the whole construction sector—and not just the so-called "intellectual professions"—so that all members of a construction team drawn from a range of European Union Member States may operate under the jurisdiction of the country in which the service is delivered, rather than subject to the various governance of different Member States.

14 March 2005

WEDNESDAY 9 MARCH 2005

Present	Cohen of Pimlico, B	Geddes, L
	(Chairman)	Haskel, L
	Eccles of Moulton, B	Swinfen, L
	Fearn, L	Walpole, L

Memorandum by Management Consultancies Association

I. INTRODUCTION

1. The Management Consultancies Association ("MCA") is grateful for the opportunity to submit evidence to Sub-Committee B's inquiry into issues raised by the European Commission's Proposal for a Directive on Services in the Internal Market (6174/04—"the draft Directive"). The scope of the draft Directive is extremely broad. It will affect management consultants, and many other providers of business and professional services (amongst others), as well as their clients operating in a very wide range of business sectors. The MCA has therefore given the European Commission's proposals particularly careful consideration.

2. Management consultancy is an increasingly important industry for the UK economy with revenues for 2003 (for which the most-up-to date information is available) estimated at £10 billion, contributing well over £1 billion to the UK's balance of payments. The MCA represents leading UK-based consulting firms which currently employ over 30,000 consultants and generate £5.8 billion in annual fee income. MCA members work for most of the FTSE 100 companies and all Government departments. The MCA is one of 22 national associations of management consultants who are members of the European Federation of Management Consultancy Associations (Feaco), many of whose members will also be affected by the draft Directive.

3. The remainder of this memorandum addresses the three main issues on which the Sub-Committee have requested views.

II. CURRENT STATE OF THE SINGLE MARKET IN SERVICES

4. The management and IT consulting sector is one of the main drivers of competitiveness in Europe. MCA members have been increasingly concerned about the growth gap between Europe and the US and Asia. As the High Level Group chaired by Wim Kok recognised in November 2004, the EU has been suffering from low growth, high unemployment and reduced productivity. Without investment in the knowledge economy, growth will not come. MCA members recognise that 70 per cent of Europe's output is accounted for by services, but at present these services account for only 20 per cent of Europe's trade. They believe that the creation of a genuine single market in services could boost growth in the EU and improve the price, choice and quality of services to clients.

5. MCA members want to support efforts to enhance prosperity in the UK and elsewhere in Europe. The expertise and reach of MCA member firms, and their multi-sector client base, provide them with powerful insights into the need to reduce burdens on business generally, cut red tape and improve administrative co-operation between EU Member State administrations. MCA members therefore welcomed the Joint Initiative on Regulatory Reform initiative last year of the Irish, Dutch, Luxembourg and UK Presidencies.

6. MCA members particularly welcome the strong lead shown by Commission President Barroso whose 5-year strategy and work plan makes better regulation a priority for the new Commission, along with creating jobs and increasing prosperity, as described in the Commission's communication to the Spring European Council, *Working together for Growth and Jobs: A new start for the Lisbon Strategy* (COM (2005) 24).

Barriers to the delivery of services

7. MCA members encounter a number of barriers in establishing a presence in another Member State (often in connection with obtaining information and understanding the appropriate administrative procedures for establishment) as well as in *delivering services* through the temporary movement of consultants—key business personnel whose specialist knowledge and skills need to be made available to clients in another Member State because they are not available locally (or available in sufficient supply).

8. The MCA therefore supports the underlying aims of the draft Directive—to overcome barriers to service providers establishing a commercial presence in other Member States, improving the free movement of services across borders within the EU and simplifying administrative procedures. A reduction in unnecessary regulation is to be welcomed.

Reduction and simplification of administrative burdens

9. The reduction and simplification of administrative burdens resulting from the creation of a "single point of contact" will be of particular benefit to small and medium-sized enterprises (SMEs) seeking business opportunities in other Member States. The costs and other burdens of obtaining and processing information, and compliance with regulatory and administrative requirements, can fall disproportionately heavily on these firms. The MCA therefore welcomes the opportunity to modernise national procedures and to facilitate the exchange of information necessary to establish a commercial presence and to conduct business in another Member State.

Barriers to the movement of persons

10. The draft Directive should also help to overcome barriers relating to the movement of persons. These barriers (which are often linked to onerous local regulatory and in some cases licensing requirements) can affect the supply of services in a wide range of service sectors. A typical long-term career secondment costs an employer approximately three or four times the annual salary of a locally hired employee. The administrative procedures relating to the "posting of workers" are considerable, covering prior notifications to labour authorities in the Member State to which a worker is to be posted; appointment of a representative in the Member State where workers are posted to handle formalities; complying with visa and work permit requirements; and managing problems which can arise owing to the differences in medical schemes between Member States, as well as pension and social security schemes, to say nothing of complying with the multiplicity of different tax regimes.

11. UK-based multi-national firms (increasingly operating global business models) need to be able to deploy professional staff (at executive and technical levels) to work away from their home country on short-term secondments and assignments (often at short notice) to meet the demands of their clients for uniformly high quality standards of service. If consulting firms, amongst others, cannot move their people to their clients at the right time, they cannot provide an efficient or an effective service. They may be prevented in practice from bidding for contracts or accepting offers to provide services which require specialist knowledge, skills and experience. The draft Directive will do much to address these barriers within the EU. The draft Directive will also ease the problems associated with the movement of employees from third countries (ie from outside the EU). Large firms often need to access their "global talent pool" to assemble teams with the right knowledge, skills and cultural fit to service clients in several countries, example in multi-country systems integration projects. Moving a third country national from one EU Member State to another for a specific purpose on a short-term basis involves obtaining work permits from each country, which is costly and time-consuming, both for the employee and their employer. The draft Directive could help to address these problems.

12. MCA members are aware of concerns about a possible lowering of labour standards in relation to the posting of workers (Article 24). The MCA does not consider that these concerns are well founded, particularly in the management and IT consulting sector which relies on highly skilled personnel. The MCA shares the view of the European Commission that the draft Directive does not change the regime for posted workers established by Directive 96/71/EC governing the minimum working conditions in the host country. Should it be necessary to address these concerns further, the MCA would urge the European Parliament and the Council to seek solutions that are consistent with the Internal Market approach proposed by the draft Directive.

Other barriers

13. How far the draft Directive will overcome other barriers that many firms actually encounter is less clear. To some extent the Commission's proposals will affect firms differently depending on their size and scale. The large consulting firms, notably the multi-national firms, have been through the process of establishment already. They will not benefit from the draft Directive's proposals very much in this respect.

14. The practical, day to day, barriers that the MCA's smaller and medium-sized member firms typically face doing business in the internal market are very different from the regulatory and administrative barriers at which the draft Directive is aimed. Different national tax regimes in the EU, different languages and cultures

exert a powerful influence over demand and supply factors involved in providing management consultancy. The key asset of management consultants is intellectual capital, in people. In practice, the smaller and medium-sized firms among the MCA membership overcome constraints on freedom of establishment by establishing joint ventures with local service providers, or by other kinds of partnering arrangements.

15. Most of these firms have neither the time nor the resources to set about establishing a commercial presence in another jurisdiction in the EU or elsewhere. Those are the real constraints in practice, not the regulatory barriers at which the draft Directive is aimed.

16. The MCA wishes to emphasise this point for two reasons. First it would be easy (and unrealistic) for policy makers to over-estimate the beneficial impact of the draft Directive on the UK management consultancy sector. Secondly, there is a real risk that some elements of the draft Directive, particularly the application of a "one size fits all" approach to quality standards, would actually add to the burdens on this sector in which there remains a strong public interest in having a broad measure of self-regulation.

III. COUNTRY OF ORIGIN PRINCIPLE

17. The MCA supports the application of the Country of Origin Principle (Article 16). This Principle provides the essential underpinning of the Directive without which it will be difficult, if not impossible, to create a genuine single market in services. The Country of Origin Principle is in keeping with the spirit of the Treaty of Rome and with the four fundamental freedoms it enshrined: freedom of goods, services, persons and capital. Combined with the removal of discriminatory regulations (Article 14) and the requirement to evaluate existing and planned regulations against the requirements of non-discrimination (Article 15), the Country of Origin Principle could help to achieve the objectives of the re-launched Lisbon Agenda, the 2004 Joint Initiative on Regulatory Reform and the Simpler Legislation in the Internal Market (SLIM) initiative.

18. Provided there are proper arrangements for its application, in a clear and consistent manner by all EU Member States, the Country of Origin Principle could provide an important boost to business confidence and help to increase cross-border trade.

19. The MCA does not share the concerns which have been expressed (for example by some public sector unions) about the possible effect of the Country of Origin Principle on moving jobs and business in favour of firms in a member state where domestic regulatory conditions are less stringent ("social dumping"). The UK management consultancy sector is now an established, mature market (with relatively few regulatory constraints on the sector as such); MCA member firms provide world class services to sophisticated buyers whose buying decisions are, and the MCA believes should remain, conditioned by market disciplines.

20. Members of the MCA are aware of opposition that surfaced about the Country of Origin Principle in connection with the proposed Unfair Commercial Practices Directive, the draft Regulation on Sales Promotions and in debate in the Council regarding a proposal for a Regulation on the Law applicable to Non-contractual Obligations (Rome II), as a result of which a proposal for a special exception for internal market matters from the general principle of Country of Destination was deleted.

21. In view of the importance that the MCA, and others, attach to the contribution of services to the EU's future prosperity and to the role which the Country of Origin Principle in services matters could perform in helping to achieve the Commission's 5-year programme to achieve the new Lisbon Agenda, the MCA would be very concerned if this essential underpinning of the draft Directive were to be weakened. The MCA hopes that the European Parliament, and especially the Legal Affairs Committee, will favour an approach that is consistent with the objectives of the Single Market.

IV. THE FUTURE

22. The market for management consultancy in the UK has for a long time been very open. There are few barriers to entry, whether regulatory or administrative. Since there is already a high level of market access into the UK from other EU Member States, the proposed changes on freedom of establishment are unlikely to have detrimental effects in principle; they could help to promote further the competitiveness of UK firms and enable those firms to take advantage of more liberalised arrangements elsewhere in the EU.

23. In practice MCA members are concerned that appropriate, market-led quality standards can continue to apply. A "one size fits all" approach to services regulation applied to quality standards runs the risk of imposing additional burdens on a dynamic business sector, one that makes a significant contribution to the competitiveness of the UK.

24. The MCA supports the underlying aims of the draft Directive—to overcome barriers to service providers establishing a commercial presence in other Member States, improving the free movement of services across borders within the EU and simplifying administrative procedures. A reduction in unnecessary regulation is to be welcomed.

25. The MCA believes that the draft Directive could make a valuable contribution to liberalising services markets and making a reality of the Single Market. With services accounting for such a high proportion of its output, it is vital for the future prosperity of the EU that services markets operate efficiently and effectively. The draft directive could cut costs involved in cross-border trade in management and IT consulting as well as other services sectors, reduce burdens on business caused by unnecessary regulation, increase the flow of trade within the EU by removing unnecessary barriers and significantly increase the amount of foreign direct investment in the EU.

10 February 2005

Examination of Witnesses

Witnesses: MR BRUCE PETTER, Chief Executive, Management Consultancies Association, MS FIONA DRISCOLL, Director of Strategy, Hedra, MR ANDREW HOOKE, Head of Government Services Group, PA Consulting, and MR MARK HATCHER, Director—Head of Public Affairs, Cubitt Consulting, Management Consultancies Association, examined.

Q279 Chairman: Let me open by saying how very good of you it is to come and talk to us. I think you can see all our nameplates. B Cohen is Baroness Cohen and L Haskel is Lord Haskel and so on, in case you had not guessed! What I would like to ask first before we dive at you with questions is do you have any general statement or general remarks you would like to make, which we would be very glad to hear?

Mr Petter: I would like to make a short opening statement, my Lord Chairman. Thank you very much indeed for inviting us to this hearing this afternoon. We very much appreciate the opportunity to elaborate on our written evidence to your Committee. Before I introduce the MCA team to you, I must apologise on behalf of the President of the MCA, Mr Lynton Barker. Mr Barker is chairing a Government Committee this afternoon and is unable to be with us. My name is Bruce Petter and I am the Chief Executive of the Management Consultancies Association, the MCA. On my left is Fiona Driscoll, Director of Strategy at Hedra, and she is also a member of the Treasury Public Services Productivity Panel. On my right is Andrew Hooke, Head of the Government Services Group at PA Consulting. On my far left here is Mark Hatcher, who is a Director of Cubitt Consulting, and Mark was formally Head of Global Public Affairs at PricewaterhouseCoopers. Mark has been advising the MCA on the draft Services Directive for some time now. The management consultancy industry is successful, dynamic and growing in the UK. The industry makes a very significant contribution to the UK's balance of payments. We support strongly the objectives of the draft Directive which we believe could make a significant contribution to the future international competitiveness of Europe. MCA

member firms work with well over 90 per cent of the FTSE 100 firms in the UK and many, many others in the private sector and all UK Government departments. MCA firms themselves range in size from large global players like PA Consulting to quite small and medium-sized enterprises. We support this liberalising measure which could also help to simplify and clarify much EU legislation as well as reduce costs and other burdens on business. As far as we are able to, my Lord Chairman, we are very happy to answer any questions you have for us.

Q280 Chairman: That is very kind. I have been reminded forcibly by your opening statement that I have failed to declare in open meeting that I am myself a non-executive director of a management consultancy group, which I think you should know, which owns two consultancies, Proudfoot and Parsons Consulting. Most of the business of both groups is in America but nonetheless you should know and I am sorry not to have declared it before.

Mr Petter: Thank you, my Lord Chairman, we were aware however of that interest.

Chairman: You had looked it up, excellent, good. The first question falls to Lord Fearn to ask. Lord Fearn?

Q281 Lord Fearn: Thank you, good afternoon. In paragraph 7 of your written evidence you say that: "MCA members encounter a number of barriers in establishing a presence in another Member State" and you go on to explain some of these. There are two parts to my question. Which barriers do you think are the most significant and would the draft Services Directive take away those barriers?

Ms Driscoll: If I can first reiterate what my colleague has said which is that the management consultancy industry is large and disparate so it covers a wide

9 March 2005   Mr Bruce Petter, Ms Fiona Driscoll, Mr Andrew Hooke
and Mr Mark Hatcher

range of firms that differ in size, in the industries they work for, the sort of services they provide, and indeed the countries that they already work in, so we have been looking at answers to the questions to cover a range. I think I would like to say that it is the SMEs (Small and Medium Sized Enterprises) that are particularly feeling those barriers most acutely. I think the barriers fall largely into two areas: one is about information and the other is about culture. On information there is quite a major task for organisations to discover what they need to know about how to establish a business in other Member States and how they might go about developing and running and servicing clients in those other areas. There are many and very different regulatory and administrative procedures and lots of the processes that one might have to go through to register or provide services are also very different. I think that leads to quite a lot of confusion. There is a perception that there is a disparity of levels of information available, there is uncertainty, there is lack of consistency, and some of our members use words like "opaque" and "complex" and "lengthy "to describe some of those procedures they have to go through. There is a slight feeling that some of them might be a little discriminatory in support of domestic interests and also somewhat disproportionate in the level of effort that has to be made sometimes for UK firms to do work overseas. They are administered by multiple bodies. Even if you can find out what information you need to know, you quite often have to go to many, many different bodies to pull together that jigsaw puzzle so finding out where you need to go to get what information is quite a substantial barrier, let alone the different environments in which you have to work.

Q282 *Lord Fearn:* That is the worst one, is it?
Ms Driscoll: I think that is the biggest. It is quite difficult to find out what you have to do, what you are going to have to comply with, how you are able to do business. The second half is around much clearer cultural differences which are more about facing the practicalities. There are practical difficulties of working in a foreign language, and understanding the customs and working practices that you may have to deal with, and although some of those are themselves to do with the regulatory environment, others are more to do with working in different environments. That again can be a particular difficulty for small and medium-sized enterprises who find it quite daunting to understand how to do business in different areas and often overcome it, rather than doing business directly, by forming alliances with local organisations. Turning, your Lordship, to the second part of the question, on whether we think that the Directive will take away

some of those barriers, I think our answer is yes and possibly to the advantage of, again, SMEs but also to large organisations. The thoughts around clarity of information, a single point of contact and streamlined procedures would be extremely valuable in enabling businesses to understand, quite simply, how they are able to do business in other territories. We would see the greater use of electronic procedures as well as opening up opportunities to access information in a simple format, and that, of itself, would certainly create greater visibility of opportunity which, in turn, should drive contestability and competition and potentially drive value. Some of the other areas are less relevant around licensing organisations but, broadly, we think the sum of the proposals would go a long way in easing the path to removing barriers.

Q283 *Lord Fearn:* Where would a person go if they did not come to your excellent organisation?
Ms Driscoll: They might go to my other colleague's excellent organisation.

Q284 *Chairman:* Two excellent organisations, right!
Ms Driscoll: In terms of the single point of contact perhaps, Andrew, you would like to answer.
Mr Hooke: I think there are a number of places that people could go to to get information. One is organisations like our own represented by the MCA but there are also Government bodies that people could go to. If you look at what the OGC (The Office of Government Commerce) is trying to do in terms of its role—it is trying to make clearer how people do business with Government so that somebody who wants to enter into the market could look to organisations such as that to try and get some clarity about how one enters into a particular market. There is maybe one other point that I think is relevant in terms of the barrier which is the process barrier, and although this framework is trying to simplify things, even what might seem to us as fairly administrative, simple things in terms of doing business such as, say, responding with fairly straightforward information at the beginning of a procurement process, to people who have not been involved either in the business of procurement or, say, from another geography they might view that as a much more complex thing than it actually is. Therein lies a significant barrier in terms of doing cross-border business. I think in terms of the point that you were asking about how does this improve things, how does it take away things, we are not a commodity business. The consultancy business is not a commodity and I think that it is easier to do business across geographies and across borders when one is talking about a commodity and many of the barriers that Fiona was alluding to I think are very

significant because we are not a commodity enterprise or a commodity business.

Q285 *Lord Walpole:* I think Mr Hooke nearly answered the question I was going to ask. Are there in fact equivalent bodies to you in all the other European countries and especially the new ones?

Mr Petter: There are in most countries but it has to be said formation in many cases, particularly in the accession countries, is very recent, and they are not effective in many cases because they do not represent a large section of the market in those countries and therefore the sort of information that we have been talking about is probably not available. It is also fair to say that in the accession countries there is also a barrier simply through the fact that the business culture is very different in those countries than it is in the more established 15 or 16 countries of the old European Union, if I can call it that.

Lord Walpole: Thank you very much.

Q286 *Lord Haskel:* When you were talking about barriers you mentioned a single point of contact. I believe there is something in the Directive about each country establishing a single point of contact. Do you feel that this would make it easier? You have said you think it will make it easier but do you think that countries would use it as some sort of barrier by not doing it very well? You seem to have disregarded it.

Ms Driscoll: No, I am saying that in principle it must be an excellent and worthy objective. The question, as Bruce has just alluded to, is that it may be implemented in a different manner with perhaps less enthusiasm in some countries than others, and it is very difficult to speculate at this stage how effective it would really be. However, as an objective, absolutely, it should make things easier if implemented robustly.

Q287 *Lord Haskel:* It is the way that it is carried out that concerns you?

Ms Driscoll: Absolutely.

Q288 *Baroness Eccles of Moulton:* Could I refer to your comments about the accession countries. It has occurred to me—maybe quite wrongly—that the accession countries, because they have not got the same tradition of working in a free market capitalist business world (and you said that there were business barriers), and that because management consultancy is quite a sophisticated part of the business world, that they might want to engage management consultants from the old EU countries, as it were, perhaps more than from the accession countries and therefore it is perhaps quite important that the barriers are overcome?

Mr Petter: I am also Secretary-General of the European grouping of management consultancy associations. My experience therefore is that in the accession countries there is a tendency to revert to old practice to ensure that consultancies when they are used, certainly in private business, are used on a "home industry is best" basis. The sort of work that large firms who have set up in the accession countries do tends to be either government or World Bank or European Union business. There is almost a divide and it is very noticeable in the membership of the Czech association for example that they have about an eight per cent market share of all the business done in the Czech Republic. The major firms doing government business and World Bank business have about 24 per cent but the major firms do not join the local firms because there is really no basis for the major firms to do business locally because it seems to be a preserve of the local firms. I think it is something which will develop through, as has already been suggested, and the major firms and indeed any smaller firms coming in will want to develop alliances with those local Czech firms in this case, or wherever, in order to crack the private sector market in those countries because that does seem to be a fairly universal business practice in the accession countries, as far as I am advised anyway.

Q289 *Baroness Eccles of Moulton:* That is very interesting. I suppose it is because there is still a big gap between the business cultures.

Mr Petter: I believe so, yes.

Q290 *Lord Geddes:* Mr Petter, that is a very interesting remark. You probably are not aware but a number of us are off on our travels next week ending up in Warsaw. In your experience, does what you have said about the Czech Republic also apply to Poland?

Mr Petter: The Polish association is much better developed than the Czech association, which is a very recent foundation. It does exist in varying degrees. Probably the most advanced is the Slovenian association and they have the job in the European Federation of which I am Secretary-General of representing the accession countries, and so therefore my experience in Poland is second hand. So the answer to your question is yes but nothing like as bad as Czechoslovakia.

Q291 *Lord Geddes:* What is the name in of the association in Poland?

Mr Petter: I do not know it but I will write to you and let you know.

Q292 *Lord Geddes:* Could you e-mail it to us because time is rather short, we are off on Monday.

Mr Petter: I will certainly e-mail it to you and, if I may, warn them that you are about to descend on them.

Chairman: They know that.

Lord Geddes: I do not know whether they know that but the Polish authorities know.

Chairman: The authorities as a whole know that.

Lord Geddes: Thank you very much.

Chairman: That completes that topic. Lord Swinfen?

Q293 *Lord Swinfen:* I want to come now to the Country of Origin Principle. We understand that this relates only to businesses operating in a non-home Member State on a temporary basis and that if the business becomes legally "established" in the other Member State, the Country of Origin Principle ceases to apply? Is that also your understanding?

Mr Hooke: That is our understanding, that the Country of Origin Principle as applied here does not apply.

Q294 *Lord Swinfen:* Thank you. What then do you understand by the meaning of the word "temporary" in this respect?

Mr Hooke: Temporary in this respect I do not think is a time period. I think it is a much more sophisticated and complex argument than that because I think there are questions that one should be asking around the duration of the service that one might provide, indeed the regularity of the service that one might provide, is it continuous or is it at a point in, say, the duration of a piece of work one might do with an organisation and indeed the continuity of the service over a period of time. So I think it is not a simple answer in terms of just articulating a five or 10-year period. It is a more sophisticated argument around the regularity and frequency of the service that one might provide.

Q295 *Lord Swinfen:* Does the UK-based management consultant already provide this service and, if so, could you give us some examples?

Mr Hooke: Can you clarify by what you mean by "already provide this service".

Lord Swinfen: A service on a temporary basis as understood by the draft Directive.

Q296 *Chairman:* Are there a lot of people doing that?

Ms Driscoll: There are many firms who are UK-based firms who second or send staff out to support clients in different countries.

Mr Petter: The way it would be worked now, if I may speak for some small members who I have been speaking to, is that this particular organisation will be sent out because it has been given a task perhaps by a UK head office and they will then ally themselves with—let's say it is in Rome—the Roman consultancy organisation, either picking from the Italian association a suitably qualified person, or in fact, moving their own staff temporarily and linking through a formal arrangement. There are a number of formal alliances in existence as there are a number of informal alliances and this association, the MCA, does try to assist where it can in the formation of informal *ad hoc* alliances for specific projects. It is not a widespread activity in the MCA but it is something that we do facilitate from time to time.

Q297 *Lord Swinfen:* You gave me the impression that the vast majority of such consultations are for subsidiaries or branches of UK firms that have smaller partners in other EU Member States. Am I right in that understanding or do they actually go to totally different non-connected businesses in the Member States?

Mr Petter: Yes, I was quoting you an example of a firm who quoted me a particular example of how it dealt with the particular problem. Consultancy projects come from a variety of sources and a variety of approaches would be appropriate according to the individual circumstances. This is very much a bespoke business in response to a client's needs.

Mr Hooke: You could be going through the subsidiary but you could of course be going direct from the UK, to advise in any of the EU states. Just to link that back to your question on the temporary operation issue, some of it might be going direct and doing a piece of work with a team for a period of three or six months to a year. On other occasions it might be a single person acting more as expert advice over a four-year period which is maybe a week here, two days here, and so on, so the nature of the work and the type of intervention that you have can be quite different from the full big team that helps on a piece of work to a single expert maybe coming in periodically to advise and cure and project manage.

Q298 *Lord Swinfen:* It sounds as though if the Directive is adopted that over the years there could be a number of disputes as to what is and what is not temporary. Do you see a body of case law building up over the years?

Mr Hooke: We see a huge question in the definition. Yes, I think there will a body of case law that arises as a result of this.

Q299 *Lord Haskel:* Of course this works two ways. Are you aware of any European companies that are giving management consultancy services in Britain on a "temporary" basis?

Ms Driscoll: Yes, I am aware of quite a number but, again, it is largely because they have a particular skill that is in short supply, or they have a particular expertise, or they have just done something to fix something for somebody that a UK client might want. There are a number of occasions.

Q300 *Lord Haskel:* So it is working both ways?

Ms Driscoll: Less so but there are a number of occasions. Equally, our people might go elsewhere in the EU and we see evidence of people coming here either as singleton businesses, as Andrew said, or because they have been asked directly or because they are part of a bigger alliance or bigger organisation.

Mr Petter: It is very common to find the offices of large and medium-sized firms in this country which you would consider head office here drawing on their networks in Europe to carry out specific projects in the UK. Your own management consultancy group, my Lord Chairman, does recruit people who are trilingual.

Q301 *Chairman:* Yes, and we do fly-ins.

Mr Petter: That is right. That is how that particular group tackles that particular problem and there is a two-way flow here.

Q302 *Chairman:* We are also established in several countries but we mix it. If it is not worth it we fly in rather than establish.

Mr Hooke: Again the ability to do that probably depends on both the type of work and maybe the issue with which one is wrestling because if you take, say, some of the work that our industry might do in the justice sector, which is quite a local country-centric sector for us because you need at least some knowledge of the justice area, it is more difficult to fly people in for that type of thing but you might get, say, the single expert who is knowledgeable about a particular issue coming in to do that. If you take a different issue or area and something which might be close to your collective hearts such as identity cards, for example, then there is interest from many parts of Europe in providing advice and input into that type of thing because they claim they have done and experienced some of the challenges that we are facing in that particular area.

Q303 *Lord Geddes:* Yet again my original question has been pre-empted by one of my colleagues but I do have another one which has only just occurred to me. You are representing the consulting industry, which is itself a service industry, but presumably you are consulted as well as about service industry problems, about goods problems, and manufacturing problems?

Mr Petter: Yes, indeed.

Q304 *Lord Geddes:* But we are looking at the draft Services Directive. I do not think any of us would want you to go on at great length, but what differences can you see between commonalty of services across the EU—and you made reference to this earlier—and goods or indeed people? The fourth plank being finance, I think, is it not, but we will leave that out of it.

Mr Hatcher: It is a broad-ranging question of course. I think it is fair to say that the issues with which service providers are concerned when they are trying to deliver services across borders are rather more complex than if you are trying to deliver goods across borders, in that case you are dealing with a physical thing, something that can be are moved very clearly from one jurisdiction to another. I think in the case of delivering a service, as the European Commission recognised when it was consulting very widely three or four years ago, you are actually looking at a number of arguably quite discrete elements in a chain of business value-adding activities right from proposing to offer the service, to presenting a proposal, to scoping up a piece of work, to delivering it, to promoting the service, advertising, and then distributing and following through in a whole sequence of steps. In the nature of service activity "delivering" the service is rather more complex and difficult to put legal boundaries around. I think that is partly why the draft Directive that you are addressing is so complex. Unlike physical goods, there are a lot more different and arguably discrete activities involved.

Q305 *Lord Geddes:* And in your opinion are there many or few lessons to be learnt from the previous Directives on goods and people?

Mr Hatcher: I think it is fair to say that at this stage in the development of the Community as it grows, as it develops, the experience gained from designing and implementing Directives across the goods, as well as the services sectors, is all leaning in the direction of greater knowledge and experience, and so arguably that must be a benefit. I think that one of the particular challenges with which the services sector is faced in the case of this Directive is that the Directive is very broadly cast. It aims to cover a very broad spectrum of activity and it is not sector specific, it is horizontal, so to the extent it covers such a broad spectrum of activity it is quite challenging for national administrations to have to get to grips with.

Q306 *Lord Geddes:* You already have indicated your favourable attitude to the Country of Origin Principle but you use very interesting words in your evidence: that you like it, it is important to business, it will boost confidence and cross-border trade "provided there are proper arrangements for its application, in a clear and consistent manner by all EU Member States". How will this Country of Origin Principle provide a boost to business confidence and how will it increase cross-border trade?

Mr Hatcher: We believe very strongly that it will provide a much needed degree of legal certainty which is so important for business decision-making and for planning investments. We believe that the Country of Origin Principle will, in fact, simplify the kind of information and knowledge that all businesses but particularly smaller-sized businesses need to assemble at the moment when they are trying to deliver a service across borders, which is information relating not only to the jurisdiction in which they are established, in which they are currently doing business, but also the regulation and the legislation and the understanding of how the administration works in the country in which it is proposed that the service be delivered. So if the Country of Origin Principle were to be implemented you would be streamlining that assembly of knowledge and information. We think that should make for greater certainty in terms of planning decisions and investments and planning service delivery. We think that the Country of Origin Principle needs to be taken into account alongside some of the other measures in the Directive, Articles 14 and 15 as well. To that extent, we believe that the combined effect of these provisions will be to increase competition, to increase innovation and the opportunities for service providers, particularly at the smaller end of the spectrum, to invest more in research and development. We believe in total that will lead to greater business confidence.

Q307 *Lord Geddes:* Turning that on its head, if the Country of Origin Principle were to be significantly amended, or even dropped, do you think that that would kill the thing stone dead?

Mr Hatcher: We see the Country of Origin Principle as being the centrepiece of this Directive. There are obviously important elements to do with mutual assistance and supervision and so forth, but this is very much at the heart of the Directive and we think, to be blunt about it, if Article 16, the Country of Origin Principle, were to be removed that would in effect emasculate the draft Directive.

Q308 *Lord Haskel:* In paragraph 19 of your written evidence you say you do not share the concerns expressed by many people that this Country of Origin Principle will lead to what they call "social dumping" or going to the place where there is the least regulation. You say that is because the UK management consultancy sector is an established,

mature market with relatively few regulatory constraints on it. Is this an argument for sector specific application of the Country of Origin Principle or is it an argument for just having the Country of Origin Principle and leaving it alone?

Ms Driscoll: We do understand the concerns about social dumping, particularly those that have been expressed by public sector unions, but we genuinely do not believe they are highly relevant in the case of management consulting. To pick up Andrew's earlier point, we are not a commodity business. This is not about driving costs down to the lowest common denominator. It is a mature profession. It is full of highly skilled, intelligent, trained people –was that a laugh, my Lord?

Q309 *Lord Geddes:* No, I can see four of you sitting there. I think what a good example!

Ms Driscoll: We are simply not about moving huge armies of people with not many qualifications and experience from country to country. We are about moving small teams of people with particular skills and expertise mainly on a temporary basis to fulfill clients' needs, and that is why we go places, because clients need help and support and advice. So I think in our case it is a rather overblown concern. Whether that means there should be something specific for management consultants or not, as my colleague has said, we very much support the Country of Origin Principle but at the moment looking at the balance between derogation and adopting principles we think the balance is pretty much all right, so we would not be pushing for anything specific at this moment.

Mr Hooke: The other side of the equation is worthy of mention here. Clearly we are dealing with procurement departments and clients as well; they are generally articulate, intelligent people and will be making a judgment on the offer and the expertise that we have and weighing up the pros and cons, and I think that that is also a mechanism which would avoid the social dumping issues.

Q310 *Lord Haskel:* I take your point that having a demanding customer will keep you on your toes but there may be some less scrupulous members of your profession, who are perhaps not members of your organisation, who feel that if they register their business in the Czech Republic, for example, where maybe regulatory standards are much less rigorous, maybe there are some standards which they could skimp on. Would some firms be tempted to do that so they could undercut your members in price?

Ms Driscoll: It is very difficult to comment on the ethics of other people in the profession if they are not fine, up-standing members of the MCA, who of course would not do anything like that. This is a competitive market place so I am sure price comes into it but actually what people are buying is expertise and skill and quality and putting people who do not have that on to clients is a hiding to nothing.

Q311 *Lord Haskel:* So the customers are keeping them on their toes?

Ms Driscoll: The customers will keep the industry up to scratch.

Mr Hatcher: If I may just add, it is fair to say that one of the most important derogations from the Country of Origin Principle is to do with posting of workers, which is a matter of considerable interest to management consultants because they do need to move people about. The draft Directive expressly provides that the protection arrangements both for employment, health and safety, and so forth, would remain in place in the current country in which the service is being delivered, so in a sense your concerns about social dumping in relation to management consulting are addressed expressly in Article 24 of the Directive.

Q312 *Lord Walpole:* If the Country of Origin Principle were to be implemented, which we assume you want, the draft Directive proposes Member State co-operation in a Mutual Assistance Framework. Is this helpful or unnecessary in your area and is it workable in practice?

Mr Petter: We feel it is unlikely to be of much use because the practice of management consultancy is not generally subject to sector specific regulation. We believe that this is in the public interest. Is it workable in practice? It is difficult to say. We fear at the MCA that it could be quite bureaucratic and costly. We understand to give practical effect to enhancement of trust and confidence in cross-border services the draft Directive recognises that Member States will need to ensure a higher degree of mutual assistance, for example, by exchanging more information with each other about their respective service sectors and co-operate in other ways to understand better the market dynamics of service sectors. Although this is unlikely to have a significant impact on individual firms, in the management consulting sector representative associations like the MCA could find themselves more involved in initiatives by government and regulators to enhance the quality of services at EC level and thereby achieve the objectives of the Services Directive. We find that time-consuming and costly and we would say to you that our method in the UK anyway is to promote best practice. I do not know if anybody would be interested in seeing that, but that is a best practice statement which we promote with the Office of Government Commerce, the National Audit Office and our sister organisation the Institute of Management Consultancy. I would be very happy to send that to you or e-mail it to you in view of your imminent departure because promotion of best practice seems to us far better than setting up a "police force".

Q313 *Lord Walpole:* Unnecessary is the answer.

Mr Petter: Quite unnecessary, yes.

Q314 *Baroness Eccles of Moulton:* In paragraph 23 of your written evidence you indicate quite clearly that a "one size fits all" approach runs the risk of imposing additional burdens on the management consultancy sector. In paragraph 23 you say that appropriate, market-led quality standards should continue to apply—which implies that there are already quality standards that relate to MCA membership—and that there would be a risk of hampering the dynamic business sector if a one-size-fits-all rule is applied. In light of your statement in paragraph 23, is it fair to say that you would resist harmonisation of standards in the management consultancy sector across the EU? Could you be more specific about the dangers?

Mr Petter: We would not resist that in principle but in practice we would be very concerned to avoid a levelling down to the lowest common denominator in the management consultancy sector. I have said already that we do try to promote best practice and we feel that this is what the draft Directive is meant to be about. We do believe that the standards applied by our member firms are very high and we believe that their firms, and more importantly perhaps their clients, are best placed to define the standards because they are close to changing market needs. As an example of the sort of common standards which might, we feel, lower the common denominator, I wonder how you would consider the standards to be applied to the management consultancy profession and the standards to be applied to the cleaning profession. There seems to be a need for a recognition of the difference. I certainly feel that I would not want my profession to be operating like that or indeed to be operating the police force within that profession—your two questions are interlinked—so we would want to be very careful of that and if and when this becomes a matter for UK enabling legislation, we would want to watch that like a hawk at that stage.

Q315 *Chairman:* I have got a sweep-up question because that is what Chairmen do. This starts from the point that your written evidence is very supportive of the draft Directive taken as a whole. Is there anything else that you would like if we were re-doing the Directive? What other provisions would you have found useful?

Mr Petter: I suppose dealing purely operationally one of the major barriers to small and medium-sized enterprises setting up in European Member States is the question of taxation and social security issues, which are all very significant barriers. When we surveyed our members earlier on in response to a consultation exercise by the European Commission, this message came across time after time, that the real barriers were cultural, which the Directive cannot do very much about in many cases, and taxation. It was the taxation and social security issues which really did cause member firms to take avoiding action when they were involved or wanted to be involved in pan-European business, the setting up of alliances, formally and informally. That is how they avoid some of the pitfalls but taxation remains a pitfall because the likelihood is that you are going to have to send people to another country and double taxation and extra costs are part of the baggage that you have to carry in doing this. With firms that have set up in a multitude of states across the Union then of course they do not have that problem, except of course where they have to pull teams in from other countries and they are faced with similar problems, although they will be more familiar with how to deal with them.

Q316 *Chairman:* Yes, so what you are saying is that you would like the tax and social security rules harmonised and simplified throughout the EU? Is that the short point?

Mr Petter: I suppose so, yes.

Q317 *Chairman:* Just checking. I think that may be asking too much.
Mr Petter: We are fully aware that we are asking for too much but you asked the specific question and that is it, yes.

Q318 *Chairman:* That is your view, right. If the Commission made significant changes to the Country of Origin Principle or even dropped it I think you have said that that would be a disaster?
Mr Petter: Yes, we say it will emasculate it.

Q319 *Chairman:* I want that down for the record. I know you have answered the question once but I would like to have it down for the record. We have managed to arrive at the end of our questions. Would any of my colleagues like to ask anything in supplement? No? Splendid. Then it remains for me to thank you and your colleagues very much for coming and adding to our understanding. We are getting a bit better as time goes on. Would any of you like to tell us anything else before you go?
Mr Hooke: We are happy.
Mr Petter: We are very happy. It only remains for us to thank you for listening so patiently to our explanations and say that we too have enjoyed sharing our views with you. Thank you again, my Lord Chairman.
Chairman: Thank you very much.

Memorandum by The Advertising Association

1. The Advertising Association (AA) is a federation of 26 trade associations and professional bodies representing the advertising and promotional marketing industries, including advertisers, agencies, the media and support services in the UK. It is the only body that speaks for all sides of an industry worth over £17.2 billion in 2003. Further information about the AA, its membership and remit is available on our website at www.adassoc.org.uk

2. The AA welcomes the opportunity to submit evidence to Sub-Committee B (Internal Market) of the House of Lords Select Committee on the European Union in order to assist the Inquiry into the European Commission Proposal for a Directive on Services in the Internal Market. This evidence should be read in conjunction with evidence submitted by individual AA member organisations.

3. General Comments: The AA has vigorously lobbied for the removal of barriers to the free movement of commercial communications across the European Union (EU). The achievement of a true Internal Market and the removal of the impeding regulations and bureaucracy are fundamental aims of our industry that will benefit business and consumers alike. The AA welcomes proposals that will serve to assist in the completion of a true Internal Market for Services, confirm the desire to work towards the goals of the Lisbon European Council, and that aim to cut the excessive red tape that continues to prevent businesses from offering their services across borders within the European Union.

THE CURRENT STATE OF THE SINGLE MARKET IN SERVICES (COMMERCIAL COMMUNICATIONS)

4. In July 2002, the Commission produced a report on the state of the Internal Market in Services following a detailed consultation with stakeholders. This report identified a large number of barriers affecting services, confirmed that these barriers occur at every stage of the business process and showed that similar barriers could be found across different sectors. The report gave special mention to problems faced in carrying out cross-border commercial communications: "The promotion of services is rendered particularly difficult because of very restrictive and detailed rules for commercial communications ranging from outright bans on advertising for certain professions to strict control on content in other cases. The large divergence of legislation between Member States impedes pan-European promotional activities for many services."

5. Commercial communication helps to break down cross-border barriers to trade throughout the EU, providing consumers with access to information about products and services. Communications of all types stimulate competition between companies and trade between countries. In particular, recourse to marketing communication allows small or new enterprises a chance of competing with established competitors. Commercial communication also provides the potential for developing a consumer-oriented European market. Strong European brands strengthen and maintain international competitiveness for European products and services. In many respects, commercial communications make and maintain the market. The ability to create and sustain trade in products and services gives commercial communication a crucial role in the operation of the market itself and therefore also in the construction of the European Internal Market as a political and economic objective.

THE COUNTRY OF ORIGIN PRINCIPLE:

6. The Commission proposal is grounded on the Internal Market Principle that being lawfully established in one Member State will allow commercial communications to be provided freely in the other 24. The Principle that a company registered to provide services in one country is automatically qualified to provide those services in any community country on the basis of home country regulation is a reasonable and realistic starting point. The Principle is workable in practice. It is this Principle that will allow companies established in the EU to be able to take full advantage of the Internal Market. Through being able to rely upon the Principle, this would by default remove obstacles, such as advertising bans and restrictions, to cross-border commercial communications that are applied in other Member States. Barriers to the freedom of movement of services deny EU citizens getting the quality of service and choice that they deserve, whilst also restricting competitiveness within the EU. The recognition of this mutuality of interest between consumers and industry is of paramount importance. The AA would wholeheartedly oppose any moves to water-down the Principle as it relates to the commercial communications sector.

7. Advertising as a Service: The AA notes in Recital 16 (and the Explanatory Memorandum Point 7 (a)) that advertising services are defined as a service for the purposes of the proposed Directive. Nonetheless, given the status of audio-visual services and the coverage within the scope of the Television Without Frontiers Directive (TVWF) to broadcasting, the AA asks the House of Lords Select Committee to seek clarification from the Commission of the reasoning behind the inclusion of broadcasting services in the Directive. There is some confusion as to the inclusion of audio-visual services in the Explanatory Memorandum Point 7 (a), but then the singling out of television broadcasting in Recital 13, and further note in Recital 47. There is no reference to the TVWF Directive in the list of derogated measures, whereas the Directive does not apply to e-commerce services governed by the EU telecom package.

8. Radio Broadcasting: In relation to commercial radio, the Services Directive would appear to require considerable change to the UK's framework for radio licensing. The AA seeks exemption from the Services Directive for radio broadcasting. The exemptions should be clear and included in both the main Articles of the Directive as well as the Recitals. Radio broadcasting is not currently regulated at EU level. The Services Directive would set an EU framework for radio licensing regulation. The ability to license radio services allows the UK to impose its own rules on the relationship of broadcasting services and the content of services. This position would be undermined without an exemption.

9. Non-Discrimination: The AA has some misgivings in respect of the "non-discrimination" provisions of Article 21 and their impact upon businesses (particularly SMEs) whose marketplace is essentially limited to a geographic area. Article 21.2 includes the proviso "without precluding the possibility of providing for differences in the conditions of access where those differences are directly justified by objective criteria" and the AA questions whether this terminology envisages that the supplier may actually refuse to provide services altogether: it may be argued that by referring to "differences in the conditions of access" the Directive intends

that a supplier may not actually refuse, but can only apply different terms to recipients in other Member States, for example by requiring a higher price to be paid.

10. In the context of the publishing industry, for instance, the publisher's right to refuse advertising is a fundamental principle. In addition to requiring all advertisements to comply with the law and the British Code of Advertising, Sales Promotion and Direct Marketing, publishers may exercise the right to refuse advertisements which, whilst they ostensibly comply with the law and the code, may in the opinion of the publisher not be in their readers" best interests, or which might, in the context of that particular local community, cause offence. For example, if a business or an individual located in another Member State were to request advertising services from a local newspaper publisher in this country, the same terms and conditions of acceptance would be applied to them as would be to a UK national. However, it might be the case that their advertising would be refused because, judged against those terms and conditions, the mere fact of their being located abroad rendered the advertising, in the opinion of the publisher, unacceptable. The AA urges the House of Lords Select Committee to seek clarifications from the Commission on Article 21, whether this would, worded in its present form, prevent or restrict their ability to refuse advertisements in this way.

11. In this context, the AA would also ask the House of Lords Select Committee to seek guidance from the Commission on the interpretation of the phrase "made available to the public at large" in the second line of Article 21.2 and whether the existence of the right to refuse advertising in effect means that advertising services are not actually being offered to the public "at large" but rather only to those who the publishers, at their discretion, chooses to contract with. The AA also asks the House of Lords Select Committee to seek clarification about the compatibility, again in the context of the "right to refuse", between Article 21.2 and existing EU competition case law on refusal to supply.

12. Information on Providers and their Services: The Directive requires service providers to make certain information available to the recipient (Article 26). The AA notes in Recital 62 that firstly "one of the means by which the provider may make the information accessible is to supply his electronic address, including that of his website" and secondly that "the obligation to present certain information in the provider's information documents presenting his services in detail does not apply to commercial communications of a general nature, such as advertising, but instead to documents giving a detailed description of the services proposed, including documents on a website". The AA encourages the House of Lords Select Committee to ensure that requirements are not onerous upon service providers, whilst the obligations remain as not required upon advertising as specified in the proposal.

13. Commercial Communications by the Regulated Professions: Article 29 requires Member States to remove all total prohibitions on commercial communications by the regulated professions. The AA supports the principle of the Commission's objective through this deregulation. Whist no professional bodies representing regulated professions are in membership of the AA's constituent bodies, the Association endorses the proposal where it provides an opportunity for the opening up of commercial communication activity in this area to the benefit of creative agencies, the media as a whole, and consumers/recipients of such services by the regulated professions that will be granted access to information through new information streams. Some similarities may be drawn with the liberalisation of advertising by opticians in the UK during the early 1980s.[1]

14. Codes of Conduct: The AA supports the use of self-regulatory mechanisms wherever practical, however recognises that the scope of Article 39 is limited only to the encouragement of codes of conduct by the regulated professions and the activities of estate agents.

15. Single Points of Contact: In essence, the suggestion to have one single point through which any formalities and procedures required to exercise service activities seems both sensible and practical in cutting bureaucratic red tape. The AA, however, is concerned how this might actually work in practice, and would ask the House of Lords Select Committee to seek further clarification from the Commission.

16. Proposals for Additional Harmonisation: The Commission proposal states (Article 40) that it shall assess within one year after adoption at the latest the possibility to present harmonising instruments in the area of gambling activities. The AA and its members have been closely involved with the UK Government and Department for Culture, Media & Sport on changes to the UK Gambling Laws. Work in this area is on-going and, with this in mind, the AA takes the offer of assistance to the European and UK Institutions in providing input in this area.

---

[1] Following investigation by the UK Office of Fair Trading and the Department of Trade in 1983, the General Optical Council updated the Rules on Publicity in 1985.

17. Implementation Timetable: The AA recognises that the Brussels European Council in March 2003 noted that "Member States should nevertheless already step up their own efforts to dismantle existing barriers". With this in mind, the Commission must be encouraged to ensure that Member States pursue such efforts to remove barriers to services alongside the approval of the Directive through the legislative process.

THE FUTURE:

18. The implementation of the Commission's proposed Directive would have a significant and beneficial impact upon the opportunities for businesses to be able to make commercial communications across borders within the European Union and operate more effectively in other Member States.

14 February 2005

Examination of Witness

Witness: MR PHIL MURPHY, Head of European Public Affairs, The Advertising Association, examined.

Q320 *Chairman:* Mr Murphy, thank you very much for coming. I am sorry you are somewhat outnumbered by us but that simply cannot be helped. Is there an opening statement you would like to make before we all start asking questions?
Mr Murphy: My Lord Chairman, thank you very much for the invitation to be here today. The Advertising Association is very supportive of what the European Commission is doing with the Services Directive. We have been lobbying vigorously for the removal of bans and restrictions on commercial communications across the European Union. We believe that the issue is about companies in the UK being able to penetrate markets and to offer increased competition in other markets which would prove beneficial to consumers because they would have more choice on their shelves and, hopefully, be paying less in terms of the products and goods that they desire themselves.

Q321 *Lord Haskel:* You have just told us that you think there are significant barriers to commercial communications. Could you tell us which barriers you think are the most significant?
Mr Murphy: The main barriers are those bans and restrictions on the free movement of advertising and sales promotions across the Member States. Other restrictions that place burdens on the UK's business relate to prior authorisations which are required in many countries, for example, Portugal, Belgium, Italy, Spain and the Netherlands. These relate to whether a promotional game may be able to be released in that country to consumers. I have a number of examples to give you, if I may.

Q322 *Chairman:* Some examples would be extremely useful since none of us is an advertising industry expert.
Mr Murphy: For example, accountants in France cannot advertise their services. In France there is a seven per cent limit placed on any premiums that may be offered. The promoter themselves may say that if you buy a certain brand of cereal they will also give

you a free watch. In Denmark you could only win a prize that is worth seven euros. I am sure you can imagine how things could be severely restricted in Denmark because of that. The prizes that we have in the UK can indeed be vast. It is about consumers' traditions and the promotions that companies wish to offer. In France lawyers cannot use letters, flyers, posters, films or TV to advertise their own services in terms of saying, "We can help you with any preparation of legal documents that you may have." In the Netherlands this prior authorisation, that I was referring to, before is needed for promotional lotteries and also for games. In Denmark there is a ban on the supply and the advertisement of gambling services and this has essentially made it impossible for any EU-based providers of sports betting services to establish their presence in Denmark. Indeed, the European Commission began to investigate this a year ago. These examples give a flavour of the different bans that are present in other EU Member States.

Q323 *Lord Haskel:* As I understand it these barriers that you have described to us are applied to firms in Belgium, Holland, Denmark and any British advertising agency which may want to do business there, so it is not really a barrier to an outside company coming into Denmark, Holland or Belgium, it is just that there are different standards in different countries and different rules. Is it harmonisation that you are asking for, that these rules should be done away with and that they should be the same in all of the European Union countries?
Mr Murphy: I think it is very much about having a mix of mutual recognition or harmonisation which we think the Services Directive provides. For example, certain countries will have certain bans. They will have these bans justified. They believe these are proportionate to the aims of public policy, consumer protection and public security, whatever that may be. For us, in terms of being able to have the advertising of the UK freely circulating throughout the Member States, it is about that mutual recognition through the Country of Origin Principle which will say that as long

as your advertising is legal, decent, honest and truthful here in the UK it should, theoretically, be able to circulate freely. I think it is those bans where we see the issue in terms of the provision of services, the idea of a temporary service being provided. Advertising and sales promotions are temporary given their very nature. It is about an advertising campaign being produced for a product or service that is going to be a specific product and temporary in nature, for example, the time it may be limited to. It is about going over there with your advertising on a temporary basis rather than establishing yourself over there.

Q324 Lord Haskel: If you are an agency and you want to start a business in another country, how easy is it to set this up?

Mr Murphy: It is not difficult for an agency to go over and establish itself in another country. However, this is not something we have information about. Smaller agencies may well decide they would like to establish in another Member State and they will have the usual hoops and burdens to cope with. For example, in Belgium it is about going there on a temporary basis first of all, putting a toe in the water, and seeing whether you want to establish yourself in Belgium. There is specific criteria and information you have to provide to the Belgian authorities in terms of who these workers may be that are coming across for you, how long they will be in the country, when they will leave, what earnings they will have and so forth. In our experience an advertising campaign will be created here in the home country. Media will originate from the UK and circulate into other countries in terms of the campaign itself. Our focus in terms of the Services Directive is about the advertising itself rather than agencies being able to go over and establish themselves.

Q325 Lord Haskel: Do I conclude, from the advertising agency's point of view, that the barriers are not so much about setting up a business but more the different regulations in each country regarding advertising itself or communications?

Mr Murphy: Very much so. Trying to create a pan-European campaign for a client is very difficult. You have to know what the laws, regulations and Codes of Practice may be in other countries. It is very difficult, if not impossible, to have a pan-European advertising campaign at the moment. We believe the Services Directive will aid this in that certain bans and restrictions may be removed as it will be the Commission that has responsibility for looking at each individual ban or restriction and asking Member States to take them down where they believe they are not proportionate.

Q326 Chairman: It is not going to fix the whole of your problem. One is not going to be able to persuade the French, for example, that it is perfectly all right to give prizes 10 times the value of the goods.

Mr Murphy: There are different cultural aspects in each Member State and in their own way each is right and proper and appropriate to that country. It is about where any bans or restrictions may be contrary to the Treaty of Rome in terms of whether they are serving the public policy initiatives which they purport to serve. For example, since 1991 the Loi Evin has implemented almost a total ban on all alcohol advertising there, but recently the French Senate agreed that French wine can be advertised in France.

Q327 Chairman: But not foreign wine?

Mr Murphy: Yes. This law is purported to be on the grounds of public health protection.

Q328 Lord Walpole: We understand that the Country of Origin Principle relates only to businesses operating in a non-home Member State on a temporary basis and that if the business becomes legally "established" in that other Member State the Country of Origin Principle would not apply to its operation. What is your understanding of that?

Mr Murphy: That is a perfect understanding of the Directive. Once a service provider establishes themselves in a different Member State those provisions of law of that Member State will apply. How we relate that to the advertising business is that we see the temporary nature of advertising circulating for a specific period, not an indefinite period because campaigns are drawn up for specific time periods.

Q329 Lord Walpole: In the advertising sector how would you define a "temporary" operation? You have just said that any advertising campaign is by itself a temporary operation.

Mr Murphy: We would say it is advertisements carried by cross-border media emanating in the UK and circulating in other Member States.

Q330 Lord Walpole: It is temporary?

Mr Murphy: Yes.

Q331 Lord Walpole: If a company has an office over there is it permanent?

Mr Murphy: Absolutely, yes.

Q332 Lord Swinfen: Mr Murphy, you have been relating the aspect of "temporary" to the individual advertising campaign. What I am interested in is the fact that the advertising agency that goes over to another country within the EU may in fact be asked to run more than one campaign, because an advertising agency in this country, if it is going to make any money, will be running several campaigns at the same time. Temporary need not necessarily refer to only one campaign. How long is "temporary", for instance?

Mr Murphy: Unfortunately we have not looked at any definition of how long temporary would be. Let us separate the two issues as we see it, the advertising itself and the agency work. I understand that other industry organisations are looking into this definition of temporary and whether it may be defined as "not being permanent".

Lord Swinfen: How permanent is permanent? None of us is here permanently.

Q333 *Chairman:* I know the advertising industry works on the basis of campaigns, but are there examples of actual agencies thinking they will just go and see how it would work in Brussels and so they go over there with a couple of people? Does that happen? Do they not go over there with a campaign, with a couple of people, and think they will give it a try for six months to a year.

Mr Murphy: It must happen. Unfortunately I do not have information in terms of how many have taken those opportunities in the last 12 months.

Q334 *Chairman:* Might it be the sort of thing that people would want to do if the Directive became law?

Mr Murphy: That is true. The larger agencies may well have satellite offices already set up in other Member States and where they do not, they may look to form some sort of partnership with other agencies that may have more expertise in those countries. The smaller agencies themselves may decide they have been successful here in London and so they would like to dabble in what may be possible overseas: and I think where that would happen the Directive would be helpful so long as the burdens that would be placed upon dabbling in another country would be lessened through the Directive in terms of information that may have to be held in terms of records and so forth.

Q335 *Lord Fearn:* In paragraph 10 of your written evidence you note the issue of editorial freedom and the problem that an advertisement from an outside source may be judged undesirable. How would you wish to see this issue resolved? I cannot see it being resolved, can you?

Mr Murphy: It is a problem. The issue here in the UK is that the right to refuse advertising does exist. For example, if you have somebody in the UK approaching a publisher saying, "I would like to place an advertisement within your publication, please", the publisher may well turn round to them and say, if it was to do with some sort of business opportunity, "We would like to have a few more details about the business proposition you are putting forward", or, "We may like to investigate any certificates relating to trade." For example, where you have somebody wanting to offer childcare a

publisher may well want to see evidence of any relevant certificates. The issue we have with Article 21.2 is to do with what sort of objective criteria could be applied where the right to refuse would be able to apply. For example, will there be different treatment by a UK publisher when somebody in Belgium wishes to place an advertisement? Will the publisher think "We would like to carry out the normal checks and verifications that we do for a UK potential advertiser"? However, because it will be much more difficult for the UK publisher to get the information from the authorities in Belgium, would they, by default, want to refuse the advertising because it will be more costly than the actual price of the advertisement in the first place for them to be able to verify that? What we are looking for is clarification that the right to refuse will still be applicable. If that means adding a third paragraph to Article 21, that may well be the clarification we are looking for. We have been seeking clarifications through the DTI and the Government and they are negotiating around the Council table and also with the European Commission. It is about providing that clarity to ensure that not all advertising has to be taken by a publisher. The publisher needs to take on board whether an advertisement is obscene or illegal or if it would be demeaning to the readership of that particular publication.

Q336 *Lord Fearn:* Who would decide that in France, Germany or Poland? Who would decide "No, we're not accepting that"?

Mr Murphy: It would be the publishers themselves.

Q337 *Lord Fearn:* If UK editors then refuse advertisements on the basis that they did not know, would barriers to the operation of advertising agencies in other Member States exist?

Mr Murphy: It could in the same way as having to cope with the different bans and restrictions that the agencies have to deal with in terms of other Member States.

Q338 *Lord Fearn:* Are editorial staff here very concerned about this? Do you see that arising all the time?

Mr Murphy: I do not have information pertaining to the number of cases that may have occurred across different publications here in the UK. I would be very happy to gather that information for you.

Lord Fearn: Thank you.

Q339 *Lord Haskel:* A growing form of advertising is on the Internet. If you are going to advertise in European countries on the Internet, it is the Internet service provider who has to make these decisions that you were saying the publisher has to make.

Would this Directive take care of that or does the E-commerce Directive try to take care of that?

Mr Murphy: My understanding is that the E-commerce Directive is outside the scope of the Services Directive. The E-commerce Directive does cover that as an issue. My understanding is that Internet service providers are dealt with under the E-commerce Directive as being a "mere conduit". For example, an advertisement may be placed on a specific website. However, the Internet service provider themselves would not be liable for that because of it being this "mere conduit".

Q340 Chairman: The only thing I can think of, in terms of the kind of discrimination that might be implied here, is that if an English publisher would turn down the kind of advertisement that a Belgian advertiser might wish to use, such as, "Send money now and we will send you back goods," where you cannot check cross-border whether that is *bona fide*. Is that the sort of thing we are worrying about?

Mr Murphy: Yes. All advertising that is published in a UK publication must comply with the law and comply with the advertising self-regulatory codes of advertising, sales promotion and direct marketing that exist here in the UK, and rigorous checks are done to ensure that they do comply, of course. Complaints may still come about. Fundamentally, it is about the publisher being able to say, "Okay, here is somebody that would like to place an advertisement with us. We have a few reservations. We would like to check the information out first of all to satisfy ourselves."

Q341 Lord Swinfen: With the Country of Origin Principle where are the matters of taste, decency or morality judged? In the country of origin of the advertising agents or in the country where the advertisement is going to be published in whatever form, if it is going to be published? Taste particularly will change.

Mr Murphy: Absolutely. This is a question that we have been labouring over for some time in terms of the free movement of advertising as a service. The example I would like to give you brings us on to mutual assistance that may be provided through the different authorities in Member States. In 1992 the European Advertising Standards Alliance (EASA), based in Brussels, was created. It set up a cross-border advertising complaints mechanism. Essentially this works using the Country of Origin Principle. How it works is that if a UK consumer receives a direct mailing from a company based in the Netherlands and the UK consumer believes that they have been misled or there is an issue in terms of taste and decency within that advertisement, in the first instance they would complain to the Advertising Standards Authority here in the UK.

The Advertising Standards Authority would then say, "This is outside our competence. This has come from another country." They would then be able to contact the European Advertising Standards Alliance and say, "We need some help with this. Please can you put us in touch with Stichting Reclame Code", which is the governing body for advertising self-regulation in the Netherlands. The Dutch would then look at the advertisement and they would judge it in terms of their own self-regulatory Codes of Practice. If they found there to be a breach of the Code, they would then take action. Essentially it is about using that Country of Origin Principle as a mechanism for resolving complaints that may come up about cross-border advertising. It is one area in which, hopefully, the Member States themselves, through the mutual assistance networks, could learn from this as an area of best practice. Best practice has been recognised by the Economic and Social Committee in their investigations on self-regulation and co-regulation and by several Directorate-Generals at the European Commission.

Q342 Lord Geddes: It seems to me from what you have just said that you hardly need this Directive. You seem to be a long way ahead of it in the advertising industry.

Mr Murphy: We wish we were. There are many different bans and restrictions that exist in other Member States. It is very difficult to penetrate those markets using what may be legal, decent, honest and truthful here in the UK. For example, if you are running a sales promotion, contest or game and you would like to penetrate different markets across Europe, effectively they could be stopped and you could be under legal proceedings in other countries purely because, even though it complies with your country of origin here, there is not that mechanism in EU law to say that that is okay. We believe the Services Directive will aid that and will encourage promoters and advertisers to advertise their products across border and penetrate those markets.

Q343 Lord Geddes: Your written evidence and all your oral evidence so far has said that as an industry you are in favour of the Country of Origin Principle. What would happen if the Directive in that context was severely amended or it dropped the Country of Origin Principle? What would be the result from your point of view in that case?

Mr Murphy: It would destroy any potential for an internal market for services specifically for commercial communications. What we have here with the Services Directive is the potential to lead towards the creation of a true internal market for commercial communications. Without that we would have severe reservations about the delivery and the drive of the European Commission and the European institutions as a whole towards the Lisbon agenda.

Q344 Lord Swinfen: If the Country of Origin Principle were to be implemented, the draft Directive proposes Member State co-operation in a Mutual Assistance Framework. I think that may be covered by the European Advertising Standards Alliance?
Mr Murphy: Indeed.

Q345 Lord Swinfen: Is that potentially helpful or is it unnecessary as far as your industry is concerned? Have you already set up a regulatory force? Are there any mechanisms, apart from what you have already told us, that would help to regulate your industry? Is it workable in practice?
Mr Murphy: The Mutual Assistance Framework could be very helpful. It is about reinforcing the cross-border complaints system operated by the EASA. In terms of whether the Country of Origin Principle itself is workable, yes, I really think it is. The precedent already exists. In 1989 the Television Without Frontiers Directive, which places the country of origin firmly at its roots, was agreed at a European level. I believe there have been six reports by the European Commission on the operation of this and each report has said that the Country of Origin Principle is working very well. In terms of the E-commerce Directive, again this has been in operation for the last five years and, again, the European Commission reports indicate that this is operating successfully. Those precedents already exist for successful operations in different sectors. The Country of Origin Principle and the Services Directive hopefully would ensure the removal of barriers in many different sectors.

Q346 Chairman: I would like to have a crack at the question we are all picking away at about advertising. We have read paragraph 6 with particular interest. I am beginning to hear that what the advertising industry regard as what would be the peculiar benefit of this Directive is that given that it is, for instance, regarded as perfectly legal, decent and truthful here to advertise cornflakes with a giveaway prize, an amount well in excess of the value of the cornflakes, this is not acceptable in Slovenia so the Country of Origin Principle would then operate, but because it is legal and decent in England Slovenia would have to accept their cornflakes with free gifts in excess of the cornflakes. Am I correct?
Mr Murphy: Yes.

Q347 Chairman: That is the benefit for the advertising agency?

Mr Murphy: Yes, absolutely. It is about providing opportunities for competitiveness in the EU.

Q348 Chairman: I see the point of it and I see the point of the competition, but that is what you think the Country of Origin Principle does, it allows you to do something that is legal, decent and truthful here, even if it is not particularly acceptable to Slovenian cultural moorings. I know nothing about Slovenian cultural moorings and so that is why I seized upon it.
Mr Murphy: My knowledge of Slovenia and its bans and restrictions is severely limited. Let us say they did have a restriction on the prize or the offer that could be included with the cornflakes in Slovenia: if that ban or restriction was justified and proportionate to the aims to which it purports to support—for example, it could be public health, consumer protection—then that would be an area in which, as long as that ban is justified, that would still be able to remain. Of course under the Directive on Services it is about Member States themselves removing, in line with the Directive, any bans and restrictions that are not proportionate and that are not justified.

Q349 Lord Geddes: If you could turn that on its head—and we are all using Slovenia as an hypothetical example and I have never been there in my life and know nothing about the country, sadly—if the restrictions in Slovenia were more severe than the restrictions, say, in the UK and the Slovenian advertising agency wanted to advertise in the UK, could they cherry pick? In other words, would they be restricted on the Country of Origin Principle by their own regulations, as you understand the Directive, or could they pick up the UK regulations?
Mr Murphy: My Lord Chairman, it would depend on how that Slovenian agency went about its business. If they were publishing their advertisement in a Slovenian publication that was circulated from Slovenia into the UK, they would be restricted to the Slovenian rules and regulations.

Q350 Lord Geddes: I understand that. What happens if they do it in the UK?
Mr Murphy: If however they wished to place an advertisement in *The Times* say, for example, then they would be able to place that separately.

Q351 Lord Geddes: Under UK regulations?
Mr Murphy: Under UK regulations.
Lord Geddes: That is what I thought it was; I just wanted clarity.

Q352 *Chairman:* To put it to you crudely Mr Murphy, are we right that you are saying it is your desire to circumvent bans on advertising of particular types in particular Member States by relying on the Country of Origin Principle?
Mr Murphy: My Lord Chairman, absolutely not. The UK advertising business does not wish to circumvent bans that may be in existence but simply to be able to advertise in countries—

Q353 *Chairman:* These are bans on advertising.
Mr Murphy:— whose bans are incompatible with the Treaty in terms of being proportionate or justified.

Q354 *Chairman:* It is a way of enforcing the Treaty?
Mr Murphy: Yes, absolutely.

Q355 *Baroness Eccles of Moulton:* I think my question is a continuation of the same debate. Much earlier on when you were asked about the country of origin I think you said that some harmonisation would be appropriate and in other cases mutual recognition would be appropriate, it would be depend what the question was. I thought at that stage you said that the legal, decent, honest and truthful principles should be harmonised?
Mr Murphy: My Lord Chairman, as I was indicating earlier, I believe that the Directive on Services itself strikes the right balance between mutual recognition and the Country of Origin Principle but also harmonisation where that is appropriate. For example, in terms of the information provisions as contained within the Directive, there have been a number of draft regulations and draft proposals for Directives over the last few years which have been looking more and more in the area of information provision and the type of information that should be set down at EU level. Where these are not especially burdensome on the industry then, yes, it is a good thing. It is about providing information to consumers and to businesses in a timely, non-misleading fashion. I think that the Country of Origin Principle here within the Directive on Services would allow UK advertising to rely on the fact that if it complies with UK law and the UK self-regulatory codes, the fundamentals of which are that all advertising should be legal, decent, honest and truthful, that should be allowed to be fully circulated. We have at a European level been working through the European Advertising Standards Alliance in terms of drawing up common principles and common best practice amongst the different advertising self-regulatory bodies, and since 1992 the different self-regulatory bodies have been talking to one another and have been looking to resolve any differences and looking into different areas in terms of mutual appreciation and mutual assistance.

Q356 *Baroness Eccles of Moulton:* Harmonisation, as I understand it, would apply across all Member States?
Mr Murphy: Yes.

Q357 *Baroness Eccles of Moulton:* So would you say that the example you have just been giving indicates that this is, as it were, a movement but that it has not quite yet been embraced all Member States?
Mr Murphy: In terms of advertising rules and self-regulation specifically?

Q358 *Baroness Eccles of Moulton:* Yes, I am obviously asking the question directly relevant to your expertise.
Mr Murphy: The International Chamber of Commerce, which is the world business organisation representative body headquartered in Paris, has since 1937 had a code of advertising practice. This is where, essentially, the principles of all advertising being legal, decent, honest and truthful come from. It is the type of code which different Member States and emerging advertising industries in different Member States have used as a basis for what they may put in terms of their own codes of conduct and practice. As a loose basis, yes, all Member States do use those principles. Self-regulation is at a different level in many different Member States across Europe. This is why the Advertising Association, and all our European partners combined, are working with and as members of the European Advertising Standards Alliance to ensure that where help may be necessary in, say, Cyprus or in the Czech Republic, that we have that expertise to share in terms of encouraging appropriate resources to be put in place for the setting up of the self-regulatory codes of conduct and for the independent adjudicatory bodies. Again it is about working together to ensure that advertising self-regulation is effective and that it is in existence in all the Member States.

Q359 *Baroness Eccles of Moulton:* Does this mean that there is an overlap between harmonisation and mutual recognition?
Mr Murphy: In some senses yes, but I believe it depends on the specific issue that you would be looking at. As I say, because the basic principles of being legal, decent, honest and truthful exist, one could say that there is some degree of harmonisation without having harmonisation across the Member States, but again the different codes of advertising practice take into account the national sensitivities of that country and the cultural diversities that we have been talking about earlier. So it is right and proper

that there are different codes across the Member States themselves.

Q360 *Baroness Eccles of Moulton:* And in your industry there will be a predominance of the sort of activities that would come under the temporary heading as opposed to the established heading?
Mr Murphy: Yes, very much so.

Q361 *Baroness Eccles of Moulton:* So all this Country of Origin Principle, harmonisation, mutual recognition, et cetera, et cetera, is particularly important to your industry because of the temporary nature of the cross-border work that is done?
Mr Murphy: The use of the Country of Origin Principle is absolutely vital to the UK advertising business.

Q362 *Baroness Eccles of Moulton:* For that reason?
Mr Murphy: For that reason.

Q363 *Chairman:* Now for a sweep-up question. People giving evidence in other service sectors (not advertising and not, as it happens, management consultancy) have told us that harmonisation, while all very well, is just going to be too slow and is a very elaborate procedure. They are much happier with mutual recognition and the Country of Origin Principle because it is quicker and you just recognise each other's standards rather than trying to agree the same standards all the way round. Does that represent more or less your position? Does the word "harmonisation" fill you with terror as it did certainly some previous witnesses because they just thought it would take too long?
Mr Murphy: My Lord Chairman, it very much does depend on the specific issue that we might be discussing. I think the problem that the advertising business has experienced in the last couple of years in terms of draft European law is that, invariably, when

you talk about harmonisation of European legislation it is nigh on impossible to get the Member States to agree and they will all say their laws, their bans, their restrictions are the best and must be followed.

Q364 *Chairman:* Yes, so really it is going to be a bit quicker and more effective if we all just agree to recognise each other's standards, if recognition of each other's standards is enforced by the Directive?
Mr Murphy: My Lord Chairman, I think the Directive provides that balance and I think the country of origin is very much the centre point of this Directive and we would not like to see it watered down at all. If I may reiterate: without the Country of Origin Principle we would have a watered down Directive and it would be terrifically difficult, if not impossible, to have a true internal market for commercial communications which is what we all seek in the advertising business.

Q365 *Chairman:* Indeed. Thank you very much. Before I give my colleagues a chance to do further sweep-up questions, can we offer you the chance to do a sweep-up statement? Are there any significant changes that you would like to see in the draft Directive as it now stands other than the clarifications that you have explained, anything new and special that the Directive is not covering?
Mr Murphy: Other than the clarifications as specified in our position paper and the answers, which I hope have been helpful to you today, there is nothing else that I would like to add.

Q366 *Chairman:* It remains for me to thank you very much for coming, Mr Murphy and all by yourself. I hope you have not found it a too anxious-making experience. We have found it very helpful.
Mr Murphy: It has been a wonderful experience. Thank you all very much.

Supplementary written evidence from The Advertising Association

Thank you again for the opportunity to have given oral evidence to the Sub-Committee. In response to two questions that arose during proceedings:

QUESTION: *How many advertising agencies have attempted to establish themselves in other EU Member States over the last 12 months?*

Having spoken to the Institute of Practitioners in Advertising, they confirm that a figure is such unknown. In practice, agencies do not generally look to establish themselves in another Member State. Campaigns are created in the home country, then advertising space bought in the media of the country in which their client wishes to promote themselves or their products or space booked in media that originates in the UK but circulates into the market concerned. Most agencies may look to create "strategic alliances" with another local agency in another Member State. Effectively any agency wishing to set up in another Member State would require the staff to be local, or at least to be fully aware of that State's individual advertising laws and regulation.

9 March 2005

QUESTION: *How many instances do you know of where a publisher has exercised the "right to refuse" to carry an advertisement, say over the last 12 months?*

Unfortunately, no figures on this subject exist. Newspaper publishers regularly refuse advertisements that do not conform with the law or the self-regulatory CAP Code or other relevant regulatory or self-regulatory provisions or their own reader protection policies. Indeed they are considered the cornerstone of the self-regulatory system because of their refusal to carry such advertisements. Even if advertisements conform to the law or relevant self-regulatory codes, subject to competition law considerations, newspaper publishers have an absolute discretion over whether they accept or refuse any advertisement. Examples of the check upon an advertiser that may be carried out by a publisher include: evidence that the advertiser can fulfil the promises made; evidence of financial controls where the potential advertisement relates to a business opportunity. Editorial and advertising content are matters within the sole discretion of the particular publication. Newspaper publishers as a whole will exercise and want to continue to be able to exercise such discretion irrespective of whether the advertiser is UK or non-UK.

Phil Murphy
Head of European Public Affairs

24 March 2005

TUESDAY 15 MARCH 2005

Present	Fearn, L	Walpole, L
	Geddes, L	Woolmer of Leeds, L (Chairman)
	Haskel, L	

Examination of Witnesses

Witnesses: MR PHILIPPE DE BUCK, Secretary General, and MS THÉRÈSE DE LIEDEKERKE, Director, Social Affairs, Union of Industrial and Employers Confederations of Europe (UNICE), examined.

Q367 Chairman: Mr de Buck, may I thank you very much indeed for so kindly agreeing to meet us today? You are a very busy person and the fact that you have fitted us in is greatly appreciated by the Committee. We have a number of questions we would like to ask you, if we may, about the draft Services Directive. What I propose to do is for us to develop our questions in a framework of probably four or five overarching themes, and no doubt my colleagues will, as a result of your answers, have a number of supplementaries that draw upon those questions—if that is agreeable to you. Shall I go straight into the questions, or is there anything that you would like to say by way of introduction?

Mr de Buck: First of all, My Lord Chairman, welcome to UNICE. It is always a big honour, and we are very pleased to be able to share some of our views with you and to give evidence on what we consider to be a very important issue, namely the services' internal market. At this point may I introduce my colleague, Thérèse de Liedekerke, who is in charge of all the industrial relations, all contacts in social affairs, in UNICE. The reason for her being here is because we are well aware that there are links between the services industry and all the related issues. In UNICE we represent the whole of business in Europe across the 25 European Member States. As you know, for your country our member is CBI. We have worked a lot on the internal market, which we consider to be the big achievement of the European Union. That has been done over the last 20 years in products and we hope that it will also be implemented for services—for two simple reasons. First, we need a complete, global internal market, as the services industries are growing faster than manufacturing industry. Secondly, more and more activities are intertwined and need also to have a link with services activities across borders. That is our main message and we can go into more detail, based on your questions. However, we think that the European Union will be discussing the re-launch—if I may so call it—of the famous Lisbon strategy. The services industry is perhaps the biggest achievement which we would like to see implemented. As Europe, compared to the United States and other parts of the world, is lacking in growth we consider that this initiative regarding services as perhaps the only one which

could help to increase the growth potential of the European Union. In the tabled documents you will not only find some documents on UNICE but also our position paper on services.

Q368 Lord Walpole: Could I ask you how active your members are in the new member countries, and how developed they are?

Mr de Buck: That is an important subject, of course. As you will see from our leaflet we now cover all the Member States with one exception, namely Latvia, where we have an observer member but not yet a fully integrated member. We have to acknowledge the fact that it is a starting point, but most of the organisations—be it in Poland, the Czech Republic, the Slovak Republic, Hungary or Lithuania—are now very settled and are participating in our work. We have also made efforts to make them better acquainted with the European Union system.

Q369 Chairman: Could I take the first theme, namely free movement of services and the Country of Origin Principle? Does UNICE believe that the free movement of services—and in order to achieve that, the Country of Origin Principle—are critical components of the draft Directive? Secondly, do you believe that the Country of Origin Principle is a realistic principle? Is it workable in practice?

Mr de Buck: That is the key question, of course. The Services Directive covers two elements. First, the establishment: which we simply want to be as smooth and as fast as possible, and with as little red tape as possible. Establishment is an important element, in terms of moving activities and jobs from one country another. The second element where the Country of Origin Principle is important is in cross-border services activities. Basically, if you want an integrated internal market, you have to allow cross-border activities. Otherwise, it is meaningless. We therefore totally endorse that principle. We consider that to be a key element of the internal market, and a key element in increasing the level of cross-border activities—with, on the one hand, all the benefits for the company and, on the other hand, for the customers, be they private or business. We know that there are some concerns and there are some derogations. An important element, which in my view is the most difficult to understand and which it is difficult to communicate, is the link between the Services Directive and the Posting of Workers Directive. Before joining UNICE, I was very active in the Belgian business industry and represented them. We have followed very closely the implementation of the single market for products, but a product is traceable and, by definition, a service is fulfilled by a person. The link between the commercial activity—the service—and the people who have to implement it is important, and therefore the link with the Posting of Workers Directive is a key element. However, we totally accept the Country of Origin Principle and would like to see it implemented.

Q370 Lord Geddes: How wide a spread of views is there amongst your members on this Country of Origin Principle? Do you get extremes from, let us say, France and Germany on the one hand and, on the other hand, the United Kingdom? Is there a big difference in your members' views?

Mr de Buck: As always in European affairs we have to try to find a common view, which is not always easy, and the task of Mrs de Liedekerke and myself is to reach that agreement. To answer your question, however, first of all we have an agreement on that principle based on our position paper. To be frank, it is true that smaller countries, for instance, will be more eager to open the market. Belgians are immediately abroad. In 120 kilometres or in 35 miles, we are abroad. For services, therefore, they need to have a larger market. That was not really a key factor, however. All the members of UNICE have supported that view. More important is not so much the question of countries, rather it is the question of activities. In some areas there are concerns. For instance, in building activities there are important concerns about the working conditions, the costs, et cetera. There is also a coincidence in terms of the calendar between the Services Directive and enlargement. If there are concerns, they come more from the western part of the European Union *vis-à-vis* the new Member States from the east. The kinds of examples being floated are examples of companies or of people coming from a new Member State and presenting their services in the former 15 European Union countries. That is a concern which some companies have.

Q371 Lord Geddes: The view has been expressed that this Directive will move businesses to countries which have, let us say, less stringent regimes, rather than to established countries which perhaps have stronger regimes. What is your view on that? Do your members fear such a movement?

Ms de Liedekerke: I think that there is a fear of that in public opinion. I think that these fears are largely unfounded and irrational in the sense that, if you

look at service markets, almost by definition they will remain very local markets. One of the obstacles to the development of the cross-border provision of services, quite apart from the administrative and legal obstacles that may exist, is also because in order to establish yourself in the market you need to be known, and there is a much stronger local element than there is for markets for goods. The fear of seeing massive movements of companies to establish themselves in countries where the rules were less stringent, therefore, would at the same time have the disadvantage of cutting those firms off from local markets elsewhere. That is a sort of natural brake on this phenomenon. However, the fear exists in public opinion, and there is a need to explain that this fear is unfounded—because of the characteristics of service markets.

Q372 Lord Geddes: Are you saying that that fear does not exist so much amongst your members?

Ms de Liedekerke: The fear amongst our members is not that fear. The fear is that there could be unfair competition if there were not the derogation from the Country of Origin Principle to allow the Posting of Workers Directive to operate. Then you could have unfair competition, in the sense of seeing undeclared work developed, with no checks and balances on it. Because the Directive foresees that the Country of Origin Principle does not apply to the matters covered by the Posting of Workers Directive, those fears are addressed. There is one remaining concern, and that is about some rules on the "don'ts" for the Member States, which could prevent them from having certain controls.

Q373 Lord Geddes: Rules on the . . .?

Ms de Liedekerke: Some rules forbidding Member States to have certain types of controls in Articles 24 and 25 of the Directives. There is a concern there, and a request from UNICE to modify and to redraft some of the elements in Articles 24 and 25.

Mr de Buck: We also believe in sound, market-driven evolution. We have had that in the Financial Services Action Plan. An expression used is a "stringent regulatory regime", but it is perhaps also the moment to ask oneself if that regime is the best one. Ahead of that you will always have the judgment of the customer, who wants a high-level, quality service for the best price.

Chairman: I am sure that we will come back to that theme. I am delighted to hear you mention the customer. A great deal of the evidence we have had has not mentioned the customer at all, and it is heartening to hear the business side mentioning it.

Q374 Lord Haskel: Thank you for drawing our attention to this Directive about the Posting of Workers. Obviously the two are very much intertwined. However, people are free to move within the European Community and people can take services from one country to another without being posted: they can just decide that they are going move, or they are going temporarily to visit countries and deliver services. As you have explained, services are delivered by people. Are your members satisfied that this kind of thing will improve the services which are given to customers, or do you see this as some sort of threat to the market in services?

Ms de Liedekerke: You mean will the Directive improve the services provided to customers?

Q375 Lord Haskel: Yes.

Ms de Liedekerke: I think that it will, because it will widen the choice for them. It could also have a positive impact in terms of widening the choice at the best possible price available for the market. That being said, however, because service markets are niche markets, you will still have this component and element in play. So there will be an opening and there will be an improvement. However, in terms of what we sometimes hear—about some sort of "sweeping wave" coming over—we do not believe that it will happen in that way.

Q376 Lord Haskel: Because . . .?
Ms de Liedekerke: Because of the niche character.

Q377 Lord Haskel: It is a local product.
Ms de Liedekerke: Yes, and they are markets of niche products.

Q378 Lord Haskel: Do you think that applies in business-to-business services as well as business to consumer?

Mr de Buck: I think that it applies in both. First, the larger the market for a provider the better, in terms of increasing the quality and reducing the cost. There is also a big benefit for the business customers—as we say, the B-to-B. Again, it all depends on what kinds of services. As Mrs de Liedekerke was pointing out, you have the locally linked issues of maintenance, for instance, where time is of the essence in logistics— even if logistics is now becoming more and more industrial. There are all kinds of evolutions, therefore, but the benefit is important. In making that link to the Posting of Workers Directive—and it is perhaps important that Mrs de Liedekerke explains this—what is its status for the people who are physically doing that work? Perhaps she could explain what the status is when people are posted elsewhere.

Ms de Liedekerke: The Posting of Workers Directive provides some protection to the workers who are posted abroad in order to carry out the work involved in the provision of a service. The first myth that needs to be corrected is that there would be

health and safety risks, because the Posting of Workers Directive foresees that a service provider going abroad to an EU Member State to provide a service has to comply, from day one, with the local health and safety regulations. The myth and the fears that there would be some sort of social dumping in the health and safety area are unfounded. With regard to the other employment conditions, obviously it would not be practical to change those terms and conditions of employment every time someone goes abroad. Basically, therefore, everything remains in accordance with what has been foreseen in the contract. Again, there is some protection foreseen in the Posting of Workers Directive, in the sense that certain public order, labour laws, and social provisions in the host country have to be complied with, and you have to compare the terms and conditions of employment with these local requirements which are considered to be fundamental public order rules on the labour market. So also from that point of view there is protection in the Posting of Workers Directive, which UNICE supports. We certainly would not like to see this Directive indirectly changing the Posting of Workers Directive.

Lord Haskel: This Country of Origin Principle is applied to temporary workers, as I understand it.
Chairman: Not temporary workers.

Q379 Lord Haskel: Temporary businesses.
Ms de Liedekerke: Business relations.

Q380 Lord Haskel: Is there any confusion between somebody being posted to do a job and whether it is a temporary or a permanent arrangement?

Ms de Liedekerke: The Posting of Workers Directive will apply regardless of whether you have a permanent contract with your employer or a temporary one. For example, if I as a permanent worker in UNICE, were posted to the CBI in the UK, this would not affect my employment contract with UNICE but I would be on a temporary mission to the UK. So it does not have an influence; it is not linked to the nature of the contracts.

Q381 Lord Fearn: There is obviously general resistance cross-border, which I think that we all accept. Looking at your document, however, it talks about encouraging necessary labour market reforms. How can you do that?

Mr de Buck: Most of the labour conditions are national, or even company rules, or rules in a branch. It depends on the system. It is different from one country to another. We work on two elements—and when I say "we", it is UNICE but it is more our members at a national level than ourselves. I think that the flexibility of the labour market must be increased; perhaps not so much in your country, but more in other countries of the European Union, because there are all kinds of rigidities. It is not linked to the Services Directive as such; it is a common problem that needs to be addressed at national level. Where the European system comes in—and now I generalise—is in favouring mobility and that for all kinds of reasons. More and more in larger companies, people have to move from one country another in their professional career. There is the fact that you have to make sure—for instance in the pensions system—that at the end of their career the pension can be properly calculated, and you need to have harmonised approaches to rules. We are therefore working on the flexibility of the labour market at a national level and also in some areas at a European level, and we are working on mobility. Flexibility of the labour contract and working conditions is one thing, but we also have to work on skills. It is always a combined approach. We have addressed that question not only to the European Parliament and to the Council, but also to our members at a national level.

Q382 Lord Geddes: Lord Haskel mentioned the temporary services. In your organisation, what is "temporary" and to what extent does it vary between the type and size of business? The follow-up is this. The Directive talks about the development of an extensive mutual assistance programme. Do you think that is workable?

Mr de Buck: I would say that what is temporary is that which is not permanent. I say that because it is very difficult at the beginning to see how long you are going to stay. We do not have answers to all of the questions, but we think that it will depend on the kinds of businesses. In the building industry, work is going on on a construction, which can last for some months, and even longer. That is one case. In others it will be shorter. As always in law it is a question of interpretation based on all kinds of criteria. You will have to find out whether or not the activity is carried out on a permanent basis, according to the kind of business it is. Another element which is linked to the Country of Origin Principle is mutual recognition and mutual assistance. I think that is a key element. If we are all together in the European Union, I presume that has been discussed between authorities; that the authorities can work together in order to achieve the same goals, putting in place the same way of organising the business, to control them, to secure them, and so on. That is an important element. There are some examples. One example which is not directly linked to services is that of customer activities. The customers of the different countries work on a mutual assistance but also a mutually recognised basis. Another example is the transport of hazardous goods. There also the whole process is based on one recognised system and governments expect each other to put the right elements in place. It is perhaps there, where the Services Directive is linked to enlargement, that some have doubts about the ability of agencies abroad to fulfil all the requirements. It is there that there is work to be carried out. We certainly would assert that it has to be done properly because, where control is necessary, we do not want there to be activities which are not properly controlled.

Ms de Liedekerke: Referring to the "temporary" issue, although it is very difficult to define, there is one limit which exists in European rules. It is the rule that in the field of social security a posted worker can only remain affiliated to the regime of the country of origin for a maximum duration of 24 months. That seems to indicate that the EU legislator considers that anything beyond 24 months is no longer purely temporary.

Q383 Chairman: Looking at the Directive and its wording, "temporary" operations appear to mean operations by a business that is not established in a Member State. If I am right, it draws a distinction between operating in another Member State but establishing there as well as in your own original Member State, or operating from your establishment in your original Member State and offering your services into other countries. The interesting question is why should any company wish to establish itself in a second Member State if it can operate with these freedoms based upon its country of origin? Why would any company wish to do that?

Mr de Buck: It is a free choice for the company to do it or not. That is one thing.

Q384 Chairman: What would be the advantage of it being established in a second Member State rather than simply operating on this Country of Origin Principle?

Mr de Buck: I think that the business leader will not do it only because of the Country of Origin Principle. It may be one of the arguments. When you are in the services industry, however, it is also a local issue, because you have to provide a service to someone or to companies. There are a lot of reasons which may arise in establishing yourself there. Perhaps in order to be closer to the customer; because the customer wishes to see somebody having a fixed establishment there; because of the pertinence of the service, and also the fact that the customer can be sure that the service will be provided at any time that he needs it. When you look at what is happening today in services—the total restructuring, be it in transport, logistics, and so on—in some areas it can be done from outside, but in some respects you have to be even closer to the companies.

Q385 *Chairman:* This is quite an important issue; there is a lot of confusion and disagreement on what the nature of a temporary operation is. As I had read the situation, it was that the free movement of services would enable a business, in any meaningful sense, to operate as if it were established in another country—not legally established in some sense, but nevertheless to have offices, a base of operations and to be seen to have that base in another Member State—that it could still be operating on the Country of Origin Principle. What do you understand in the Directive as the meaning of "established" as opposed to "temporary"? What does your organisation understand by that?

Mr de Buck: The establishment is to have a permanent activity somewhere settled. You do not necessarily need to have a company registered to have an establishment. In terms of tax, if you are providing an activity from outside you are taxed on a different basis from that of a stable establishment. It is a well recognised principle in tax law. So those elements will be taken into account. I think that the facts will also be taken into account. By whom? By the tax authorities; by social security people; even by the people who are employed. It will be different if they can prove that their employer has an establishment in a country or not, and those elements will intervene.

Q386 *Chairman:* That is very helpful. So the taxman, as everywhere, will catch up with everybody eventually. Like death!

Mr de Buck: Certainly.

Q387 *Lord Walpole:* Are you talking about a company moving to another country or are you talking about them opening a branch, which will be subject to the laws of the country in which they open the branch?

Mr de Buck: Both. You can have a company moving from one country to another. That would be a relocation of activities. However, in terms of the business, you have to see if you can provide all of your business in the same way as you have before. What we expect—because it is not the matter of relocation which is important for us—is that you put in place an internal market, so that one company can provide more services to more customers in more countries. The second branch of your alternative is perhaps more likely.

Q388 *Lord Walpole:* That is what you expect to happen?

Mr de Buck: Yes.

Q389 *Chairman:* Can we carry on with the mutual assistance issue? There are many critics of the Mutual Assistance Framework. We have heard evidence

from people who say that it simply is not workable, in that a Member State of the country of origin could supervise in any meaningful sense—or have the incentive to supervise—the operations of a business operating across the board in another country. So is it a workable framework? What would be your answer to the critics of the Mutual Assistance Framework, who say, "All very well in theory, but simply impracticable"?

Ms de Liedekerke: The country of origin would not be in charge of supervising the operations in the other country. To go back to the example of health and safety, it would be the local labour inspectorate on the host country that would be in charge of making sure that health and safety regulations are respected. What the country of origin would be responsible for would be, for example, checking if there are authorisations, requirements, for the activity of that company in that particular country; to provide the evidence to the host country that these have been fulfilled properly; to provide evidence that there is an employment contract which links the worker posted to the host country to the company—those sorts of elements. So it is a question of co-operation. There is not a sort of reversal of the system of checks. The host country would still be allowed to carry out a number of controls but, for certain information, it would turn to the country of origin for those matters which are covered by the law of the country of origin. It is a question of organising the co-operation, therefore.

Mr de Buck: And trust.

Ms de Liedekerke: It is true that at present there are problems, but it is also perhaps because some of the resources are devoted to a lot of paperwork. In Belgium, for example, you have to have prior authorisation before sending a worker to provide services cross-border. If you were to shift the resources of the people who are doing all the paperwork required for granting these prior authorisations to other tasks, and to improve and enhance co-operation with the country of origin, you could have the same efficiency in control but by other means. It is therefore a question of fine-tuning and reorganising your system of checks and balances.

Q390 *Chairman:* So you think the Mutual Assistance Framework is eminently workable?

Ms de Liedekerke: It can work, but it will require adaptations in the way in which Member States work.

Q391 *Lord Haskel:* Perhaps I may pursue this matter of mutual assistance a little further. Do your members think that it should also apply to mutual recognition of qualifications? In some countries, some suppliers of services have to be qualified; in others, they do not. Do you see this as a difficulty?

Ms de Liedekerke: The mutual recognition of qualifications is not covered by this Services Directive at all. There is an explicit total derogation for these matters. In this case the Country of Origin Principle would not apply, because these matters are completely outside the scope of this directive.

Q392 *Lord Geddes:* What changes, if any, would you like to see to the draft Directive?

Ms de Liedekerke: There is definitely a need to clarify and introduce changes in Articles 24 and 25 on the interface with the Posting of Workers Directive, because there are some wordings which could be misunderstood as implying an undermining of the Directive—so the lists of the "don'ts".

Mr de Buck: The "do nots".

Q393 *Lord Geddes:* Any other changes?

Ms de Liedekerke: There is also a need for fine-tuning of wording in Article 16, which is also partly linked to the Posting of Workers Directive.

Mr de Buck: However, what we would not like to see is a dismantling of the Directive. That would be really bad for the European Union internal market.

Q394 *Lord Geddes:* What would happen if the Country of Origin Principle was dropped?

Mr de Buck: Then we can leave the system as it is.

Q395 *Chairman:* You were asked what changes you would like to see. What changes would you not wish to see? Clearly in your view there could be so many changes that, effectively, it is destroyed as a worthwhile venture; but what changes would you not like to see that are short of absolute disaster, as it were, from your point of view?

Mr de Buck: We would not like to see the dropping of the Country of Origin Principle. Secondly, we would not like to see a dismantling of the link between the Services Directive and the Posting of Workers Directive. That has to be better clarified, as has been said. Thirdly, we would not like to see a transformation of this horizontal Directive into a lot of vertical approaches. We then go back to 25 years ago, when we had it for products and it was an endless exercise.

Q396 *Chairman:* So you would not be in favour of a harmonisation approach: seeking to harmonise the standards and details of each and every individual service?

Mr de Buck: Standardisation in services is a difficult exercise. You can imagine standardisation for products, to have compatibility—but that is another subject. For services, however, we think that by opening the market there will be an evolution, based on sound competition, going in the same direction in terms of control and regulation. However, I do not think that we have to start the whole process with a big effort in terms of all kinds of harmonisation, because then we shall miss the goal of opening the market as soon as possible.

Ms de Liedekerke: There is a fourth thing. Working on the scope of the Directive—and there are elements which currently require clarification, as has been described—if, in order to solve some problems, the route taken were to empty the Directive of its content by introducing all sorts of exclusions from its scope, that would also be a very bad development.

Q397 *Chairman:* You have been generous with your time. I fear that our time has run out. I am sorry that we were late in starting; because of that, we have not been able to ask you all that we would like. However, you have been frank and helpful, and we are most grateful to you.

Mr de Buck: Thank you, and thank you for giving us that opportunity.

TUESDAY 15 MARCH 2005

Present   Fearn, L   Walpole, L
       Geddes, L   Woolmer of Leeds, L (Chairman)
       Haskel, L

Examination of Witness

Witness: MR MALCOLM HARBOUR, a Member of the European Parliament, examined.

Q398 *Chairman:* We are very grateful to you for meeting with us. This is a very important Directive and we know that there are many views on it. We are hoping that in something like 50 minutes, we might be able to explore a number of themes and to get some details. Is there anything that you would want to say by way of background before we go into the questions?

Mr Harbour: I very much welcome this opportunity and I am delighted that you have come over here. I know that you are seeing a number of my colleagues, so I think that you will get a flavour of the range of issues involved in this. Perhaps I should position myself, for your record. I am Conservative Member for the West Midlands and I am the Conservative spokesman on the Internal Market and Consumer Protection Committee. I am also the co-ordinator for the European People's Party and European Democrat Group in the European Parliament, which is the political grouping of which the Conservatives are members. So I am the senior spokesman for the biggest group in the Parliament on the Committee and lead our group on the Committee. On top of that, I am also the shadow rapporteur to Mrs Gebhardt, whom you are about to meet, who is my colleague and who is also the Socialist co-ordinator. It is an interesting debate in the Committee. The two lead spokesmen for the two biggest groups are both working on this proposal. We have been working on it, between us, since before the election. We had the draft proposal in February and we had some initial skirmishes on it back then, so we have been working on it for quite a long time. We have also done work on the preparatory discussions with the Commission within the framework of the whole internal market strategy. I think that the key document—which anyone who wants to understand this Directive needs to look at—is the June 2002 document sprepared by the Commission in their analysis about barriers to trade and services within the internal market. You can see the flow-through from that into the proposals and the structure of this Directive. The problem with quite a lot of the arguments we are currently hearing about the Directive is because people have not actually gone back to the source document, looked at how the Commission has tried to follow it through, and the basis for why they have decided to go for a bold approach of having a major horizontal Directive. It is essentially because there are so many barriers—I think over 90 which they have identified—that they felt that was the best way of dealing with it. That is just a bit of context; then we can perhaps go into the detail.

Q399 *Chairman:* That is very helpful. It reflects the views also, I think, of certainly some on this inquiry Committee. The way in which I propose to go about things is to ensure that one or two of us keep a bit of a structure with some thematic questions and then, from your responses, there will undoubtedly be a series of supplementaries, and so on. Could I start with the Country of Origin Principle? In your view, is the Country of Origin Principle critical to the success of this Directive in freeing up and creating an operating single market in services? If it is critical, is it workable in practice? In other words, critical, desirable, but not workable?

Mr Harbour: Yes. The reason why is that the critical barrier which has been identified is the fact that companies that are legitimately established and delivering services—and in many cases satisfying customers, complying with quality standards—are essentially inhibited at the moment from providing those services across borders. That is because many of the administrative formalities they are required to go through relate to things like having to re-establish business subsidiaries; having to get pre-authorisation to provide services; having to notify authorities before they post people there—the whole range of things that you have seen. I think that the first Principle in terms of Country of Origin—that a company which is legitimately registered and trading actively in one country should, in principle, be able to go and trade in another country—is fundamental. That therefore requires the establishment of the Country of Origin Principle, and also the Member States accepting as part of this next development of the internal market that they have to step up their co-operation mechanisms in order for that to happen. There are legal obligations included in this Directive—on the basis that the Directive goes through in close to its present form—which will require Member States to set up that legal co-operation. What has been interesting in our discussions with Member States and the Council is that there are many Member States who are keen to do that. This is not without precedent. At the end of the last Parliament we agreed the Consumer Co-operation Directive, which required Member States to set up co-operation in that area. I think that we are now entitled to say to the Member States, "It is now time for you to trust each other in how we manage the development of the internal market, and this is the next step forward". In summary, Country of Origin is an integral part of the whole operation of the Directive, and there is no valid reason for rejecting that Principle on the basis we cannot make it work.

Q400 *Lord Fearn:* Is there an alternative?

Mr Harbour: I am not sure there is, if you are going to deal with the barriers that are set down there. Let us remember that this Directive is basically bringing into practice the established case law of the treaties on the internal market. Companies have, under the treaties and under the internal market, the right to go and provide and deliver services in any other country. So I think that is why it is an integral part of this proposal.

Q401 *Lord Haskel:* Is an alternative to chip away at the barriers?

Mr Harbour: I think that would not achieve what we want. I liken this to the 1985 Lord Cockfield programme. If you remember, we had reached the stage then in the evolution of the single market for goods where it was clear that we needed to make a significant step up in activity, because we were not making any progress on large-scale harmonisation under unanimity, and the ability of one country to veto it. We have now moved into an economy where services are becoming more and more important, and this proposal is the next evolution of the internal market, where we take this major step forward where Member States have to engage in administrative co-operation and take it to a new level, in order to make the internal market for services work. The Country of Origin Principle is, in a way, equivalent to mutual recognition of technical standards and goods. It is a fundamental step forward. We are not seeing it in that context, but in my view that is the context in which it should be seen.

Q402 *Chairman:* Why are some people saying that it is effectively not workable? That there are too many serious problems about it?

Mr Harbour: Because I do not think that they have looked in detail at what the provisions say and what they are intended to do. That is the core of the issue. If you look at the clarified text that the Council has produced—which I think is extremely helpful in this respect—where we have the recitals and the text in counterpart, you will see where the recitals clearly describe the issues that are at stake here. I think that administrative co-operation will work successfully.

We should not ignore the technological developments that will enable it to work successfully, in terms of electronic interchange of data and ease of access of data. There are all of those sorts of factors which the Commission has built into the proposal and which are extremely important. They are not being looked at in detail, partly because we have not got beyond the principles. Also, we have to look at what are the core objectives. There have been a whole lot of, I think, very unhelpful ideas put around which suggest that Member States' fundamental rights to manage and control service providers in areas like public health and safety, for example, are not clearly outlined here. The one that has been put about is around issues to do with building sites: that companies coming from, shall we say, Latvia—I think there has been a case in Sweden—apply the building site safety law from Latvia and not the Swedish law. That is not correct. It is specifically set out in here. It is not correct. In some cases people have made a very emotional response, but have not actually looked at what the specific provisions are here. The basic provisions are that if you are legally established and delivering a service in one country of the European Union, you are then able to go and deliver that service in another with a minimum of formalities. That is the core of it.

Q403 *Chairman:* Is that saying that the Country of Origin Principle is important because it says, "Yes, you are qualified to do business in another Member State, you do not have to prove that again, but, when you do do business in the Member State you have to adhere to the rules of that Member State"? Is that what you are saying? Are you saying that Country of Origin is important because it gives a business, as it were, authority to operate, but when it operates it is under host country rules? Is that right? The critics appear to be concerned that the Country of Origin Principle means not only that you can operate but that you will operate under your own country rules. You have said that in health and safety, no, that is not the case; but are there other areas where that is the case?

Mr Harbour: There is a whole range of important areas where they also have to comply with other home country rules: specifically, employment. We have a Posting of Workers Directive already. It is not operated very consistently across Member States—which, by the way, is one of the problems we have. If you look at how different Member States have transposed the Posting of Workers Directive, there is a huge range of discrepancies; but essentially what the Posting of Workers Directive says—and I think that it has been in since 1996—is that if I post people to work in a Member State, in terms of key employment standards I have to comply with the host country's standards. In other words, things like minimum wage, holiday entitlement, and those sorts of areas—I have to comply with those. So it does not give me a blanket.

Q404 Lord Geddes: Immediately?
Mr Harbour: Yes.

Q405 Lord Geddes: Then what is the point of the word "temporary" in the draft Directive—you can work temporarily?
Mr Harbour: You can work temporarily, yes, but you still have to comply with the core standards.

Q406 Lord Geddes: The Posting of Workers Directive and health and safety.
Mr Harbour: Yes.

Q407 Lord Geddes: What are the others? What other derogations are there?
Mr Harbour: Those are the key derogations, yes. If you are a professional, where you are working in a profession where your qualifications have to be authorised, then of course it does not override that at all. In other words, if I am a law firm, then obviously to practise as a lawyer I have to have my qualifications recognised. That is already covered separately. I would have to have my qualifications recognised; but if I had a professional establishment, a firm established in one country, I could go and set up a subsidiary or I could practise in another country, provided that my legal qualifications were verified.

Q408 Lord Geddes: The implication of what you are saying is that the oft-voiced fear that businesses will move to regimes that are less stringent is really a false fear; it is null and void?
Mr Harbour: Yes.

Q409 Lord Geddes: I am putting words into your mouth, but that is the implication of what you are saying.
Mr Harbour: I agree with you entirely. Not only that, if you read the Directive you will see that the definition of your country of establishment is very carefully defined. The Commission accepted from the beginning—with our support—that this was not to be a charter for letterbox companies, where you would go and establish somewhere with a letterbox and that would then entitle you to apply lower standards everywhere. Your right of establishment, if you like, is clearly defined in the provisions of the Directive. We may want to have them tidied up a bit, but the country where you actually carry out activity, not a letterbox, is very specifically and clearly defined. In other words, the whole proposal is intended to benefit people who are running legitimate, successful businesses in one Member State to be able to go to another far more easily than they

do at the moment, because of the sort of barriers that are put in their way. To come to the Posting of Workers Directive—and this is an area which shows you the sort of problems we are trying to contend with—it has specific obligations that, if you post workers, that has to comply with a core set of minimum standards, including minimum wages. There are some detailed provisions in that about people on short-term postings and so on, and you can read about them. Some countries, however, in complying with that, have said, "If I send people to work in Belgium I have to apply five days in advance, or I have to register the names of the people I am going to send five days in advance to the authorities". In some countries, you have to have a local establishment registered; you have to fill in paperwork; you have to comply with all these bureaucratic obstacles. These are the areas which service companies find the most onerous. They are not required under the provisions of the Posting of Workers Directive, but this is the way that Member States have implemented them. One of the difficult parts of this Directive is that it is being suggested that, because the Commission has banned some specific practices in Member States in connection with the Posting of Workers Directive, it is therefore trying to undermine it. I do not see it like that. That is one of the most difficult areas and those are the areas which are causing some of the most controversy. I come back to the point I made earlier. If you look at why we have this Directive, you have to understand the provisions that the Commission is trying to remove, and those are the sorts of provisions that are stopping companies from exercising their internal market rights.

Q410 Lord Geddes: So you, in that context, define this Directive as de-gilding the gold plating?
Mr Harbour: In that particular respect, yes. It is removing barriers. That is what this is all about. It is removing barriers but at the same time protecting Member States' justifiable rights to be able still to enforce some of their own Member State provision on public interest.

Q411 Chairman: Referring to the working document of your Committee on the Internal Market and Consumer Protection—
Mr Harbour: Ms Gebhardt's document.

Q412 Lord Geddes: Not yours?
Mr Harbour: We never voted on it. You said that it was from my Committee. It is not a document that we have ever voted on. It is Ms Gebhardt's opening shots in the debate, and we had a very lively and interesting debate about it, I can tell you, when she tabled it.

Q413 Chairman: Let me mention one item in here, and it would be useful to have your view about it. It says two things. In relation to mutual assistance it says, " . . . does the country where a service provider is established have any interest at all in supervising services provided outside its own territory?". In a sense, that is an assault upon the workability of the ideas there. The other matter—which is what I want to draw your attention to at the moment—is where she says, "There are no common . . . standards. In the interest of fair competition, common rules, ie a combination of harmonisation and recognition, are essential. Only in this way might it be conceivable to introduce the Country of Origin Principle in particular areas". For example, someone has quoted the problem that a German bricklayer has to be extremely highly qualified and a British bricklayer—and quite possibly a Polish bricklayer—may not have to be. Under the Country of Origin Principle, is it not possible for a Polish building company or bricklaying business to be sub-contracted to lay bricks on a construction, to bring in its own Polish labour, completely differently qualified to the Germans? Is not that the kind of thing that German trade unions and builders might be bothered about?

Mr Harbour: I think that they are bothered about it, but the question is whether they are justified to be bothered about it. The question then is whether Polish bricklayers can produce equal quality work, under the right supervision and conditions, as German bricklayers. I think that the jury is very much out on that. In the end, it is the customers who will decide. It does not absolve the people managing the building site from ensuring the quality of the work. This is the issue at stake. There is no question—and the Commission's report will demonstrate this—that quite a number of the restrictions that Member States currently have in place to stop, or to discourage shall we say, service providers from moving across borders are protectionist, and I think that is a good example. My question then is this. Look at the other provisions in here which relate to issues like quality, quality certifications measures, and other aspects. The Directive is quite clear that part of the work which has to be done between Member States and the Commission is to step up and encourage the development of quality standards and norms at a European level.

Q414 Chairman: So they emphasise voluntary codes, in general?

Mr Harbour: Yes. I think that is the way we will get this moving forward much more quickly. On Evelyne's point, I disagree with her because, if we waited for harmonisation—I refer you back to what I said earlier about the original Single Market programme—we would be in exactly the same

position. If we try to harmonise everything, we will wait forever. We will not make progress. In any case, we are not talking about Country of Origin as being the sole instrument here, because there are a number of areas. We have already talked about mutual recognition of qualifications. There are quite a number of professions where we do already have harmonised standards, through the Mutual Recognition of Professional Qualifications Directive, and this does not override that in any way. I think that we need to take a much more mature attitude to this. I understand the issues—and in Germany it is particularly true—where they have a very well-developed set of craft skills. My argument to them, however, is, "You need to be promoting your craft skills as a higher and better-quality standard, and you need to be selling that to your customers. If you are producing better-quality work, then your customers will pay for it". That is part of what having a competitive market is all about. That is what has happened in goods, and why should it not happen in services?

Q415 Lord Fearn: What does "to operate on a virtual basis" mean?

Mr Harbour: You are talking about internet trading, and so on?

Q416 Lord Fearn: Yes.

Mr Harbour: We already have that enshrined through the E-Commerce Directive anyway. There are many services where there is a possibility to deliver services through virtual means. However, I think that the point I made earlier about quality standards and certification is much more important in the on-line world, because on-line consumers need to have more of that sort of reassurance if they are not meeting somebody face to face. Therefore, quality certification of some kind, or an independent quality testament, or a star rating system, or whatever, will be much more important. These are the sorts of things that we need to be encouraging. It also hooks into the Unfair Commercial Practices Directive, which we have just agreed, where compliance with codes of practice which are laid down, or non-compliance with them, or claiming that you comply with them when you do not, will now become a standard offence across the European Union. So we have some weapons there. Plus the consumer co-operation provision, where the Member States have already agreed to step up dealing with cross-border complaints—quite a lot of which will arise through on-line trading. So it is not as if we were not tackling all these things at the same time, and putting in place a series of counterpart frameworks to enable the services market to move forward.

Q417 *Lord Fearn:* They are all being accepted?

Mr Harbour: Yes. We voted on the Unfair Commercial Practices Directive three weeks ago, and the consumer co-operation regulation was agreed in April. It was one of the last things we did. Ironically, Evelyne Gebhardt was the rapporteur—so you should ask her about it when you see her.

Q418 *Lord Haskel:* Ms Gebhardt also says that there is no clear distinction between the social economy and general interest services. We have been looking at this Directive on general interest services. Is there a clear line between these two—between general interest services and this Directive on services—or is there a sort of grey area in the middle?

Mr Harbour: I think the first point to make is that this Directive does not in any way impose on Member States any sort of ownership format for the delivery of public services—despite what has been claimed, astonishingly enough. I could not find any reference to that. Some people say that it is a charter for liberalising public service. It is not at all. Member States are still free in areas where liberalisation has not been agreed—as opposed to communications or energy for example—to manage and run public services in the way they wish to continue to do so. So this Directive is aimed at services that are provided for commercial considerations; in other words, delivered by organisations. Those organisations could be publicly owned organisations, if they are trading on a commercial basis, and that is not excluded. The next question relates to the groups of services that are delivered as part of public services. For example, care for elderly people which is delivered on a commercial basis, in facilities that might be provided by the state but where private contractors deliver services. It seems to me that there is absolutely no reason at all why those should be excluded. Why should companies who run elderly care services on a commercial basis be excluded from providing services in another country? Given that they will then provide services within a fixed establishment, they will have to comply with all the standards and norms that the managers of that establishment require of them. There is nothing in this Directive that in any way prevents that. In any case, that is the requirement of the managers of that establishment. They cannot be overridden by any Country of Origin Principle. This is a practical point. If people can provide suitably qualified people—they may be qualified by mutual recognition of qualifications, so that they have qualifications from another country in nursing which are mutually recognised, and they go through the procedures of having them recognised—why should they not be entitled to provide services?

Q419 *Lord Geddes:* On timing, when do you see Commissioner McCreevy issuing any amendments to this draft Directive?

Mr Harbour: He will not issue any separate amendments until we vote it. Even then, it will be part of the normal co-decision process. The Commission is not intending to override the normal processes of co-decision. They have made that clear. I think that there has been a bit of confusion about the Commission indicating that it wants to make changes, but has now made it clear, following a certain amount of pressure from myself and others, that the normal co-decision processes will proceed. Evelyne is the rapporteur. She has not yet produced her final report. We are having various debates with her about the content, including one the day after tomorrow. I think that she is now promising to produce it next month; so you will hear that from her. I think that her intention is that we should try to vote on it in Committee before the summer recess in July, and then maybe in plenary in September. Meanwhile the Council is, quite rightly in my view, continuing to work through aspects of it. I was asked my opinion on it, and I said that I thought the area in which we would very much welcome engagement with the Council is on this whole area of mutual co-operation. After all, the requirements that the Commission has set down on the Member States are for the Member States to say whether they will be workable and effective. I think that it would be very good, in terms of external perception, if the Member States in Council were seen to be giving serious attention to how they are going to make the mutual co-operation provisions work satisfactorily, and make some suggestions for amendments to that. I hope all of that will then come together in September, and I rather hope then that we may, under the British Presidency, make some serious progress towards a Common Position, which I would like to see us have before the end of the British Presidency. I cannot see us getting the whole job done within the British Presidency, but I would hope that we would try to have an agreement with Council in Second Reading, some time during the Austrian Presidency. Certainly I would like to have seen this dealt with in a year's time.

Q420 *Chairman:* What do you regard as the main difficult issues which do have to be resolved in those coming months?

Mr Harbour: I think that the operation of the Country of Origin Principle and the clarification of where that applies, and where it does not, will be the most difficult issue. There are some people, including the rapporteur, who want to alter that fundamentally, in a way which I think is not workable. I think that will be the major political battle that we will have. The second thing is in relation to issues around the Posting of Workers

Directive. I agree very much with what the Commission has proposed, in terms of preventing Member States from gold-plating that Directive, or rather removing some of the existing gold-plating; but there is undoubtedly some resistance to what people see as retrospective changes to that Directive. We may have to look at those provisions, in order to get them through. I am disappointed about that because I think that they are pretty clear but, in the end, I am politically realistic enough to know that we have to make some compromises. So I think that those are the two major areas, and some of that will be linked particularly to the construction sector— about whether we need any specific measures to deal with issues in the construction sector. That is the one where there has been quite a lot of debate and discussion, and that is coming from two directions. Our colleagues in the new Member States are extremely keen that these provisions are not watered down and they are extremely supportive of this proposal. As Charlie McCreevy said in our House last week, who are we to try to block the benefits of the Single Market from the ten new Member States when we have been enjoying them ourselves for the last 20 or 30 years?

Q421 *Chairman:* I think that the words you used were "the operation of the Country of Origin Principle". Was there anything else about the working of the Principle that you had in mind, other than those two points?
Mr Harbour: Those seem to me to be at the core of the problems that we are having. We do have broad political agreement that we need to liberate the service market. We have moved beyond the stage where certain groups were calling for the whole Directive to be withdrawn— even though the Green Group still want it to be withdrawn—but they do not have a majority for that in the Parliament. We now have to come up with a piece of legislation, therefore, which will deliver some serious benefits. If we start to move away from some of these or overcomplicate some of the provisions, we will not achieve the benefits. This is a Directive about delivering opportunities to relatively smaller companies. It is very much a Directive that ought to be effective for small and medium enterprises. Large companies have the lawyers, they have the funds, and they can set up, and may want to set up subsidiaries, in different countries. It might make their life easier but, if we really want the dynamic effect, it is the small and medium-sized enterprises at which we have to target this. If we cannot get agreement on some relatively simple provisions that will deal with these 91 barriers, one has to say, "Why are we bothering at all?". I hope that it will not come to that, because I am hoping that people will see sense in this and say that this is no more than giving people their existing rights of

establishment. We need to tackle these barriers; we need to make the administrative procedures as simple as possible; and we clearly need to be sure that the Member States will collaborate effectively. I think they can demonstrate that to us by the work they do over the next few months.

Q422 *Chairman:* Are there any changes that the critics of the Country of Origin Principle want? Are there any changes that they are seeking that, in your view, would effectively be changes too far, which would leave you with a piece of paper that is not able to be implemented?
Mr Harbour: I think that some of the ideas that are floating around about applying this on a sector-by-sector basis are almost entirely unworkable, because of problems of definition. There are also some new proposals that have just surfaced about Member States applying some of their own priority lists to sectors they want deregulated. That seems to me to be a charter for complete and utter confusion. Anything like that, which tries to apply the Country of Origin process or the procedures of local establishment in a selective or a timetabled way, just will not work. If there is an issue around the Country of Origin Principle, it should be focused on making the principle workable and making it clear what it covers and what it does not cover, in terms of the service being provided in the host countries as opposed to the home country.

Q423 *Lord Haskel:* Where all this could fall down is if there is no co-operation, no mutual assistance?
Mr Harbour: Yes.

Q424 *Lord Haskel:* Is the real purpose of the Country of Origin Principle to put pressure on people to participate and to step up the mutual assistance?
Mr Harbour: No, I do not think that I would put it like that. I think that it is a natural evolution of the way that the Single Market has been going. I come back to what I said earlier, that this is not new. Interestingly, the 1996 Directive on Posting Workers already has provisions for co-operation. I come back to the consumer regulation which I think is of extreme importance. If we are to make the Single Market work successfully, we have to step up the level of mutual co-operation between administrations at all levels. This has already gone on in areas dealing with internal market cases anyway. We have the SOLVIT process— of which I am a great admirer of and which is still relatively unknown— where administrations have stepped up their co-operation in a much more effective way, in giving people a single-point access to deal with Single Market complaints. I have access to it through my office here. I am one of the leading people who submit cases to SOLVIT. Indeed, one of my cases,

anonymised, is included in the last Single Market report, so I know that it works. This is not forcing this to happen; it is a natural evolution of the process of making the Single Market better, because we are getting Member State administrations to trust each other, to exchange information, and to use the technology which is now available to enable them to do that. After all, information technology is a great enabler of co-operation. It also enables you to deal with complaints referred in different languages in a much simpler way, to transmit information in a simple way, and indeed, to give people access to databases. To give you a simple example, suppose we have a simple on-line form which, when you want to provide a service, you have to complete in a standard format; embedded in that you can have a direct linkage to your registration in your home country's database and company registration. Then, if I work in Sweden and somebody comes to me saying, "Confirm to me that you are complying with the requirements and your company is legitimate", I can say, "Here is my form, here is my computer. You click there and you will find the information". The concern I have is that part of the debate we are having on this seems to be deeply rooted in some of our protectionist thinking about creating the Single Market more than 30 years ago. I sometimes despair about some of the rhetoric I hear coming out. I was with the Deputy Prime Minister of the Czech Republic yesterday. We had a meeting with Mr Barroso, and he is quoted on the front page of the *Financial Times* today—and I agree with him— saying that within the Single European Market we should not be using words like "social dumping". After all, we have put in place a common set of *acquis communautaires* on employment regulations. How can we claim, therefore, that a Directive which is encouraging people to exercise their rights is social dumping? It is ridiculous. We have to elevate our sights about what we are trying to do here in making the Single Market work successfully, and services has to be the next major area in which we move forward.

Q425 *Lord Geddes:* Is there anything else which, in an ideal world, you would like to see in the Directive, or anything you would like not to see in the Directive?
Mr Harbour: No. I am an admirer of the basic construction and ideas behind the Directive. I think that it is a very ambitious and well-integrated proposal. If we try to unravel bits of it, we are in danger of making the whole structure ugly and difficult to work. There are some provisions that I think we need to clarify, but I think that, fundamentally, it is an imaginative and important step that moves in the right direction. The area which we do need to look at—and this is an area which is more difficult, because in the Directive it is an encouragement rather than a legal requirement—is

this whole area we were talking about, namely encouraging the development of quality standards and codes of practice, and getting them to start operating across borders. However, it seems to me that those will follow on behind the evolution of the market itself, and we need to find ways of facilitating and encouraging providers of services to collaborate together more extensively to do these things, because it will be good for consumers.

Q426 *Lord Geddes:* Do you think that it will go through in, give or take, the form it is in at the moment?
Mr Harbour: I remain confident. I am always a "cup-half-full" man in politics! But we have to keep at it, and we have to remind ourselves what it is all about. The recent Danish study has been helpful, and I am sure you have seen that. We have now had a comprehensive study from the Danish institute and I think that there will be other studies which show the potential benefits from this. In a way, why should we be surprised that, if we start to liberate markets, it will generate more employment, raise economic activity, and reduce prices? This is what the existing internal market has already delivered. I am slightly tired of going to meetings and hearing people say, "We believe in the internal market but we are worried about some of these provisions". Why do we have the internal market at all? I think that we are at a very critical stage of this now. My biggest worry is if the Council does not come in with us on this, because the Council has already rowed back from things like the Sales Promotion Directive—which also ought to be part of this—because there are issues about sales promotion in here too. The provision on mutual recognition of sales promotion legislation was finished by us two years ago, and essentially the Council has given up on it because they cannot get agreement on it. This Directive is putting pressure on the Council to say that we do need to step up our engagement in a different way, and we do need to look at these anti-competitive restrictions. However, I know that it is politically difficult for some of them.

Q427 *Chairman:* Why do you think that, after so many years of Green Papers, consultations, assessments and so on, the position appears to have been reached where there are some fundamental disagreements about the Directive, even to the degree that some voices are proposing changes which would appear to be so fundamental as to question its value at all? Why do you think that has happened? Are there any lessons from that for the way in which proposals from now on—major proposals—come forward?
Mr Harbour: I think that there are quite a lot, and part of the problem has been the whole way in which the release of this has been handled. It is very easy to

be right in hindsight, but I think that the Commission should never have released a Directive of such fundamental importance in the dying days of the last Commission. We were not able to give it any serious consideration. They have not positioned or promoted the benefits of it very seriously in any way, and shown how important it is, even though they are now starting to do that. I think that the people who have read the Directive are astonished at some of the allegations that are being made about it. I sometimes get a sense of unreality when I read what is being suggested, when people come to see me about it, and when I read the Directive. Then, of course, we ran into an election period, where there was no Commission to advocate it; the Parliament was not meeting; none of us were working on it; and then we come back here and, in the meantime, a whole lot of opposition has been stirred up, and most of the publicity about it has been almost entirely adverse. It is now given to a new Commission and a new Commissioner, Charlie McCreevy, who has had no involvement in its development, and who is expected to come charging out, advocating it. That is part of the problem we have had. There are two things, therefore. For a Directive of such fundamental importance, probably the right thing to have done would have been to have had a strategic paper before we got the final Directive. In other words, we had the analysis from June 2002 and I think the Commission would have done well to have had a Green Paper on approaches to dealing with it, which we could then have debated and discussed. We could have agreed the principles, and then moved into the substantive Directive itself. That is what I would have done and I think, in terms of best or better regulatory practice, that would have been much more satisfactory. If you look at the vastly extended timetable now, I do not think that it would have cost us any time. The time we would have taken in reviewing the strategic document and looking at ways of doing it would have meant that by the time we then had the legislation, we would have got basic agreement to it and it would have gone through much more quickly. This is a fundamental principle of legislature practice that all public administrations need to learn. I liken it to my days in the car industry. Regulation is a development process. When I was designing and developing new cars, it was always much better to put in time up front to sort out all your design choices and do all your consumer research, before you finalise your design solutions. The more time and effort you spent on that early part, the many fewer quality problems you had when you got it into production. Legislation is no different in that respect.

Q428 *Chairman:* I think that we have come to the end of our questions. Is there anything you would like to add by way of summary or in pointing us to key issues that we should still have in mind?

Mr Harbour: I think that I have probably covered most of it, apart from saying this. First of all, I am delighted to have the opportunity to meet you. A more general issue, however—because you and I have talked about it, My Lord Chairman—is how we might deepen our engagement on a more regular basis, maybe in terms of talking more broadly on some of the issues about the strategy for the internal market—we have a new document from the Commission—and maybe aligning our two work programmes, your work and ours, much more closely together. In particular, bearing in mind that there are senior British colleagues, you are meeting my colleague Philip Whitehead shortly as the Chairman of the Committee, myself as the co-ordinator, and I think that we are the only Committee in the Parliament where there is that conjunction of UK members; we would like to be able to meet you and exchange views on a much more regular basis, because I think that it is extremely valuable. You have given me some good opportunities to expose my ideas on this, sprobably in a more challenging way than I might have in my Committees here sometimes. So I think that we should try to do that.

Chairman: Could I say how grateful we are for your time, for the frankness and clarity with which you have both identified issues and given us your opinions on them? I am sure that they will be extremely important when we come to consider the views of the Committee.

Examination of Witnesses

Witnesses: Ms EVELYNE GEBHARDT, a Member of the European Parliament, and Mr PHILIP WHITEHEAD, a Member of the European Parliament, examined.

Q429 *Chairman:* Could I say a very warm thank you to both of you for agreeing to see us today? You will not know the details, but you do know that we are undertaking an inquiry into the draft Services Directive. We have been taking oral evidence now for some weeks. This week we are visiting Brussels and seeing yourselves and the Commission. We are going on to Berlin tonight, and then on to Warsaw tomorrow night. We will then meet with the British Minister next Monday, and that then concludes our oral hearings. For the record, it would be very helpful if you could introduce yourselves to the Committee.

Ms Gebhardt: I am Evelyne Gebhardt, Member of the European Parliament for the SPD, the German PSE, and I am the rapporteur for the Services Directive. It is therefore very good that we have the opportunity to talk together about it, because it is a very important piece of legislation. I do not think that I have to introduce Philip Whitehead. He is the Chairman of our Committee on the Internal Market and Consumer Protection and he works well with all the members of that Committee. There are others here: Joe Dunne, who is the first secretary—

Mr Whitehead: It is the equivalent to the Clerk of a Committee. My assistant is David O'Leary.

Ms Gebhardt: And my assistant is Birte Dedden.

Chairman: Perhaps my colleagues would like to introduce themselves briefly?

Lord Geddes: Euan Geddes, a Member of the House of Lords. I previously had the honour to chair this Committee in 1997–99, and I must say that I am very glad to be back on it again.

Lord Fearn: The Lord Fearn, Member of the Committee.

Lord Haskel: Lord Haskel, a new Member of the Committee.

Lord Walpole: Lord Walpole, the only independent member of the Committee!

Q430 *Chairman:* Can I start by going straight to one of the hearts of the matter, and that is the Country of Origin Principle? You may not have the same view, and I will pose this to both of you. Do you regard the free movement of services and the Country of Origin Principle to be inextricably linked? Is the Country of Origin Principle critical to the success of the Directive aiming to create a single market in services?

Ms Gebhardt: First, it is important to have a Services Directive, because we have a good deal of protectionism in Member States and we do not really have an open market for services. We therefore have a need to do something. Myself and my political group are very—how can I say it? Not opposed, but—

Mr Whitehead: Sceptical.

Ms Gebhardt: Yes, sceptical about the Country of Origin. There are many reasons for that, and I will raise three of them. The first is that this Principle is not a common principle. It is saying that we have 25 countries with their own laws, and these laws are in competition with each other. That is not a good way to take decisions in this matter, because we want fair competition between the countries and not to have the countries looking at who has the lowest level socially, who pays the workers least, and so on. My view is that the best way is, if possible, to have more harmonisation or mutual recognition. The second problem with the Country of Origin Principle is that it goes against juridical certainty. If in one country there are three or four service providers coming from three or four countries, the consumer may not know which law is in place in terms of providing for those services. There is therefore uncertainty for the consumers in knowing which the right one is. We also

have many specific problems in countries. I understand that Great Britain has a big problem with healthcare matters. If we have the Country of Origin Principle there, then it may be that your healthcare systems will no longer be protected as they are now. I think that it is necessary to make provision in relation to these problems and the problems in other countries. We know that in Great Britain and Germany healthcare is something which is in the hands of the state. In Portugal, it is private. So if we have the Country of Origin Principle, we do not know on what basis someone coming from Portugal to Great Britain will provide his services. We therefore have to be careful about such matters. Our political group decided to say—though Labour abstained and one voted against the proposal—that the Country of Origin Principle is not the basic principle of this Directive. That is, we have to be careful about harmonisation and mutual recognition, but we did not say that we are absolutely against this Principle, because I think that there are some cases where it will be necessary to have it. We have it in matters of e-commerce and also television without frontiers, but there are specific clauses there, and I think that we have to give some good answers regarding the problems we have. I hope that, with my poor English, I can take some questions, but I will give you the paper, so that you can read it in better English than mine.

Mr Whitehead: I think that is a very good survey from the rapporteur's point of view of the misgivings. We have to ask ourselves why these misgivings are there, and whether they are all to be taken seriously. The Labour Group within the Socialist Group here, broadly speaking, is aligned with the British Government view, namely that the passing of the Services Directive will be a major step forward in the establishment of the internal market for something between 60 and 70 per cent of all our transactions. That cannot be gainsaid; it is an important element. The problem with the Country of Origin Principle, as it has emerged, is that it was an attempt—a daring attempt, I think—to introduce a unilateral principle across a very wide range of different activities. That has proved to be the problem with it. On the one hand, there are people who say that you cannot possibly risk the serious damage to some services—the so-called "race to the bottom"—if healthcare and matters of that kind, for example, were to be included within it. A number of professions have raised issues of this kind. The fact is, of course, that healthcare and some other services of social and welfare import would be excluded, but not entirely. There is always the possibility that, if these things become matters of dispute at law, under the continental system more than our own, the European Court of Justice will become a replacement for the executive. It will start deciding what might be changed round. The sheer boldness of what Commissioner Bolkestein proposed has been, in a way, the undoing of the full proposal. This was an attempt to go way beyond the movement towards harmonisation and the insistence that such a movement should reach, within a defined period of time, full harmonisation; at which point you then had the various mutual agreements at an acceptable level. We have never said that harmonisation should simply leave derogations which absolve Member States from moving towards greater harmony over a period of time. We have just done that with the Unfair Commercial Practices Directive, and that did not use any Country of Origin provisions in the end. Our problem with this proposal, however, is that it was attempting to go the whole way in one burst. My analogy would be to say that, with these proposals here, you cannot imagine that you are on a speedboat in the open sea. You are on a narrowboat on a canal, and you are being nudged forward for much of the time. There was not much nudging here; there was a great desire to go very hard for it. I think that Evelyne has set forward very fairly the reservations that were held, not just on the left but also amongst the trade unions and others, who saw the possibility that a service provider with lower standards would come into any given country. There was great doubt about the extent to which they had to be established in the country of delivery. So making some linkage between the country of origin and the country of delivery seems to me to be a prerequisite for this progressing. I agree that it should not just be scrapped; I think that we have to improve it. It is also fair to say that if Malcolm Harbour, the Conservative representative who is a great enthusiast for this legislation, were here, he would have said that Commissioner McCreevy, and indeed the Commission in general, should not have expressed any doubt about the proposal: that they had a duty to proceed with it, even if it was eventually voted down; and that that hesitancy has been quite fatal to its prospects. I do not think that it has been, but it is fair to say that that is the opposed view in the Committee.

Chairman: As you would expect, there are a number of questions that we would like to fire at you about that; some about your reservations, some about your implied alternative solution.

Q431 *Lord Geddes:* Could I come in on what Ms Gebhardt had to say about the lowering of standards? Is it your belief that the Country of Origin Principle will encourage and result in businesses moving to regimes which have less stringent standards?
Ms Gebhardt: Yes.

Q432 *Lord Geddes:* If it is—and I am not surprised at your answer—on what basis do you come to that conclusion? Do you have any evidence of that?

Ms Gebhardt: Yes, I do, because I have spoken with many people, and also with owners of enterprises. Some of them have said to me, "We are against the Country of Origin Principle but, even if it is included in this law, we will accept it, because it is clear that we have to see that we are competitive in our countries. If enterprises coming from other countries are in competition with us, we have to have the same basis as them". So I would say that if it were only that, it might be okay; but many of the very small enterprises, which do not have the finances and logistics to do the same as the bigger enterprises, will have to take into account the higher laws in those countries. They will not then have the opportunity to be competitive with these bigger enterprises. This was said to me by entrepreneurs, and so I have to take that into account.

Q433 *Lord Geddes:* Can you give us any specific examples? I am sure that you do not want to mention companies' names, but in what field of business? In construction? In hairdressing?
Ms Gebhardt: One of these companies was a cleaning company; others came from the social care area.

Q434 *Lord Geddes:* Care for the elderly?
Ms Gebhardt: Care for the elderly, yes, and also healthcare. This is what they were saying in these areas. There was also another one.

Q435 *Chairman:* Can you explain something, because I am certainly puzzled by this? What do you mean by "lower standards"? If a cleaning company from—let me pluck a country from the air—Poland, which operates in Poland, went into Germany and offered cleaning services that were cheaper and just as good, if they were not as good, they would not get the work. Why do you call that "lower standards"? A lower standard of what?
Ms Gebhardt: I do not want to take Poland specifically as an example in this discussion. I will give another example. In Finland there is a very high level of education in relation to healthcare; but in Germany, for the elderly, it is not so high. Any pupil who wishes to do so can do it, though they do not have to have a special education for it. Such people, who are not so well educated, are not paid as much as they are in Finland, where they have that high level and are very expensive. Finnish people say, "We are angry about that. If we have the Country of Origin Principle, then the less well educated Germans will come to Finland, creating greater competitiveness". I put it that way, because I do not want to say it is simply a question of the new Member States and the older Member States. You can find examples in every country where you can say that is the case.

Mr Whitehead: Obviously we do have an obligation to those people who aspire to offer services in the enlarged Community and who come from the new Member States. You could not see the process of enlargement through without offering that. You will take away with you the record of the debate following Mr McCreevy's statement recently. There was a very strong speech by Mr Kaminski, a senior Polish representative, saying, "You cannot turn your back on us now and refuse us the right to operate". What I would say here—and it is an important element in this picture—is that there are of course great anxieties if the operation is based only on competition according to cost. In a way, the answer to the question to Evelyne is this. If it is just a cost equation, a far cheaper service may or may not be as good, but if it is not as good and it still got the contract because it is cheap, then it may be retained. That is a particular worry in Germany—five million unemployed.

Ms Gebhardt: And not only because of that. Because I am German, it does not mean that I am thinking only about Germany. We have to be careful if we have the Country of Origin Principle—and I say this because of the British healthcare position—because of the case of Portugal, for instance, where they are privatised. In Great Britain, they are not. It is not just a problem for Germany; you can find problems in all countries. If we continued to speak about this, we would find other matters. Poland would say, "We do not want the Country of Origin Principle because the Germans are causing problems for us"—because many Germans are going to Poland for their dentistry, because it is very cheap there. Insurers in Germany pay well, and this is now causing an increase in prices in Poland. The Polish people are not able to pay those prices, which then creates a problem for them.

Mr Whitehead: I am sure that is right. I am not saying that you are speaking as a German; you are speaking as the rapporteur, of course. However, there are two things which have to be seen in parallel with this Directive, which I think slightly alters the picture. One is the Posting of Workers Directive, which means that there is absolute employment protection in the country of delivery and it is not just a matter of shipping people in, like the illegal workers in the UK found dead on Morecambe Sands, and so on. I think that does offer some protection. Secondly, if you are looking at the professions—something we are debating this week in our Committee—there is the mutual recognition of qualifications. Provided the emphasis there is on the qualifications as well as the mutual recognition, it will ease many of the reservations that people have. But we have to have the whole thing together. You cannot just proceed with the Services Directive alone.

Q436 *Lord Haskel:* Looking at this from the point of view of the consumer, obviously there must be certain standards of service and these standards differ from country to country. Presumably, if you are going to offer a service in another country—and these things are very local—you have to deliver a standard which is in keeping with the standards expected in that country. From that point of view, are the consumers protected? It would seem to me that the Country of Origin Principle does not stand in the way of that.

Ms Gebhardt: That is a real problem for the consumers. We have two things to develop there. The first is that if service providers come from a different country, there are different qualities and standards proposed. If there were a problem involving the courts, which law should be taken into account? That is not stated in the Commission's proposal and nobody knows how to manage that. We therefore have to ensure that it is clear, so that there is no judicial uncertainty. The other point we have to deal with is the problem of controls. With the Country of Origin Principle, the controls are in the Country of Origin but the service is provided in another country. How do you ensure that, if there is a need for control, that control is properly taken? I cannot imagine that the Country of Origin would have enough money for taking controls in another country. We therefore have to make sure that is managed. I think that there is a great majority in our Parliament who would wish to make profound amendments to that, and to ensure that there is good administrative co-operation between the countries on that matter. However, it is a very difficult point and there will have to be further discussions on it.

Mr Whitehead: That is correct. Does the consumer gain? In theory, yes, because competition in services will lead to wider choice and probably better choice. If the Polish plumber, who will come round to your house in half an hour instead of five days and do you just as good a job, is also legally established, paying his taxes, and so on, the consumer gains. However, we have found that for consumer protection legislation—and this was particularly true of the Unfair Commercial Practical Directive, which has just gone through all its stages—that harmonisation at the highest possible level you can achieve among the Member States was the chosen route, with a process of derogation: that is, four or five years to get everyone up to that higher level. In that sense, country by country, you can probably move in the same way as had been suggested by the once-for-all switchover to the Country of Origin Principle. It may be that now we have to find a different route to the same objective, which will also give rather more certainty to the consumer. We particularly need it in fields like agent liability. We need to know exactly who is liable when these problems arise.

Q437 *Lord Fearn:* Clearly a firm can establish themselves in another European market and have a presence there, or they can have a temporary situation. What do you understand by "temporary"?

Ms Gebhardt: That is a very difficult discussion. In the law on the mutual recognition of qualifications, the European Commission proposed that 16 weeks in one year is "temporary". However, the European Parliament says that it cannot be taken as such, because if you are a plumber it is possible to finish the work within 16 weeks, but if you are an architect and you are building a house, then it will take more than 16 weeks. We therefore said that we have to consider how long and how often it was proposed. We did not define it; it will be taken sector by sector. The Council's Common Position will be the same as the European Parliament in that regard.

Q438 *Lord Fearn:* We read the working document, in which there is an alarming phrase which says that it may be withdrawn or redrafted. Is that really on the cards?

Ms Gebhardt: No. There was a problem which arose when I wrote my text. I thought that I had seven pages on which to write it. I did not know that the first and second pages, which are administrative matters, were included in that. I therefore had to summarise my own proposal, and I withdrew the opening, in which were the positive aspects. In one of the conclusions, I took out too many words. So it is possible to read it as if I were saying that we have to withdraw the whole of the text, but that was not what I wanted to say. I wanted to say that we have to work profoundly on this text. I am sorry that, in summarising my own paper, this has caused a problem.

Mr Whitehead: Our clear understanding now is that the proposal will not be withdrawn but it can be excised. Some things will go.

Q439 *Lord Geddes:* Does "excised" mean amended?

Ms Gebhardt: Amended, yes.

Q440 *Lord Walpole:* What has come up on several occasions is the combination of harmonisation and mutual recognition. What did you actually mean by that? Both of you have used that expression.

Ms Gebhardt: There are some points on which we have further work to do. We have finished the Unfair Commercial Practices Directive. That is a harmonisation that has been well done, I think. We have to consider liability and so on, so that we have a high level of common standards in our countries. In cases of mutual recognition, it is what we are saying in relation to the mutual recognition of Professional Qualifications Directive; namely, if somebody has a qualification in his own country it has to be accepted in the other countries. It is a part of the Country of Origin Principle there—which I absolutely agree is a very good thing in that case—but it is defined in the recognition. We therefore have the opportunity to see the other qualifications and if there are sufficient qualifications to be taken into account in the other countries. We have said that we want to have a pro forma presence in the country, so that the countries know that the provider is there; not new tests and so on for the qualifications, but to say that it is recognised. So that we know the plumber from Poland is a plumber, and if he wants to provide his services in Germany or Great Britain it has to be agreed. I am clear about that. If the qualification is the same—why not?

Q441 *Lord Geddes:* In your 2 March paper, which you have kindly given us (*not printed*), you make six demands, of which the fourth demand is that the Country of Origin Principle—which incidentally I call COOP—cannot be the basic Principle of the internal market in services. We have heard evidence from others who have said that if there is not the Country of Origin Principle, then the whole of the draft Directive is a complete waste of time and it might just as well be torn up. What are your comments on that?

Ms Gebhardt: That would be the case if we were to remove this Country of Origin Principle without having another proposal on that. However, I do have other proposals on that: harmonisation and mutual recognition. Some people have said that they want simply to remove Article 16. I would say that is not satisfactory, because we then do not have a principle in this Services Directive and it would not work. However, if we say that we are changing or amending the principles which are taken into account in this Services Directive, then it is good to have a Services Directive. My colleague Mr Würmeling suggested that we should take the Country of Origin Principle as the basic principle, but he then proposed a very long list of exemptions. If you read those exemptions, the question you ask is, "What then?". It is as if you are saying that you are making a new proposal on the principles which are working today, harmonisation and mutual recognition. I think that it would be better to have a principle which works than one which has many exemptions and which does not work.

Mr Whitehead: We are having to do some rethinking, because of the boldness of the original proposal. Joe Dunne will correct me if these figures are wrong, but I think that it took about ten years to produce an internal market in goods. You will remember Mrs Thatcher signing the Single Act, and all of that. That led to something like 250 or more sectoral proposals coming out. This proposal is to go the whole way in one step. It is extremely difficult to do that, as has now emerged. We have this problem with people's anxieties that one size does not fit all; one proposal does not fit all. One of the things that we are proposing in the Committee, and it will come up this afternoon, is that we are allowed to commission studies and we would like to do a study fairly quickly of what the actual impact has been of those pieces of legislation which have used the Country of Origin Principle but have done it sectorally. Curiously enough, some of those who now vehemently argue against the Country of Origin Principle in general were very much for it in things like the TV without frontiers. They saw the point there. To make it apply to everything at this stage, however, is very difficult. *Ms Gebhardt:* I spoke with Mr Delors on this, because I thought it would be very important to have his point of view. I heard about his many pieces of legislation and I said to him that I thought it would be workable with about 12. He said, "No, that is too much". He thinks that it can be done with four, five, maybe six pieces of legislation. It would perhaps be interesting to ask Mr Delors to give his opinion, because he would be the one who would know about these things. Regarding television without frontiers and e-commerce, there is a technical point of view as to why

it has to be the Country of Origin Principle, which is because it is going on the air or by internet. These are not services which are going to a specific country, as with cleaning or other services, where people go elsewhere in order to give their services. It is something else and cannot be said to be the same, or to have the same arrangements.

Chairman: As I expected, the time over which we have been able to meet with you is hopelessly insufficient. It is entirely of our making, because you have been generous with your time. I suspect that we could go on for a long time, because there are many matters to discuss. If we did want to correspond briefly with you, I hope that we might be able to do that, because there are one or two things we wanted to explore with you. With regret, however, we have to conclude. On behalf of the Committee, may I extend to both of you our warmest appreciation? It has given us an insight into how you see things, and that is often as important as words. Meeting people is always better, and we are grateful to you.

Memorandum by Internal Market Directorate-General, European Commission

INTRODUCTION

In reading this response, it should be borne in mind that, in its recent Communication to the Spring European Council, the Commission has signalled that, in order to ensure the smooth discussion of this important proposal, it will work constructively with the European Parliament, the Council and other stakeholders in the run up to the adoption of the first reading by the Parliament. It will be focusing in particular on concerns raised in areas such as the operation of the country of origin provisions and the potential impact for certain sectors.

In the light of these discussions, the Commission may revisit its approach on some of these areas, including possibly those addressed by the written Call for Evidence. Therefore, the answers given by Commission services in its response shall not prejudice any decision that may be taken in relation to these areas.

A. THE CURRENT STATE OF THE SINGLE MARKET IN SERVICES

ARE THERE SIGNIFICANT BARRIERS TO FIRMS SEEKING TO OFFER THEIR SERVICES IN OTHER MEMBER STATES OF THE EUROPEAN UNION? IF SO, WHAT ARE THE MOST IMPORTANT OF THOSE BARRIERS? WHAT MEASURES ARE NEED TO OVERCOME THOSE BARRIERS? DOES THE COMMISSION'S PROPOSED DIRECTIVE ADEQUATELY ADDRESS THOSE ISSUES?

1. Yes. It has not so far been possible to fully exploit the growth potential of services because of the many obstacles hampering the development of services activities between the Member States. In our report on "The State of the Internal Market for Services",[1] the Commission listed these obstacles, which affect a wide range of services such as distributive trades, employment agencies, certification, laboratories, construction services, estate agencies, craft industries, tourism, the regulated professions etc and SMEs, which are predominant in the services sector, who are particularly hard-hit. SMEs are too often discouraged from exploiting the opportunities afforded by the internal market because they do not have the means to evaluate, and protect themselves against, the legal risks involved in cross-border activity or to cope with the administrative complexities. The report, and the impact assessment which accompanied the draft Services Directive, shows the economic impact of this dysfunction, emphasising that it amounts to a considerable drag on the EU economy and its potential for growth, competitiveness and job creation.

2. These obstacles to the development of service activities between Member States occur in particular in two types of situation:

---

[1] COM(2002) 441 final, 30 July 2002.

— when a service provider from one Member states wishes to establish himself in another Member State in order to provide his services. (For example, he may be subject to over-burdensome authorisation schemes, excessive red tape, discriminatory requirements, case-by-case application of an economic needs test etc); and

— when a service provider wishes to provide a service from his Member State of origin into another Member State, particularly by moving to the other Member State on a temporary basis. (For example, he may be subject to a legal obligation to establish himself in the other Member State, need to obtain an authorisation there, or be subject to the application of its rules on the conditions for the exercise of the activity in question or to disproportionate procedures in connection with the posting of workers).

3. Accordingly, the aim of this proposal for a Directive is to establish a legal framework to facilitate the exercise of freedom of establishment for service providers in the Member States and the free movement of services between Member States. It aims to eliminate certain legal obstacles to the achievement of a genuine internal market in services and to guarantee service providers and recipients the legal certainty they need in order to exercise these two fundamental freedoms enshrined in the Treaty in practice.

B. THE COUNTRY OF ORIGIN PRINCIPLE

IS THE PRINCIPLE THAT A COMPANY REGISTERED TO PROVIDE SERVICES IN ONE COUNTRY IS AUTOMATICALLY QUALIFIED TO PROVIDE THOSE SERVICES IN ANY OTHER COMMUNITY COUNTRY ON THE BASIS OF HOME COUNTRY REGULATION A REASONABLE AND/OR REALISTIC STARTING POINT? WHAT SIGNIFICANT BENEFITS TO BUSINESSES AND CONSUMERS ARE LIKELY TO OCCUR AS A RESULT OF THE ADOPTION OF THE COUNTRY OF ORIGIN PRINCIPLE? IS THE PRINCIPLE WORKABLE IN PRACTICE?

4. Yes. To clarify, the Country of Origin Principle applies only to operators providing cross-border services into another Member State, without establishing there permanently. The proposal provides that the principle's application is combined with derogations for particularly sensitive areas and concerns, for example, the applicable working conditions in the case of the posting of workers, consumer contracts, public health and the safety of building sites. This means that the member State where the service is provided will retain the right to apply its national laws to incoming service providers in these specific areas.

5. For areas not covered by derogations—in particular many business-to-business activities—a service provider would be subject only to the rules and regulations of the Member State where it is established without being subjected to other Member States' rules every time it crosses a border. This would considerably increase legal certainty. Simply by checking where the derogations apply, a service provider could easily find out whether and for which activities he would have to comply with national rules. This would considerably reduce legal search and compliance costs, and encourage businesses (particularly SMEs) to operate across borders.

6. Underpinning the Country of Origin Principle, and to enhance trust and confidence in cross-border services, the proposed Directive provides for some key, harmonised, EU-wide quality requirements covering professional indemnity insurance for service providers, the information they must provide to regulators and customers and commercial communications by regulated professions.

7. In order to make the principle workable in practice, the proposal also provides for enhanced administrative co-operation requirements between Member States, removing the current duplicative requirements and controls and ensuring that national authorities work directly together. This is outlined in further detail below.

8. The Country of Origin Principle is not a novelty. Its source is found in the principle of freedom to provide services provided in Article 49 of the Treaty, as developed over the years by abundant case law of the European Court of Justice. It is an efficient way to give full effect to this Internal Market freedom and to establish a genuine area without internal frontiers. The Country of Origin Principle is an integral part of the Community legal approach which relies on trust and confidence between Member States, including in areas which are not harmonised at Community level.

9. This principal has already been adopted and successfully implemented in other Internal Market directives in particular in Directive 89/552/CEE (television without frontiers), Directive 95/46/CE (protection of personal data), Directive 99/93/CE (electronic signatures) and Directive 2000/31/CE (electronic commerce). These Directives have proved to be successful both in terms of facilitating the development of cross-border activites between Member States and in terms of ensuring a better protection of general interest objectives at Community level. Compared to the Services Directive, these Directives contain a more limited number of derogations from the Country of Origin Principle.

10. In addition, the alternative to Country of Origin, ie launching a large-scale and detailed harmonisation process, is not feasible, nor desirable. to attempt to harmonise every single piece of national legislation relating to such a broad variety of services which are covered by the Services Directive would be unnecessary, unrealistic and inconsistent with better regulation policy.

WILL THE APPLICATION OF THE COUNTRY OF ORIGIN PRINCIPLE MOVE BUSINESS IN FAVOUR OF FIRMS BASED IN MEMBER STATES WITH THE LEAST STRINGENT REGULATORY REGIMES? WHAT ISSUES DOES THIS RAISE FOR BUSINESS AND CONSUMERS? HOW MIGHT THOSE ISSUES BE RESOLVED?

11. There is no evidence to suggest that business will move to Member States with the least stringent regulatory regimes. Indeed this does not correspond to past experience in the field of the free movement of goods, where the principle of mutual recognition has been a well established one for many years, and where benefits have been experienced across the EU. A recent economic study ("Copenhagen Economics" study, commissioned by the Commission[2]) of the likely impact of implementing the Services Directive (for further details see C. below) shows that there are important benefits to be achieved by all Member States from a full implementation of the Services Directive. Furthermore, it estimated that economic gains will be greatest in the sectors and Member States where existing regulation is currently heaviest.

12. It is important to note that the Country of Origin Principle only applies to the temporary cross-border provision of services. For services provided via an establishment in another Member State, the service provider will have to comply with all the relevant rules in that Member State. In addition, the proposal provides that the principle is combined with a large number of derogations, harmonisation and enhanced administrative co-operation between Member States. Derogations from the Country of Origin Princple cover, for instance, the applicable working conditions in the context of posting of workers, consumer contracts, health and safety on building sites and public Health. Harmonisation of national laws concerns, eg requirements relating to the information which service providers must make available both to consumers and to competent authorities, and provisions relating to professional indemnity insurance.

THE APPLICATION OF THE PRINCIPLE RELIES ON THE DEVELOPMENT OF AN EXTENSIVE MUTUAL ASSISTANCE FRAMEWORK, WHEREBY MEMBER STATES CO-OPERATE IN SUPERVISING ENTERPRISES BASED IN THEIR COUNTRY IN RESPECT OF OPERATIONS IN OTHER COUNTRIES. IS THAT A WORKABLE FRAMEWORK?

13. Yes. As the question implies, effective administrative co-operation mechanisms are essential to the effective application of the Country of Origin Principle. Today this does not exist and Member States often submit companies from other Member States systematically to their entire national body of rules and regulations. Duplication of rules and controls result in higher costs and complication for service providers without necessarily ensuring that traders are properly supervised or that the law is genuinely enforced. The lack of co-operation between Member States is also used by rogue traders to avoid supervision, thereby creating risks or harm to the health, safety or financial wellbeing of users of their services.

14. Under the Services proposal, Member State authorities will be explicitly responsible for supervising the activities of service providers established on their territory, including where they provide services into other Member States. This means that they will no longer be able to turn a blind eye to unlawful conduct by these service providers which results in harm to consumers in other Member States. This will help to combat rogue traders who escape control by moving around from one Member State to the next and thus result in better protection for consumers who want to use cross-border services.

15. This does not mean that Member States will have to send out "flying squads" to carry out factual checks and controls in other Member States. These checks and controls will be carried out by the authorities of the country where the service provider is temporarily operating.

WHAT OTHER SIGNIFICANT CONCERNS ARE THERE REGARDING THE PRACTICAL IMPLEMENTATION OF THE COUNTRY OF ORIGIN PRINCIPLE AND HOW MIGHT THESE BE ADDRESSED?

16. As regards the practical implementation of this, there is a need for further work and modern technological tools will be use as far as possible. The Commission is currently working on a project drawing up a prototype

---

[2] http://europa.eu.int/comm/internal_market/services/docs/strategy/2004-propdir/2005-01-cph-study_en.pdf

system to demonstrate how the electronic information exchange system will work in practice, based on the model already proven to be successful in the context of the SOLVIT system. It is also important that there is a strong commitment from Member States on the overall objective of ensuring effective co-operation between national administrations in support of a better-functioning Internal Market.

ASSUMING EFFICIENT OPERATION OF THE COUNTRY OF ORIGIN PRINCIPLE, WHAT SIGNIFICANT BARRIERS TO TRADING IN OTHER MEMBER STATES ARE LIKELY TO REMAIN, SO FAR AS FIRMS IN THE RELEVANT BUSINESS SECTORS ARE CONCERNED?

17. In theory, barriers to trading in other Member States could remain in some of the areas covered by derogations to the Country of Origin Principle. However, these derogations are carefully targeted, for instance to take account of some other Community instruments relating to particular aspects of service activities, or relate to areas where the divergence of national laws is such that the freedom toprovide services cannot be fully ensured. Further derogations of a temporary nature apply to cash-in-transit services, gambling activities and the judicial recovery of debts. It is envisaged that instruments harmonising these areas may be brought in. Once these instruments are adopted, the derogations will cease to apply. The question underlines the importance of ensuring that derogations to the Country of Origin Principle are carefully limited to areas where this is strictly necessary.

C. THE FUTURE

DO YOU EXPECT THE IMPLEMENTATION OF THE COMMISSION'S PROPOSED DIRECTIVE TO HAVE A SIGNIFICANT IMPACT ON TRADE IN THE SERVICES SECTOR WITHIN THE EUROPEAN UNION? IN WHICH SERVICES INDUSTRIES DO YOU EXPECT THE LEAST AND LARGEST MOVEMENT TOWARDS A EUROPEAN UNION SINGLE MARKET IN THE NEXT FIVE TO 10 YEARS.

18. Once implemented, the Services Directive could give a considerable boost to trade, competitiveness and growth in the services sector. It could also give a boost to high-quality jobs in a sector which already accounts for a majority of employment within the EU.

19. Recent economic research has backed this up. For instance, the CPB Netherlands Institute for Economic Policy Analysis[3] has found that the implementation of the proposal will lead to about at 15–35 per cent increase in bilateral trade and foreign direct investment in commercial services.

20. Most recently, an independent study by Copenhagen Economics[4] has found that a reduction of barriers in the field of services, as proposed in the Directive, could yield significant economic gains, estimating *inter alia* that, the total "welfare gain" for the EU economy would be 0.6 per cent (corresponding to a money equivalent of €37 billion); prices of services will fall in the sectors covered by the Directive (price falls range from 7.6 per cent for the regulated professions, to 0.3 per cent for business services); output and value added will increase across all sectors (in money terms, value added will increase by around €33 billion); and all EU countries will profit from more jobs. Net employment will increase by around 0.3 per cent, or 600,000 jobs, across the EU. Also, workers will benefit from higher wages, which will increase by approximately 0.4 per cent in the services sectors covered.

21. The results of the study by Copenhagen Economics indicate that all services sectors will benefit from increased intra-EU cross border activities. However, it estimates that those services sectors which are currently regulated most heavily in Member States could experience the largest increase in intra-EU trade and investment. Depending on the type of service provided, the positive trade effect may be more important than the establishment growth and *vice-versa*. For example, it is estimated that the Directive will increase intra-EU cross-border trade in professional services (legal, accounting, business and management consultancy) by 9.4 per cent. Cross-border establishment in this sector is expected to increase by 2.7 per cent. For less regulated sectors such as IT services, recruitment, cleaning and real estate, the Directive will increase cross-border trade by 1 per cent but prompt an increase of 2.5 per cent in terms of cross-border establishment.

February 2005

---

[3] http://www.cpb.nl/eng/pub/notice/23sep2004/notitie.pdf
[4] http://europa.eu.int/comm/internal_market/services/docs/strategy/2004-prodir/2005-01-cph-study_en.pdf

TUESDAY 15 MARCH 2005

Present   Fearn, L   Walpole, L
            Geddes, L   Woolmer of Leeds, L (Chairman)
            Haskel, L

Examination of Witnesses

Witnesses: MR THIERRY STOLL, Deputy Director General, DR MARGOT FRÖHLINGER, Head of Unit, E1 Services, MR JEAN BERGEVIN, Head of Unit, E2 Services, and MR HUGO DE CHASSIRON, member of E1 Services Unit, European Commission, examined.

Q442 Chairman: Welcome.

Mr Stoll: Allow me to say a few words; first of all to welcome you, to say how much we appreciate your interest in this very important proposal, the Services Directive, and for taking the trouble to travel, I understand not only to Brussels but also to other places, to learn more and to understand this proposal. I had the opportunity and privilege of attending a Select Committee quite some time ago about Schengen, the free movement of people, which is probably the issue that compares best with the provision of services in terms of trickiness and political sensitivity. I am therefore very glad to have the opportunity to discuss the Services Directive with you. There is one important caveat, or health warning, I want to give. As you are aware, this is a very controversial proposal which has been discussed extensively, including public opinion, sometimes with very fierce attacks against the Directive or some of its principles. This has led to the slightly unusual step taken by the Commission chaired by President Barroso, indicating that the Commission had heard the anxieties that this proposed Directive was creating. It has led to the step that the Commission has announced a certain margin of flexibility in relation to the further negotiation of this Directive, even before the Parliament has produced its opinion at First Reading and the Council has reached its Common Position. As I say, this is to reflect the sensitivities surrounding some of the aspects of the Directive. The Commission, from the lips of both President Barroso and Commissioner McCreevy, has indicated three areas of concern to which the Commission would be particularly sensitive. The first was to ensure that, whatever the reality about the present proposal, the final result should not lead to social dumping or to something called "social dumping", whatever we may wish to call it. In other words, it should preserve workers' rights in the country of destination. That concern must be absolutely safeguarded in the end result. That was a very strong and clear message. The second indication of flexibility was in relation to so-called sensitive sectors that will or might be

affected by the draft Directive. In particular, the Commission has highlighted the whole of the health sector and the so-called publicly funded services of general interest as sectors that may possibly be left out of the scope of the Directive, because there are very strong feelings about the degree to which these sectors should or could be affected by the Directive. The third area that was highlighted by the Commission was the famous, or infamous, Country of Origin Principle. There, the Commission stated that it was aware of the concerns surrounding the operation of the Country of Origin Principle and while it felt that the Country of Origin Principle should be maintained in the Directive, there would have to be guarantees that it did not lead to uncertainty—for business and for users, consumers, citizens—as to what exactly is the law applicable to certain situations covered by the Directive, whilst retaining the Principle as a guiding principle for the Directive. President Barroso has returned to this particular element, I think no later than yesterday and even this morning. I think that you need to be aware of these three signals of flexibility, because they mean that when the Parliament comes up with its report and its amendments, these are the areas where the Commission will be particularly sensitive to any changes that the Parliament might wish to propose, without wanting to prejudge what the outcome of the First Reading in the Parliament will be. What I will say in relation to the Directive, therefore, will refer to the Directive as it was proposed by the Commission and, I stress, does not prejudge in which direction this Commission may go when looking at the Parliament's opinion. My last word as a matter of introduction is that this is obviously one of the most important proposals to be discussed at the moment in the European Union, certainly when it comes to delivering the Lisbon Agenda, the objective of improving the competitiveness of the European economy. If we do not get it right on this proposal, I think that the overall Lisbon Agenda will be in peril. So this is to underline the importance of this proposal but, again, because it is so far-reaching and ambitious, it has also given rise to very vocal concerns. I am now in your hands as to how we should proceed.

Q443 Chairman: First of all, could I express on behalf of my colleagues our deep appreciation of the fact that you have been able to spare your time today to meet us. We are very grateful indeed. It is most important to us that we are able to meet to discuss the Directive. So thank you again for that, and for your helpful introductory remarks. We appreciate that we are meeting you at a sensitive time on these matters, and therefore perhaps the way in which you may feel you are able to respond will be even more measured than usual. You will understand, however, that if we are asking questions it is to seek clarification and to seek guidance. We understand that there are limits to how far you can help us in these matters today, but you will certainly see some of the things that we are interested in. Do I take it from your remarks that the free movement of services, as dealt with in the draft Directive, and the Country of Origin Principle do remain, in the view of the Commission, very important, indeed if not critical, matters to be addressed and followed through, if a single market in services is to be forthcoming in a reasonable time frame under the Lisbon Agenda? Can I take it that remains the position of the Commission?

Mr Stoll: Yes, definitely. First of all, there is the importance of the services sector as a major contributor to growth and competitiveness. It has untapped potential because, unlike the free movement of goods, we have not proceeded with any in-depth harmonisation. The figures are there to show the untapped potential, more than two-thirds of the EU's Gross Domestic Product and only 20 per cent in terms of trade. This shows that there is not enough cross-border provision of services. Why is that? The unanimous assessment is that it is simply too difficult for businesses to engage in cross-border provision of services: whether through establishment, because of the red tape with which they are confronted and the multiplication of red tape, or by direct cross-border temporary provision of services, because of the red tape but also, let us be very clear, because of the protectionism and the way that Member States like to look at their national markets as being national and not part of the wider market. In terms of the Services Directive, I think we remain convinced that we do not have much alternative but to proceed in the way we have started to proceed, which is via one horizontal instrument covering all the sectors that we want not to exclude; and there are a few exclusions, because they are being dealt with by other parts of Community policy. So it is one horizontal

instrument covering a great number of services, some of which may appear to be minute and, as such, not very important with regard to competitiveness. For instance, I get the question, "Why would chimneysweeps be a concern of yours?" because chimneysweeps are regulated and because citizens ask, "Why can I not have my chimney swept by the cheapest offer, just the other side of the border?", to take a caricature of an example. Based on the country of origin—because I think this is essential—we do not have the possibility of harmonising across 20 or 30 different sectors in the EU. With 25 Member States, I do not think that we would get very far. It would be time-consuming and would probably be impossible. Also, we believe that it would not be desirable. If there is one difference between the times we are in now and, say, the Eighties when we harmonised extensively to allow for the free movement of goods, it is that notions like subsidiarity, over-regulation and over-harmonisation have become much more important. Therefore, we believe that the starting point should be that Member States accept that, give or take a couple of exceptions, their legislative regimes are basically comparable and do not subject their citizens to unreasonable risks. Full harmonisation prior to free movement is therefore not required. We believe that, yes, a single horizontal instrument, based on the country of origin—provided we get all the flanking measures in place, like administrative co-operation—is the right and probably the only way to achieve something reasonable within a reasonable amount of time. We still have the Lisbon Agenda. 2010 may be a bit optimistic, but we do not have all the time in the world to achieve it. If you would allow me, My Lord Chairman, I would like to introduce my colleagues. They are Margot Fröhlinger, who is the Head of unit in charge of the drafting and the negotiation of the Directive, Jean Bergevin, who is the Head of unit who was also associated with the preparation, but more with looking at the economic dimension of it, and Hugo de Chassiron, a colleague in Margot Fröhlinger's unit.

Q444 Chairman: If any of your colleagues wish to contribute at any time, please do so. Let me ask one further question on this particular issue, and then my colleagues will, I am sure, have further questions. You said in your introductory remarks that you recognised some areas of concern. You mentioned the concern of other people about possible social dumping, the issue of certain sensitive sectors, and also the matter of legal certainty. Are there any other issues that the Commission regards as significant hurdles, which either have to be overcome or, on the other hand, perhaps in persuading those who have

concerns that their concerns are not necessarily well-founded? Are there any other issues out there that you think are potential hurdles or stumbling blocks?
Mr Stoll: The three areas signalled obviously have not been invented by the Commission; they reflect the very acute debate. There is one area which, when we come to discussions about it in more detail, I would not say might be a source of insurmountable difficulties but which clearly will take some time to discuss. That is the whole operation of the administrative co-operation.

Q445 *Chairman:* Yes, we will come to that.
Mr Stoll: Because some Member States think that this may, okay, be all about competitiveness, but perhaps at the cost of putting excessive burdens on Member States' administrations.
Chairman: You obviously read our mind well. We certainly will be coming to that.

Q446 *Lord Fearn:* You do admit that the programme is ambitious. Dealing with the Country of Origin Principle, would you say that the principle is workable in practice? If it is not, is there an alternative?
Mr Stoll: Part of the answer to the first question is also in the answer to the second question. I think we agree that we do not have much of an alternative; we do not have much of a choice. However, let me say a little more about the operation of the Country of Origin Principle. First of all, this is the best way to prime the pump, if I may say so, for the development of cross-border provision of services. This is a bit of a chicken-and-egg discussion of course. However, unless Member States are convinced that they can start offering their services on a broader scale than simply to their local or their national markets, there is not much chance that they will be offering these services on a wider scale, entering into competition with each other, provoking a very healthy competition that will drive down prices, increase consumer choice, and make the benefits develop across the Union, including for consumers. The businesses are now very much restrained in thinking of the internal market as an internal market—as a single market, I should say—because, even before offering their services in other Member States, very often the first step they have to take is to engage a lawyer to give them advice as to what the situation will be in possibly all of the 24 other Member States into which they would like to provide their services. Also, what the conditions will be; what the legal requirements will be; what the administrative requirements will be. They have to pay fairly high legal fees, just to be informed that it will be quite a nightmare if they want to overcome those hurdles in, potentially, 24 Member States. That works as a

disincentive. They do not even think of advertising their services across the borders. In particular, small and medium-sized companies find it very difficult. Big companies will always find a way round. They will open establishments; they have the means to pay legal fees. The small and the medium-sized companies are the ones that are, at present, very much afraid of engaging in activities across borders. The small and medium-sized companies are also the ones that hold the most potential, and which will be the most sensitive to the benefits accruing from the Country of Origin Principle. Knowing that they are legally established in their home country and that, bar a number of exceptions, they can engage in cross-border activities without having to confront 24 paper chases, legal requirements in the other Member States, will be a tremendous boost, providing tremendous legal certainty, for them to embark on offering services cross-border. As I say, the competition then will take over and also make sure that there is more on offer, a better choice for consumers, and lower prices. However, that requires a number of things to happen. First of all, I want to stress that the Country of Origin is not an unqualified Principle. It does not apply across the board. With such a broad Directive, this would not work and would not be acceptable. There are areas where the Country of Origin Principle cannot be applied—or, at least, not for the time being—possibly pending further harmonisation, and we have identified a number of areas where this is the case; but it should at least be the starting point. What do the reactions against the Country of Origin Principle show? It shows a huge lack of confidence of Member States in each other's regulatory systems. That is a bit of a contradiction, especially now after enlargement. What we find, and thank goodness there have been some pretty good press articles in the last few days highlighting this, is that we have decided to allow 10 new Member States to join us and we are now telling them, "If our companies want to do business in your location that is de-localisation", with all the negative connotations; "If you send companies over here, that is social dumping". I think that we have to look at the EU, the 25 Member States, as a whole. The alternative is that we will lose out, not to Slovakia or Slovenia or Poland, but to India, China, Brazil, Malaysia, Singapore and the rest. So, yes, the Country of Origin Principle needs to be the guiding principle, but it has to be underpinned, in particular by administrative co-operation. It is the one key instrument that we believe is best suited to create the conditions of mutual trust between the Member States. If we just expect the Country of Origin to apply in isolation, without a little bit of help, then the concerns will not allow it to take place. We must therefore make sure that there is this mutual trust. It is not just an act of faith, but has to be underpinned by very concrete co-operation tools which allow administrations to talk to each other and get more information about who the other service provider is, what is his status, does he have a track record and so on, all these detailed questions that will create mutual trust and mutual confidence.

Q447 *Lord Geddes:* Mr Stoll, we have been told that an announcement had been made in the last 24 hours of further moves regarding the draft Directive. Perhaps I can ask you some specifics on that. First, on "social dumping". Would you say that the opportunities for businesses to move their operations, their business, into third countries within the EU which have less stringent regulations are now virtually dead? Is that what it is aimed to achieve? On the sensitive sectors, you have mentioned health. I was not quite sure whether in that respect you meant health and safety. You went on to talk about publicly funded social interests. Did that mean provision of health care, whereas your first "health" meant health and safety? I was not quite clear on that. On the Country of Origin Principle and the guarantees regarding uncertainties; I wonder if you could expand that a little. I think I understand what you mean, but I would love to hear some more.

Mr Stoll: First of all, I should say that this is not a sign of flexibility that has been made by the Commission. It does not translate into a modified proposal. In other words, we are not in the process of drafting very concrete changes to Article X, Y or Z, to translate these. These signals have been drafted in fairly open and, let us admit, vague terms, so as not to limit excessively the scope of further debate in the Parliament. It is a door that has been opened but it remains to be seen how much we shall allow to pass through that door at the end of the day. On your first point, I am afraid that each time we use the phrase "social dumping" we are not doing a service to anybody: to the Services Directive; to our economies; to our overall understanding of what the EU is about. However, for convenience's sake that is the term which is used by everybody. The first point is that we will probably need to go on clarifying that the Directive as such, in its present formulation, does not lead to social dumping, because of the relationship with the Posting of Workers Directive. That makes abundantly clear that a Polish company, working on a building site in Germany, will not be able to do so with Polish workers paid at the level of Polish wages and subjected to Polish labour law or labour standards. Even today in the press, I continue to see the same examples used against the Directive. So I think we will have to continue to explain that even in its present form there is no such thing as social dumping. The second point to make is that there may

be one or two loopholes in the interaction between the Services Directive and the Posting of Workers Directive. I would say—and this is not rocket science—these amount to perhaps five per cent of the whole spectrum of the relationship between the Services Directive and the Posting of Workers Directive. I think that we will probably have to fill that gap of five per cent of uncertainty—in particular, the way collective bargaining applies in different Member States—to make abundantly clear that in no way can the Services Directive lead to a situation where companies can bring their labour force from a cheaper country and create a sort of unfair competition in that sense, for instance, on a building site. Does that mean that the Services Directive would not allow companies to choose where to operate from? Again, we have to make a very fundamental distinction here. The Services Directive of course cannot, and does not aim to, prevent business operators from choosing how they want to conduct their business across Europe. They do so based on a number of reasons, which have to do with proximity to the customers, linguistic situations, the dimension of the company, also the legal and tax environment, including the red tape, and the quality of the administrations with whom they have to deal. I think it is absolutely clear that, in an internal market, companies should have the choice to decide from where they want to operate. What the Services Directive does not allow—and there are very specific provisions—is to artificially select a place from where you want to conduct your business, for instance, by opening a letterbox operation there. The Directive makes it abundantly clear that you must have a physical location in that country. Therefore, under that proviso, companies should be able to apply a certain form of decision-making about where is the most beneficial place to do business. The Services Directive is not the latest instrument that will allow this. It is perfectly legitimate for the European Union to be made up of Member States which have different traditions. The alternative is that we would have to harmonise absolutely everything: taxation, which is not on; even labour law, which may be an objective worth pursuing, but we have quite a number of labour standards already in Europe, some would say possibly too many. Collectively, we believe that these create enough of a level playing field but allow for differences in systems. There must be some competition of national systems in a healthy economic environment. If you want to have everybody starting from exactly the same position, then you lose the whole incentive of competition and you stifle innovation. This is simply not the solution. On health—again, this is a very broad indication—the idea was meant to signal that the provision of health services as such could be excluded. The

Commission has not said that it felt they had to be excluded. It is more a sign that, should the Parliament go in that direction, the Commission would probably go along. However, should the Parliament say that the health services ought to stay in the Directive—because there may be benefits in having this in the Directive rather than outside it—then I think that, again, the Commission would reflect very seriously and accept that they have to stay in. The other services are the much wider category of services of general interest, the publicly funded ones. The signal there is to say to Member States who are concerned, and who do not believe what is already said in the Directive, that nowhere does this Directive force Member States to open up to competition services that they have decided they want to keep within the public domain. It is not a privatisation Directive; it is not even a liberalisation Directive, I would say. It is a Directive that aims at facilitating the provision of services. It is an empowering Directive. It says that where services are provided on an economic basis, they should be allowed to be provided in a much freer legal environment than is the case today. Where Member States choose not to have these services provided on an economic basis, however, nowhere does the Directive force them to do so.

Q448 Lord Geddes: Can you give one or two instances of what you mean by that?
Mr Stoll: Local transport. In Member States, local transport can be very much in the hands of the public authority, local government. Nowhere does the Directive say that you would now have to open up the sector to purely economic activities. Of course, the health services are one very sensitive area. There is also the water supply. They are already taken out from the Country of Origin Principle in the present Directive. The Commission has signalled that it could even consider keeping them out completely from the scope of the Directive; in other words, also excluding them from the provisions on establishment. I think that this is aimed at answering the concerns that are voiced, in some Member States more than in others, about the degree to which services of general interest might be affected by this Directive. The third one was . . . ?

Q449 Lord Geddes: The third one was whether you could give us any specifics, when you mentioned the Country of Origin guarantee regarding uncertainties.
Mr Stoll: Where the Country of Origin applies, I think that it is fairly straightforward. It simply means that a company can only be subject to the legislation of its Member State of establishment and cannot be subjected to legislation in the country of destination. However, there are a number of exceptions: in fact, quite a number, 23 at present in the Article. The

question then arises what happens in those situations. What is the applicable law? In many situations, that applicable law will be determined by the so-called private international law rules of the Member State concerned, which in turn might also be subject to some harmonisation at Community level. There is work—

Q450 Chairman: May I interrupt you for a moment? Which situations are you talking about? Are you talking about the 23 derogated areas? You are saying what law applies there—is that what you are now talking about?
Mr Stoll: Yes, that is one area where there might be uncertainty. It is quite certain where the Country of Origin applies. That means it is the law of the country of establishment that applies. However, if we are in the situation of a derogation from the Country of Origin Principle, then the question arises what law does apply. In most cases, this will be determined by private international law instruments. Maybe this needs to be spelt out more clearly in the Directive. Another way of clarifying—but I am not sure whether this falls under the heading of clarification—is perhaps to add further derogations to the application of the Country of Origin Principle. There, of course, we will be confronted sooner or later with the question mark, "Have we reached a point where we are throwing away the baby with the bathwater?". I think that the Commission has deliberately not wanted to indicate where this threshold might be, but this will have to be thrashed out in the ongoing negotiations. Margot, is there anything else to add on this, on the clarification of the operation?
Dr Fröhlinger: No, but one should perhaps explain this. It may seem quite significant that we have 23 derogations from the Country of Origin Principle, but these derogations do not all apply at the same time. Many activities will come under no derogation or under only one derogation for one aspect of their activity. For instance, let us take a management consultancy firm established in the United Kingdom, or an IT consultancy firm established in the United Kingdom, wanting to provide services in Germany or in France, without having a permanent presence there. They would go through the list of derogations. They would say, "I am not a regulated profession. I do not need a specific professional qualification in these countries. I do not come under that derogation. I do not do consumer contracts. I do not come under that derogation. I do send employees, but there are no minimum working conditions for consultants. So I do not need to bother about the derogation for the posting of workers. At the end of the day, basically I do not need to bother. I just go across the Channel and I do business in France and Germany as I do in

the United Kingdom". However, the situation right now is that they could potentially be subject to many divergent rules in these countries. For instance, if they do marketing and advertising in Germany, they could come under rules in Germany where you cannot even send unsolicited mail or faxes to companies, because that is considered as being unfair competition. In France, if you are an environmental consultancy for instance, you may be subject to language requirements, or all sorts of requirements which you do not normally know about. So either you take very expensive legal advice about all the requirements which are potentially applicable to you, or you just cross the Channel and do your business, but the risk being on the one hand, prison, or on the other hand, appearing before a civil court in Germany, because a competitor may take you before a civil court on the grounds of unfair competition, just because you have sent faxes. The Country of Origin Principle is very important in that it provides this legal certainty to companies, except for cases where they can identify precisely defined derogations, where they have to comply with the laws in another country. They are on the safe side. There is legal certainty, and the legal complexity is very much reduced.

Q451 Chairman: On that theme, can you explain to us what a business which is operating under the Country of Origin Principle can do in a host Member State; not its Member State of origin? What can it do that is not bound by the rules and conditions applying in the host Member State? What can a business actually do? It has to abide by health and safety regulations; if it goes into Germany, there are all kinds of things about labour law, and so on; it has to meet other regulations. I am beginning to be a little puzzled as to quite what the advantages are—the so-called advantages—of Country of Origin. It appears as if it enables a company to say, "We are qualified to operate in your country, because we are already registered and so on. We are qualified to and nobody can stop us seeking it but, once we do offer services, we have to meet all the conditions of that Member State". Am I right? I am a bit puzzled by this.
Mr Stoll: It will depend on the sectors, of course. If you are working in the construction sector obviously you are providing the service for a couple of days, weeks, months possibly; and there the labour laws, the minimum wages and so on, of the country of destination will apply. However, the one big advantage is the legal certainty.

Q452 Chairman: Legal certainty to do what?
Mr Stoll: Knowing that—for instance, if you are in the construction sector—you will have to abide by the social laws in the country of destination. All the

steps that you are otherwise required to take in order to provide a service, or all the restrictions to which you are subjected in many Member States, you would know that they can no longer be opposed to you.

Q453 Chairman: You presented it to us at the start as being a great simplification for small companies. They do not have to check this or that. What you have told us, however, is that far from this being a blanket, "You can go and operate in another country as if you were in your own country", it is not that way at all. You have to find out what the labour laws are; you have to follow health and safety; you have to do all the checks that you would have had to do before. I am becoming a little puzzled, and I think the layman, the person who is not an expert in this, will begin to say, "Quite what are these freedoms?". The opponents of the Directive and Country of Origin Principle present this as if it is a *carte blanche* to do anything you want. You are presenting it as a great simplification, but "Don't worry, these businesses still have to abide by a lot of rules". The poor small and medium-sized businesses have to do all this checking. They have to check your list of thirty derogations—
Mr Stoll: Twenty-three.

Q454 Chairman: Twenty-three derogations; they have to look at all the labour laws, and so on. I have to say that this does not sound like a big, liberalising, freeing-up, simplifying of the marketplace to me. What is the reaction to that?
Dr Fröhlinger: They do not have to check the labour law in a systematic way. If they are in a sector, such as business-to-business services, consultancy, legal, accounting, et cetera, they do not have to bother about labour law. Minimum working conditions, which are covered by the Posting of Workers Directive, have to be accepted if they are minimum working conditions; but such minimum working conditions exist only for some blue-collar activities, such as the construction industry, which is the most important. If you are, as I said, a management consultancy firm or an IT consultancy firm, you do not have to bother about labour law in another country and you do not have to bother about health and safety, because you are not yourself causing a risk by providing your service. Your client may have to respect some health and safety legislation, but you yourself, as a consultancy firm, are not doing anything that will—

Q455 Chairman: It depends on what service you are offering? There must be some services where you have to meet health and safety conditions?

Dr Fröhlinger: Yes, of course there are services where you have to meet health and safety conditions. Certainly the construction sector is a sector where you have to meet safety conditions; health services are a sector where you have to meet health conditions. But if you are in the IT sector or if you are a real estate agent, for instance, you are not yourself subject to safety conditions. So there you can just go. Right now, you cannot. If you are a real estate agent established in the United Kingdom, you cannot operate nor can you advertise your services in a number of other Member States. In order to operate there, in order to advertise there, you need to be registered with local authorities and you have to comply with all the applicable advertising rules, et cetera.

Q456 *Chairman:* The agents, whoever they are—you say estate agents, for example—they could advertise, because that is what they can do in the Country of Origin?
Dr Fröhlinger: Yes.

Q457 *Chairman:* But a business that is based in that other Member State cannot advertise, because it is bound by the rules of their game?
Dr Fröhlinger: Yes.

Q458 *Chairman:* You may get some objection to that from the construction industry.
Dr Fröhlinger: That is where the objections come from.
Mr Stoll: But the Directive will also lead to reform in some over-regulated Member States. We have seen this happen on previous occasions.
Dr Fröhlinger: What you have to understand there is that that is already a principle on which the free movement of products is based today. We had the same objections with the free movement of products. For instance, it was a revolution in Germany when the European Court of Justice imposed that they had to allow the importation of beer from the United Kingdom, from Ireland and from France, which was not subject to the German law of purity. That is the whole system of the Common Market, that you have to allow for the free flow of products and services.
Mr Stoll: The single most important benefit of the Directive is to replace case-by-case clarification provided by court decisions by a set of rules which are known in advance. Of course there will be something of a learning curve. Every trader knows under which conditions it is operating today and under which conditions it will be allowed to operate under the Services Directive. A construction company will know full well that each time it goes on a building site in another Member State, there will have to be respect for the local worker; but consultants will

never ask the questions, because they will never be confronted with a similar situation.

Q459 *Chairman:* It is extremely interesting how many times construction is mentioned, which we will return to later. I suggest to you—although obviously you are, or somebody is, putting a lot more public relations effort into it—that you do need to get away from just talking about the construction industry all the time, because that is what the opponents are raising. There are a lot more services out there than construction and the more times you keep beating on that, it makes people think that that is the one issue. It is like taking on Real Madrid or playing Manchester United. Choose an easier team to take on!
Mr Stoll: There is a reason. Even big business—that supposedly should be fully supporting this—is rather lukewarm, because of the construction sector. If you talk to UNICE, they will say, "Yes, this is a pretty good idea, but what about the construction sector?". That is also where the protectionist element comes out more clearly.

Q460 *Lord Haskel:* In your opening remarks you said that you are seeking some guidance from public opinion. Does this mean that you are doing some polling? Do you have it in mind to try to persuade the public of the other side of it?
Mr Stoll: There are two questions there. One, are we receptive to what public opinion is expressing on this? I think the fact that the Commission has indicated a certain flexibility, at an unusual moment during the negotiation of such a Directive, is an indication that we take these concerns very seriously. That is what Commissioner McCreevy said very clearly. He was convinced that, in the present climate of discussion, the Directive would not fly, as he said. Nobody wants to take the chance of allowing for more time to go through the complexity to make sure that it is understood and accepted, because we have a number of difficult situations in Member States, a Referendum in France, for instance. If we are to lose everything because the Services Directive is a key object of discussion in the Referendum, then obviously we lose everywhere: we lose the constitution; we lose any hope of getting a Services Directive. In terms of what we have to do regarding more promotion; I think that it will be easier now that the Commission has indicated a willingness to allow compromises. We need to be able to explain more thoroughly what the Directive does and does not do. The difficulty is that not everybody is prepared to listen to the arguments; and that is because it is sometimes very convenient to use this proposal as a symbol of what has been labelled the neo-liberal approach of the Commission. This is forgetting of

course that, in that case, the Treaty of Rome was neo-liberal. It was simply based on sound competition, and not competition at any price. One does forget about the checks and balances that existed even in the Treaty of Rome. I have to admit that it is probably a confession we can make, that we have not always been good at explaining European integration to our citizens. However, this is not just the Services Directive; this is an issue at large. If I may say so, our Member States do not help us. I have not heard many Member States or ministers trying to explain, in fairly objective terms, what this is all about. I would mention a couple of press articles. The one article that I thought was the most honest, and the first such I have read in recent times, was an article in *Le Monde* last Friday, which signalled that this was all to do with the fears created by enlargement: have we decided on enlargement without knowing what we were doing?

Q461 Lord Haskel: Is it your intention to try to win hearts and minds? You did say that in the past it is something which you could have done rather better. Are you going to try to put it right on this occasion?
Mr Stoll: Yes. One example is that today the *Financial Times* draws on the experience of the last couple of days, including the economic analysis, and does quite a good job of it, that is, the *Financial Times*, not the Commission. However, we should be much more professional about it.
Chairman: I can confirm that this is the third time we have been told about that article today, so that is a triumph for publicity. So seldom in any of your literature, or that of the critics, is the customer mentioned. It is all in terms of the producers. It is all about producers, whether it is as workers' or as employers' vested interests. Whatever view one takes, this is trying to introduce competition. That means that some vested interests will lose out, as you rightly say. The consumer gets very little mention, I have to say, including in your introductory memorandum. It was noteworthy also in the economic work done. In fairness, your opponents rarely mention the consumer, except by implication, as a threat to them. A threat is because of the threat to the producer's interest, which is quite interesting.
Lord Haskel: It has not been made clear that the standards which consumers expect will in fact be maintained, as you explained to us before.

Q462 Chairman: It may or may not be. It is very interesting when harmonisation is talked about. I would put this to you as a question. People who propose alternatives to this speak of harmonisation. When you seek to understand what is meant by harmonisation, they actually mean harmonisation of standards of education, or the qualifications of

producers. They do not mean harmonisation of the output because, of course, that is monstrously difficult even to begin to conceptualise. There is this presumption that if only everybody had a degree before they did hairdressing, we would be full of superb hairdressers—extremely expensive hairdressers!—whereas you can be a very good hairdresser without having a degree. But there is this extraordinary—to the British mind, not elsewhere in Europe—concentration on issues of the producer. When you hear the word "harmonisation", and when people put forward an alternative, what do you think they mean? There is a paper by Mrs Gebhardt, who concludes her seven-page "think piece" by saying, "The Services Directive should . . . prepare the way for harmonisation or mutual recognition at a high level of quality". What do you think people in the European Parliament mean when they talk about harmonisation?
Mr Stoll: Not only people in the European Parliament. Some Member States, France in particular, have the same approach.

Q463 Chairman: Which is what?
Mr Stoll: That, before you allow mutual recognition and indeed free provision of services, you should have prior harmonisation.

Q464 Chairman: Of what?
Mr Stoll: That is the issue. What is important for the customer of a service is indeed to have some degree of certainty about the qualifications of the person who is providing the service. However, where qualifications differ too widely and where there is a need to ensure that you do not expose consumers to qualifications which are too wide-ranging, the Qualifications Directive which is about to be adopted in the Council and the Parliament will provide all the necessary safeguards. That is, either by having provided for harmonisation of the actual requirements before being able to perform a profession in another Member State or, where harmonisation of the content, the curriculum, is not deemed necessary, by making sure that where there is too big a difference in the training of professionals, the Member State can ask for compensatory measures; which are either a test or a traineeship, a probation period. The other important element, outside the qualification as such, is the quality of the service. Can you rely on the person who is providing the service? The Services Directive has one chapter, which I accept has gone very much unnoticed, which deals with the quality of the services and, in particular, the information about who will provide the service. It is unlike goods. For instance, lawnmowers have to have a maximum level of noise production. That can be fixed; that can be expressed

in decibels and then the engineers provide engines which do not exceed that particular amount of noise. Then you provide the harmonisation which makes sure that these lawnmowers can circulate. It is much more difficult to harmonise services. What do you harmonise in services? What you are interested in is the quality and reliability; and of course you do not want all service providers to be equal. You are looking for different types of service providers. The price will be an important element. If you have a tiler from across the border who can lay your tiles at a much cheaper price, many customers will be interested. Of course they will want to know whether this is somebody who is completely unknown in the Country of Origin or if there is some means of getting information on that particular company, for instance. That is where the administrative co-operation will be all-important, in order not to expose consumers to just any service provider coming from anywhere in the Union.

Dr Fröhlinger: You have to bear in mind that everyone who talks about the need for harmonisation is talking about something different. There are people—the trade unions and some Socialist Members of the European Parliament—talking about more harmonisation in the field of labour law and social security. That is what they are focusing on. Because they feel that the Commission is no longer proactive in this area they are taking the Services Directive hostage in order to put pressure on the Commission to come up with more proposals in the field of labour law and social security. However, there is also a discussion about harmonising the output. There is now the idea that for a number of services activities there should be quality standards, either harmonised by law or by standardisation, as we have done in the area of products. Everyone knows, however, that for many services standardisation cannot be the right thing. Standardisation would be too heavy, too costly, and anti-competitive. There are those who seriously consider that we should have harmonisation of output, in terms of harmonisation of quality standards and harmonisation of deontological rules for the liberal professions; others talk about more harmonisation regarding professional qualifications. So they are all talking about different things and, most of the time, they are not very specific. They are either saying that we need more harmonisation of labour law and social security—even talking about tax harmonisation—or they are talking about harmonisation of output, or they are talking about more harmonisation of professional qualifications. However, none of this is realistic. We therefore think that sometimes these requests for more harmonisation are also a means to hide a fundamental opposition to a freer movement of

services, because they know that it is not realistic, and they are just trying to bargain for time.

Q465 *Chairman:* Without wishing to be discourteous, I do think that on that issue you are losing the argument. We have heard all of that said. There is no rebuttal, no questioning, no challenging, clarification, and so on. A number of witnesses have given evidence before us and have said, "There is an alternative, namely harmonisation". You must know that it is being said. I have to say that it seems plausible, until you start to raise it. If you said this in the UK, and if it were suggested that Brussels was going to start laying down harmonised standards for travel agents, trade fairs, tour guides, leisure services, sports centres—and that this would be determined by the quality of the gymnasium equipment and that it had to be the same in every country—you only have to say it to know that, certainly in my country, there would be uproar. I would say to you that one does need to think proactively in a number of directions.
Mr Stoll: Some Member States like harmonisation very much, not regulation.

Q466 *Chairman:* But what most people mean is harmonisation to their standards. They really mean "our standards". Everyone thinks that their standards are the best!
Mr Stoll: It all boils down to the point I was making earlier about confidence. We accept that there are areas where you have too big a difference in Member States' legislations and that this can expose consumers. However, that analysis is not being done by those who ask for more harmonisation. They use it as a blanket pre-requirement and, as you say, it could be anything under the sun, including taxation. All the conditions being equal, then there is no harm in having your hair cut by an Estonian, a Frenchman, an Italian or a Maltese. Again, this is not feasible, not realistic, not desirable, because we would be over-regulating in many areas. It is not feasible because there would not be an agreement between 25 Member States about whose standards should be lowered and to what level. What level below your level is still acceptable for your consumers? There will not be a consensus among 25 Member States on where that average, acceptable-to-all, level is.
Chairman: Could we move on to the Mutual Assistance Framework?

Q467 *Lord Geddes:* Could I make that my second question, if I may? I want to ask whether in your consideration the Mutual Assistance Framework is workable, but perhaps I could put ahead of that congratulations to you—and I am not being facetious—that in one hour of oral evidence, we have not yet asked the very first question that we have always asked, namely what is your definition of "temporary"?

Dr Fröhlinger: We do not have a definition of "temporary", because—

Q468 Chairman: There are two issues. What is the significance of the use of the word, and then what do you mean by it?

Dr Fröhlinger: We do not use the term "temporary" in the legal text of the Directive to draw the distinction between freedom of establishment and the free movement of services. We have taken the opposite approach. We have defined what an establishment is; if you are an establishment then you are subject to the law of the country where you are established. Establishment is not a formal concept; it is a qualitative concept. As soon as you have a permanent infrastructure through which you carry out economic activity, then you are considered as being established, regardless of the legal form; regardless of whether this is just an office, a laboratory, a subsidiary, a branch, or whatever. By contrast, the free movement of services, where the service provider is in principle subject only to the law of his country of establishment, takes place where a service provider goes into another Member State to provide services without having a fixed and permanent infrastructure there. This has to be evaluated on a case-by-case basis, however. The Court of Justice has decided that service provision can take many months; it can be longer than a year. It is dependent on the individual case. In the past, we have tried to define what is temporary. In the Professional Qualifications Directive, we tried to define temporary as meaning 16 weeks. We have been told by everybody in the European Parliament that that is not possible, because you may have a permanent infrastructure and then from day one you are established, or you may have no infrastructure but you are working on a building site and the work takes 12 or 14 months, and this is still temporary, because you are not there permanently. Therefore, we have defined the concept of establishment, and everything which is service provision without an establishment, is considered as being free movement of services.

Lord Geddes: Could I now come to the Mutual Assistance Framework, which is clearly an integral part of the Country of Origin Principle. Is it workable?

Q469 Chairman: Your critics say not.

Dr Fröhlinger: Yes.

Mr Stoll: Partly because they are influenced by the people who say that it cannot work because they do not want to make it work. We are aware that this is a sea change; it is a major structural reform that has to take place in Member States' administrations. It is not just the sum of 25 national markets, but that they have a shared ownership, a shared responsibility for managing that internal market, all of them together. We are also aware that it will bring about a steep learning curve and a certain amount of investment, and change at the beginning. That is probably also an element that is frightening some Member States, who do not like accepting that they will have their administrations change the way they behave. As to the second element, why is it difficult? It is because administrations are not used to talking to each other. They are used to negotiating with each other when they meet in Brussels, but they are not used to co-operating when they sit in their respective offices. It is partly also because the underlying tools—the informatics tools, for instance—are very complex to build up. This is one area where I think that the Commission can be helpful. We have launched a pilot project—which was not devised as a pilot project for the Services Directive but rather to deal with the daily mis-applications of Community law—where we put in place and offered the IT infrastructure to help national administrations raise concrete problems that their users encounter, the SOLVIT network. I must say that we are quite surprised to see that it actually works. There have been about 700 cases so far. To take a concrete example, an architect who has a diploma in his Member State but is prevented from providing his architectural services in another Member State, despite the fact that the Directives are entirely clear that he should be allowed to do so. More often this is now put into the system; the two administrations talk to each other; they do this with a certain amount of good faith, and we have a success rate of about 70 per cent. Seven hundred cases may not sound much, but this has to be compared with about 800 infringements that we deal with on a yearly basis, which are from big and small companies in Member States. It is therefore not out of proportion to the difficulties encountered in the real world. Our idea is to try to convince Member States that by supplying some of the hardware or the IT instruments, we might take away from them some of the more material problems they will encounter; but there will have to be the psychological sea change in the mindset, accepting that it should be discussed. I think that the pressure will come from the Member States themselves. We have also witnessed this in the Qualifications Directive. It is the Member States who are now coming to us and saying, "The Directive says that we should co-operate, but how can we do this? Commission, could you help us to sort this out?", because they believe that this is the only way to make the Qualifications Directive work.

Dr Fröhlinger: I would like to add that, interestingly, the point about administrative co-operation and mutual assistance not working is not raised by

Member States; it is raised in the European Parliament and by vested interests. Member States in the Council accept that it will work, because they are willing to make it work. Our critics raise two issues. One is the willingness of Member States to make it work; the other is the feasibility. As far as the willingness is concerned, they say that Member States are not interested in controlling what a service provider does if he causes harm in other Member States. Member States are willing, under the Services Directive, to accept a legal obligation to do exactly that: to make sure that their service providers behave in a lawful way wherever they are providing services in Europe. In terms of this question about willingness, therefore, we think that it is just bad faith because Member States are themselves saying, "We are prepared to do that. We acknowledge that it is necessary to do that". The second issue is that of feasibility. That is of course a serious concern because, under the Directive, a municipality, let us say in the south of Bavaria, may have to communicate with an authority in Spain or in the United Kingdom. However, we think that these practical difficulties can be overcome by software-based technological systems, as mentioned by Mr Stoll, which are already in place for SOLVIT. We are working at the request of Member States, drawing up a pilot project where, by giving the alleged location and the alleged activity of the company, you have the competent authority and then you can communicate directly with the competent authority. There will be standardised questions, available in all languages. Even if another language is used, they will be able to understand your request. They can use their own language to fill in the replies, but there is free automatic translation of text. Where automatic translation is not workable, for instance, between some of the languages of our new Member States and old Member States, we will have to provide for some sort of related translation service. However, we think that these practical difficulties can be overcome.

Q470 Lord Fearn: What are the daily infringements that you have mentioned, of which you are getting so many?

Mr Stoll: We handle about 800 infringements, most of them based on complaints. Not all of them, but some we launch ourselves. This is an indication that even where there is *acquis communautaire*, where there are Directives in place, Member States do not always transpose it. I think that the application problem can be brought under control. The SOLVIT system deals only with application. The law is perfectly in line with Community law, but it is daily application by administrations. There is also

training to be done, of course. The greatest problem we have, however, is when Member States do not transpose on time or when they transpose Directives erroneously. That is where we either have to persuade them to transpose in time, transpose correctly, or else take them to court, which is not our preferred option. We try to solve the problems without having to go all the way to the court.

Q471 Chairman: Can I raise one thing arising from this particular theme of mutual assistance? Does this mean that, for this to work, each Member State has to collect quite a bit of information on all small and medium-sized enterprises in its country, just in case they ever want to offer a service abroad? There is a concern among the small businesses in the UK that they may get caught up in having to provide information, get involved in checks and so on, and have no intention of operating in any other Member State. If you do not, how does a Member State mutual assistance agency—whatever it is called—know that an SME is temporarily offering a service abroad? Say a hairdresser or a dentist goes abroad—let us get away from construction for a change—how does a Member State government know that? After all, this is supposed to be freeing things up. I am trying to understand this. Is this a bureaucracy waiting to break out? That is a serious question because, for it to be efficient, you have to have information. It is no good having information too late; the only way to have information is in a timely way. To your mind, how will this work? This looks to me like a state register of operations of every small and medium-sized business in the country. You are not just being asked about whether it is registered in some way, which in Britain really means for VAT and for tax. In a lot of businesses you have no idea what they do, frankly, if they are not a limited company. All you have is a statement of what they do, is it a partnership or whatever. What is it in the United Kingdom that this agency is going to collect by way of information?

Mr Stoll: First of all, I do not think that there should be *a priori* registration for all companies. There should be some discretion left to companies as to whether they even want to consider being active outside the borders of the UK. The second element is that in many cases—and again we have the benefit of the discussions in relation to the professional qualifications Directive—it is quite clear that the putting into operation of the system will be primed by the country where the service is being provided. It will say, "We have a possible suspicion or doubt about a certain service provider", because, for instance, there have been complaints by customers, "and we would like to ensure that this service provider is registered, is fully compliant with the regulations of the Country of Origin". I think that it should not be a systematic imposition of requirements on all operators, whether they are active in trans-border services or not.

Q472 *Chairman:* I have to say to you that that sounds to me an exceedingly weak thing, if a small business is still determined to get away with it. Say it is an amusement park, a sports centre, a tour guide, or whatever, and somebody in France complains that a British two-person business has offered some services and they did not do it very well, and somebody calls your agency—with whatever name it is going to be given—saying, "We didn't get a very good service from this business and we want to complain about it". I am trying to understand how it will work. A real concern was expressed to us by representatives of small business that all small businesses will be asked to register with something, and they do not have to do that currently.
Mr Stoll: You do not do it nationally. You may have similar difficulties. Not all the services provide the sort of quality service that you might expect.
Dr Fröhlinger: Nobody needs to collect data about companies in a systematic way. What will happen here is, for instance, if in Italy—where they are particularly keen to stop and arrest tour guides from other Member States—they come across a tour guide from another Member State and the tour guide says, "I am a British tour guide; I have been legally working in the United Kingdom for a number of years, and that is my business", and if the Italian authorities have doubts about whether this is really a tour guide established in the United Kingdom and whether he is carrying out activities from the United Kingdom, or whether this is just a circumvention of Italian law and in reality he is permanently in Italy, the Italian authorities can go to the competent UK authority in relation to this tour guide, and ask them, "Is this tour guide really established in the UK and does he legally carry out his activities there?"; and if employed persons are involved, "Are these employees registered in the United Kingdom?". They can ask these types of questions. However, they can ask these questions only if they come across somebody who supplies a service in Italy, where they have doubts about whether this is really a tour guide from the United Kingdom and whether it is someone who is legally carrying out his activities.

Q473 *Chairman:* I must say that it seems to me this has all the makings of a gargantuan monster that will grow, because it will inexorably lead to different authorities wanting more information. Thinking about the UK, the UK has a very flexible, very often unregulated, business environment. I use my example deliberately because it does not raise a number of

issues, but if you wanted information you are likely to be told, "It is registered for VAT", or it may not be, as a small business, "It is registered with the Inland Revenue", and that is all we could tell you. Then there will be pressure from people who bother about this in some Member States, "We don't think that you keep very much information about tour guides. We think that you should keep more". My observation from the Chair on our side is that this is either very weak—it sounds good but it is not very effective, which the critics would say—or, in order to become effective, it will seek to collect a lot of information about businesses on which it does not need any information at all, but it needs it just in case, or it will seek to collect more information, certainly in the UK. You do not think that?
Mr Bergevin: The key thing to know is that the company is registered in that Member State.

Q474 *Chairman:* The business.
Mr Bergevin: That the business is actually registered in the United Kingdom. In the same way as if you had an operator coming into the UK who says he is French and is acting in a questionable manner, the key issue is to know that he is actually registered in France. I think that is the key requirement. The other thing relates to information. I cannot speak for the UK but I would suspect that in the UK—for example if there are trading standards officers who stop somebody acting, and I am not referring to the building trade—but let us say a trader in Scotland, and that company is established in the south of England, there is a way by which you can enforce—

Q475 *Chairman:* I knew that you would come back to building!
Mr Bergevin: Let us say an accountant. The other important issue is that companies themselves—and this is interesting in terms of what you were saying about SME companies or whatever—in order to develop business, will themselves seek to give themselves either quality marks, or be involved in different quality marks or, more importantly, will be registered with a chamber of commerce. If they are not going beyond their local market, I would agree with you. Generally speaking, however, just the fact that you can know and you have to know that the company is registered in order to enforce law on it, that is the key issue.

Q476 *Chairman:* I press this because this issue is presented as the way in which you seek to reassure politicians, trade unionists, consumer groups, that the Country of Origin Principle can work. This is supposed to reassure; it is providing reassurance about quality, about reliability and so on. The information we collect in the United Kingdom might tell you nothing about the quality of their services or their reliability as service providers. It simply would not give you that information. You said at the start, if I may paraphrase "We have to get the Mutual Assistance Framework right because, if we get that right, it will reassure people when we go ahead with the Country of Origin Principle". In relation to the UK, I am not sure whether you would have a framework that gives you that. I am sorry to say that, but we must be frank about this. If that is put up, you will find that the searchlight will go on this. If there is this reassurance, the thing that says, "The Country of Origin Principle can work and this is the thing that will make it work", the searchlight will come on to this. After all, some critics of the Commission have said, "It's very ambitious. This thing wasn't sold very well and it was all put out into the domain when it came out. There is a lot here to swallow. The Country of Origin Principle is a big issue and it wasn't sold with sufficient care in advance", and perhaps the mutual assistance one could backfire on you too?

Mr Stoll: Underlying all of this debate is something that comes back to one of your initial questions: do we have an alternative? Harmonising is not an alternative. The other alternative, which we have not mentioned, is to continue as we do today, with infringements. We will continue to have court decisions, which may go much further than what the Commission is proposing, which has some benefits and some disadvantages. It is good for the service provider who happens to be the source of that particular court decision, because he will have a clear statement that, yes, he is entitled to provide his services and, no, Member States are not entitled under certain conditions—very restrictively dictated by the courts—to prevent him from providing that service. However, that would only be good for that particular Member State, and would have to be repeated. I must emphasise that it is not just the Commission; it is not just that we bring cases before the court. The national courts refer matters to the European Court of Justice. Again, that is not satisfactory from the point of view which is our starting point, namely, how can we make sure that the level of provision of services is generally made easier? It will not come free. It will not be entirely free on the part of Member States, for instance. There will have to be some initial investments, in psychology, mindset, and probably in infrastructure. At the end of the day, however, you will have to make a calculation whether this is the one-off investment which has to be made, in order to ensure that your service providers can provide these services without

too much impediment, or certainly fewer impediments than they confront today.

Q477 *Lord Geddes:* How do you see the timetable?
Mr Stoll: We expect the Parliament to provide its opinion either before the summer, although that may be optimistic, but I understand that there is work going on by Mrs Gebhardt; have you met her?

Q478 *Lord Geddes:* Yes.
Mr Stoll: The indication we have is that she may produce a first report by the end of this month, but I do not think that will be the one which will lead to the adoption of the Parliament's opinion. So it will be either before the summer or immediately after the summer. I suspect that the Council will aim for the same sort of timetable. We will not agree this at First Reading, so we will be looking for a Second Reading, possibly starting under the UK presidency. Then very much will depend on whether the climate has eased a little and whether we can expect adoption in the normal 18 months to two years that we usually take to negotiate this.

Q479 *Chairman:* Clearly, as with any group of people from a Parliament, there are subtle differences in how we see things; but you will know that in general terms we are, in the United Kingdom, very much in favour of the Directive and we are very much in favour of the Country of Origin Principle. Certainly my remarks were in no way other than to make sure that the case is robust. We have flexible markets, a light touch on regulation, because we believe in letting the consumer and the market take a decision. Occasionally in life, people buy the wrong product from the wrong person—whether it is a washing machine or a service—and we cannot run people's lives by regulation, and so on. This has been enormously helpful to us. We will keep the closest of interest in it, and we will try to report probably during the course of July, perhaps at the end of June. Your advice today will be one of the important parts of the evidence that we have taken. Thank you very much indeed.
Mr Stoll: My Lord Chairman, I wish to thank you for the interest shown and also for your very kind remarks. I must say that I was not expecting to hear such kindness, but I take them seriously and I am very grateful for them, because they are absolutely to the point. The United Kingdom stands to benefit a lot from this Directive, but I think that you are also aware that some of the fears which have been expressed in some Member States relate to Member States which are less regulated than others.

MONDAY 21 MARCH 2005

Present	Cohen of Pimlico, B	Haskel, L
	Eccles of Moulton, B	St John of Bletso, L
	Fearn, L	Walpole, L
	Geddes, L	Woolmer of Leeds (Chairman)

Memorandum by the Department of Trade and Industry (DTI)

A. The Current State of the Single Market in Services

ARE THERE SIGNIFICANT BARRIERS TO FIRMS SEEKING TO OFFER THEIR SERVICES IN OTHER MEMBER STATES OF THE EUROPEAN UNION? IF SO, WHAT ARE THE MOST IMPORTANT OF THOSE BARRIERS? WHAT MEASURES ARE NEEDED TO OVERCOME THOSE BARRIERS? DOES THE COMMISSION'S PROPOSED DIRECTIVE ADEQUATELY ADDRESS THOSE ISSUES?

The analysis in our Regulatory Impact Assessment (RIA) provides evidence that there are many barriers that are holding back cross-border trade in services in the European Union. Whilst accounting for 71 per cent of Gross Value Added (GVA) in the United Kingdom economy in 2002, services only accounted for 32 per cent of total exports and 23 per cent of total imports. In an economy like the United Kingdom where the service sector is important to continuing economic success, a more liberal European Union regulatory regime for services has to be a welcome goal.

The Lisbon European Council 2000 adopted an economic reform programme with the aim of making the European Union the most competitive and dynamic knowledge-based economy in the world by 2010. A key part of the programme is to make the Internal Market a reality for services. As a result the Commission undertook a large-scale survey that involved the European Institutions, Member States and other interested parties. The Commission published its report, *"The State of the Internal Market for Services"* (*not printed*), in July 2002.

The report identified 91 different barriers to trade in services. Amongst the more important barriers were the often complicated and lengthy licensing and authorisation procedures that businesses seeking to provide services in another Member State are required to complete. These procedures often require multiple visits to the Member State with no guarantee of a positive result. Another problem is the heterogeneity of regulation: where different countries have slightly different procedures all meeting the same objective. The resulting costs often deter small business from trading across borders or establishing in another Member State. (Commission document: practical examples) (*not printed*).

DTI believes these barriers can only be overcome by the removal of disproportionate and discriminatory legislation (thereby enshrining the principles of Article 43 TEC on the Freedom of Establishment into Member States' national legislation), and in order to deliver the free movement of services promised in Article 48 TEC by allowing businesses to provide cross-border services temporarily (or remotely) on the basis of their home state rules (with certain important exceptions). This Country of Origin Principle will reduce the burden of having to comply 25 times over with different sets of regulations designed to achieve the same purpose, an administrative burden that is particularly difficult for small enterprises.

Looking first at the issue of "Establishment", the reduction in the costs and time associated with establishing a business in another European Union country is tackled in the Directive by the requirement on Member States to review all authorisations associated with the operation of a service and remove those authorisations that are discriminatory, cannot be objectively justified or where the objective can be attained by less restrictive means. The Directive also requires Member States to streamline their processes for granting authorisations and make information about them more accessible.

This will be of particular benefit for small business who have fewer resources to devote to lengthy negotiations with competent authorities. Although the exact form of the proposed "Single Points of Contact" (SpoC) has yet to be fleshed out, they will provide easy and convenient access, at a single point, to all the information a business requires to operate in that Member State. The requirement to make all procedures and formalities relating to the exercise of a service activity easily available at a distance and by electronic means will further reduce the administrative burden.

The resulting reduction in bureaucracy fits well with our Better Regulation agenda and will have the extra benefit of reducing red tape for United Kingdom service providers who trade only at home.

Secondly, as regards provision of services without being established, the application of the Country of Origin Principle (CoOP) will provide business and other providers with a means of "testing the water" in a new market on a temporary basis. The costs associated with establishment are often prohibitive for small businesses who might otherwise expand if they could do so under the law of their state of establishment.

The United Kingdom Government agree with the Commission that their proposal would remove many of the barriers to cross-border service provision and make progress in the direction of achieving the Lisbon goals. However, there are a number of aspects of the Directive that we would like to see changed and details of these have already been submitted to the Committee as part of the response to the public consultation.

B. THE COUNTRY OF ORIGIN PRINCIPLE
IS THE PRINCIPLE THAT A COMPANY REGISTERED TO PROVIDE SERVICES IN ONE COUNTRY IS AUTOMATICALLY QUALIFIED TO PROVIDE THOSE SERVICES IN ANY COMMUNITY COUNTRY ON THE BASIS OF HOME COUNTRY REGULATION A REASONABLE AND/OR REALISTIC STARTING POINT? WHAT SIGNIFICANT BENEFITS TO BUSINESS AND CONSUMERS ARE LIKELY TO OCCUR AS A RESULT OF THE ADOPTION OF THE COUNTRY OF ORIGIN PRINCIPLE? IS THE PRINCIPLE WORKABLE IN PRACTICE?

The Country of Origin Principle (CoOP) is a principle originally developed by the European Court of Justice (ECJ) to give effect to the free movement of goods in cases like Cassis de Dijon[1]. More recently it has been used in other European Union legislation such as the television without frontiers Directive and the E-commerce Directive, but the provision in Article 16 of the Services Directive to facilitate free movement of services is the most ambitious use of the principle by the Commission to date.

The Commission has chosen this route because it wants to see a speedy reduction in regulatory barriers to trade in services, and because Member States are committed, by the Lisbon Agenda, to creating a properly functioning Internal Market for services. Continued sector by sector harmonisation is an unattractive alternative: first it would take many years, perhaps decades to achieve; and second, harmonisation of standards across a huge range of services is neither necessary nor appropriate. Provided key issues such as health and safety and protection of the public, workers and the environment are secured, and standards across the European Union are broadly compatible, the consumer should be able to choose the standard of service s/he wants. An alternative would be to leave things as they are and continue to let the Commission pursue breaches of the Internal Market using the existing and future case law of the Court. However, the very reason that a Directive on services has been deemed necessary is that this approach has not had the desired effect and is both hugely time-consuming and costly.

Given that much of the essential legislation that protects United Kingdom citizens and consumers is already harmonised at European Union level, we think the CoOP is a realistic starting point for delivering the free movement of services. There is widespread recognition that the derogations from the principle need further negotiation and the United Kingdom has stated its intention to seek changes to the Directive in its response to the public consultation.

The consumer will benefit from a greater choice of service providers and the likely increase in service quality and reduction in price that increased competition brings.

CoOP will also provide an opportunity for businesses, especially Small and Medium sized Enterprises (SMEs), to assess market demand for their service in another Member State through temporary service provision and without having to go to the expense of becoming permanently established in that country.

WILL THE APPLICATION OF THE COUNTRY OF ORIGIN PRINCIPLE MOVE BUSINESS IN FAVOUR OF FIRMS BASED IN MEMBERS STATES WITH THE LEAST STRINGENT REGULATORY REGIMES? WHAT ISSUES DOES THIS RAISE FOR BUSINESSES AND CONSUMERS? HOW MIGHT THESE ISSUES BE RESOLVED?

Much of the legislation that protects European Union citizens either as employees or as consumers is already harmonised to one level or another within the Community. Consequently, service providers will be bound by this legislation regardless of which Member State they are established in [under CoOP it is the country of establishment that determines the applicable law]. Those Member States who have recently joined the

[1] The case referred to as Cassis de Dijon (Case C-120/78) concerned an importer of the French fruit liqueur into Germany. Germany had a law that such drinks had to have a *minimum* alcoholic strength of 25 per cent, the French liquor has around 15 per cent. The Court ruled that the German law was a measure having equivalent effect to a quantities restriction on imports. It did not accept that there was a general interest ground justifying the German rule. The effect of the ruling was that products lawfully marketed and produced in one Member State should generally be permitted to be marketed in all other Member States.

European Union are committed to implementing all current European Union legislation. All Member States have an interest in maintaining high standards of domestic legislation to protect their own consumers and workers and there is little prospect of a race to reduce standards amongst Member States.

In order to protect against companies "brass plating" themselves in states at the lower end of the European Union spectrum of national regulation, the Directive makes it clear that it will not be sufficient for a business to register a "post box" in one Member State to qualify as established there. Businesses must be carrying out genuine economic activity in the Member State in question. The United Kingdom would not want to see companies abuse the fundamental freedoms in the EC Treaty and we are looking at the practicality of introducing, in the Recitals, a provision on the "evasion of home country legislation". This would stop service providers from setting up in another Member State with the primary objective of offering services back to their home Member State thereby avoiding home Member State legislation. A similar Recital is included in the E-commerce Directive.

Chapter IV of the Directive (Quality of Services) requires Member States to ensure that service providers give clear and unambiguous information about themselves and the service they provide. Recipients of services will have to be provided with specified information by service providers, including contact details, details of the supervising competent authority or professional body, legal status, contractual clauses and details of dispute resolution procedures and the law applicable to the contract. Consumers are further protected by Article 17(21) that provides for a derogation from the CoOP for "contracts concluded by consumers to the extent that the provisions governing them are not completely harmonised at Community level." The United Kingdom wants to see the qualification about harmonisation removed so that all contracts concluded by consumers are derogated.

This Directive recognises the need to open up the Internal Market for services whilst maintaining adequate protections for European Union citizens. With the exception of areas where we will seek to negotiate changes to the text, the Directive strikes a good balance between the needs of business and the consumer.

THE APPLICATION OF THE PRINCIPLE RELIES ON THE DEVELOPMENT OF AN EXTENSIVE MUTUAL ASSISTANCE FRAMEWORK, WHEREBY MEMBER STATES COOPERATE IN SUPERVISING ENTERPRISES BASED IN THEIR COUNTRY IN RESPECT OF THEIR OPERATIONS IN OTHER COUNTRIES. IS THIS A WORKABLE FRAMEWORK?

This Directive is strongly linked to the Lisbon Agenda and achieving its goals will require a massive effort from Member States. There is no doubt that some provisions like those outlined in Chapter V (Supervision) on mutual assistance will pose a challenge to Member States. However, if Member States are serious about achieving the Lisbon target then they will have to find ways to make provisions like this work.

The framework outlined in Chapter V (Article 35) is a sensible basis on which to negotiate although we are still at the beginning of this process. Whilst difficult, it is not beyond Member States to achieve a workable solution to the issue of mutual assistance.

The SOLVIT network that currently works to resolve problems with the Internal Market for goods has proved to be a successful example of how Member States can cooperate when faced with difficult issues.

WHAT OTHER SIGNIFICANT CONCERNS ARE THERE REGARDING THE PRACTICAL IMPLEMENTATION OF THE COUNTRY OF ORIGIN PRINCIPLE AND HOW MIGHT THESE BE ADDRESSED?

The United Kingdom has identified in its response to the Public Consultation several areas of concern. These include the relationship between the Services Directive and Private International Law and United Kingdom criminal law, the potential impact on health and safety legislation and the protection of animals.

DTI is cooperating closely with other Government departments and stakeholders and will seek to ensure that essential changes are made to the text of the Directive to ensure United Kingdom concerns are met. Negotiations are at a very early stage.

ASSUMING EFFICIENT OPERATION OF THE COUNTRY OF ORIGIN PRINCIPLE, WHAT SIGNIFICANT BARRIERS TO TRADING IN OTHER MEMBER STATES ARE LIKELY TO REMAIN, SO FAR AS FIRMS IN THE RELEVANT BUSINESS SECTORS ARE CONCERNED?

Whilst acting as a significant deterrent to cross border trade in services, the barriers tackled by the CoOP are not the only ones holding back the development of the Internal Market for services. Some barriers such as culture, language and, for some services, the requirement of physical proximity between service provider and recipient (co-location) will remain and cannot be tackled by European Union legislation. The full economic benefits of the CoOP will take time to be realised as consumers become more confident in the procedures Member States establish to properly supervise service providers and business becomes more comfortable with the new and less burdensome regulatory regime.

It is important to remember that this Directive is about much more than just the CoOP. Some services simply cannot be provided on a temporary basis or at a distance; the provisions that remove barriers to establishment will have a significant impact on the burden of regulation faced by both businesses who export services and businesses who trade domestically.

C. THE FUTURE

DO YOU EXPECT THE IMPLEMENTATION OF THE COMMISSION'S PROPOSED DIRECTIVE TO HAVE A SIGNIFICANT IMPACT UPON TRADE IN THE SERVICES SECTOR WITHIN THE EUROPEAN UNION? IN WHICH SERVICE INDUSTRIES DO YOU EXPECT THE LEAST AND THE LARGEST MOVEMENT TOWARDS A EUROPEAN UNION SINGLE MARKET IN THE NEXT FIVE TO 10 YEARS?

The level of services traded domestically is very much higher than that traded across European Union borders and there are currently a significant number of barriers to the free movement of services. Services account for over 70 per cent of GDP and employment in most Member States. However, trade in services is currently relatively low accounting for only 20 per cent of total trade within the European Union. This cross-cutting framework Directive will impact on all service industries that are not specifically excluded. Perhaps the greatest impact will be on those services that are easiest to export, for example IT and business services.

Data on the service industries is not easy to come by. To make a better assessment of sectoral impacts we need to build on the economic analysis of the effects of the Directive carried out for the Regulatory Impact Assessment. To this end we are looking again at the main barriers to cross-border trade facing United Kingdom service providers and evaluating the extent to which these barriers would be reduced by the Commission's proposals. We are referring to the OECD International Regulation Database that contains detailed information on sector-specific regulation in different countries and will be making use of the evidence we gather from the case studies we have commissioned on the barriers faced by United Kingdom firms in the construction and business services sectors. We hope to present the results of our findings around May.

The next stage of our analysis will be to try to estimate the potential economic effects of the Commission's proposals and service sector liberalisation more generally on the European Union and Member States—for instance, the impact on output, employment, prices, trade and investment. We are discussing possible ideas with academics and professional economists and hope to commission some analysis in February. We would look to report the findings of this analysis in late spring.

Accurate estimation of the effects of the Directive is hampered by insufficient data and a lack of suitable economic models. However, several other Member States are also making encouraging progress. The Dutch, Irish and the European Commission have focused on trying to quantify the economic benefits of the Commission's proposals by developing and running their own economic models, whilst Germany has commissioned case studies to explore the potential impact on the German services providers. The Dutch have published their work and the others are expected to present the results of their analyses over the next few months.

Despite the practical difficulties that will need to be overcome, the proposed Services Directive will, on the basis of past experience from the Single Market Programme for goods and liberalisation of the European Union's network industries, have the potential to deliver significant economic benefits to the European Union's economy and its citizens. (See recent DTI/FCO/HMT paper on *The Proposed Directive on Services in the Internal Market: what are the benefits?* (*not printed*).

February 2005

Examination of Witnesses

Witnesses: MR DOUGLAS ALEXANDER, a Member of the House of Commons, Minister of State for Trade and Investment and Foreign Affairs, MR PAUL BAKER, Lawyer, MR TIM HOGAN, Economist, DR FIONA HARRISON and MR HEINZ KESSEL, Services Directive Team, Department of Trade and Industry, examined.

Q480 *Chairman:* Good afternoon, Minister, and your colleagues. Can I give you a very warm welcome to Sub-Committee B. I think it is the first time that we have met with you. Thank you for kindly agreeing to meet us for longer than originally anticipated. This is entirely because we recognise that this is an important issue, and I know you have the same view. We thought it very important to ensure that it was fully aired at this stage in this House. Minister, I think you would like to make an introductory statement.

Mr Alexander: Thank you very much indeed. I am grateful for the opportunity to address the Committee. Whether it was an error of judgment on my part to accept the invitation to answer questions for another 45 minutes, only time will tell; but I was very happy to do so. With your kind permission, I will make a brief introductory statement setting out the Government's view of the Draft Services Directive, but before doing so, can I introduce my colleagues? On my extreme left is Heinz Kessel, chief negotiator for the UK and the Council working group; on my immediate left is Fiona Harrison who, like Heinz Kessel, is the policy lead within the DTI team, working with and co-ordinating this Directive. On my immediate right I have Paul Baker, legal advisor on this Directive, and Tim Hogan on my far right who is responsible for economic advice in relation to this Directive. There may be various technical issues when I will call on the advice and support of officials to ensure that not just the issues but also the thinking of the officials is shared with the Committee today. Clearly, I have had the opportunity to see the unamended transcripts of the witnesses that have been before the Committee already on this matter, and it is already a matter of record that services account for 70 per cent of the EU's GDP and employment. While that is the case, they only represent 20 per cent of services and trade between EU Member States. A large part of the reason for this, we believe in Government, is that there are simply too many barriers in the way to effective trade and services. Existing case law of the European Court of Justice contains many such examples of those barriers. Service providers, both large and small, bear unnecessary costs and face unnecessary obstacles, and recipients get less choice and less quality and increased prices as a result. The Services Directive aims to eliminate barriers to establishment by applying better regulation principles and facilitating the free movement of services by allowing operators to provide a temporary service in another Member State under

the Country of Origin Principle. A recent study, again already discussed before this Committee, by the Copenhagen Economics Institute estimates that the sum of economic benefits to consumers and producers would rise by some £26 billion, create at least 600,000 new jobs; and there would be productivity improvements which would lead to an increase in real wages and a fall in the price of services across the European Union. The Government's position therefore is one of strong support for the Directive's market opening objectives, in particular its provisions for Member States to simplify their administrative procedures and the Country of Origin Principle. We seek to maximise the benefits of the Directive but we do have important concerns, which are shared by other Member States and their domestic stakeholders that need to be addressed in the Directive. For instance, we want to look again at the scope of the Directive. We believe that tax, publicly-funded healthcare and occupational pensions should not be governed by this instrument. We will also seek necessary sectoral exclusions for water, where our liberalised regime would otherwise be disadvantaged against operators from much less open or state-dominated European Union Member States without any obvious benefit to UK operators abroad; and gas and electricity, where there is a very recent liberalising piece of legislation. We also need to look carefully at the Country of Origin Principle and we must ensure that this does not compromise our high standards of protection for the environment, health and safety, workers, animals and vulnerable people in our society. However, in order to reap the benefits of the Directive we must ensure that the right balance between the market opening potential of the Country of Origin Principle and legitimate levels of protection is struck. Equally, we must ensure that we retain the right to apply UK criminal law in areas that are not specifically related to regulating service activities. The Country of Origin Principle should not apply to criminal law, which is not specifically linked to access or to the exercise of the service activity. We recognise that a lot of work still needs to be done on the practical implications of mutual assistance, and we continue to work closely with the domestic stakeholders, the European Union and other Member States, to find workable solutions that do not lead to additional burdens to business. In conclusion, My Lord Chairman, the Services Directive has great potential to provide a significant contribution to growth, competitiveness and indeed employment within the European Union. There are of course areas where the Directive in its current form would require further work in/order to provide the expected benefits without compromising on essential protections.

Q481 *Chairman:* Thank you, Minister, for that helpful introduction. How important do you believe it is for the European Union to achieve a single market in services speedily and by 2010 at the latest? *Mr Alexander:* I do think it is important, and that is clearly the view of the Government. Let me try and offer you some statistical evidence in support of that. Clearly, in order to make the European Union the most competitive and dynamic economy in the world by 2010—the Lisbon objectives—it is vital that we create a true internal market for services. The recent study conducted by the Association of European Chambers of Commerce and Industry highlights the scale of the gap in economic performance presently between the European Union and the United States. It suggests that the European Union will take decades to catch up with US levels of employment, income and productivity, and only then if growth consistently outstrips that of the United States by 0.45 per cent per annum. Services clearly are an immediate driver of growth and job creation and have been for over two decades, and now account for over 70 per cent of EU GDP. However, cross-border trade in services, as I reflected in my introductory remarks, only accounts for 20 per cent. We therefore believe that services form a very significant contribution to the pursuit and achievement for the Lisbon objectives. Since 1992 intra-European trade in goods—and this is an interesting comparison—has increased by a third, and added 1.8 per cent to EU GDP, worth around £300 per person within the United Kingdom. About 2.5 million jobs have been created across the European Union as a result of the opening up of the markets for goods. If gains of anywhere near this scale could be realised in the service sector through the opening up of European trading services, I believe the effect would also be significant. Again, the Copenhagen Economics Institute study, which has been a matter of some discussion before the Committee, estimates that the sum of economic benefits to consumers and producers would rise to some £26 billion and at least 600,000 new jobs across the European Union. These results, it could be argued, should be seen as the lower estimates of the potential impact on the European Union and indeed on individual Member States, because the study only covers two-thirds of the sectors covered by the proposed Directive and does not incorporate the long-term effects of the proposed Directive itself. A fuller study would potentially show significant additional benefits. In conclusion, a reduction in the barriers to trade and services would mean a more competitive service sector that we believe would lead to increased productivity, more choice and lower prices, and increased investment in R&D and job-creation across the European Union.

Q482 *Chairman:* You faithfully and vigorously put the UK case. Without for the moment commenting on the merits or de-merits of different views, we formed the strong impression that in France there is no desire to have anything to do with this Directive, certainly not this side of their Referendum. The Germans probably want to put it back even further, past next year's elections in Germany. How on earth can this Directive get approved and agreed in time to take effect and have single market services by 2010? The question was, do you think it is important to achieve it speedily by 2010 at the latest? Are not the forces of dragging feet a lot stronger than those that want to go forward? *Mr Alexander:* I am fairly aware of the recent commentary that has been covered, not least in our own newspapers, as to the respective positions being adopted both in France and in Germany. You will appreciate that my responsibility today is to represent the views of the British Government. Increasingly, in a European Union of 25, there is often a wide range of views expressed on individual Directives. The robustness of the case that I seek to advance today reflects our own conviction about the scale of the contribution that further movement in the area of intra-Union services trade could make. I am cognisant of the fact that there will be other Member States that take given views; but given the range of work that has to be taken forward, not in relation to just this Directive but over the months to come on issues like the financial perspective, structural funds and other matters for which I have responsibility, I would be pre-judging the discussions that have yet to take place. In addition, avoiding straying into the domestic politics of our European Union partners in France and in Germany, one of the merits of this Committee's investigation is to be able to examine some of the detail and some of the facts underlying some of the perceptions that have developed around this Directive. That affords the opportunity this afternoon for us to set out, hopefully with clarity and some rigour, the basis on which the British Government has reached its position, although I am very respectful of the point that you make, that it is a negotiating position for the British Government, and we cannot pre-judge the outcome of those negotiations or indeed the time-scale by which those negotiations will be concluded.

Q483 *Lord Haskel:* Accepting that you want to see the free movement of services throughout the Member States, what changes do you think are important to be made in order to secure this free movement?

Mr Alexander: As I sought to reflect in my introductory remarks, we are firmly of the view that there are a number of significant barriers, as identified in the European Commission's own survey of 2002 that hamper present free movement of services, as enshrined in the European Union Treaty. In some instances, for example, operators are effectively prevented from providing the temporary services by the department for permanent authorisation to provide services within another Member State. One of the reasons that we are of the view that these changes need to be made is the particular impact on small and medium size enterprises. It is often the case that, notwithstanding the scale of the barriers faced to trade and services within the European market place, larger companies are better able to overcome those barriers. If you recognise that up to 90 per cent of service providers are themselves SMEs, if we are serious about ensuring that there is a much wider opportunity for services to be triggered across the European Union, our concern was not simply for the larger providers of services but also for those SMEs. In particular, SMEs at the moment are often deterred from providing a service in other Member States because of lengthy and costly authorisation procedures. Changes to enable them to effectively test the water in another Member State on a temporary basis, without having to fully commit to permanent establishment, we believe could make a vital contribution to fully opening up the European market in this area.

Q484 *Lord Haskel:* One of the barriers that we came across when we travelled, particularly in France and Germany, is a fear that it is unacceptable that companies in lower cost countries would have the opportunity of eroding the higher standards of social protection in the richer Member States. How do you feel this could be changed?

Mr Alexander: I have sought, obviously, to look at this matter in terms of the position of the British Government in relation to the position of workers, and health and safety. I hope I have already offered the Committee some assurance on those matters. But it is fair to say that in the case of some of the concerns that have been expressed, we simply take exception and disagree with some of the analysis underpinning the concern where we are respectful of the basis of the concern and have reached a different view as to how seriously threatening those particular aspects would be. One of the most frequently heard arguments is the suggestion that, somehow, there would be a race to the bottom; that there would be a desire to establish base competitiveness by certain Member States, who

would in turn seek to provide lower standards of protection.

The Committee suspended from 4.49 pm to 5.00 pm for a Division in the House

Q485 Lord Haskel: We were talking about changes that might be necessary to overcome some of the barriers that you spoke about, and I was making the point that we have learnt in France and Germany that they are concerned that companies in lower cost countries will erode the higher standards of social protection in the richer Member States, and we were discussing how you might overcome these barriers.

Mr Alexander: Let me endeavour to reply to Lord Haskel by making a number of points: and with the forbearance of the Committee I will speak at some length because clearly it is a matter of some contention and concern, not just in the Member States that Lord Haskel mentioned, but also in the United Kingdom. There are a number of reasons why we would take issue with the analysis of some of the concern that has been expressed. First, the Country of Origin Principle does not apply to the terms and conditions for posted workers. There does appear to have been some confusion in the minds of some of the critics of the Services Directive as to whether that is the case. Therefore, the Country of Destination Rule as set out in the Posting of Workers Directive will continue to apply. I will be happy to speak more about the position of posted workers in due course. Second, all Member States subscribe to the same EC law. Therefore, the Country of Origin Principle will be based on similar labour law, given the coverage of EC labour law at present, similar consumer protection laws, similar environmental protection law, across the range. In relation to the position of new Member States, which has been the basis of some of the concerns in particular, we have had to work very hard during the accession process to ensure their legal systems properly reflect the European Union *acquis* and in that sense some of the concern is misplaced. Third, to make use of the Country of Origin Principle an economic operator must be established in a Member State. The definition of establishment, the technical definition, requires actual economic activity. A postal address, a brass plate, in a particular accession country's capital would clearly not be sufficient to meet that criterion. Finally on this point, there is a vein of internal market case law concerned with the abuse of Community rights, which we believe would be relevant and ought to be referred to specifically in the Directive. This is necessary to ensure that service providers do not wrongfully seek to erode regulations by relocating to another Member State, and often that has not been clearly reflected in the concerns that have been articulated. The authors of the Copenhagen

Economics Study did not find any significant evidence of job shifting as a result of the implementation of the Directive. In their opinion, if this were to happen, the effect would be, as they put it, "drowned in the job creation effect of the Directive". However, they could not rule out jobs moving, but in their view this would be limited and not important, as service jobs usually have to be close to the market.

The Committee suspended from 5.03 pm to 5.13 pm for a Division in the House

Q486 Chairman: Minister, you were part way through a very important section of your remarks.
Mr Alexander: Let me preface what I was going on to say with one or two observations, given your concern in relation to the specific subject of race to the bottom. I have to say that I think there is something of an analogy to be drawn between some of the commentary that has been made around the risk under the Services Directive of a race to the bottom with some of the previous public debate that took place in the United Kingdom on the issue of off-shoring. One of the things that is striking is the extent to which the public conversation and debate around off-shoring has moved on in the United Kingdom relative to other very highly developed industrialised economies. I had the opportunity to spend some time in the United States last summer amidst the controversies of the American presidential election. One of the things that was most striking to me was the disparity between the public conversation around off-shoring in the United States, which one would think of as an extraordinarily open and free-trading country, and the position here within the United Kingdom. The discourse involved the suggestion of the great threat of the exporting of American jobs, the extent to which protectionism was a necessary and appropriate response to the challenge of competitiveness of other developing economies. I came back to the United Kingdom with a much clearer sense of the extent to which—albeit particular off-shoring decisions are often painful for the communities affected—there is a fairly broad consensus amongst not just policy-makers but the public; that we have a great deal to gain by the kind of open trade, not just in manufacturing but also in services, that would be envisaged by the kind of Directive that we are discussing today. The other aspect that contextualises our discussion on the specific *acquis* within the European Union is a point more relevant to Europe itself, and that is the extent to which the British model of regulation in particular—albeit that I would argue as a Government Minister—has contributed greatly to the levels of economic stability, economic growth and employment that have been reached in recent years within the United Kingdom appear to have had very little effect on some of our fellow Member State countries in terms of their approach to regulation in recent years. Therefore the suggestion that there would be somehow a domino effect or knock-on effect as implied by the race to the bottom thesis is contested by contemporary experience, where within the European Union a very wide range of standards and levels of business regulation continue to exist within the European Union and single market. A further point in relation to the European question, in particular, is that much of the conversation around the race to the bottom has become almost inextricably linked to discussions of the European Social Model, as it is described. Again, having had the opportunity, not in least in preparation for my appearance before this Committee today and previous research on this subject, one of the points that emerge when discussions take place on the European Social Model is that it is more often discussed than defined. In that sense, there is often a wide range of opinions as to what constitutes the European Social Model. With those words as context, let me move on to the specific point you raised before the Division in terms of the *acquis* and its position across Europe and some of the points that I touched on. It is the case of course that there is a framework Directive on health and safety standards, plus a range of sectoral Directives that impact on the issue of health and safety. In relation to consumer protection, one of the other areas I mentioned, the Services Directive as presently drafted contains a degree of harmonisation in relation to information-sharing, the notion of empowering the consumer with further information. There are also a large number of Directives which provide minimum standards of harmonisation across Member States where Member States individually then choose to have more stringent measures in place as well. On the issue of workers, there are of course many Directives on social protection, particularly in relation to posted workers in the Posting of Workers Directive. It sets out terms and conditions for minimum wages, minimum holiday periods, equality laws between men and women, and health and safety law in general; so there is a broad canon of European law in this area. As I say, my sense is that some of the concerns that have been expressed, while understandable, are not entirely founded on a clear understanding of how the present European Union single market is working.
Chairman: Thank you for your comprehensive reply. Issues related to this will come up in   later questions, so we will come back to the matters you raise.

Q487 *Lord Walpole:* Is the Country of Origin Principle critical to achieving free movement of services, or are there any alternatives to the Country of Origin Principles that you have thought about which would achieve the same results?

Mr Alexander: We do believe that the Country of Origin Principle is extremely important, but of course there could be alternatives. I would be happy to try and explain both the basis on which we believe the Country of Origin Principle is so important, but equally what the alternatives might be. In terms of why we believe it is important, I return to my earlier answer on the particular position of small and medium size enterprises, approximately 90 per cent of service providers. We believe that if the Directive is genuinely to address the concerns of SMEs in particular, and their capacity to trade effectively across borders and services within the European Union, then the Country of Origin Principle has a very vital contribution to make to their endeavours— the capacity to effectively test the waters; the ability not to find themselves constrained by a range of other obligations. While other alternatives have been mooted, we do not find favour with them as a Government. One alternative would be to continue the process of sectoral legislation, of which there has been some to date, but not least given the concerns that have been expressed in terms of timing and the time-scales envisaged by the original Lisbon European Council, we believe that the framework approach suggested by the Services Directive is a preferable way forward by far. The risk with the sectoral approach would be to effectively create a patchwork of service provision; sub-sectors that generate potentially complex and contradictory legislation, dependent on particular areas of concern and particular sectors.

Q488 *Lord Walpole:* Presumably, the time-scale is important there, is it not, or would be against that?

Mr Alexander: Absolutely. While, clearly, the ambition envisaged within the Services Directive as drafted has its critics, as has been suggested already to the Committee, the virtue of an ambitious approach is to ensure that if consensus can be reached and a way forward found, then you can have a comprehensive approach within the time-scales envisaged, as distinct from the more incremental approach envisaged inevitably by a sectoral approach to legislation whereby it would necessarily take a longer period. There is also a point to be made in that regard in relation to the strength of a framework approach, as distinct from a sectoral approach, is your capacity within a carefully drafted framework approach, to better foolproof the Directive in terms of future change, whereby it is fair to say that a sectoral approach is less capable of being future-proofed effectively than a sectoral approach. There is, of course, an alternative argued by some, which is not to advance the sectoral approach but to

effectively do nothing; to leave the position as at presently constituted whereby the Commission can pursue breaches of the internal market using the existing and future case law of the European Court of Justice. However, we believe, for the very reason that the Services Directive is necessary, an even more incremental approach than that envisaged by a sectoral approach would not produce the pace or scale of change necessary, given the scale of our economic ambitions for reform within the European Union.

Q489 *Chairman:* In terms of the language that has generally been used, I take the sectoral approach to be the harmonisation approach, which has certainly been used by a number of witnesses, including the TUC before us here. I hope I am right?

Mr Alexander: One of the points that I discussed with officials prior to my arrival was the evidence given before this Committee by the TUC in terms of, if I may say so, a rather adept question as to how they define the sector. Perhaps I can invite Paul to set out the position in relation to the sectors, because it is a matter which, not least in the light of the question asked, I thought important to clarify on a legal basis.

Q490 *Chairman:* While he does that, one of the questions that we posed as we have been around Europe is, for those who want to harmonise, what do they want to harmonise?

Mr Baker: Often sectors will be very obvious. For example, we had energy sectoral legislation in 2003, they will be the most natural definition of a sector, so are the Gas and Electricity Liberalisation Directives; or the telecoms package in 2002 which is carved out of the Services Directive, as you will probably notice, in Article 2. Both packages are about liberalisation and better regulation, and in the case of the telecoms package they are about removing authorisation schemes altogether. So rather than having to go through costly authorisation procedures, you notify the competent authorities that you wish to start providing a telecoms service in certain areas, and after a certain period you are allowed to do that. Sectors will be very obvious, but sometimes when people are talking about sectors they are not necessarily talking about an industrial sector like gas and electricity or telecoms, they are talking about something a bit different, so one has to define one's terms. Obviously, depending on what you are talking about will depend the answer as to what you are going to harmonise. In the case of telecoms it was about removal of authorisation schemes.

Mr Alexander: In relation to your specific question about the interaction between harmonisation and a sectoral-specific approach to legislation, there would be a degree of risk for the United Kingdom in such an approach, not least given the extent to which, consistent with the flexibility of the British economy, we believe that we are both more likely to be and are better regulated than, with respect, some of our European partners. In that sense, if we were to take a sectoral legislation approach whereby we will achieve harmonisation, then the risk to the United Kingdom's position would be that that harmonisation would come at the cost of some of the flexibilities which we believe have served the United Kingdom well in recent years.

Chairman: The Financial Services Framework, as I recall, had about 40 Directives. The thought that harmonising a sector means a Directive to cover a sector is, on past evidence, not entirely realistic. Even then, as you said Minister, we would be very concerned to ensure that there still is flexibility to allow the light-touch approach in this country. It is a difficult route to go, but nevertheless it has been suggested by some people to us.

Q491 *Lord Geddes:* On the subject of definitions—and we have asked this question of all witnesses, both in this country and on the Continent—can you confirm that in your opinion the Country of Origin Principle only works on a temporary basis, and that once a company has been established, it then abides by the laws of the host country?

Mr Alexander: Yes. I am happy to give that confirmation, although clearly implicit in that answer is a subsequent question as to how—

Q492 *Lord Geddes:* Quite so. Can I ask that question?

Mr Alexander: That, I am afraid I cannot answer in a single word in a way I can confirm that we do accept it. Again, this is a matter that I have discussed at some length with officials in terms of both how that clarity would be derived in terms of European case law. I turn again to the lawyer supporting me on this to offer clarity in terms of how the ECJ has defined temporary in terms of sectors previously, because clearly it will be a matter of legal definition.

Mr Baker: It is clear from the Services Directive, as well as in a number of key areas, that the Services Directive is reliant on the case law of the Court. There is a particular recital that refers to the test used in the key case to do with the difference between temporary service provision where you move to another Member State and permanent establishment there. That is a case called *Gebhart*, about a German lawyer. The European Court of Justice said that the temporary nature of activities in question must be determined in the light not only of the duration of the provision of the service, but also of its regularity, periodical nature or continuity. What we are talking about here is the question of the provider, the competent authority that would be looking at regulating that provider, but also in the final analysis the national courts and potentially the ECJ as well, looking at the facts of the case. They would be looking at whether the provider has permanent infrastructure in the Member State in question; whether it employs local labour; to what extent, if they have moved to France, they intend to have a stable and continuous connection to the French economy. That is the test that has been used in front of the ECJ, whether there is a stable and continuous basis to the activity with the Member State in question. The Services Directive relies on the case law of the Court; there is no number of weeks that I can say to you that after that number of weeks the person would be established. It will be a question of looking at the facts of the case.

Q493 *Lord Geddes:* It has been put to us—and it is not the first time we have heard that—that that situation will act against the interests of the SMEs in that they will certainly for quite a period of time, until sufficient case law has come down from the ECJ, not know where they stand. Being an SME by definition, they will not be able to afford to be prosecuted in a host country, not their own. Have you any thoughts on that subject? They are in the horns of a dilemma.

Mr Alexander: On this general issue perhaps there is more work to be done, and it is for exactly that reason that we continue to discuss this particular point both with the Commission and Member States. I appreciate the point you are making in terms of trying to, in advance of European Union jurisprudence moving on, providing as much certainty as can reasonably be expected by those who we are asking to work on the basis of the Directive; but clearly we are one of 25 and continue to discuss this matter with the Commission.

Mr Baker: That is absolutely right. Your point is a very interesting one, but I think the interesting point is that it is not one that has been put to us very much. The vast majority of people who have put the point are regulators being concerned about the situation the opposite way round; the fact that they are going to have loads of people challenging them on the basis that they are temporary providers, not permanent established providers. That shows to me that we have to be very, very careful in what we do. For example, we could put on the table a suggestion that we have a number of weeks, as a presumption. Some Member States might well say, "let us make it four weeks", and we might say, "let us make it six months". I am not suggesting it would be those numbers, but you can see that different Member States would have very different views. Different sectors will be amenable to different numbers. We have to be very, very careful, in delivering the sort of benefits that we need here;

whilst giving the sort of people you are talking about, who are the key audience, the security that they need.

Q494 *Baroness Eccles of Moulton:* Would the tendency be for a provider that was operating on a temporary basis and therefore coming under the Country of Origin Principle, to stay in that mode, or would they want to be recognised as established? Would there be a general rule? Would there be one desire on the part of SMEs and another on the part of non-SMEs; or would it be impossible to say which way people would want to be?
Mr Baker: There is no particular rule. The Services Directive—although we have spent quite a lot of time talking about SMEs—is not just about SMEs. There is no specific rule for SMEs versus large companies. There is no particular distinction of that type. In terms of moving from one mode of provision to another; to an extent, given what I have said it will be a question of fact, but, clearly, economic providers will have decided in their own mind at some stage, either to commit to establish themselves in France and want to permanently establish there. They might have bought property; they might start thinking, "I now need to use local labour" or something of that nature; so they will need to be careful themselves about the basis on which they are operating in that Member State. There is no doubt of that, but it will be a question of fact.

Q495 *Lord Geddes:* Minister, you have already touched on the juxtaposition between this draft Directive and the one on the Posting of Workers. Do you think that those two are clear enough in their own definitions to split them apart, or do you think that the Services Directive needs amendment to make it even clearer?
Mr Alexander: It is fair to acknowledge that there has been some confusion on the relationship between the provisions on posting of workers as set out in the Services Directive, and those that are set out in the Posting of Workers Directive itself. The Services Directive does not intend to apply to employment law *per se* as set out in the recitals; it only seeks to cover posted workers to the extent that the service providers should not be subject to cumbersome administrative burdens when posting workers to another Member State. In that sense, as I worked through the proposals with officials, it became increasingly clear to me that a fairly clear distinction can be drawn, albeit that some of the commentary at the moment suggests that one cannot be drawn. The Posting of Workers Directive is derogated from the Country of Origin Principle and the Services Directive and therefore applies in full. This means that posted workers will continue to be subject to the terms and conditions of the Member State to which

the worker is posted, the country of destination, or the host Member country. These working conditions cover minimum wages, working time, minimum paid holidays, hiring out of workers, health and safety standards, protection of young people and pregnant women, equality of treatment between men and women, and other non-discrimination provisions. We therefore believe that concerns in this area are not as justified as some of the commentary would suggest.

Q496 *Lord Geddes:* Why do you think there is such concern?
Mr Alexander: Candidly, I think there are issues, unrelated to the Services Directive in terms of the Posting of Workers Directive, which have unfortunately become rather mixed up in discussions with the Services Directive. The opportunity for there to be discussion of the Services Directive has allowed some to advance arguments which are more appropriately directed in terms of the Posting of Workers Directive rather than the Services Directive. In that sense, it has been an opportunity to further ventilate some of the concerns people have in terms of implementation of the Posting of Workers Directive.

Q497 *Lord Geddes:* Do you have discussions with your opposite numbers—and let us be quite blunt about it—particularly in France and Germany?
Mr Alexander: As a matter of course in terms of European negotiations officials are speaking very regularly to not just the Commission but other Member States.

Q498 *Lord Geddes:* Has this particular problem come up?
Mr Alexander: Of course there are issues of disagreement and agreement between us, and this is one of the matters on which there has been discussion.
Chairman: The point was made to us in Germany that they do not have a minimum wage.
Lord Geddes: *De Jure.*

Q499 *Chairman:* In law. Hence, one of your assurances, on the face of it, would not be a reassurance in Germany. There is no reason, Minister, why you should know the law of 24 other countries, but that point was certainly put to us. Although individual industries may have bi-industry agreements and some minimum wage structures, in general in Germany overall there is not minimum wage legislation.
Mr Alexander: I am respectful of the point you make in terms of the statutory framework or lack of a statutory basis for a minimum wage in Germany. I have to say that it is a fairly novel critique of the

German labour market that wage rates are dangerously low; and in that sense I would be intrigued in terms of the impact of German wage rates on the British economy. If that is the point the Germans are making, it is one we can no doubt consider in the future.

Q500 *Chairman:* I would not attempt to discuss the point the particular German witness was making at that time; but am I right that operating on a temporary basis, a business from a different Member State working in a host Member State, could bring in employees from his own country and pay them at salaries that reflected their country of origin on a temporary basis, rather than the wage rates of the host country?
Mr Alexander: It may fall within the provisions of the Posting of Workers Directive and the protections derived from that. As I say, I am respectful of the fact that there are some critics of the Posting of Workers Directive, but that does not bear directly on the operation of the Services Directive as much as the view of the Posting of Workers Directive.

Q501 *Chairman:* Are you saying the operation of the Country of Origin Principle and the Services Directive means that if a business, say, from Lithuania—to take a country absolutely at random—came to this country on a temporary basis of operating, it would have to pay those temporary workers coming from Lithuania for, say, six months at some wage rate or salary that reflected salaries in this country? Who would decide what they would be? How would that operate? Then they could go back to Lithuania after six months and be paid at Lithuanian rates under the Services Directive.
Mr Alexander: The Posting of Workers Directive is the key Directive in this regard and in that sense the protections afforded to them would be those set out in that Directive.
Mr Kessel: That is entirely correct. The Posting of Workers Directive differentiates between three types of different temporary postings. The first one is where a foreign corporate entity goes across and provides a service directly to an end customer. The second one is where this corporate entity posts workers to a subsidiary into the other Member State, and a third one is where these workers are posted by a temporary workers' agency. It strikes me that your example falls clearly into the category of the first example, whereby the corporate entity hosts the worker and takes the workers with them into the other Member State. It is clearly the national minimum wage and other terms and conditions set out in the Posting of Workers Directive that would apply.

Q502 *Chairman:* In this country I understand that, but most jobs that most service providers would be bringing people in to do would not be at a national minimum wage, but it would be the minimum wage. There would be no way in which we could tell an IT business from Lithuania; who is going to tell them what rates to pay, other than they must pay at least the minimum wage?
Mr Kessel: At least, yes.

Q503 *Chairman:* But in Germany, where they have no national minimum wage, adjacent to Poland, whether justified or not they say that that very minimum level is not a safeguard. I do not ask the Minister at all to comment on your situation, simply to help explain to the Committee how companies are supposed to operate under the Country of Origin Principle. Surely, nobody could tell an SME; there is nobody who can tell them what to pay other than, for example, in this country where they must pay a minimum wage and that is all. It could significantly undercut existing British producers, for example, as long as he is paid at least the minimum wage.
Mr Alexander: Our labour market whether involving posted workers or not, has for some time set a minimum floor, which we uphold and believe is the right way forward, as a Government, for the British labour market. That said, it is inherent in the nature of an functioning market that there will be alternative rates of pay offered by respective producers, and in that sense we would not wish to undermine flexibility of the market and services within the United Kingdom; with the important caveat that the protections that are provided both to British workers for the minimum wage would continue to endure, and indeed the protections afforded to posted workers under the Posting of Workers Directive would also apply. With respect, the greatest concern that has been expressed by some has not been in relation to the competitiveness of the market place above the level of the minimum wage, but a misplaced concern that within the United Kingdom the operation of the Services Directive could involve people undercutting the minimum wage. That is why, on the temporary basis on which these people would potentially be posted in your example, it is a very important to recognise that the Posting of Workers Directive gives the assurance that many of the critics of the Services Directive have been seeking.

Q504 *Lord Fearn:* My question is in four sections, which roll together, and so I will ask them all together. What are the remaining major objections within the other Member States to the Country of Origin Principle approach? Which of these do you think are based on a misunderstanding of the draft Directive? I think you have touched on that. What are the other significant objections? Does the UK share any of these latter concerns; and, if not, in particular cases why not? You have mentioned health and safety as well.

Mr Alexander: I am grateful for the question. The first point I would make would obviously be the issue of the race to the bottom, although with the acceptance of the Committee, given the extent to which I have commented on those, perhaps I could recognise race to the bottom as one of those issues where concern has been expressed, and offer other areas. The second main area of concern that I would identify would be the operation of the Country of Origin Principle, this time in relation to sensitive areas. There is widespread concern that the Country of Origin Principle will lead to lower levels of protection in a number of sensitive areas, for example the environment, health and safety, and the care we extend to vulnerable people within our own society. You asked us for the British Government's position and we share those concerns, but we believe that a high level of protection can be maintained by textual amendments of existing derogations within the Services Directive as drafted. We think that that is both realistic and achievable, but we recognise that that is a genuine concern that must be addressed within the Services Directive.

Q505 Lord Fearn: What makes you think that?

Mr Alexander: Because the scope is there, if I recollect, under 17.17 for there to be further specific textual amendments in relation to areas that would effectively be derogated from the operation of the Services Directive as drafted. As I reflected in my earlier comments, there is a great deal of discussion taking place at the moment, not just between the British Government and the Commission, but between the British Government and other Member States. In that sense, albeit we are keen to see progress in relation to this Directive, there is still a lot of negotiating to do, and in that sense the Government's position that I set out at the beginning is one we would negotiate very hard for in terms of taking forward this Directive. The third area involves the issue of private international law where there have been a number of legal concerns raised in relation to the interaction of the proposed "Rome II" regulation and its conception of how to deal with applicable law concerning non-contractual liability within the European Union and, on the other hand, the Country of Origin Principle that we have just been discussing. We believe that the concerns that have been raised in relation to this area reflect the fact that there is a tension between the Country of Origin Principle and the general rule of applicable law; that the law is that of the country where the damage occurs in relation to "Rome II" as presently drafted.

On that basis, in principle the Country of Origin Principle should not apply to the areas covered by "Rome II", and we believe that is the way forward in terms of how to reconcile the present draft "Rome II" regulation and the present draft Directive on Services. There might be a case to be made in relation to certain discrete areas within the field covered by "Rome II" for treatment under the Country of Origin Principle. An area where this might be possible is in relation to unfair competition rules and possibly advertising; but in principle the Country of Origin Principle should not apply to the areas covered by "Rome II". The third area which I would identify would be in relation to when activity is temporary service provision, and when there is an establishment of a service provider within a country. It has certainly been a recurring theme in terms of the discussions between Member States as to where that distinction can be drawn between temporary service provision and establishment. As I have suggested, further work needs to be done, not least in the light of the concern that was suggested may afflict SMEs that would otherwise be keen to be able to use the Services Directive. So in all of those areas I hope I have reflected both where there is further scope for work and where there are areas of genuine concern, but those would be the main areas that I would identify.

Q506 Baroness Eccles of Moulton: Minister, the next question takes derogation a little further, even proposing that it could become a Directive wrecker. There are already many derogations from the Country of Origin Principle approach and it appears that more are being considered. Is the UK looking for any further derogations? At what point does an accumulation of derogation significantly affect this drive to achieve free movement of services?

Mr Alexander: The position in terms of the derogations that the British Government seeks I sought to reflect in my introductory statement. In relation to the points we have already raised, we also believe that greater certainty can be provided by clarifying the "co-ordinated field" referred to in Article 16; in other words, the requirements which apply to, access to and exercise of a service activity, and which are covered by the Country of Origin Principle. Greater certainty in that regard would be helpful. To take one example of criminal law, at the moment there is a danger that the co-ordinated field covers more than is intended. Whilst we are still working on the issue, we think the proper scope should be to cover what we might call regulatory criminal law. Therefore the co-ordinated field would clearly exclude general crimes, for example, manslaughter, assault, fraud and many other crimes, so we do think there are ways that the definitions can be tightened; but in terms of the specific derogations those are the ones that I spoke of at the beginning. With regard to the question of whether there is in some way a tipping point, at which point the effect of the cumulative derogations is to undermine the approach of the framework, then if there were to be an excessively large number of derogations, this would potentially render the Country of Origin Principle ineffectual; but the determination of that point is almost, by definition, very difficult to determine in advance of the discussions and negotiations that are taking place at the moment. That is why it is important that we proceed with respect and also caution, in terms of seeking to establish the number of derogations required, and to avoid a situation whereby unnecessary derogations are added to the draft Directive.

Q507 *Baroness Eccles of Moulton:* Minister, at the beginning of our discussions the derogations that you referred to were the three big utilities: water, gas and electricity. They presumably would be common ground across the whole of the EU membership. Everybody presumably has these three utilities as good candidates for derogation, or is that not the case?

Mr Alexander: With respect, in terms of the terminology that is appropriate in this area, the derogations we seek are in relation to issues such as tax and publicly-funded healthcare. There are exclusions, which I sought to differentiate in my introductory remarks, in relation to the utilities you mentioned. For example, there are certain areas where we are categoric that the appropriate response is derogation and one is, for example, on the issue of taxation. There are however other instrumental arguments, for example the relative liberalisation of the English water industry relative to that elsewhere in the European Union, which means we would be seeking exclusions; but that clearly is a subject for discussion with our European partners[1].

Q508 *Chairman:* I notice on your list of exclusions that construction services are not included. Do I take it that the UK is opposed to construction services being excluded?

Mr Alexander: In terms of the position we are adopting at the moment I did not refer to construction services, you are right. I would not at this stage pre-judge further discussions that might take place with our European Union partners, or indeed, with the Commission. As of today, that is not

a case that I am pressing nor would I seek to suggest that to the Committee.

Q509 *Chairman:* You mentioned publicly-funded healthcare. How do you define that meaningfully? That is a derogation that you are seeking. For example, would healthcare and looking after elderly people in an elderly persons' home in the private sector be excluded?

Mr Alexander: I hope I can offer a commonsensical answer to this, the NHS. In that sense, clearly, there could be instances where there are accountants providing commercial services to the National Health Service whereby you could claim that there were cross-border services that were appropriate within the scope of the Services Directive. The substantive meaning that is reflected in the particular language that I used reflects the distinctive nature of the provision of healthcare within the United Kingdom.

Mr Baker: That is exactly the point. The DTI was convinced very early on about the case to exclude the NHS from the implications of the Directive; but on the other hand we felt there was a good case to be made for the opportunity to include private healthcare.

Q510 *Chairman:* SMEs from elsewhere in Europe would not be able on a temporary basis to bid for outsourced work within the NHS for example?

Mr Baker: I do not think we would see this as excluding the ability for people to use the Treaty freedoms. All we are saying here is that we would exclude the NHS from the workings of the Directive. It would not mean that there would be a prohibition, and in fact you could not do that under the Treaty as it stands. We are not talking about black and white here.

Q511 *Chairman:* Certainly in this country we do have quite a degree of the use of outsourcing and so on, and on a large scale PFIs. So these elements of the NHS that provide a lot of flexibility would not be open to SMEs or businesses from elsewhere in Europe, on the basis of the Country of Origin Principle and on a temporary basis?

Mr Alexander: A point to be reflected here is that even in terms of any major public procurement, one is obliged to put notification in the official journal. We are not seeking to undermine the freedoms provided in terms of the European treaties. That being said, I sought to reflect accurately to you the policy thinking; which was that the NHS was not up for negotiation in terms of the Services Directive as envisaged in terms of policy-makers. Indeed, we were keen to ensure that there was a very clear demarcation drawn between the notion of services as

---

[1] The reference to derogations in Q.507 and the answer, as opposed to exclusions, is somewhat unclear. The United Kingdom position is to exclude tax, publicly-funded healthcare, water (and wastewater), electricity and gas services. Derogations in the context of the Services Directive refer to derogation from the Country of Origin Principle.

described by someone who advocated the Services Directive and what we take to be the very particular nature of the provision of healthcare within the United Kingdom, of which we are proud and determined to protect.

Q512 Chairman: Taken to the logical conclusion, the exclusion of public services in that sense by all Member States would leave an enormous hole. You talked earlier on about 70 per cent of services.

Mr Alexander: With respect, a very great distinction can be drawn between the nature of the provision of healthcare within the United Kingdom and the system of healthcare that is provided within other Member States. That is why, in terms of private healthcare there may be scope for other Member States to advocate their respective views on that, but in terms of the nature of the provision of healthcare within the United Kingdom the British Government has taken a very robust view. As I say, these matters will continue to be discussed with our European partners.

Q513 Baroness Cohen of Pimlico: Can I get at this question in a different way? We had all thought that this was going to be a terrific Directive, because, after all, only 21 per cent of services were freely traded and there was another 70 per cent to go—except there is not, is there, by the time you have taken out gas, water, electricity, the National Health Service—and other countries have doubtless taken out some? Do we have any numerical percentage estimate of how narrow this has now become?

Mr Alexander: It would be unfair of me to read Fiona's statistic without acknowledging her before the Committee!

Dr Harrison: We think the figure drops from 70 to 50 if you take out the public sector. Whether or not it will drop further if you take out some of the utilities that are part private, part public; we are still trying to get a handle on that exactly.

Q514 Baroness Cohen of Pimlico: Is this in the UK or EU-wide?

Dr Harrison: EU-wide.

Q515 Chairman: If a derogation were achieved by the UK for publicly-funded healthcare, that would have to be agreed by all Member States and it would apply to publicly-funded healthcare throughout the EU I assume? The answer to that must be "yes".

Dr Harrison: Yes. It is also worth saying that the majority of Member States want all of healthcare out, and many feel they cannot distinguish between public and private in the way that we have managed to. I am sure you know that Commissioner McCreevy has said he thinks all of healthcare will come out of the

scope of the Directive, so to a certain extent trying to keep private healthcare in, is probably not a negotiating position we are going to succeed in delivering.

Q516 Baroness Cohen of Pimlico: By the time we have taken out everything we are going to derogate on—and presumably the whole of financial services is covered by another Directive—professional services is on the whole covered by another Directive yet. I am sorry, but is there rather little left for this Directive to focus on?

Dr Harrison: For something like financial services that is true. But although the qualifications and exercise of a service are covered by the Directive on Mutual Recognition of Professional Services, it is not the case that they are excluded from the scope of the Services Directive. With a horizontal Directive you read it alongside existing sectoral pieces of legislation. For example, the better regulation benefits associated with countries' authorisation schemes benefit the regulated professions. There are very specific disapplications of particular bits of the Services Directive—to do, for example, with requiring original copies of documents—where there is derogation in favour of the Directive on Mutual Recognition of Professional Qualifications; but the Services Directive as a whole will bring benefits to regulated professions.

Q517 Chairman: We are at the end of our time. Would you be agreeable for us to touch on the question of the Mutual Assistance Framework because it is very important? We will not, I promise you, take the time that you might think implied by the enormous long text, but this was described to us by the European Commission as an essential part of achieving success in the application of the Country of Origin Principle. Indeed, they said it was central to the success of it. We will deal with the whole thing in nine minutes!

Mr Alexander: With respect, I have another meeting, but I am respectful of my appearance before the Committee and I will endeavour to answer your points as quickly as I can.

Q518 Lord St John of Bletso: On the Mutual Assistance Framework, we had evidence from the Construction Industry Council. They had concerns that there would be inadequate provision of their services provided in other Member States, and that this could threaten standards. Considerable emphasis is placed on the Mutual Assistance Framework as the basis for establishing confidence in a principle of free movement of services based on the Country of Origin Principle. Do you agree that such a workable framework is critical in this matter?

Mr Alexander: Yes, we would be in agreement on that point. The Country of Origin Principle is based on the concept of the Member State where the provider is established being responsible for the supervising of those activities, even where he provides those services temporarily in another Member State. Furthermore, the Member State must exercise its supervisory powers over a provider who moves temporarily to another Member State. It would not therefore work for a foreign competent authority to seek to supervise a provider under the rules of another Member State. We are of the view that it would be a challenge to make the framework function in practice, but interesting work has already been done by the Commission in this area to facilitate exchange of information and translation concerning providers, based to an extent on existing internal market information systems. I am respectful of the point you make in terms of the Construction Industry Association's evidence before you; but in fact some of the commentary that I have been able to read has reflected not a concern that there will be inadequate supervision, but somehow that you would by the Mutual Assistance Framework see flying regulators going around Europe seeking to over-regulate and to weigh a greater administrative burden upon those bodies that were being regulated. In that sense, the Mutual Assistance Framework represents the best way forward, but there is still further work to be done both in terms of the point of contact, and how the agencies in respect of Member States will work collaboratively together; and that is why we are working very closely with the Commission on these questions at the moment.

Q519 *Lord St John of Bletso:* We have severe constraints of time, so my comment was really on lack of inadequate supervision which certainly would threaten standards, and that would be a problem right across the board, but I will not draw the issue.

Baroness Cohen of Pimlico: Most of these questions are about numbers and how we are going do the Mutual Assistance Framework. Are we going to collect the data; are we going to burden SMEs with collecting data, the sort of SME that would not dream of working out of the United Kingdom? Perhaps I could cheat and ask if we could have the answer in writing. Would that be a way through?

Chairman: Minister, you have been very, very accommodating. You will appreciate that two Divisions played havoc with what we thought was a planned timetable. Can we have a written response to these two questions?

Baroness Cohen of Pimlico: They are based largely on statistics.

Chairman: Yes, but I have to say that this was regarded as extremely important, and we did observe a very different approach and state of preparedness and forward-thinking on this in different countries. Minister, can I thank you and your colleagues for, as always, a detailed and forthright response to our questions. We are grateful to you. Thank you for overstaying your time. I hope it is not too much inconvenience to you in your next meeting.

Supplementary written memorandum by the Department of Trade and Industry (DTI)

COULD YOU EXPLAIN HOW YOU CURRENTLY THINK THE MUTUAL ASSISTANCE FRAMEWORK WOULD WORK?

Firstly, what we don't think would happen. There has been a considerable amount of concern about the need to set up a cadre of flying regulators—we don't think that is what is required and it is certainly not intended by the Commission. Article 36 provides the key to the supervision of providers who move abroad temporarily to provide a service—it makes clear that the competent authorities of the host Member State shall participate in supervising the provider. That is in contrast to the general rule for country of origin which is that it is the role of the home Member State to supervise its providers. Article 36 goes on to distinguish between the tasks allotted to the home and host Member States.

At European level it is clear that the thinking on this issue is still at an early stage on this important subject. The Commission included Article 38 so that it could develop the way Member States' implement the working of the mutual assistance system. We think much more thinking needs to be done now and set out in the Directive, rather than left for Comitology.

For example, we think it needs to be clear that the supervision provided for in the Directive will not lead to more regulation for business to deal with—therefore in a case where a derogation allows a host Member State to supervise a provider, the home state should not also supervise that provider.

It should not significantly add to the costs of supervision for business or indeed for Government, therefore the obligations on Member States need to be practical. There are also issues that need to be resolved concerning the type of information that should flow between Member States and the trigger points for such exchanges.

The mutual assistance obligations should be an advantage to consumers and recipients. At present, there is cross-border service provision and there is no accompanying obligation on Member States to assist each other in the event of problems arising with the service. Under the Services Directive there would be a mechanism for dealing with such problems.

How Would this be Established in the United Kingdom? How many Points of Contact for how many Sectors would need to be Established Within the United Kingdom in Order to make the Framework Workable?

Article 35 as currently drafted allows for one or more contact points for the mutual assistance system. We think that flexibility is right. There will be many different situations, some where there is a United Kingdom wide supervisory body that might be an obvious contact point for its sector, others where each United Kingdom jurisdiction has its own supervisory body or bodies, for example, in relation to lawyers and finally other situations where the United Kingdom has no overall supervisor at all.

Given the heterogeneous nature of supervision that suggests that different services will need to be dealt with differently. There is a precedent in the internal market area for mutual assistance called SOLVIT. This is a problem-solving tool—there is one SOLVIT point in each Member State—the United Kingdom's is at DTI. These points have problems identified to them by their nationals and send them to their opposite number in the relevant Member State via the IT system—the system can translate on the basis of fixed data fields and has had considerable success in dealing with low level internal market issues.

Although that suggests a single contact point, for the reasons identified above we do not think at this stage in our thinking that a single point would be appropriate or acceptable for all services covered by the Directive.

What Information or Data would be Collected from Businesses Established in the United Kingdom as a Base of Information for each Mutual Assistance Unit in the United Kingdom?

The Directive makes specific provision in relation to exchanging data with Member States where there is unlawful behaviour or for Member States to provide information as to whether a provider has been subject to criminal convictions or other sanctions or actions. We do not believe the Directive imposes an obligation beyond applying national provisions to service provision abroad, therefore we do not believe this will involve a large data collection regime concerning the activities of providers.

Information in relation to regulated professions will of course exist at their regulatory bodies. There will also be information about service providers at Companies House and on databases concerning criminal convictions. Implementation will require a system able to provide joined-up answers concerning such information.

Therefore the information necessary largely exists within the Government or regulatory sphere, the principal issue for implementation is how the contact point would be able to access the information.

For which Businesses would that Information be Collected and at what point in their Operations?

As noted above we would see the information referred to in the Directive as being collected within the scope of existing United Kingdom regulatory schemes.

In Practical Terms how would the United Kingdom Government and/or the Relevant Unit Assisting a Mutual Assistance Activity know if and when a United Kingdom Established Business is Undertaking "Temporary" or "Non-Established" Activities in Another Member State?

The Directive as it stands relies on the case law of the European Court of Justice to make the distinction between situations where the Country of Origin Principle will apply and those where a provider is established in the host Member State.

The distinction between a situation where the Country of Origin Principle in Article 16 applies and where the establishment provisions, Articles 5–15 apply is made by the use of the phrase "Member State of origin" in Article 16 which makes clear that the only Member State which in principle can apply its laws to a provider is the Member State where the provider in question is established.

The reliance on the case law is clear from recital 19 which notes that "the temporary nature of the activities in question must be determined in the light not only of the duration of the provision of the service, but also of its regularity, periodical nature or continuity". The leading case on the issue, *Gebhard,* concerned a German lawyer practicing in Milan on what the Court described as a stable and continuous basis. Mr Gebhard practiced in Italy for 13 years. The Milan Bar argued Gebhard was not established in Italy because he did not belong to the Italian professional body. The Court not surprisingly did not accept the point and the case was decided under the establishment provisions of the Treaty.

There will be many situations where it is very obvious from the facts of the case whether a provider is established in a Member State or whether the provider has moved temporarily to the Member State. For example, the provider may have a permanent office, local staff and substantial infrastructure; in which case he will be established in the Member State. On the other hand a provider may be providing services by travelling to see a client in another Member State and travelling back to his home country, that scenario is highly likely in relation to the work of professionals of many types.

However, there will be cases where the situation is much more difficult, for example, the provider may be providing his service for a considerable period, but he merely rents offices on a short-term basis to the extent it casts doubt upon whether he has "a fixed establishment for an indefinite period". Some work has been done on this point in working documents to make clear that the fact that a provider rents his office does not automatically mean that he is not established in a Member State.

These points are essentially technical in nature, but there is also the issue of abuse. Here the definition of establishment assists because to be established there must be "actual pursuit of an economic activity". Therefore it would not be possible to set up merely a mailing address in, for example, a new Member State and thereby benefit from the Country of Origin Principle. It would be necessary to have a permanent base there, as the Court says to exercise the activity there on a stable and continuous basis. This point needs to be made clearer in the recitals concerning establishment—that has happened in Council working documents.

There is still perhaps more work to be done because it will be difficult to advise with certainty on whether a person is established or not in the difficult cases referred to above—this is an issue we wish to pursue with the Commission and other Member States.

COULD YOU EXPLAIN HOW AN EQUIVALENT MUTUAL ASSISTANCE UNIT IN ANOTHER MEMBER STATE WOULD INTERACT WITH A UNITED KINGDOM UNIT IF AND WHEN ANY PROBLEMS AROSE IN ANOTHER MEMBER STATE?

There is work going on concerning the practicalities of how contact points might work together at European level. A sub-group of the Internal Market Advisory Committee has been set up to consider how a system might be developed to meet the objectives set out in these articles. This is likely to be built on the successes of the SOLVIT system, which deals with resolving internal market problems and has a track record of doing so quickly.

That system works by direct contact between each of the Member States' SOLVIT centres. In that system where a problem arises the enquirer is directed to the national SOLVIT centre which after analysis of the issue enters it into the system, it is then dealt with by the relevant Member State's centre, who will contact the relevant parts of that Member State's government.

As I mentioned, however, the position under the Services Directive is more complex and therefore it is likely that a single centre would not be appropriate. That said, it is also clear that there would need to be a contact point of last resort, perhaps to deal with situations where there is no obvious competent authority for a given provider.

There is clearly a lot of work to be done on these Articles, but there is also a clear benefit to recipients of services, including consumers. This looks like a major task, but there are examples of functioning mutual assistance regimes in other areas of EC activity, for example, there is a long-standing scheme in the area of tax. We think it will be possible, and is necessary, to provide for an effective scheme here.

April 2005

MONDAY 4 APRIL 2005

Present	Cohen of Pimlico, B	St John of Bletso, L
	Eccles of Moulton, B	Swinfen, L
	Fearn, L	Walpole, L
	Geddes, L	Woolmer of Leeds, L (Chairman)
	Haskel, L	

Examination of Witnesses

Witnesses: MR OLIVER BRETZ and MR JOHN OSBORNE, Partners, European Competition and Regulatory Group, Clifford Chance, London, examined.

Q520 Chairman: Good afternoon and I welcome Oliver Bretz and John Osborne from Clifford Chance. I always extend a warm welcome but on this occasion I will also extend a double thanks in that you agreed kindly to the postponement of the original date when you were due to come before us and you agreed kindly to a complete change of direction in our line of questions. I think that is a first and you did so with typical Clifford Chance aplomb. You are very warmly welcome. There is quite a bit to get through and the questions that we will pose to you are ones where we feel, given the evidence we have heard from elsewhere, that you could probably best advise us and explain. We have been around Europe and listened to various things and we thought it would be jolly useful to get your take on some of these things. We understand entirely that you are as not, as it were, officials of Clifford Chance but that this evidence is given as your considered views as experienced people. Is there anything you want to say at all by way of general introduction as to how you see things before we go into questions?

Mr Bretz: My Lord Chairman, we thought rather than making an opening statement we would perhaps spend two minutes going through some concepts and how they apply at present before the draft Directive comes into effect. The first concept we want to talk about is the concept of harmonisation. The terms we are going to use are "full harmonisation" and "minimum harmonisation"; these are very important concepts because full harmonisation is a holy grail which everyone is always looking for but which really never happens. It is a situation where the rules for a particular field are completely set out in harmonised legislation. At that point the particular field of application is harmonised for the EU as a whole and what that means is that Member States cannot have more restrictive rules that go over and above the harmonised rules. As I said before, this very rarely happens and certainly in the services field it is not really a concept that has ever been achieved. Instead, what the political process often yields is a degree of minimum harmonisation. The concept of

minimum harmonisation allows the Member States to agree on what level of minimum protection is necessary in order to allow the free movement of whatever it is—goods or services—across border and you can immediately see that this links in very closely with the Country of Origin Principle. So in an area where there is no full harmonisation, but where there may be minimum harmonisation or no harmonisation, it is in those areas that even at present the Country of Origin Principle will apply under the settled Case Law of the European Court of Justice. It is very simple. It emanated from the goods field where after a lot of debate the courts took the lead and said once a good is marketed in one Member State it should be good enough for all other Member States, unless there is some overriding interest that that other Member State is seeking to protect. Very briefly the Country of Origin Principle applies at present to services. That is the settled Case Law of the European Court of Justice. My Lord Chairman, with your kind permission, I want to read one quote from the European Court of Justice. This is from case C58 of 1998 which was a German case called *Corsten* and in that case the Court said: "It is settled Case Law that even if there no harmonisation in the field, a restriction on the fundamental principle of freedom to provide services can be based only on rules justified by overriding requirements relating to the public interest and applicable to all persons and undertakings operating in the territory of the state where the service is provided, but only insofar as that interest is not safeguarded by the rules to which the provider of such a service is subject in his home Member State. I have changed this ever so slightly but the fundamental point we wanted to make right at the beginning is that the Country of Origin Principle, which we are going to spend a lot of time talking about, applies today to services. Thank you.

Chairman: Okay, that is extremely helpful. Lord Fearn?

Q521 Lord Fearn: Good afternoon. My question really centres on the word "established" so if I might roll three questions into one, it would be helpful. If a business established in its "home" Member State also becomes an "established" business in another Member State what, under the draft Services Directive, do you say "established" means in the second Member State? What would be required for a business to be established in the second Member State? Would such a business operating in the second Member State be subject to all the laws and regulations of the second Member State in precisely the same way as a business for which the second Member State is its home Member State? There are three parts to the question

Mr Osborne: The Directive defines "establishment" in Article 4 as being "the actual pursuit of an economic activity through a fixed establishment of a provider for an indefinite period". It is very difficult to define clearly across all industries what "temporary" provision of a service means, and therefore what the Commission has done is to focus on "establishment" because they believe that would be easier to actually define. So they have defined establishment through a fixed establishment for an indefinite period, and that is probably as close as you are likely to get because the European Court has actually found that there is no clear rule in the Treaty and has set out at least four factors which are used to try and ascertain whether there is temporary provision or whether there is establishment. They look at duration, continuity, periodicity, regularity. They have insisted that you must do the analysis on a case-by-case basis. The Council of Ministers have followed that, the Commission has followed that, and there was an attempt in an earlier draft of the Mutual Recognition of Professional Qualifications Directive to have a presumption saying that if you provided services in another Member State for not more than 16 weeks then that would be a service provision, with the implication that if you did it for longer then you would have an establishment. So they focused on having an establishment, ie some sort of fixed infrastructure, in that other Member State. You can provide services in a second Member State and you can have offices there without having an establishment but I think that is probably as good as you are likely to get. If you form an establishment in a second Member State the question then is are you subject to exactly the same rules as every other business in that host Member State? If you look at the Treaty Article, that is correct because the Treaty Article says that you can establish in that other Member State, subject to the same conditions as the nationals of that Member State, but in practice you will find that someone creating a secondary establishment is in a slightly more favourable position than nationals of that Member State and that is because various national rules may be disapplied. The obvious national rules would be national rules which set some requirement

based upon nationality or upon residence which the Treaty would actually prohibit. There may be other rules which on their face apply to everyone but where under the Case Law of the Court the Court says that if there are any national rules which hinder it or make it less attractive for someone to move across border, then those rules will not apply unless they can be justified as meeting an overriding requirement of a general good and they are objectively necessary and they are proportionate. So people who go cross-border, whether they provide services or indeed whether they establish themselves, may be subject to a lighter touch than the nationals of that host Member State.

Q522 Lord Fearn: You used the word "fixed" several times. Does that appear in the Directive?

Mr Osborne: Yes, the Directive says through a "fixed establishment". The reference is Article 4, sub-paragraph 5 of the draft Directive.

Lord Fearn: Thank you very much.

Q523 Lord Walpole: Unless you have totally lost me, which you probably have, could you explain the position about tax in the second Member State? Do companies once they are established have to pay the same tax and to whom, particularly for instance, VAT levels?

Mr Osborne: Tax is not dealt with in the draft Directive so one would assume as a matter of principle that a business should be taxed according to its operations within the host state, ie looking at its revenues and costs attributable to its activities in the host state. Of course a lot would depend whether it establishes itself through a branch or through a separate subsidiary and also the nature of its business. In principle, one would expect to be taxed upon the profits attributable to its operations in the host state.

Q524 Lord Walpole: And the charging of VAT, which of course varies?

Mr Osborne: One would imagine that would be a separate issue as to whether they would have to register for VAT in the host state and you would have to look at those rules, but all the VAT rules are harmonised because VAT is a European Community tax system which all Member States had to sign up to upon accession to the EU.

Q525 Lord Walpole: But the rates are not all the same?

Mr Osborne: The rates differ obviously from Member State to Member State. Greece has certainly increased its VAT rates to in part recover the cost of the Olympic Games.

Q526 *Lord Swinfen:* You mentioned registering for VAT. If you registered for VAT in the host state does that establish you in that state?

Mr Osborne: It would I think be an indicia of permanence that you are likely to be operating there for an indefinite period.

Mr Bretz: My Lord Chairman, I think it is probably worth just explaining a little bit more how the factoral assessment of permanence is carried out because I think there is almost an assumption that you have to second guess the state of mind of the business of the service provider at that particular point in time, and I do not believe that is the case. What you need to look at is all the factoral circumstances surrounding the particular business concerned in order to decide whether this business is participating in the economic life of the host Member State and is therefore providing services on an indefinite basis. The Case Law is quite interesting on this because the Case Law looks at whether you have a permanent infrastructure, so, for example, if you run a nursing home which has patients in it that is a good indication that you are providing those services on an indefinite basis because you have an infrastructure which by its nature is indefinite. However, if you were a travelling hairdresser who goes to a Member State once a week and maintains a salon in that Member State—and this is not something that is uncommon in for example the German/Belgian border—you would not be established because the existence of a salon in which you work one or two days a week or whenever you happened to be there is not an indication of a permanent presence.

Chairman: Could we, before we go into that, take the second series of questions because it has started to come together and if we can get both the temporary and the established on the table, there are certainly one or two things we can pursue with other colleagues.

Q527 *Lord Geddes:* That last statement that you made, Mr Bretz, was really very indicative about the hairdresser and, if I may, I will come back to that because that seems to be the nub of the question I want to ask which is the reverse side of "established" or the other side of the coin. You rightly said in your opening comments that most of our questions will home in on the Country of Origin Principle because that is where the big question mark is. That very helpful opening statement you made obviates the first part of my question. In other words, if you are established then you are not temporary. The established bit comes first; the temporary bit comes second, I do not mean chronologically but from a definition point of view. Then we come down to the question of how temporary is temporary? What is

temporary? How do you define temporary? Can I stop there before I go on to what I want to ask next.

Mr Bretz: One of the problems which the Commission is facing in drafting this Directive is that it is almost impossible to define "temporary". You have made exactly the right point which is that the first question that you have to ask is are you established, and it is only really if you are not established that that part of the Services Directive that relates to services becomes relevant.

Mr Osborne: It may vary and it would also vary depending upon the activity. As to the activity you need to carry out in a second Member State, it very much depends upon the occupation or the profession which you are conducting. If you are a subcontractor performing a subcontract on a large site you may have lots of things there but your operation can still be temporary, whereas if you are a professional like a lawyer you do not need very much. Nowadays with your mobile phone and your Blackberry, et cetera, you can travel across border and you do not actually need a physical infrastructure. It is very difficult to have a general definition which encompasses the enormous variety of different services and how they are actually delivered on a cross-border basis.

Q528 *Lord Geddes:* So would you advise us to try and get out of our minds defining "temporary", as one does say as a layman, as a matter of time?

Mr Osborne: I think that is probably right. There is one case which involved a plastering subcontractor from Portugal working for a German contractor in Bavaria over a period of nearly two years but who was only working on that one contract for that one German contractor. The implication of the Court's judgment was that that was temporary. So if you go back and look at it in terms of the first principle, here is somebody working cross border but only on one contract only for one contractor. It is not as though he was saying, "I can do work for anybody in this country," he was just doing that one project.

Q529 *Lord Geddes:* I would love to come back to the hairdresser but I do not want to hog this. Is there, in your opinion, sufficient Case Law from the ECJ? Let us assume (which is not going to happen) that the draft Directive goes ahead exactly as presently drafted, is there sufficient Case Law, in your opinion, to make it workable?

Mr Bretz: The Case Law is there. The Case Law, however, says that you need to look at the question of establishment on a case-by-case basis, looking at the permanence of the particular operation that is there and the periodicity of the operation that is there, what is actually being done and then comparing it to what is normal for that type of business. So if you are asking has the Case Law established any hard-and-fast rules that can be used service-by-service to determine whether someone is established or merely providing a service, then the clear answer would be no. If you are asking has the Case Law set out some general principles that can be applied on a case-by-case basis, then the answer is yes.

Lord Geddes: That is very interesting, thank you.

Chairman: A great lawyer's answer! Absolutely clear but still leaving some questions to come—and they will! Baroness Eccles, Baroness Cohen and then Lord Swinfen.

Q530 *Baroness Eccles of Moulton:* Lord Geddes asked the first part of the question that I was about to ask, about whether there was enough established Case Law because both your definitions of "established" and "temporary" have left, apparently, a lot of scope for judgment. Your answer implies that there will still be a great deal of judgment needed when the existing Case Law, as it is building up, is applied in its framework form. Presumably this will have to take place in the courts?

Mr Bretz: I think it is highly likely that on a case-by-case basis ultimately this will be determined by the courts. The situation after the Directive in that respect will be no different from the way that the Country of Origin Principle operates today. It will be a service provider going to another Member State and the Member State saying, "You are established here," and the service provider saying, "No, I am not." At that point there are a number of different options but the most likely route is that it will go to a national court in the host Member State as an issue. In the German case, for example, it was by way of prosecution so the person who had the Portuguese labourers in Germany plastering this very large-scale building was prosecuted under the black market labour laws and at that point as a defence he said, "No, these people are not established here so they are not subject to these rules," and the national court can then make a reference to the European Court of Justice. As you can feel from all of this, it is not very satisfactory for the poor service provider.

Q531 *Chairman:* You say the national court can or should?

Mr Bretz: It is quite a complicated set of rules. A national court may make a reference to the European Court of Justice, but it is only once it comes to the last Court of Appeal—and in a UK context, for example, that could be the Court of Justice in a situation where leave to appeal to the House of Lords is refused the Court of Justice becomes the last Court of Appeal—that an obligation to a firm arises, unless the question of European Community law is sufficiently clear not to require a reference, and it will be the national judge who will ultimately decide whether the question of Community law based on the precedent is sufficiently clear for the duty to refer not to arise.

Q532 *Chairman:* Is this a normal way in which Directives are established or is this a very unusual Directive in that it is going to have to have recourse to the courts to such an extent in order to determine what is temporary and what is established? Is this common practice?

Mr Osborne: It is common practice in many Directives for the difficult issues to be resolved by reference to the European Court simply because at the end of the day Directives are agreed in a political environment, ie in the Council of Ministers, which leads to a lot of debate behind the scenes, horse-trading, coming up with drafting which can accommodate different points of view. The drafting is not by any means ideal in many cases and as a result that naturally generates litigation.

Q533 *Baroness Eccles of Moulton:* This seems to be such a central pillar of the whole Directive that it is really rather confusing that it needs such a lot of legal determination.

Mr Osborne: I think the problem is that the European Court has said that the Treaty provides no clear answer and the Court is unwilling to do more than say, "These are the factors that we take into account," and to give a clear steer into individual cases. It is unwilling to write down its own judgment on something where the Treaty has failed to do it.

Mr Bretz: It is probably worth adding at this point that the Directive is of course always subject to the primary sources of Community law, which is the Treaty as interpreted by the Court, so coming back to John's example of a presumption, you could not have a presumption that says after 16 weeks, or whatever, you will be deemed established because such a presumption would not be compatible with the Case Law of the Court, so you cannot in secondary legislation seek to change the primary source of Community law, which is the Treaty Article.

Baroness Eccles of Moulton: There is one conclusion one could come to as a result of that!

Q534 *Chairman:* Do the Treaties embody the freedom of provision of services?

Mr Bretz: Yes.

Chairman: They do. Baroness Cohen?

Baroness Cohen of Pimlico: This leads me on to a key question I have begun to see staring me in the face. I thought I saw that the Directive in some sense does not do anything on this point. There always was a Country of Origin Principle. The establishment point has always been fought out in the courts. The Directive has made no change to this position whatsoever, so what use is it?

Q535 *Chairman:* Can I rephrase that in another way—that it was put to us and I think the Commission, but I may be wrong—that the case-by-case basis is certainly there but that is a hopelessly slow way of obtaining an effective single market in services. After all, Case Law has not got very far in providing free movement and free provision of services, and therefore the Directive is intended to seek to establish greater certainty than in its absence to try and prevent the case-by-case basis. I suppose the other side of that coin is, in principle, does the Directive in its present form provide any greater confidence to providers of services on a temporary basis than would otherwise exist through the case-by-case basis?
Mr Osborne: I think it does, my Lord Chairman, in the sense that although the basic principles do no more than reflect the Case Law, what it does in various Articles is to say that various provisions which you will find dotted around national laws are unlawful which would make it a lot easier for people who want to go cross-border when they find that barrier to say, "That is unlawful, see Article so-and-so of the Services Directive." Secondly, what it does is to try and encourage service providers to go cross-border. Because it makes it clearer that they can go cross-border relying on the Country of Origin rules and providing information centres and single points of contact et cetera, so that service providers who want to establish themselves in another Member State would go to one single point of contact, obtain the requisite information, apply for any requisite authorizations; it does make life easier for service providers, and it does encourage them to actually go cross-border. The more encouragement and activity you have the more that will generate life under the Services Directive and will lead to cases which will help to clarify some of the principles which are at the moment not entirely clear.

Q536 *Chairman:* John, you talk there about—and Oliver jumped slightly when you said it—businesses wanting to become established and you talked about barriers, but of course we are not at the moment talking about businesses wanting to become established. There are parts of the draft Directive dealing with reducing the barriers to becoming established but the question here is in relation to operating temporarily. It is the free movement of services side of the Directive. Does it help those companies and businesses?
Mr Osborne: Yes, I think it does because they can see that they can go cross-border and the Country of Origin rules generally will apply to them and therefore it is positive encouragement for people to actually do that. A lot will depend upon their willingness to take up that particular option.
Mr Bretz: I just want to add one thing. I think one has to focus on the role that the Directive plays in all of this. The Commission, if it wanted to and had the human and financial resources to do it, could go after each and every single one of the restrictions and say to the Member State either you abolish this restriction or we will take you to court. I would argue that this would be a highly inefficient and very costly process. The advantage of the Directive is that it almost switches the burden to the Member States because it says we have a Directive, this Directive basically forces you to do certain things and if you fail to do them it will be directly applicable in your local court and you do not want to under-estimate the significance of that particular fact. So if I am a service provider and I go to France or Greece, or wherever I go to, and I feel aggrieved, I can invoke my Directive rights in the local court of that country, even if the Member State concerned has done absolutely nothing to implement it. I think in that respect it has a very significant use because you can point to specific articles as opposed to general principles set out by the Community courts, which by their nature are much more difficult to interpret and much more open to being circumvented.
Lord Swinfen: The position of your hairdresser who goes over for one haircut I can understand. What is the position of the contractor who is contracted to design, build and commission an atomic power station, shall we say, that could take ten years or more to build and to commission and might even involve members of staff having to move to the second country and live there for that length of time, but all the rest of their business is in their home country? Is that still temporary?

Q537 *Baroness Cohen of Pimlico:* Is it in Case Law?
Mr Bretz: Putting my European Court of Justice hat on I would say it is a matter for the national court to decide having regard to the duration, regularity, periodicity and continuity of the project.

Q538 *Lord Swinfen:* That is a lawyer's answer.
Mr Bretz: It would be a Judge's answer. If you went to the European Court of Justice with that particular question that would be the European Court of Justice's answer to that question. My feeling is that obviously the longer the project and the more significant the investment required *in situ*, the more likely you are to be established. I would say

personally, weighing up both sides of the debate on this particular question that you have posed, that you would have to become established because it would be very difficult to provide that sort of project as a service provider.

Q539 Chairman: Can I just try this on you. Is it not clear that the intention of the temporary provision is to enable businesses to examine and consider whether it can build up some business in another Member State or not, or perhaps, offer it very temporarily and then leave? That is the intention of the temporary concept. It is not that a business can call itself temporary even if it is operating very clearly for a very long time on a very, very long-scale project. That could not be said to be breaking into a market or otherwise. Is there something about that in the Directive or am I quite wrong about that?

Mr Osborne: In commercial and practical terms, my Lord Chairman, I would agree fully with you that it is the first step, it is the toe in the water.

Chairman: That is the intention. The intention is not that the business can keep saying it is temporary but it has been there for 30 years. That would be on the face of it outside the spirit of the Directive?

Q540 Lord Geddes: That is exactly my question. How long can the Belgian hairdresser go once a fortnight to Germany and remain temporary?

Mr Bretz: So long as the services are not being provided on an indefinite basis they will be provided, under the Directive, in a temporary capacity. There will come a point where the person has had the infrastructure in the Member State for so long and has established a customer base, comes to the country on certain days every week to the same salon. What I cannot do—and clearly we come back to the same point—is I cannot tell you at what point in time that will be. In Belgium it would probably be the point where she is invited to get a *permit de sejour* and register with the local tax authorities. It is basically up to the Member State to at some point say enough is enough.

Q541 Lord Geddes: It is up to the host state surely?

Mr Bretz: Yes, the host state to say, "Enough is enough; at this point you are established."

Lord Geddes: Thank you.

Q542 Lord Swinfen: What happens if she goes to the clients' homes?

Mr Bretz: Again it is just another factoral ingredient. There would not be any infrastructure so on the Court test she would be less likely to be established than if she had an infrastructure, but it is really just one ingredient. I would not focus too much on the infrastructure because all we know is if you have a permanent infrastructure then you are likely to be

established but there are lots of forms of infrastructure so I would not focus too much on that point.

Chairman: All that is by way of introduction, scene setting, if I may say. We come to the nub of the matter and that is why it is that people in some Member States are getting bothered about temporary versus established. Lord Haskel is going to start us off on this group of questions.

Q543 Lord Haskel: Of course the reason why people are getting exercised about this is that we have had it put to us that if you have a temporary worker coming from one state to another, he or she may bring with them the standards of that country and eventually those standards will have to become the standards of the host state. Now defenders of the Country of Origin Principle say that any business operating on a temporary basis in another Member State is still bound by the *acquis* of the European Union and these provide certain basic accepted standards in relation to matters such as health and safety, workers' rights, environmental matters, the social standards which are the concern in France and Germany when they may get workers coming on a temporary basis from Poland or some of the newer Member States. Could you tell us what is the position in law? What are the key elements of the *acquis* which would apply to a business operating on a temporary basis in another Member State and would these elements of the *acquis* then be embodied in the law of the host Member State so that, in fact, there should be no concern about people coming from less developed parts of the European Union into the more developed parts of the Union because those basic standards remain the same?

Mr Osborne: The EU *acquis* should be the law in all Member States, including the ten new members who joined on 1 May last year because as part of the enlargement process they worked extensively in changing their law to bring in and adopt the various EU laws which they would need to have in place as of the date of accession. Thus the *acquis* should be common to all Member States. There may be odd bits of law which a particular Member State has not yet implemented—Germany on the EU Energy Liberalisation Directives for example—but those are relatively isolated examples so it should be the same law. So if I as a self-employed person go to Germany, for example, to do a particular job, there is not too much which could apply to me as a lawyer but if I am a subcontractor and I send a group of people, ie, I post workers to do this project in Germany, then all of those workers are going to be subject to the Posting of Workers Directive and they will be subject to the basic employment laws of the host Member State. That would be various things like wages in Germany where you have national collective labour agreements and they would be beneficiaries of those agreements, et cetera, and health and safety and construction regulations on site, and all of that will actually apply to those people. So why are certain potential host Member States like France and Germany concerned? It may be that they may have doubts about the quality of work to be performed. If you look generically at certain of the older Member States—France and Germany—there has been a lot more regulation of the standards and qualifications and training required for individual occupations, far more than we have in the UK, and therefore there may be an expectation that German and French workers who have been through this process of training and then experience may be better workers and may produce better quality work, and there may be a fear that these potential cowboys coming from other Member States may be producing work which will not be of the same quality. There may also be a concern that, okay, if you post workers to, say, Germany, then in terms of wages you may be subject to the minimum rates of pay in Germany but that the posted workers will just get the minimum whereas, in practice, German workers get considerably more than the minimum; therefore there is the ability of the foreign service provider to undercut the businesses established in the host Member State.

Mr Bretz: May I just add one very small point on the Posting of Workers Directive because I think it is very important. A posted worker means a worker who for a limited period carries out work in the territory of another Member State, ie, a Member State in which he does not normally work. It is up to the host Member State to decide whether someone is a posted worker. So it is the host Member State that decides whether the posted worker provisions apply. That is often ignored and I think it is a very important fact.

Mr Osborne: Because that means in effect you can have the authorities, competitors, et cetera, in the host Member State who can effectively monitor provision by foreign service providers. If they think the rules are not being complied with they can complain to the local regulators, et cetera, et cetera. That is a sort of self-monitoring really by the national industry. They can keep an eye on that sort of thing and complain if they believe that the rules are not being complied with and the host Member State can then decide whether these posted workers are in fact genuine posted workers.

Q544 *Lord Haskel:* So the whole purpose of the Directive from your explanation is to let the market work and if there is a shortage of plumbers in Germany then let's get some plumbers from Poland and if they will come at a cheaper rate that is the market working and it is really nothing at all to do with the law?

Mr Osborne: I think that is right. If you look at the free movement of goods, you will see that the price differentials between Member States of ordinary common or garden products which all of us do buy may be three to five times greater than the differential within one Member State. In terms of services the amount of free movement of services is not that great and we all know services constitute something like 70 per cent of the different national economies. Therefore there is perceived to be considerable scope for cross-border service provision bringing in additional competition into those markets. It is a way to create a genuine internal market across services, which is absolutely vital.

Q545 *Lord Haskel:* So, from a legal point of view then, is there any point in differentiating between services and other products, because from what you say the same rules apply? In fact, if you talk to business people they feel that it is a false differentiation anyway because many manufactured goods depend on the services that go with them and many services depend on the manufactured goods being supplied which they then have to service.

Mr Osborne: Absolutely because many manufacturers will be providing service and maintenance on their products for many years after the product has been supplied. Many service providers will be supplying goods as part of the service contract, so why should we have different rules applying to different elements?

Q546 *Lord Haskel:* So from a legal point of view in fact there is really no difference?

Mr Bretz: In fact, the rules of European Community law apply in an almost identical way to goods and services. If you look at the Case Law, the words used by the European Court of Justice are identical for goods and services. It is the same principles that apply. I wanted to pick up very briefly on your Polish plumber because I think it is a good example and we should use it to explain the interaction of posted workers and services.

Chairman: We are going to come to the Posting of Workers Directive and I am a bit concerned that we are moving into this area of the relationship between the Posting of Workers Directive and the Services Directive. Can we wait until later and then we will get to that then. Let us try to stick to the question of the Services Directive. Lord Haskel, have you anything else on that one?

Lord Haskel: I think we have covered the point really. The laws and regulations of the host Member State and of its country of origin I think have already been discussed.

Chairman: Okay. Baroness Eccles?

Q547 *Baroness Eccles of Moulton:* You have talked about France and Germany in relation to, to put it crudely, cheap labour coming in from Poland and we could move on but, in the meantime, there is just one question that occurred to me, which is highly relevant. If the *acquis* were broader and more all-embracing there would be no need for the Country of Origin Principle, would there?

Mr Osborne: I think in that case we are talking more about full harmonisation, which is something which is impracticable to actually adopt. The European Community today is perhaps less willing to take an enormous raft of measures because it would encounter resistance amongst the Council of Ministers. Even measures like the Working Time Directive have created enormous difficulty in agreeing the original Directive and then the various amendments to the Directive. If you try and tackle each of the different elements in terms of what you need to do to work in different Member States you would be creating an enormous raft of law. I think that is probably an impracticable (although ideal) position.

Q548 *Baroness Eccles of Moulton:* It did seem when we came up against questions like wages and health and safety that the *acquis* had already dealt with them. They seem to be two of the more fundamental principles that the code would have had to cope with if the *acquis* had not been in place. I would like to ask what the situation would be in two contrasting examples. The first is what would be the situation if a Polish business were to provide services on a temporary basis under the Country of Origin Principle in the United Kingdom, which would be one situation, and what would be the situation if a UK-based business were to operate in France on a temporary basis under the Country of Origin Principle? That is the question.

Mr Bretz: My Lord Chairman, with your kind permission, we will pick up the Polish plumber point again at this point. If you had a self-employed Polish plumber who is contracted to provide a commercial service—and I am intentionally using the word "commercial" as opposed to a service to a consumer, so he is carrying out a service in a commercial building and the client is a business—and that self-employed Polish plumber is subject to the Country of Origin rules, the Country of Origin Principle will operate at that point. However, if we take a slightly different example and we have a Polish company that employs the very same plumber and sends him off for three or four months to the UK to perform a plumbing job in the same building, that posted worker will be subject to the UK employment rules.

Q549 *Chairman:* Because of the Posting of Workers Directive?

Mr Bretz: Because of the Posting of Workers Directive. So the difference is between the truly self-employed and the service provider who uses posted workers. We should not forget in this context the cross-border service. There are lots of services that can be provided without ever having a physical presence in the host Member State. Again the Country of Origin Principle can apply in those circumstances. So that is really a fundamental distinction. If you turn it around and you talk about an English plumber going to Germany and France, one additional hurdle or obstacle that one will face is that in Germany being a plumber is indeed a regulated profession and at that point you basically say, "What qualifications do you need in order to perform plumbing services in Germany?" And that is where the draft Directive on Professional Qualifications will come in useful because you can provide evidence that you are entitled to supply that plumbing service in Germany. Can you call yourself a German plumber? Insofar as the use of that word in German is a regulated title you may not use it but you can provide plumbing services. It is a slightly arcane distinction but it is very important to the draft Directive on Professional Qualifications.

Q550 *Baroness Eccles of Moulton:* So that would be described as a barrier, the fact that in order to operate as a plumber in regulated Germany you would have to produce various qualifications, certificates or whatever that would not be considered necessary elsewhere?

Mr Bretz: You can provide the service.

Q551 *Chairman:* Under the Services Directive.

Mr Bretz: But the actual title.

Lord Swinfen: You would call yourself a "water engineer"!

Q552 *Chairman:* Or a "Polish plumber".

Mr Bretz: I suppose it is the same in my profession, if I go to Belgium I cannot call myself an avocat for example because that is a regulated title.

Q553 *Baroness Eccles of Moulton:* But you can still perform the service?

Mr Bretz: Provided I am qualified to perform the service I can provide the service, yes. That is the fundamental basis of the Services Directive.

Q554 *Baroness Eccles of Moulton:* Does that mean there are indemnity problems in some areas? Why does one have to worry at all about going to particular areas if it is just a question of the title and you are allowed to perform the service anyway?

Mr Bretz: Because the title is often fundamental to market recognition. There is a good example in the accountancy field where in the UK "accountant" is not a regulated title but "chartered accountant" is, and you may well be an accountant but unless you are a member of the institute or association nobody will employ you as an accountant so you still need to have the regulated title in order to be accepted by the market.

Q555 *Lord Swinfen:* At the very beginning of your answer to this question you stressed that the Polish plumber was going to work in a commercial building. Would there be any change to your answer if he was going work in a residential building in a domestic setting in somebody's house?
Mr Bretz: Yes because the provisions on consumer contracts will apply and I think it is important to stress that in the Services Directive the Country of Origin Principle will not apply to consumer contracts. I do not know whether I should spend some time now going through that.

Q556 *Chairman:* Yes please.
Mr Bretz: When you look at the exceptions in Article 17—

Q557 *Chairman:* I apologise, I have asked Baroness Cohen to deal with this, but by all means carry on. You have got a head of steam!
Mr Bretz: The point I was going to make is that if you look at Community legislation whenever the Country of Origin Principle comes up, as a general rule there is usually a specific exception related to consumer contracts and the idea is that a consumer should effectively benefit from the ability to invoke the rules of his home country even when the service provider is from another Member State unless—unless—there is actually complete harmonisation in relation to the particular point. There is no consumer contracts harmonisation in place at the moment but there could be in the future and until such time if a foreign service provider is dealing with a consumer, it will always be the host country's consumer rules that apply.

Q558 *Lord St John of Bletso:* I have a very minor point. Just on the issue of a practising solicitor or an accountant, how would that affect your professional indemnity insurance?
Mr Osborne: To be honest, I am not sure. We would obtain, and do have, global professional indemnity insurance cover. Currently Clifford Chance operates in 29 different countries ranging from China to Russia to Singapore and the UK; and I do not think we have had any difficulty in securing appropriate cover for practising in those different jurisdictions. Indeed, quite often we might be working on a project in, say, India where we do not have an office but yet we still have cover for that particular work. The only issues in relation to indemnity that tend to arise are

in relation to practice in the US where the market, as you are well aware, has certain different features.

Q559 *Chairman:* Can I come back to the question of dumbing down or rush to the bottom of standards and so on. It has always been rather difficult to establish from listening to people which laws and regulations they think that temporary operators in their country would not be subject to. There seems to be a general feeling that somehow businesses operating on a temporary basis are not going to be subject to the same laws as us. When you ask what are the laws that they are not liable to, it is often difficult to know. So my question is this: if a business is operating on a temporary basis in another Member State, which of its activities and processes are subject to the laws and regulations of the host Member State and which are the laws and regulations where the Country of Origin Principle would apply? What is it that businesses operating on a temporary basis "get away with", in the words of people that have been pejorative about it?
Mr Osborne: Probably the main thing, my Lord Chairman, would be that if one takes the skilled crafts of let's say Germany, you have a skilled crafts register where to get on that register people may have to go through a period of training and then a period of experience before they are recognised as being a master of their craft. You do not really have the same position in the UK. Anyone in the UK, for example, can set up as a plumber without even having an NVQ qualification. So there will be a concern that cross-border service provision can come from people who do not have the depth and range of qualification and training, et cetera, and therefore that affects the quality of the work that you perform.

Q560 *Chairman:* Sorry, we are moving on to the question of alleged consequences. My question is: is it possible to say of a business operating on a temporary basis in a host Member State what laws of the host Member State apply to that business and what laws of the Country of Origin apply to that business? After all, all this is about the argument that the Country of Origin Principle applies and yet we are often told that although the Country of Origin Principle applies there are some laws of the host Member State that apply to you, for example, consumer protection if it is sales to consumers. Is there any generalisation possible because when the European Parliament discusses these things, for example, there will be a host of allegations made about "the laws of our country do not apply because it is operating on a temporary basis". What generalisations can one make about this?
Mr Osborne: If you have cross-border service provision and a self-employed person goes to another Member State to perform a service, probably the

things in the laws of the host Member State which would apply would relate to, let's say, if you are working on a building site, to construction, building regulations, that sort of thing. If he is sending posted workers there then you have the whole raft of posted workers' rights. The same with contracts. If he is contracting with a consumer he will have the national host Member State consumer protection laws. The Member State of origin will be dealing with things like qualifications and experience and dealing with any regulatory enforcement measures. In terms of business contracts it is likely that a service provider will seek to contract under its own laws giving jurisdiction to its own courts. If they want to sue him they would have to go to the home Member State and that country's law would govern his contract and that country's courts would deal with any lawsuits. So those are in general terms what the situation is. There will be variances depending on the nature of the activity.

Q561 *Chairman:* So, in general terms, consumer protection would be by the host country, and in general terms, health and safety would be covered by the host country?
Mr Osborne: The detail, particularly working on sites—

Q562 *Chairman:* --- I am trying to get away from construction because every time we mention it construction comes up.
Mr Osborne: My Lord Chairman, the Commission has been looking at the issue of safety in relation to services and unfortunately there is very little data so it is a bit of a black hole. Article 16 of the Services Directive says the Country of Origin rules apply, and in particular they cover such matters as behaviour of the provider, quality or content of the service, advertising, contracts and providers' liability, so that is implying that a number of safety issues would be a matter for the Country of Origin. If you are working on a site, it should be the law of the host Member State. I am not sure how much more additional help we can give in terms of divvying up the different laws as between the host Member State and the home Member State.
Mr Bretz: You did ask us later on, Chairman, to identify areas of the Directive where a bit more clarity might be helpful and certainly on the definition of the co-ordinated field, which is the only area to which the Country of Origin Principle applies, John has read the non-exhaustive list in Article 16. It would obviously be very helpful to get a better idea of what the co-ordinated field is. For example, in our preparation we had a discussion internally as to, for example, whether the general legal provisions, including the law of the contract, will be home Member State or host Member State in the absence

of an express choice of law. John and I came to the conclusion that that would probably be part of the co-ordinated field but reading the definition of co-ordinated field, namely "any requirement applicable to access to service activities or the exercise thereof", it is not entirely clear that the law would be that of the home Member State.

Q563 *Lord Haskel:* But you did make the point earlier, and I wrote it down because I thought it was rather an interesting point, that one of the differences is that for some host countries the rules are applied with a lighter touch to a temporary worker or company which is coming into their country.
Mr Bretz: That would be in a situation where the rule is applicable to all providers—national providers and foreign providers—but has the effect of discriminating against the foreign provider. So for example where a standard is very easy to meet for a national but much more difficult to meet for a foreign provider, even though it applies to everyone, it could effectively discriminate and therefore go against the Case Law of the European Court. That is where this reverse discrimination point comes in.

Q564 *Lord Haskel:* It is a matter of discrimination?
Mr Bretz: It is effectively discrimination but without being expressly discriminatory. A good example is the German rules on lawyers where they have to be affiliated to a particular federal state or particular länd within Germany but that would not apply to someone who was coming into Germany to provide legal services. They could provide legal services without being affiliated to a particular länd because in restricting to a particular länd you would limit their freedom to provide services or their freedom of establishment.

Q565 *Lord Walpole:* Is there any basis for the argument that the Country of Origin Principle would permit businesses operating in another (in other words not their own home) Member State on a temporary basis to drive down standards of health and safety, conditions of employment, wages, salary levels and environmental protection? I particularly wanted to ask this because this was a question we were asking both in Berlin and Warsaw recently and you can imagine that the answers were extremely different. For instance, in Germany they were really worried that contractors coming in from other places would pour pesticides all over the place. I am sure in my own mind that comes under the *acquis* anyway but it was certainly brought up with us. On the other hand, when we went to Warsaw we discovered that the way that the old Soviet Union operated was that the Poles were the constructors of very many buildings all over the Soviet Union. I do not know how good or bad they were, that is not the point, but that was what they had always done and always expected to go abroad to work. So is there any basis and can this argument be agreed or is there no basis to it and can it be elaborated? Or is there a basis, in which case should the draft Services Directive be changed a bit to overcome reasonable concerns?

Mr Bretz: My Lord Chairman, with your kind permission, I think we should leave the working conditions aside for a moment because we are going to discuss that as part of the posted workers. The question is related to the quality of the service provided so that the question is if a service provider from another Member State comes to your country, do you have any control over the quality of the service provided or do you lose control and thereby start a race to the bottom? I think the answer to that is that once you have a free trade area such as the European Union and you have Case Law of the European Court of Justice that provides for the free movement of services, it is inevitable for an unregulated service, and this is what we are talking about, we are not talking about a regulated profession such as a doctor or accountant or lawyer to be provided on the basis of Country of Origin and therefore there will be a trade-off between the price of the service and the quality of the service. That is not necessarily a bad thing because there may be people who are currently foregoing the service in Germany because the price point is set at a level which is above their willingness to pay. The whole concept underlying the free movement of unregulated services is that you will increase welfare ultimately by allowing more consumers—let me rephrase that because I am not going to talk about consumers—by allowing more service providers to provide services at different price levels. There may be variations in quality. Insofar as it is a regulated service which has to be provided by qualified professions—and obviously the immediate connotation is that there is a connection between the qualification that you have to possess and the quality of the service you provide but unfortunately there is also a connotation between that and price—at that point you come back to do you possess the necessary qualification under the draft Directive on the Recognition of Professional Qualifications to provide this service? So those are the elements but for an unregulated service the assertion is absolutely right that subject to the exclusions in Article 17 and subsequent you will be able to provide that service on a Country of Origin Principle and you could be doing that at a much cheaper price point and you may be providing a much lower quality of service.

Q566 *Lord Walpole:* You may be providing just as good a service though. Incidentally, there is no minimum wage in Germany, is there, although I understand that the majority of construction workers do work under a union agreement?

Mr Bretz: There is a collective agreement.

Q567 *Lord Walpole:* Collective, organised wage levels?

Mr Bretz: But we always come back to the Posting of Workers Directive. I do apologise. At the end of the day if you start posting workers to Germany and they are posted workers, then the collective wage agreements will apply to their working conditions. There is no doubt it will apply. This is one of the reasons I think why Commissioner McCreevy reacted so angrily in the European Parliament because he was faced with the social dumping argument. He said, "I do not want to hear about social dumping because that should be guaranteed as a result of the Posting of Workers Directive."

Q568 *Lord Walpole:* As far as throwing chemicals around the place where they should not, presumably that is covered by the EU *acquis*, is it not?

Mr Bretz: It should be. I am not an expert on how the throwing around of chemicals is regulated specifically . I do not know if John can help you.

Mr Osborne: Certainly I think the environmental protection laws on matters like waste are all matters of Community *acquis*. The other point to make is that the Services Directive does not change the current situation. It will be exactly the same as it is today under the Services Directive.

Chairman: Let us turn to the question of posted workers.

Q569 *Lord St John of Bletso:* You have in fact covered partly the application and definition of the Posting of Workers Directive but what is the relationship between this Directive and the draft Services Directive? Does the draft Services Directive in any way compromise or reduce the effect of the Posting of Workers Directive? What degree, if any, is there a lack of clarity (since as lawyers certainty is key to you) in the draft Services Directive? If there is a lack of clarity, what amendments would you recommend to overcome these problems?

Mr Osborne: My Lord Chairman, the two Directives are actually separate and parallel. I think the Posting of Workers Directive is covered by derogation in Article 17 and the only changes made to that Directive under the Services Directive are those set out in Article 24 which are essentially dealing with a slight change in allocation of tasks between host Member State and home Member State and supervisory responsibility. I think that would open up a different Pandora's Box if in dealing with the Services Directive you tried to re-open the Posting of Workers Directive so the Services Directive does not change the Posting of Workers Directive.

Q570 *Lord St John of Bletso:* What about the issue of lack of certainty?

Mr Osborne: I do not think there is any lack of certainty on that particular point. If more and more people take advantage of the provision of services across borders then inevitably that will raise issues which may require reconsideration of the Posting of Workers Directive, but that is a separate thing.

Q571 *Lord St John of Bletso:* I want to move on to the mutual recognition of professional qualifications. You have already mentioned the example of you practising in Brussels. What are the principal provisions of this Directive? How does it interface with the draft Services Directive? Finally, would the draft Services Directive change the position of businesses including individuals by providing business services on a temporary basis?

Mr Bretz: I will make a start and then John can come in as appropriate. I think the first question we have to ask is what type of regulated service are you talking about? Is it regulated in a home Member State as well as a host Member State or is it not regulated in a home Member State but regulated in a host Member State? And really I think we come back to the fundamental problem which is there is such a different regulation in particular in France and Germany of certain professions. That could be, for example, the hairdresser that we have spoken about. In order to be a hairdresser in Germany you have to have done a long-term apprenticeship and be a master hairdresser otherwise you cannot call yourself a hairdresser. The problem is that not all Member States have that type of regulation. Essentially what the draft Directive on Professional Qualifications does is it applies a Country of Origin Principle to professional qualifications as well. The basic presumption is if you come from an unregulated Member State—I am going to use that term and apologies for its vagueness—if you have performed that particular profession in two of the last ten years you will be able to go to another Member State and also perform that profession. If you have not done your German apprenticeship but you have been a hairdresser in the UK for two years, and I must confess I am not familiar with what requirements there are in the UK for hairdressers but I expect it is unregulated—

Q572 *Baroness Cohen of Pimlico:* It is.

Mr Bretz: --- You can go to Germany and become a hairdresser without having to pass the master hairdressing qualification, so it is a major door-opening exercise in those countries where there are very high barriers to entry in terms of qualification.

Q573 *Lord Geddes:* Does that exist now or is this coming in as part of the Directive?

Mr Bretz: That is currently in draft.

Q574 *Lord Geddes:* So that does not exist at the moment?

Mr Osborne: There are various Directives covering a wide range of occupations which have been agreed over many years and this new Directive is a logical carry on from that. As to particular occupations, I am afraid that we are not completely up-to-date with all the different occupations that are covered but architects, doctors and lawyers have all been covered by prior Directives. The other point to add is that if you provide services cross-border under the Mutual Recognition Directive then you will be subject to a certain amount of, let's say, regulation in the host state in terms of the title you can use, for example, and also in terms of if you commit serious professional malpractice in the host state you will be subject to their disciplinary rules. You may have to register with a national association of the host state but that is a pure formality. There will be a declaration and you will have to register. So it is a parallel process and it is separate to the Services Directive because the Services Directive deals with all other services apart from those encompassed by the Mutual Recognition Directive.

Q575 *Lord St John of Bletso:* To what degree on the second side of the question would the draft Services Directive change the position of individuals and businesses operating? You have mentioned about the hairdresser bringing on the two-year rule but how else would it change the position?

Mr Bretz: The fundamental point is that you get access to the title and we have mentioned title before as being of fundamental importance to the market. At present, in the absence of the draft Directive on Professional Qualifications, which is the one that we are talking about at the moment, you can go to Germany and provide your hairdressing services but what you cannot do is call yourself a "friseur", which is the regulated German title which means "hairdresser". You can imagine how difficult it is to provide hairdressing services if you cannot call yourself a hairdresser. Most Germans would not understand your home title which is "hairdresser". There may be some basic disadvantages in getting access to that title. I think that is a most fundamental aspect. John has mentioned that there are some secondary aspects in terms of the regulations that you become subject to but that is the major door-opening aspect of that particular proposed Directive.

Q576 *Lord St John of Bletso:* If I could ask a personal question. I trained as a lawyer under the corpus of Roman and Dutch law. I can practise in Scotland; however I cannot practice in England. To what degree could I, with the draft Services Directive,

4 April 2005   Mr Oliver Bretz and Mr John Osborne

now avail of my qualifications to practice in other parts of the European Union?

Mr Osborne: I would believe, without being absolutely certain, that if you are qualified in Scotland you should therefore be able to provide services in other Member States just as an English solicitor would be able to provide services.

Q577 *Baroness Cohen of Pimlico:* Is that under the Professional Services Directive?

Mr Osborne: Yes.

Lord Walpole: Can I ask a quick one while we are on that subject?

Chairman: You are third in line. Lord Haskel has been waiting patiently, Baroness Eccles and then you.

Q578 *Lord Haskel:* From what you have been telling us this whole question about qualifications on the one hand, and regulations on the other, means that as an English lawyer you would be saying they had a right to go and work in Germany and if the qualifications are such that unless they have had a certain amount of experience they cannot practice, insisting on qualifications is a matter of discrimination and that would be illegal under European law? If you were a German lawyer sitting there, would not the German law say, no, that is not quite right because we have certain standards in Germany and it is not a matter of discrimination, it is a matter of maintaining our legal requirements and maintaining our legal standards; so who wins?

Mr Bretz: Legal services is probably not a perfect example because there is a specific Directive on legal services. To summarise it in two seconds, if I go to Germany and I wanted to call myself a Rechtsanwalt, I have to work under a German lawyer for five years or pass an aptitude test. Those are the two choices given in the Directive and I could avail myself of either/or. Most people work under a German lawyer for five years and then apply to transfer their England and Wales solicitor title to the recognised title after five years. That is the specific answer on legal services. In relation to other services, you end up with the same debate again which is how does the qualification relate to the quality of the service? I think it is very, very important to remember that the third part in that particular equation is the price of the service.

Q579 *Lord Haskel:* So it is a matter for the market?

Mr Bretz: Essentially, what are people willing to pay for a particular service in that Member State and is it really necessary for people to have the very high level of qualification in order to perform that service because what you are effectively saying is by requiring such a high level of qualification there will be people losing out because their price point is below the price point that has been set for that service.

Baroness Eccles of Moulton: My question has been more or less asked by Lord Haskel. I would be going over some of the same ground so I will withdraw.

Lord Walpole: While we are on about Lord St John's qualifications for the law, what is the position about Irish citizens in this country? Are there no restrictions, as there never have been, and how does this work out in EU law.

Chairman: Is this in services?

Q580 *Lord Walpole:* Yes. There is nothing to stop anyone from Ireland coming over to England, is there?

Mr Bretz: Just to give you an example. I am a German national. I have lived and worked here for a very, very long time. There is nothing to stop any Community national from coming to the UK and working here. There is no requirement for a work permit and no requirement to register. I can simply come to this country and perform my profession.

Q581 *Lord Walpole:* So Ireland is no more particular or peculiar than anywhere else?

Mr Bretz: It is exactly the same.

Chairman: We have had the Irish question. Let's push on. It is not central to this inquiry but the Irish question is always important. Baroness Cohen?

Q582 *Baroness Cohen of Pimlico:* I am now going to try and unpick the rights of consumers. We are back now to the draft Services Directive for this one. I think you said earlier that under the draft Services Directive if you are providing a service to a consumer all of the law of the state in which the consumer is resident applies. If I am a consumer and I wish to sue you, is it under my law that I am suing you?

Mr Osborne: The Directive gives a derogation for consumer contracts and therefore it would be the host Member State law which would actually govern those sorts of contracts.

Q583 *Baroness Cohen of Pimlico:* If I had my hair done atrociously by a temporarily resident German hairdresser, it is English law that applies?

Mr Osborne: Under the Brussels Convention you would be able to sue in your own Member State.

Q584 *Baroness Cohen of Pimlico:* Under my own law.

Mr Bretz: In the absence of choice of law. Effectively what I said before is absolutely true, if you are a consumer none of this Country of Origin stuff would apply to you.

Mr Osborne: The only practical difficulty would be if you sue in your own country and you get judgment in your own country, under the Brussels Convention you have to enforce it in the other Member State where the person is established, and the Services

Directive will help there because it will require professional indemnity insurance for services, so ultimately there should be somebody to pick up the tab.

Q585 Baroness Cohen of Pimlico: That is helpful nonetheless. If however I am a business and the Polish plumbing firm temporarily resident here has done a really bad job, what then happens?
Mr Bretz: Assuming at the moment we are talking about the UK, plumbing is an unregulated profession and the Country of Origin Principle will apply. Assuming for a moment that none of the derogations will apply, just for the sake of argument, at that point it is likely, in the absence of a specific choice of law in your contract, that it is governed by Polish law.

Q586 Baroness Cohen of Pimlico: Right, so that is a radical difference from being an individual consumer. Unless you choose your law, you are going to be governed by the—
Mr Bretz: --- Unless you have a specific choice of jurisdiction, it is also likely that the courts in Poland may have jurisdiction over the matter. Whether they have exclusive jurisdiction is another matter and is hugely complicated, and I do not want to get into it.

Q587 Baroness Cohen of Pimlico: Is that a change to the draft Services Directive? Or was that always the position?
Mr Osborne: That is the situation today. The Rome Convention deals with the applicable law in a contract and the Brussels Convention deals with where you sue.

Q588 Baroness Cohen of Pimlico: That is no change. The Services Directive has not made life any different and if you are contracting with my incoming Polish firm I had better be careful to specify then, as now, what sort of law we are operating under?
Mr Bretz: John has already mentioned the Rome Convention and the Brussels Convention. Both contain the same derogation for consumer contracts to a greater or lesser extent. There are minor variations in it

Q589 Baroness Cohen of Pimlico: Can I ask a sweep-up question. Are there other Directives that deal with consumer protection? Is consumer protection used here both for individuals and for businesses and, if so, does the Services Directive qualify, reduce or improve the rights of consumers of services, whether they be individual consumers or business consumers, provided by businesses operating on a temporary basis in another Member State?
Mr Osborne: There is a raft of Directives covering in one form or another different elements of safety from the Product Liability Directive, which is embodied in the Consumer Protection Act 1987, to Directives on a whole range of things like cosmetics, food, food additives, organic products.

Q590 Baroness Cohen of Pimlico: Those are goods not services, however.
Mr Osborne: Yes, but as we discussed earlier the term "service provision" often refers to the provision of goods and services as well. There is no general law in relation to pure provision of services but the Commission has a separate consumer protection priority programme that is going on at the moment where it is looking at further measures which might apply in terms of safety rules in service provision. One good thing which the Services Directive would do is this provision about professional indemnity insurance under Article 27. This is where the services provided pose a particular risk to the health and safety of the recipient or a financial risk to the recipient, and in that situation the Member State shall ensure that the service provider is covered by professional indemnity insurance or some other equivalent. I am not quite sure how a Member State is going to be able to ensure all cross-border service providers are actually covered but that is what the Directive says.

Q591 Baroness Cohen of Pimlico: If I go to a salon in Germany—
Mr Osborne: --- They might use particular chemicals which might destroy someone's hair.

Q592 Baroness Cohen of Pimlico: Indeed, one lives in dread, yes!
Mr Osborne: There are other provisions in the Services Directive which are fairly bland. They talk about service providers providing information. They talk about providing information about any service guarantees they may offer. They encourage voluntary codes of practice, voluntary self-certification of quality, but they are all fairly bland, they do not really bite.
Mr Bretz: It is interesting that the particular words in the provision that John mentioned are also mirrored in the draft Directive on Professional Qualifications because they are basically saying that where the service has public health or public safety implications at that point the host Member State may at least check the qualifications of the provider to establish they have got the qualifications. However, they cannot go beyond that and if the qualifications are met then under the draft Directive on Professional Qualifications that person can exercise that service in the host Member State.

Q593 Baroness Cohen of Pimlico: What I keep probing for is that I cannot quite see what all the fuss is about in the Services Directive. It seems to me that the real impact on some of the countries with very strict regulated professions is not provided by the Services Directive at all; it is provided by the Professional Services Directive. What is John Monks on about, roughly speaking?

Mr Bretz: I would absolutely agree with the statement that there is nothing in the Services Directive itself that gives rise to these concerns. The Country of Origin Principle really only operates to its full extent in a very, very limited number of circumstances, namely where you have an unregulated service being provided without the posting of workers in a way that is not subject to any of the exceptions in the Directives. Conceptually that will be a smaller number of cases than all the other cases.

Q594 *Baroness Eccles of Moulton:* From what you have just said, it makes one wonder about what appear to be the hugely extravagant claims about the results of the application of the Services Directive. It is said that something like 66 billion euros are going to be added to the economy as a result of the application of the Services Directive. It does all seem quite strange really in view of what has just been discussed in the last few minutes. I suppose that is an observation not a question but the question really is just dawning on me—and I am sure it has dawned on everybody else ages ago—that a consumer is a different person to a business purchaser of services. You could interchange the two descriptions. You could be a consumer of a business or you could be a purchaser of services as a private individual. So we have to get the actual terminology clear in our minds first. Is there a grey area where the two overlap and where you could not be absolutely sure whether the person you were talking about, or the purchaser you were talking about, was a private individual or a business?

Mr Osborne: There may always be slight grey areas but we have exactly the same problem under the UK consumer protection legislation which provides rights to consumers. There may always be the odd cases where there will be fringe issues but it is a situation common to our own national law at the moment. The Directive will not have any impact upon that.

Q595 *Baroness Eccles of Moulton:* Is our consumer protection law only applicable to the individual or can it apply to a business?

Mr Osborne: Most of it will apply primarily to consumers buying for their own consumption as opposed to businesses who are using something in the course of their business. However, there are rules, for example, under the unfair contract terms legislation on standard terms of business. There are various pieces of UK legislation which would also impact on business-to-business terms.

Q596 *Lord Swinfen:* Coming to nearly the last fence, there are conflicting views of the Country of Origin Principle. Some witnesses have told us that it is the cornerstone of the Services Directive and that they would resist all attempts to water it down. Others claim that it is completely unworkable. Looking at the Services Directive, particularly the sections dealing with the Country of Origin Principle and the free movement of services, is it possible to identify issues of law that might explain these two drastically different views? If there are, what are they?

Mr Bretz: My Lord Chairman, I come back to my introductory statement which is that the Country of Origin Principle is not new. It has existed for a long time in particular in the goods sphere. It was introduced by the European Court of Justice in a case called *Cassis de Dijon* in relation to goods, mainly as a result of the realisation by the Court and others within the European institutions that full harmonisation was simply never going to happen. So there was a fundamental change of approach at that particular point in time. Minimum harmonisation is what people are looking for now where you basically guarantee a minimum set of standards that are part of the *acquis communautaire* that apply to all Member States, including the new Member States, and beyond that the Country of Origin Principle will apply. It is probably worth mentioning that the Country of Origin Principle also already applies in relation to broadcasting. It is contained within TV Without Frontiers, a Directive which I am sure you will have heard about. It is contained in the E-Commerce Directive. In the virtual world, as it were, it was hugely important for service providers to know that they could rely on the Country of Origin Principle. The Case Law says it also applies to other services and what the Directive does is it tries to implement that Case Law of the Court in a more specific and certain manner rather than trying to bring individual cases to establish the law, which would be costly and inappropriate. Concerns that have been expressed about social dumping in particular are mostly dealt with by the Posting of Workers Directive insofar as the service is provided using posted workers. There is obviously still an area of loophole here which is if a service can be provided cross-border or provided by someone who really is self-employed, then the Country of Origin Principle will apply to its full extent. The example that I used recently was a commercial laundry service because again I am trying not to make it a consumer contract, which picks up bed linen and tablecloths in Germany, puts them into a van and drives them across the border where all the washing and ironing is done in Poland. It is only the person that picks up the laundry that will be the posted worker because they will be spending two days a week in Germany picking up laundry. All the other services are provided in Poland and the laundry is returned clean. That is a typical service where the Country of Origin Principle is a very powerful way of making sure it is home country regulation that will apply. In conclusion, I do not think there is anything radically new in the Services Directive and I think that the concerns about quality of service, which is the other area that is often mentioned, and we have talked about the social side, working conditions and the Posting of Workers Directive, then you are talking about regulated services because it is certain that services which pose risks in terms of quality are more likely to be regulated, and then you are basically into the field of the draft Directive on Professional Qualifications and that will be dealt with within the scope of that particular Directive. So I do not think there is much here that is in this particular draft Directive that is new.

Lord Swinfen: Thank you very much. I do not think I need ask my final question.

Q597 *Chairman:* Is the Country of Origin Principle workable in practice?

Mr Osborne: My Lord Chairman, I would make one point which is that one of the reasons for scepticism will be that the Country of Origin Principle relies on a degree of trust that the regulators in the home Member State will be able to perform the necessary regulatory discipline over service providers established within the state. The question is do all Member State have sufficient confidence in the ability and willingness of regulators in different Member States to properly regulate service providers within their jurisdiction so when a list of complaints comes up about a particular service provider providing services to Member States and they are referred by the host Member State back to the home Member State, will anything actually be done about those and will it be in fact practicable to have this single point of contact? Will it be practicable to provide all this information? Will it be practicable to provide a single point of authorisation? Will it be practicable to ensure that all service providers actually have professional indemnity insurance in place? The UK Government could not possibly know the identity of all service providers carrying on business in this country. How do they check that everybody has appropriate professional indemnity insurance? There are questions about the workability of different aspects. There are questions about how much trust and confidence you can have in the regulators in different Member States, but in principle there is no

reason why it should not work because it is merely a codification of the situation we have today.

Q598 *Chairman:* If I can summarise that. You have said on consumer protection that for the individual consumer there is really no cause for concern at all. For the business purchaser of services it will be for them, as it is now, to decide whose law applies. Any sensible business person would ask that question in the contract. Nothing has changed there. On the question of social dumping your advice to us is that the laws that apply are effectively such that the social dumping argument appears not to be robust, to put it that way, and not to have a lot of substance to it. Where there are issues and where there is a trade-off is in the quality of service. The quality of service may be better or worse. It may be at a higher or lower price but that is the trade-off for the purchaser to decide for themselves rather than protection to stop them doing it. And there is the issue of trust. Is it fair to assume that the Country of Origin state government service will reasonably supervise and ensure that the supervisory process is undertaken? That last point is one we have not talked to you about, not because we have not been concerned about it but because it seems it is not a matter of law but a matter of administration and fact. So to summarise, social dumping and the consumer protection issue should not be a cause of concern on the basis of any change in the legal position. The issue of quality of service and the trade-off is certainly one that opens up issues but that is not a matter of law it, it is a matter of choice and you make a decision as to whether or not you use it. On the question of trust and supervision it is not so much a matter of law, it is a matter of administration and is it likely to be carried through. Is that a reasonable assessment of your advice?

Mr Bretz: Yes, I would agree with your statements. The only small change I would make to your statement is about social dumping. I would say insofar as the posting of workers is part of the provision of services there is no concern about social dumping. There clearly could be in a situation where a service is fully cross-border or where it can be supplied in such a way to not require the posting of workers.

Q599 *Chairman:* I am sorry to use the Polish example because it is the most sharp but let me just ask this question: if a subcontractor employed 50 Polish workers to go and do a job in Germany, for example, and it took six months to undertake whatever business it was in, would that come under the posting of workers?

Mr Bretz: My Lord Chairman, absolutely, those workers would be posted workers for the duration of their stay in Germany. It would be the host Member State, ie in this example Germany, that could determine their status as posted workers.

Q600 *Chairman:* Is the Posting of Workers Directive in place or is it a draft, just remind me?

Mr Bretz: It is in place.

Chairman: I do not think there is anything further. You have been exceptionally generous with your time and we thank you for that. It is an indication of how much we have benefited by the fact we have kept going way beyond our normal time. Thank you very, very much indeed.

Written Evidence

Memorandum by Alliance of UK Health Regulators on Europe (AURE)

This paper has been produced by the Alliance of UK Health Regulators on Europe (AURE) in response to the Select Committee's Inquiry into the European Commission's proposal for a Directive on Services.

As regulators, AURE members have statutory responsibility for the protection of patients and service users. Our functions embrace the education and registration of health and social care professionals, the maintenance of professional standards and action against individuals who fall short of those standards.

AURE supports the aim of the proposal for a Directive on Services as a positive step towards facilitating service provision across the EU. Nevertheless, we firmly believe that in pursuing this goal, it is necessary to find the optimum balance between removing unnecessary barriers to cross-border service provision and at the same time ensuring the protection of the public interest (including public health).

Whilst we are please to note the inclusion of some checks and balances in the Commission's proposal, there remain certain areas of the text that need to be strengthened in order to enable competent authorities to carry out their regulatory functions and ensure patient safety across Europe.

This paper outlines in further detail AURE's concerns as listed in the table.

Measures of Concern in AURE
- — Single points of contact (Article 6)
- — Authorisation schemes (Article 10)
- — Cost of the authorisation procedure (Article 13(2))
- — Deemed authorisation (Article 13(4))
- — Derogations from the Country of Origin Principle (Articles 17 and 19).
- — Exchange of information (Articles 33 and 35)

SINGLE POINT OF CONTACT (ARTICLES 6 AND 7)

Article 6 states that a service provider must be able to compete "all procedures and formalities needed for access to his service activities" and "any applications for authorisation needed to exercise his service activities" at a single point of contact. This seems to imply that the contact point would orchestrate all the procedures, formalities and applications that a service provider might need to complete, liaising as necessary with regulators/competent authorities and others. AURE is concerned that, operating as an intermediary in this way, the contact point would in fact become an additional tier of bureaucracy between the service provider and the regulator potentially creating delay and/or misunderstanding.

We also note that the proposed role of the contact point goes much further than that envisaged in Article 57 (regulating contact points) of the most recent draft[1] of the proposed Directive on the recognition of professional qualifications. It is clearly essential that there should be a consistent approach across both Directives. The approach described in the Directive on the recognition of professional qualifications offers a more practical, and less bureaucratic, way forward.

In this context, AURE welcomes the recent Dutch Presidency working document (16 November) currently under discussion at Council Working Group level. This document adds a second paragraph in Article 6, which states that "The creation of single points of contact does not interfere with the allocation of functions or competences among competent authorities". However, AURE would like to see this provision strengthened even further to state clearly that the provisions on single points of contact in the proposed Directive on Services shall not interfere with the allocation of functions or competences among competent authorities, or their pursuit of those functions.

AURE would like to see explicit reference in the text to national competent authorities/regulators and the possibility for these bodies to play the role of the single point of contact where appropriate. AURE also asks that the relationship with the provisions on contact points in the proposed Directive on the Recognition of Professional Qualifications be more clearly defined.

---

[1] Council Common Position of 21 December 2004, 2002/0061 (COD) Council Doc 13781/2/04.

AUTHORISATION SCHEMES—ARTICLES 9 AND 10

Generally speaking, AURE supports the criteria laid down in Articles 9 and 10 for applying and operating authorisation schemes. We would take the view that the authorisation schemes operated by AURE members satisfy these criteria. Nevertheless, to ensure the protection of recipients of services in the health and social care sectors (who are often vulnerable patients), we wish to see it put beyond doubt in the text of the proposed Directive that authorisation schemes are acceptable for professions with implication for public health and safety.

The Directive must also make clear that nothing in the provisions of Articles 9 and 10—or, indeed, Articles 14 and 15 on Black and Grey lists)—shall prejudice the ability of competent authorities to require service providers who have been authorised to pursue a service activity from demonstrating, from time to time, that they remain fit and competent to continue to pursue that activity. This is particularly important in the field of healthcare where competent authorities are now developing systems intended to ensure that healthcare professionals remain competent to practise throughout their working lives. Not only is this essential for the proper protection of patients, but it is also consistent with the provisions of the proposed Directive on the Recognition of Professional Qualifications which highlights the importance of life-long learning.

AURE calls for Article 10 explicitly to permit the application of authorisation schemes for professions with implications for public health and safety and for the Directive to make clear that it is without prejudice to the ability of competent authorities in the health field to require service providers to demonstrate, at set intervals, their continuing competence to practise.

AUTHORISATION PROCEDURES (ARTICLE 13)

AURE endorses the requirements laid down in Article 13 that authorisation procedures should be clear, accessible, objective and impartial. However, we have two areas of concern:

Cost of the authorisation procedure (Article 13(2))

Article 13(2) states that any charges which may be incurred from an application "shall be proportionate to the cost of the authorisation procedures in question".

The UK competent authorities represented in AURE are responsible for a wide range of regulatory functions which are undertaken in the public interest. These include not only the granting of registration/authorisation to practise to healthcare professionals, but also responsibility for education, maintenance of professional standards and the operation of fitness to practise/disciplinary procedures for individuals who fall below those standards.

AURE's members are independent of the UK Government. They receive no funding other than through the fees paid by their registrants. These fees cover not merely the cost of registering/authorising an individual to practise, but they also take account of the wider regulatory functions that AURE's members are required to undertake in the public interest. AURE's members fully accept that they must ensure that the registration and annual retention fees they set are reasonable and proportionate to the costs of the responsibilities they are required to fulfil in protecting the public interests. However, this cannot be limited simply to the unit cost of the authorisation process itself and must reflect the full range of regulatory responsibilities to be carried out.

Since the definitions in Article 4 explicitly state that authorisation schemes cover both access to a service activity and the exercise thereof, it is essential that Article 13(4) makes clear that charges levied on applications may be proportionate to the costs of ongoing regulation by the competent authorities, not just to the unit cost of authorisation of access.

AURE would like to see Article 13(2) amended to make clear that health and social care regulators who are independent of Government can continue to charge fees that fairly and accurately take into account the costs entailed by the full range of their regulatory functions.

Deemed authorisation (Article 13(4))

Article 13(4) introduces the concept of "deemed" registration/authorisation in cares where a regulator fails to respond to an application within a specified time-scale. The processing of applications from EEA nationals is usually straightforward and completed within a brief timeframe. However, allowing health and social care professionals to practise in the absence of a response from the relevant regulator would encourage abuse of the system, undermine confidence in the registers, put patients at risk, and lead to confusion for both patients and employers.

We note that this Article permits different arrangements where there are objectively justified "by overriding reasons relating to the public interest". It is essential that the Directive makes clear that the definition "public interest" covers cases concerned with public health and safety.

In this context, AURE welcomes as a positive step the introduction of a new recital 28(a) in the recent Dutch Presidency working document in the Council, which makes direct reference to the possibility of exempting health services from rules on deemed authorisation by reason of public interest. However, to ensure fully that patient safety is not compromised, it is necessary that this clarification be also included in the text of Article 13(4).

Moreover, we also take the view that the concept of an "implied decision" should not be embedded in the definition of an authorisation scheme given in Article 4(6). If necessary, it should be contained in a separate definition which specifically excludes its application to professions with public health or safety implications.

Article 51 of the proposed Directive on the recognition of professional qualifications provides for an appeal under national law in cases where regulators do not respond to applications for authorisation within a specified time limit. We consider that, where public health and safety are at stake, this will provide a mechanism for holding regulators to account without undermining the regulatory regime which exists for the protection of the public. In any event, it seems appropriate that there should be consistency of approach across the two Directives.

AURE calls for Article 13(4) to make clear that health and social care services are exempt from rules on deemed authorisation for reasons of overriding public interest. In the same context, we also request that the concept of an "implied decision" should not be embedded in the definition of an authorisation scheme given in Article 4(6).

Free Movement of Services: Country of Origin Principle and Derogations (Articles 16–19)

In discussions on the proposed Directive on the recognition of professional qualifications, it has been widely acknowledged that if health and social care professionals were able to practise temporarily in other Member States without being subject to regulation in the host State, patients would be put at risk. This view is reflected in the Council Common Position[2] reached on that proposed Directive where Articles 6 and 7 now provide for the temporary registration of individuals in professions which have implications for public health and safety.

AURE therefore welcomes the recent working documents of the Dutch and Luxembourg Presidencies in the Council of Ministers which seek to clarify further and confirm that the Country of Origin Principle will not apply to professions with implications for public health and safety and will not affect the rules on the free provision of services as laid down in the proposed Directive on the Recognition of Professional Qualifications.

AURE is calling for the European Parliament to strengthen the Commission proposal by further clarifying the exemption of healthcare professions and Title II of the proposed Directive on the Recognition of Professional Qualifications from the Country of Origin Principle, as reflected in the recent working documents of the Dutch and Luxembourg Presidencies.

Exchange of Information (Articles 33 and 35(3))

AURE is encouraged to see, in Article 33, that provision has been made for the exchange of information between competent authorities in different Member States about disciplinary measures against a professional. However, for professions with implications for public health and safety, it is not sufficient for this information to be provided on a reactive basis, "at the request of a competent authority in another Member State". Rather, competent authorities must be proactive in disseminating information to all Member States where they have taken action against an individual who is unfit or unsafe to practise. This is vital if vulnerable patients are to be protected. Furthermore, a decision to communicate such information should not be based on a judgment about whether the individual "is likely to provide services in other Member States" (as suggested in Article 35) since the competent authority will not be in a position to make such a judgment and also because the individual may hold registration in more than one Member State.

It should also be emphasised that the goal of effective information exchange is likely to be impeded in cases where professions are not regulated in all Member States.

AURE would like to see the provisions on information exchange strengthened to provide for compulsory proactive information exchange among Member State competent authorities where an individual's fitness to pursue his or her profession is in question.

---

[2] *Ibid.*

The Alliance of UK Health Regulators in Europe: Who are We?

The Alliance of UK Health Regulators was established to safeguard the health and well-being of patients and service users to ensure that members of the public have access to and are treated by adequately qualified and competent professionals. As Regulators we are required to register for practice only those with the appropriate training and qualifications and who are able to communicate effectively with patients and service users. The Alliance lobbies on a range of European issues to protect patient safety.

Members of AURE

General Medical Council	http://www.gmc-uk.org
General Dental Council	http://www.gdc-uk.org/
General Optical Council	http://www.optical.org/
General Osteopathic Council	http://www.osteopathy.org.uk/
General Chiropractic Council	http://www.gcc-uk.org/
Health Professions Council[3]	http://www.hpcuk.org/
Nursing and Midwifery Council	http://www.nmc-uk.org/
Royal Pharmaceutical Society of Great Britain	http://www.rpsgb.org.uk/
General Social Care Council	http://www.gscc.org.uk/
Pharmaceutical Society of Northern Ireland	http://www.dotpharmacy.com/psni/
AURE	http://www.aure.org.uk

11 February 2005

Memorandum by Amicus

Country of Origin Principle

1. The proposed Directive is based on the Country of Origin Principle, which means that the service provider is subject to the laws, rules and regulations of the Member State where they are established or registered and not by the laws, rules and regulations of the Member State where they are providing the service. Article 16 specifies that Member States of posting shall not impose requirements "governing the behaviour of the provider, the quality or content of the service." This implies that measures introduced by a Member State of posting to ensure that all businesses, operating within its territory, do so on the same basis with regards to health and safety, the behaviour of the company, the quality and content of the service, the technical and financial capacity of the company, the payment of fiscal and social charges etc will not apply to services providers registered in another Member State but who are providing a service in the Member State of posting.

2. This situation is ambiguous and suggests that external services providers will gain a competitive advantage over a local service provider, because they will not be subject to the same criteria. The potential long-term consequence of such a situation will be the eradication of all local measures, which protect against potential abuses and ensure a decent standard of service.

3. Amicus is concerned that many experts have raised serious apprehensions regarding the application of the Services Directive, especially with regards to the Country of Origin Principle. At a recent European Parliament hearing a number of experts stated the following:

4. Berned Jan Drijer, Attorney Bar of The Hague, former member of the Legal Services of the European Commission and legal advisor of the Dutch Representation to the EU stated:

5. "Giving up one's own rules is fine, providing you get commonly agreed rules in return (which does not happen with this Directive). If common standards are missing the country having the lowest standards may set the standard for all. What is more, when national rules can no longer be applied to incoming services their application may also become untenable on a purely domestic level".

6. "The suggestion that country of origin is prerequisite for a level playing field is contestable, if—like here— common rules are lacking. One may even end up with the opposite of a level playing field; each service provider will carry its own national rules into the host state, which may be source of distortions of competition among providers and of legal uncertainty for recipients of services."

---

[3] The Health Professions Council regulates the following 12 health professions: arts therapists, chiropodists/podiatrists, clinical scientists, dieticians, medical laboratory scientific officers (MLSOs), occupational therapists, orthoptists, prosthetists and orthorists, paramedics, physiotherapists, radiographers and speech and language therapists.

7. "What I do say is that this proposal is flawed and that one needs to restore the balance, precisely in order to make the Country of Origin Principle work".

8. BEUC, the European Consumers Organisation stated that:

9. "While appreciating the logic behind the country of origin approach in a single market, there are considerable doubts as to how well it will work in practice to prevent or stop specific abuses or to resolve specific complaints. The gap between theory and practice could be large".

10. "Even in cases where the country of origin rule may seem appropriate in principle, it may not actually work in practice" ... "The country of origin approach cannot work without the appropriate legal, institutional and practical framework for administrative cooperation; in most services areas no such framework exists."

11. Onno Brouwer the Attorney at the Bars of Amsterdam and Brussels, former legal secretary of the European Court of Justice and President of the permanent delegation of the Council of the Bars and Law society of the EU to the EU Court of Justice, stated that:

12. "It could be feared that the implementation of the proposed Country of Origin Principle will lead to a lowering of standards in comparison with the present situation. Such fears particularly exist with regard to the fields of consumer protection, the posting of workers and social security. These fears are not wholly unjustified."

13. The Platform of European Social NGO's said:

14. "The fact that providers would be subject only to the national standards in their Member State of origin could lead to a "race to the bottom" in quality standards, as Member States compete to attract service providers" ... "to forge ahead with the Services Directive ... would be counterproductive and irresponsible".

15. Amicus believes that there is overwhelming evidence that suggests that in its current form the Services Directive is impractical, dangerous and certainly unworkable and is an invitation for abuse and manipulation and threatens to undermine the European Social Model. Furthermore the Services Directive undoubtedly contradicts and undermines the Lisbon strategy of "more and better jobs and with greater social cohesion". Amicus believes that instead of harmonising upwards, it stipulates aggressive competition between Member States, resulting in a downward spiral to the lowest common denominator of protection provisions within the EU, which will be to the detriment of workers, consumers and the environment.

16. Of particular concern is the relationship between the posting of workers and the Country of Origin Principle.

17. The Directive attempts to protect posted workers by applying a derogation from the Country of Origin Principle to the Posting of Workers Directive 96/71/EC. However the effectiveness of the Posting of Workers Directive is undermined within the text of this proposed Directive. In one aspect it states that "Member State of posting shall carry out in its territory the checks, inspections and investigations necessary to ensure compliance with the employment working conditions applicable under Directive 96/71/EC", however it then limits the Member State of posting's ability to carry out these obligations by specifying that the Member State of posting cannot subject the provider or posted worker to "hold and keep employment documents in its territory". Furthermore it then requests that the Member State of origin should ensure that the provider takes all measures necessary, to be able to communicate the relevant information ie "the employment and working conditions applied to the posted worker"; however only after the end of posting.

18. This situation is absurd and totally undermines the obligations laid out in the Posting of Workers Directive. In one instance it is suggested that the Member State of posting shall monitor the behaviour of the service provider, however it then blocks the opportunity to obtain the necessary information to establish whether or not abuses are taking place.

19. The current text of the Directive fails to address potential abuses that could take place. For example under the current proposed provisions there is nothing to stop a company establishing in a Member State with the lowest social requirements and then providing a service to another Member State. It can post workers to that Member State and undermine the basic social and employment terms and conditions. Once the contract has finished and before the provider is requested to supply the relevant employment information the business can simply dissolve.

20. This situation will endeavour to take away any power Members States of posting have to ensure that all workers working within its territory are entitled to certain or minimum terms and conditions of employment. In addition it will undoubtedly result in a downward spiral of terms and conditions of employment to the lowest common denominator in the European Union.

21. Amicus is also particularly concerned about the actual application of the Posting of Workers Directive in the UK. Unlike all other EU Member States, the UK decided against fully transposing the Posting of Workers Directive, claiming that the UK already provided minimum employment standards for all employees working in the UK. However in Britain, the only principle legislation relevant to the Posting of Workers Directive is:

— The Working Time Regulations 1998.

— The National Minimum Wage Act and Regulations.

— The Sex Discrimination Act 1975.

— The Race Relations Act 1976.

— The Disability Act 1995.

— The Employment Equality (Sexual Orientation) Regulations 2003.

— The Employment Equality (Religion or Belief) Regulations 2003.

— Health and Safety Legislation.

— Legislation on the employment of children.

22. This means that posted workers are not covered by other pieces of employment legislation, especially relating to individual rights and trade union and recognition rights:

— Employment Rights Act 1996.

— Employment Tribunals Act 1996.

— Employment Rights (Dispute Resolution) Act 1999.

— Employment Relations Act 1999.

23. Amicus believes that any worker posted to the UK should be covered by all UK social employment legislation, including those mentioned above. In addition, Member State of posting should have the right to monitor and investigate the application of labour standards within its territory and should be entitled, where necessary, to impose preventative regulatory measures to ensure that external services providers do not gain a competitive advantage via social dumping.

Monitoring Services under the Country of Origin Principle

24. One of the key concerns surrounding the Country of Origin Principle is the monitoring of the service provider. Article 16.2 of the Directive specifies that:

25. The Member State of origin shall be responsible for supervising the provider and services provided by him, including services provided by him in another Member State. This indicates that the Member State of posting will have a minimum impact on the:

— The behaviour of the provider.

— The quality, standard and content of the provider.

— The liability of the provider.

26. The practicality of the Member State of origin having the capability to "supervise" the service provider in another Member State is ambiguous and raises a number of questions:

(a) What interest or encouragement will a Member State of origin have to supervise service providers, which are performing in another country?

(b) How would a Member State of origin monitor how a service provider is operating in another country?

(c) What action can the Member State of origin take when they detect service providers operating in an unprofessional or illegal manner?

(d) What action can the Member State of posting take, should the Member State of origin not take its "supervising task" seriously?

27. The "Country of Origin Principle" removes any control the Member State of posting has over the behaviour and actions of the service provider. Amicus believes that the Directive should be amended accordingly to address these issues.

23 February 2005

Memorandum by the Association of British Insurers (ABI)

SUMMARY

1. The proposal for a Directive is aimed at providing a legal framework to eliminate the barriers to the freedom of establishment for service providers and the free movement of services between Member States.

2. Financial services, including insurance, are excluded from the scope of the proposed Directive. However, Article 27 of the proposed Directive requires certain service providers to carry professional indemnity insurance where there is a health and safety risk, or a financial risk, to the service recipient.

3. ABI believes that Article 27, as drafted, is based on a fundamental misunderstanding of how insurance markets work and that it may act as a disincentive to the cross-border provision of services:

— ABI is opposed in principle to the introduction of compulsory insurance. In the UK, experience with compulsory insurance has been problematic;

— the differences between Member States' liability laws, propensity to claim and level of awards are such that most UK insurers are reluctant to write non-UK risks or risks on a cross-border basis; and

— cross-border service providers may therefore have difficulties in obtaining appropriate liability insurance and will not be able to comply with Article 27.

Article 27 should therefore be deleted.

INTRODUCTION

4. The Association of British Insurers (ABI) is the trade body for insurance companies operating in the United Kingdom. ABI has 390 members who provide approximately 95 per cent of the insurance business written by companies in the UK, and are responsible for over 17 per cent of the investments on the London Stock Exchange. ABI is grateful for the opportunity to contribute to the Sub-Committee's inquiry into the Proposal for a Directive on Services in the Internal Market.

5. While financial services, including insurance, are excluded from the services covered by the Directive, Article 27(1) of the Directive states that "Member States shall ensure that providers whose services present a particular risk to the health or safety of the recipient, or a particular financial risk to the recipient, are covered by professional indemnity insurance appropriate to the nature and extent of the risk, or by any other guarantee or compensatory provision which is equivalent or essentially comparable as regards its purpose".

6. Unfortunately, Article 27 is based on a fundamental misunderstanding of how insurance markets work. The mere creation of an insurance requirement will not address the fundamental reasons why insurance on a cross-border basis may be difficult or expensive to find. ABI is aware of the popular myth that anything is insurable; this is not the case in practice.

INSURANCE FOR CROSS-BORDER ACTIVITIES

7. Risk appetite, expertise and pricing capability are all geared to the experience of the insurer. Most insurance business transacted in the UK is for businesses based in the UK and conducting their business activities in the UK. These insurers are familiar with UK liability laws, the circumstances under which they may be required to pay claims and the amount they will pay. Risk assessment and evaluation is very much geared to UK claims potential. Policy wordings have developed to reflect UK law and usually operate on a "losses occurring"[1] basis for public and products liability and "claims made"[2] for professional indemnity.

8. London is also an international insurance market, and some of its members have experience in writing business located outside the UK. Such insurers are usually specialists, with the expertise and infrastructure to service large risks, including the collection and payment of overseas taxes. This is a different market from domestic risks.

9. Liability laws, propensity to claim and level of awards vary greatly from country to country. Legal procedures are also different. Most UK insurers are unfamiliar with the underwriting principles necessary to write non-UK risks and are therefore reluctant to write such business. Furthermore, vital reinsurance may not be available to support insurers writing business beyond their competence: shareholders may not be happy with their capital being utilised in this way, and regulators may require extra capital to support insurers writing such business because of the extra risks involved.

---

[1] A "losses occuring" policy covers injury or damage that happens during the policy period. Thus, if the claim is not made until a later date, it will still be covered.

[2] A "claims made" policy covers claims that are made against the insured during the policy period.

10. Most insurance policies are also arranged on an annual basis, and the offering of insurance for shorter periods, particularly for a single contract being performed by the insured, attracts a much higher risk premium.

11. These fundamental difficulties in the way of supplying insurance on a cross-border basis are compounded by a number of practical issues that arise from the drafting of Article 27.

PROFESSIONAL INDEMNITY INSURANCE

12. In the UK, a professional indemnity policy covers the legal liability of the insured to pay damages by way of compensation for economic losses as a consequence of a breach of professional duty. With the exception of medical liability, policies do not cover bodily injury or damage to property; these claims are covered by a public or products liability policy. In other Member States, professional and public liability are defined differently. It is important, therefore, that the Commission is absolutely clear about the scope of its proposal. As currently drafted, Article 27 currently calls for both financial risks and health and safety risks to be covered.

TO WHICH SERVICE PROVIDERS WILL ARTICLE 27 APPLY?

13. The Directive does not state which service providers will fall under Article 27. It proposes that a committee should be established to determine this. The Commission has suggested informally that it should apply to a relatively small number of activities, principally leisure, construction, medical and some professional risks.

14. The proposal to determine coverage by committee will inevitably lead to an increase in compulsory insurance in the UK, which has much fewer compulsory insurances than other Member States. This is a concern to the insurance industry, and also to our policyholders, particularly as the experience with compulsory insurance in the UK has been problematic. Recent experiences with compulsory Employers' Liability insurance, where the capacity in the insurance market has been severely stretched, demonstrate the difficulties that can arise. Riding schools have also encountered problems in taking out Public Liability insurance. Likewise, the construction industry and Independent Financial Advisers have also experienced problems in finding, and affording, appropriate cover. ABI is therefore concerned that the insurance for these bodies to operate cross-border, may not be available or affordable, and thus this provision will prevent them from operating on a cross-border basis at all.

IMPACT OF ARTICLE 27 ON THE BRITISH AUTHORITIES

15. In practice, the enforcement of Article 27 may also be problematic. The drafting of Article 27 and Recital 63 suggests that Member States are taking on an obligation to ensure that cross-border providers of dangerous services have adequate liability insurance cover for their activities in other Member States. Yet, how are national authorities realistically supposed to enforce this? Will there be sanctions for a service provider found to be in breach of another Member State's requirements?

16. Article 27 (3) states that "When a provider establishes himself in their territory, Member States may not require professional insurance or a financial guarantee from the provider where he is already covered by a guarantee which is equivalent, or essentially comparable as regards its purpose, in another Member State in which the provider is already established". The British Government envisages that the "Single Points of Contact"[3] will be where this "equivalence" is verified. ABI is concerned that "equivalence" will be extremely difficult to measure in practice; particularly where policies may be written in a foreign language and where knowledge of a service providers' home country liability laws may be minimal.

17. Article 27(3) further states that "Where equivalence is only partial, Member States may require a supplementary guarantee to cover those aspects not already covered". The insurance industry does not typically cover this type of requirement. There are instances where risk is shared by a number of insurers writing business in layers to enable the insured to buy an appropriate amount of cover. The business however,

---

[3] Article 6: "Member States shall ensure that, by 31 December 2008 at the latest, it is possible for a service provider to complete the following procedures and formalities at a contact point known as a "single point of contact: (a) all procedures and formalities needed for access to his service activities, in particular, the necessary declarations, notifications or applications for authorisation from the competent authorities, including applications for inclusion in a register, a roll or a database, or for registration with a professional body or association; (b) any applications for authorisation needed to exercise his service activities."

tends to be written in a single market and it is fairly rare for an overseas market to "top up" the cover written in the UK market. The UK market does however provide "top up" cover to business written in overseas markets because of the international nature of the London market for large risks.

CONCLUSION

18. ABI believes that Article 27 will not address the reasons for the limited availability of liability insurance on a cross-border basis: the differences between Member States' liability regimes, propensity to claim and level of awards are too great at present to be resolved through regulation. ABI understands that the Commission's motives for the drafting of Article 27 were ones of consumer protection, yet Article 17(21)[4] excludes contracts for the provision of services concluded by consumers from the Country of Origin Principle. Article 27 will therefore have no added benefit for consumers, and in practice may prevent potential cross-border service providers from offering their services, where they are unable to obtain appropriate cover or where it is priced prohibitively. ABI therefore believes that Article 27 should be deleted, and that the market should remain free to develop appropriate liability products to meet consumers' needs.

March 2005

Memorandum by Association of Building Engineers

The following are comments received from responding members. The comments are general as it is proving very difficult to get to specifics as once problems arise members alter their approach and intent.

A. THE STATE OF THE SINGLE MARKET IN SERVICES

Are there significant barriers to firms seeking to offer their services in other Member States of the European Union?

Yes. We are a Professional Association operating in the construction sector, offering professional qualifications across a range of construction related disciplines. In addition, we offer education, training, support and "Continuing Professional Development" for our members and other construction professionals.

If so, what are the most important of those barriers?

— Acceptance of qualificational and educational standards across Member States.

What measures are needed to overcome those barriers?

— Acceptance of qualificational and educational standards across Member States.

— A common format, understanding and assessment of qualifications and associated academic standards across Member States.

B. THE COUNTRY OF ORIGIN PRINCIPLE

Is the principle that a company registered to provide services in one country is automatically qualified to provide those services in any community country on the basis of home country regulation a reasonable and/or realistic starting point?

Yes.

What significant benefits to businesses and consumers are likely to occur as a result of the adoption of the Country of Origin Principle?

More choice of service provider and potential for reduced cost.

Is the Principle workable in practice?

Not until there is an EU-wide system of cross-country acceptance of qualifications.

---

[4] "Contracts for the provision of services concluded by consumers to the extent that the provisions governing them are not completely harmonised at Community level".

Will the application of the Country of Origin Principle move business in favour of firms based in Member States with the least stringent regulatory regimes?

There needs to be an EU-wide system for cross-country acceptance of qualifications.

C. THE FUTURE

Do you expect the implementation of the Commission's proposed Directive to have a significant impact upon trade in the services sector within the European Union?

In which services industries do you expect the least and the largest movement towards a European Union single market in the next five to 10 years?

Within the context of the Building Expert we were founder members of a pan-European organisation, the AEEBC. The AEEBC has already undertaken significant development work to create a system capable of providing a credible cross-boundary approach to the equalisation of the skills and qualifications of Building Experts across the EU.

The Association is working with others to progress the avenue of greater mobility within Europe through links within the various European Member States, both academic and technical.

February 2005

Memorandum by Construction Confederation

INTRODUCTION

The Construction Confederation represents the interests of building and civil engineering contractors in the UK. Its membership comprises:

— British Woodworking Federation

— Civil Engineering Contractors Association

— Major Contractors Group

— National Contractors Federation

— National Federation of Builders

— Scottish Building

A SINGLE MARKET IN CONSTRUCTION

By its very nature construction is not an easily tradeable service. It generally requires a large volume of materials, some of which are expensive and cumbersome to transport and a local supply of skilled labour. Companies tend therefore to become established in whatever country they are carrying on construction rather than trade across borders, even within the European Union.

At present the value of overseas contracts at £4.57 billion represents 6.4 per cent of construction turnover and the majority of these contracts are carried out by larger international contractors. The majority of companies operating in the UK are SMEs (Small and Medium Sized Enterprises) that would not have the resources to establish overseas.

We do not therefore believe that the Services Directorate is likely to have a major impact on UK contractors' ability to access other EU markets.

Within Europe the public sector is a major source of work for contractors—in the UK it is over 40 per cent of turnover. There are already procurement rules in play that help provide access to other European public sector markets. Even so, as the review undertaken by Alan Wood for the Chancellor (November 2004)[1] indicated there is still unfair discrimination against foreign contractors, even when they are established within EU markets.

It is not clear that the measures proposed in the Services Directorate would overcome these barriers. It is hard to see how the proposals on a single point of contact would provide any real practical value. Indeed, they appear merely to add another layer of bureaucracy.

[1] Wood Review: *Investigating UK business experiences of competing for public contracts in other EU countries.*

THE COUNTRY OF ORIGIN PRINCIPLE

The Directive covers a wide range of sectors, each with its individual characteristics and its "one size fits all" approach does throw up problems for the construction industry in the UK. We are particularly concerned that the proposed Directive risks undermining health and safety in construction.

HEALTH AND SAFETY

The construction industry often has a complex chain of service providers, due to the regular practice of sub-contracting. This structure could include the situation that one or more temporary service providers are included in the chain and therefore could be subject to home Member State regulation. Whereas the other contractors in the chain must comply with the applicable national law. In the case of the Posting of Workers Directive, workers sent to work in another Member State are subject to the host Member State health and safety regulations. This approach is logical and should be adopted for the Services Directive. We understand that this is the intention of the derogation provided for in Article 17(16), however, we believe that greater clarification is required.

SOCIAL EMPLOYMENT

The EU Posting of Workers Directive is an important piece of legislation for the European construction market. The Construction Confederation supports the derogation from the Country of Origin Principle in Article 17(5). Nevertheless, where possible we believe that these latest proposals should correlate with the existing Posting of Workers Directive, to avoid confusion. We believe that the Services Directive also refers to the "host country" as opposed to "Member States of posting" in Article 4(11).

Similarly to the concerns presented in the section above on health and safety, the Confederation would like to highlight the importance of host country authorities having the right to inspect construction sites. It would not be practical for on-site inspections to be carried out by the home country authority. This is both for geographical reasons and also as the home country inspectors would not have sufficient knowledge of the applicable national laws and collective agreements. For control measures to be effective we believe that documentation should be readily available for inspection. The specific proposals contained in Article 24 appear not to provide such a practical approach.

PROFESSIONAL INSURANCE

The construction industry recognises the importance of appropriate professional indemnity insurance, particularly due to the health and safety risks, and welcomes the Commission's proposals for equivalence. In the case of temporary service providers establishing in the UK construction market, we are currently unable to comment if other EU requirements are equivalent to the UK health and safety insurance requirements. For example, under UK law parties are unable to exclude liability for injury or death. We have urged the UK Government to ascertain if in such cases there is equivalenace to the UK insurance market.

CONCLUSION

The Construction Confederation is very concerned by these latest EU proposals. We support the Commission's aim of removing unnecessary barriers to achieve a genuine internal market in services. However, the practical implications of what is currently proposed, particularly in the area of health and safety, far outweigh the benefits we believe could be created for the UK construction industry. In addition to all the specific points raised above, we believe that such proposed changes, could provide an incentive for companies to establish in a Member State with low standards, whilst gaining access to all other Member States. For the UK, which generally is a Member State with high standards, this could have serious economic and social consequences.

11 February 2005

Memorandum by General Dental Council

B. The Country of Origin Principle

1. It is our understanding that regulated healthcare professions will be exempt from the Country of Origin Principle by virtue of a derogation cross-referring to the Directive on the recognition of professional qualifications. The clear provision of such a derogation in the Directive is vital.

2. Whilst the General Dental Council (GDC) is supportive of the freedom of movement of professionals, freedom of movement must be achieved in a way which does not undermine the protective measures which Parliament has established for patients in the United Kingdom, and which other European parliaments have established in their countries. The Country of Origin Principle would threaten patients across Europe were it to be applied to regulated healthcare professionals.

3. We envisage practical problems with the arrangements for mutual assistance covered in Articles 35 and 36 which are intended to support the operation of the Country of Origin Principle. In particular, we consider it unlikely that the competent authorities in the country of origin would have either the incentive or the practical ability to provide the monitoring and supervision in the host State which appears to be envisaged. The Country of Origin Principle places a worrying physical and legislative distance between the competent authority (the supervisory authority) and the activities falling under its jurisdiction (the activities to be supervised). The relevant competent authority in the host State would have the practical ability to regulate activities in its territory but, where the Country of Origin Principle applies, might be unable to take swift and decisive action to address problems. The host State might even be unaware that the service provider is operating within its territory.

4. Moreover, the Country of Origin Principle could potentially lead to a situation in a Member State where, for example, dentists are practising under differing codes of conduct. This would be a confusing and unacceptable situation for patients.

5. From a patient's point of view it would be difficult to know how to pursue a complaint about a healthcare professional practising under the Country of Origin Principle, if he or she was thought to be performing below standards if the patient were expected to file a complaint with the competent authority in the country of origin, this would entail obvious complications in terms of knowing which authority to contact and use of language. Such obstacles might mean the patients would not pursue their concerns and that suspected professional misconduct might go unheard.

6. Such factors suggest there could be serious practical obstacles to the effective operation of the Country of Origin Principle potentially leading to a deterioration of standards and possibly putting the public at risk.

7. Whilst the GDC fully supports the principle of mutual assistance between Member States, we consider that the extent and complexity of the co-operation required under the Country of Origin Principle could make that Principle unworkable.

8. For these reasons, the GDC strongly argues for a clear exemption from the Country of Origin Principle for regulated healthcare professions (see paragraph 1). The solution to the problem is in effective and prompt registration systems to enable the mutual recognition of European qualifications.

8 February 2005

Memorandum by General Osteopathic Council

Introduction

1. The General Osteopathic Council (GOsC) was established under the Osteopaths Act 1993 to regulate, promote and develop the osteopathic profession in the UK, maintaining a Statutory Register of those entitled to practise osteopathy.

2. Whilst we recognise the importance of facilitating service provision across the European Union (EU), what sets osteopathy apart is that there are no formalised common standards of osteopathic training and practice across the EU.

3. As one of two competent authorities across the whole of the EU, we have a number of concerns about aspects of this draft Directive which could jeopardise patient safety. The GOsC's written evidence relates to those issues relevant to GOsC functions.

BACKGROUND

4. Only practitioners meeting the GOsC standards of safety and competency are eligible for registration. Proof of good health, good character and professional indemnity insurance cover is also a requirement.

5. It is an offence for anyone to describe themselves as an osteopath and practise as such, unless registered with the GOsC. The public can, therefore, be confident in visiting an osteopath in the UK that they will experience safe and competent treatment from a practitioner who adheres to a strict Code of Conduct.

6. Osteopathic training in the UK comprises a four to five-year BSc Honours degree programme with extensive clinical training. UK osteopaths are also committed to a mandatory programme of Continuing Professional Development.

SCOPE OF THE SERVICE IN THE INTERNAL MARKET DIRECTIVE

7. We would respectfully urge the House of Lords to press the UK Government to support the removal of healthcare from the scope of this Directive, thereby ensuring the GOsC is able to fulfill its role to protect the public.

SINGLE POINTS OF CONTACT (ARTICLE 6)

8. Whilst a single point of contact providing information to service providers has merit, the proposal goes beyond this to encompass the completion of all procedures required to carry out service activities, such as liaison with the competent authority. This goes further than the draft Directive on Mutual Recognition of Professional Qualifications,[1] and may in fact complicate rather than simplify administrative procedures through added red tape. We would press for the European Commission to amend this proposal so its objectives of simplifying procedures and cutting bureaucracy can be met.

AUTHORISATION (ARTICLES 9 TO 13)

9. We support the fact that authorisation schemes are permitted for reasons of public interest, but does this include patient safety? As a health regulator we would automatically assume that patient safety is of public interest and thus GOsC registration procedures, for example, would meet these criteria.

10. We strongly disagree if a regulator fails to respond to an application within the time-scale, then this would equate to the individual having met the minimum standards. We note that this does provide for different arrangements in the public interest and we consider it essential to make it clear that this includes public safety and health. Deemed registration does not allow for the unforeseen, nor protect the public—only serving to undermine our regulatory role.

THE COUNTRY OF ORIGIN PRINCIPLE (ARTICLES 16 TO 19)

11. We fully support what we consider to be derogation for professions with implications for public health and safety from the Country of Origin Principle. If this were not the case, we believe this would have serious implications on patient safety, particularly in the light of the lack of regulation framework for the osteopathic profession across the EU.

12. In order to emphasise the importance of this exemption, in the case of a complaint against a practitioner from outside the UK, the GOsC would be powerless to take action against him/her under the proposed arrangements. If osteopathy is not regulated in his/her country of origin—where is the competent authority to take action? This is of particular concern when one considers that patients can refer themselves directly to an osteopath, without having seeing their GP first.

MUTUAL ASSISTANCE (ARTICLE 35)

13. Whilst we fully support the principle of mutual assistance, in the case of the GOsC—apart from the Finnish Ministry of Health—there are no competent authorities to "mutually assist" or receive assistance from. We believe this is a potential risk for patients, which is why we are looking to establish a European alliance of osteopathic regulators as a strategic priority.

14. We would welcome any support from the House of Lords in encouraging the UK Government to press Member State governments to regulate osteopathy. We also hope that the European Commission will assist in identifying those competent authorities in relation to osteopathy in the rest of the EU.

---

[1] Proposal for a Directive of the European Parliament and of the Council on the recognition of professional qualifications. COM(2002)119 final.

EUROPEAN-LEVEL CODES OF CONDUCT (ARTICLE 39)

15. We encourage the development of voluntary European standards including Codes of Conduct at European level; however, as mentioned above, there are currently no formalised common standards in the training and practice of osteopathy across the EU. We cannot underestimate the difficulties this presents. These barriers are not only linguistic and cultural, but also legal as the autonomy and scope of osteopathic practice differs between Member States.

16. In the same way the latest text of the draft Directive on Mutual Recognition of Professional Qualifications stipulates the inclusion of regulatory bodies in the establishment of common platforms, all regulatory bodies should be involved in the development of these codes, along with professional associations and patient groups.

17. As part of the forthcoming UK Presidency of the EU, we would welcome assistance from the UK Government (and European Commission) to encourage the regulation of osteopathy across the European Union and to help identify those designated bodies with which we can build links.

14 February 2005

Memorandum by Griffiths & Armour Professional Risks

We write regarding evidence on Article 27 of the draft Directive in Services in the Internal Market.

We are commenting in our own right as a leading firm of Professional Indemnity Insurance Brokers and on behalf of the Construction Industry Council (CIC) whom we advise. We submit this evidence from the point of view of construction professionals as service providers within the Internal European Market.

CIC are submitting evidence separately on common concerns with other aspects of the proposed Directive.

ARTICLE 27.1

This appears to require Member States to introduce mandatory professional indemnity insurance [PII] schemes for professional service providers in their country of origin. The qualification is that the PII needs to address "a particular risk to health and safety . . . or particular financial risk to the recipient".

1. As the PI insurance will be a bespoke policy, unique to the service providers and their business needs, there will need to be a clear definition of the "particular" risks to be covered. It is clear that to comply with the intent of this Article there will need to be statutory limits on liability for those particular risks to ensure that all the liability arising is contained within the cover of the PII policy of the service provider. This is to be applauded but it has to be recognised that such a cap is not the custom and practice of purchasers in the various Member States. (It is believed that it is only Spain that offers a limit of liability on professional service providers but that is only in relation to Public Procurement Contracts.)

2. It would appear that to comply with Article 27, the Member States are required to establish some form of registration for all service providers with a provision to maintain PII. In addition, Article 7.1 requires a single point of contact for all professional service providers for the benefit of those seeking establishment other than in their country of origin. Such registration and a single point of contact does not exist at present in the UK.

3. Member States are expected to ensure that insurance is available although they have no control over what insurance is available within the market of each Member State. To be effective and to ensure there are no new barriers created by this provision, it is clear that similar costs of cover will be required in each Member State even though the global insurance market is not structured in this way. It cannot be assumed that insurers will provide the level of cover required by Article 27, putting the logical basis of the Article into some doubt.

4. PII operates on a claims made basis and renews annually (ie it is the policy that is in place when a claim is notified that bears the risk, not the policy that was in place when the service was provided). The expectation on Member States is to have a continuing duty to ensure insurance is being provided by the service provider once they have established themselves. There will therefore need to be further requirements regarding the period of time the insurance has to run. Member States will need to have a continuing duty to monitor the PII of the service provider.

5. Certain liabilities are not covered by available PII (including certain Health and Safety risks). Further, criminal acts arise from breach of Health and Safety Regulations and are uninsurable.

ARTICLE 27.2

1. It is not in the service provider's best interests to grant direct access to his insurers by a potential claimant. It will also give the insurers an administrative burden which can only be transferred to the service provider in the premium and thereafter incorporated into the costs of the services to be provided to the distinct disadvantage of the service purchaser. The privity of the service provider's insurance contract must be maintained.

2. In keeping with global custom and practice on insurance, the intended position of the intermediary/broker needs to be clearly stated.

ARTICLE 27.3

1. Mention is made of "professional insurance". Clarification is needed to establish whether this is different from the "professional indemnity insurance" stated in Article 27.1.

2. Where a "supplementary guarantee" is required, it is not stated whether this is in accordance with the requirements of the country of origin or of the Member State and the extent of the guarantee. It has to be recognised that many "guarantees" lie outside the protection of PII cover and would therefore not be covered by the principles established by Article 27.1.

3. The consequences of the service provider failing to comply needs to be stated.

We, as Professional Indemnity Insurance brokers, have over 2,000 construction professionals as clients and they are concerned that the currently drafted proposal will attract additional costs to their business and will restrict their ability to work competitively in other Member States.

We would be more than happy to give further evidence in this matter or develop our concerns in response to any comments you may have.

11 February 2005

Memorandum by the Health and Safety Commission

SUMMARY

1. The Health and Safety Commission (HSC) considers that the draft Services Directive will encourage better regulation across Europe through its simplification and establishment provisions. This will promote sensible health and safety measures, and a more level playing field for UK business abroad. HSC welcomes the Directive's broad intent. HSC comments address issues in the draft Directive as published last year with the Department of Trade and Industry's (DTI) consultation paper. But, this memorandum also discusses potential improvements in the Directive which appear to be emerging from discussions in Europe.

2. HSC has also considered the likely impact of the Country of Origin approach to opening markets to temporary service providers. HSC is concerned that this approach, as it stands, risks seriously undermining sensible UK controls on work-related health and safety risks. HSC therefore welcomes the Government's declared negotiating stance, which, in the context of an overall wish to promote the economic benefits of the Directive, seeks to uphold UK standards on health and safety in all circumstances.

THE ROLE OF HSC

3. HSC is responsible in Great Britain for advancing effective strategies for reducing work-related injuries, ill-health and deaths. 235 workers and 167 members of the public[1] were killed in work-related incidents in 2003–04; and 30,666 workers suffered major injury. A total of 39 million working days were lost to work-related injury and ill-health. These figures represent unacceptable and largely preventable levels of individual suffering, and economic cost between £13.1 and £22.2 billion per year. Many of these incidents do not come to the notice of the wider public. Sometimes they are front page news, for example when 21 cockle pickers drowned in Morecambe Bay.

4. HSC promotes sensible measures to manage work-related risks. This benefits employees and others affected by work. It also benefits employers, whose investment in risk management is repaid in higher productivity, lower costs, and enhanced reputation.

---

[1] Excluding suicides and trespassers on the railways.

5. These risks arise from work activities which include the wide range of services within scope of the draft Directive. These services include suppliers of labour in agriculture and shellfish harvesting, as well as architectural, construction, engineering and maintenance services, and the distributive trades and fairgrounds. DTI's 2004 consultation paper indicates that about half of all enterprises in the UK are in "market services", as are 49 per cent of all UK employee jobs. This underlines the importance of sensible risk controls.

6. HSC makes proposals to Government for improving and simplifying the statutory and voluntary framework for health and safety regulation based on wide public consultation and expert advice. HSC is committed to regulation which fully reflects better regulation principles. HSC is assisted by the Health and Safety Executive (HSE). HSE is also responsible for proportionate enforcement in accordance with the HSC Enforcement Policy Statement.

"Simplification" and "Establishment"

7. The Directive's simplification and establishment provisions would require easy access to regulatory services for all businesses, and equitable treatment of competitor service providers moving in permanently from another Member State. Experience in health and safety regulation leads HSC to support the idea of single points of contact, electronic access to regulatory services, and requirements to ensure that authorisations are objectively necessary, proportionate, and non-discriminatory. In health and safety regulation, authorisations include licences for asbestos removal, explosives manufacture and storage, and nuclear installations.

8. HSE already has a single point of contact, *Infoline*, which deals with more than 270,000 enquiries per year from business and other stakeholders. The European Commission (EC) may wish to draw on this experience in its proposed administrative pilot in this area. HSE has also been developing electronic access in response to the Modernising Government agenda.

9. However, these provisions need to be made more workable. For example, further developments in electronic access under the Directive should allow Member State authorities to prioritise and select projects on the basis of cost-benefit considerations, not a blanket requirement. HSC believes the EC intend single points of contact to provide ready access to expert decisions on health and safety authorisations. But the current wording of Article 6 suggests single points of contact could be new authorities. This needs to be clarified.

10. As the draft Directive indicates, authorisations should be used only when objectively necessary and proportionate, and they should not be used to discriminate against other Member States' service providers. HSC believes that authorisations used in GB health and safety regulation will readily meet these criteria. But, one aspect of Article 10, on conditions for granting authorisations, gives HSC cause for concern. Article 10(3) would prevent a Member State from applying authorisation requirements to a business if its home Member State already applies controls "equivalent or essentially comparable" in purpose.

11. Authorisations are only used under health and safety at work regulation where no less stringent measure will be enough to ensure that serious risk is adequately controlled. The authorisation process is vital to an effective working relationship between business and HSE in high risk areas. There is thus a strong argument that other Member State authorisations, dealing with asbestos stripping for example, could not be equivalent or essentially comparable. However, HSC wishes to see the intentions of Article 10(3) clarified, in favour of ensuring UK standards of health and safety continue to apply. Otherwise, Article 10(3) risks undermining the coherence of controls on high risk work activities, creating potential problems similar to those the Article 17(17) derogation needs to overcome in country of origin.

Country of Origin

12. HSC believes that the balance of opportunities and risk, and benefits and costs, to business, to employees and to others affected by work does not generally support extending the Country of Origin approach to work-related health and safety risks.

13. Country of Origin seeks to assist service providers operating temporarily in another Member State by making them subject to their home Member State requirements. But harmonisation of health and safety regulation across Europe is no more than work in progress in many sectors. The health and safety record in Great Britain is among the best in the European Union. Country of Origin risks importing poor health and safety practices in some temporary service providers' operations. It risks undermining standards more widely when temporary providers supply services to other businesses. It also risks undercutting responsible businesses.

14. Construction is one example where risks can be controlled only by professionals, clients, sub-contractors, suppliers and workers co-operating in the management of risks. Doing this effectively requires everyone to sing from the same sheet, in this case the same health and safety requirements. There are welcome indications that the EC does not intend building sites at least to be subject to Country of Origin. But, this kind of co-operation and cordination is needed in many other spheres too, for example anywhere one or more contractors carry out maintenance of buildings, machinery, process plant, electrical or electronic systems.

15. HSC understands that a further draft of the Directive being discussed in Brussels working groups may effectively exclude regulation of conditions for workers from Country of Origin, including work-related health, safety and welfare requirements. This would be a sensible and welcome development.

16. The draft Directive as sent out for consultation last year would have increased bureaucracy for business in this area, as well as adversely affecting risk controls. Health and safety and other conditions for "posted workers", those sent by a service provider to another Member State, are to be regulated by the host Member State under the Posting of Workers Directive, as now. But Country of Origin as formulated appeared to mean that workers recruited by a temporary provider in the host Member State would be subject to the home Member State health and safety requirements. The temporary provider would then face two sets of requirements. HSE and DTI drew EC attention to this. The Posting of Workers Directive approach allows for sensible and effective control of risks to workers—HSC hopes the final Directive will indeed adopt it for all workers.

17. However, Country of Origin would still apply to regulation of risks to non-employees such as members of the public affected by work activities, eg people in the vicinity of scaffolding work in the street, or who risk inhaling legionella bacteria from an ill-maintained office cooling unit. European Union legislation does not deal consistently with risks to the self-employed, and says little or nothing about risks to members of the public. Other Member States' requirements appear to vary considerably. Again Country of Origin would introduce damaging discontinuities to health and safety regulation.

18. In the experience of HSC and HSE, the vast majority of employers wish to comply with health and safety requirements, which are no more than what sensible business should do anyway to control risks. Most employers actively seek to manage risks. But there are a minority who have no respect for people's health and safety, or who deliberately cut corners. HSC is concerned that such unscrupulous businesses will seek to exploit temporary service provider status. Some will claim to be subject to Country of Origin even when they continuously or regularly operate in a Member State, and may well succeed in staying one step ahead of the regulator. Country of Origin risks introducing uncertainties in relation to health and safety regulation which unscrupulous businesses would seek to exploit.

19. The regulation of work-related health and safety risks is designed to safeguard people, so far as is reasonably practicable, from risks which can lead to harm, sometimes to a lifetime of serious ill-health or to death. This is good for individuals and it is good for business. As regards health and safety at work, HSC considers that the modest increase in certainty for temporary service providers from Country of Origin in its unmodified form is outweighed by confusion of requirements, damage to effective employer communication about risk, increased risks of harm, and consequent costs.

20. Article 17(17) currently appears to offer a partial derogation from Country of Origin for health and safety requirements, targeted on especially serious risks. But, Article 17(17) does not yet appear to be worded so as to take account properly of the issues raised above. HSE is working with DTI to seek to address these kinds of problem. HSC understands there are some positive signals emerging from discussions in Europe, but HSC also considers it should comment on the draft Directive as it is publicly available. A priority for the EC in developing the Directive should be to ensure that the extent of the Article 17(17) derogation safeguards necessary and proportionate controls on work-related risks to people's health and safety.

ENFORCER COSTS

21. Under the Directive, Country of Origin would be made to work by means of requirements for mutual assistance between Member State enforcing authorities. The Sub-Committee may wish to note HSE's current estimate of the resources which HSE would need to devote to mutual assistance, based on the way the Country of Origin approach currently appears to impact on health and safety. HSE estimates that the annual cost would be at least £1.25 million. This raises the question whether all 25 Member States' authorities would be able to find the resources to support their end of the mutual assistance process.

22. Local authorities also enforce health and safety requirements in certain sectors—HSC understands that local authorities are considering the impact of the draft Services Directive and the potential cost implications.

17 February 2005

Memorandum by Institute of Practitioners in Advertising

The Institute of Practitioners in Advertising (the "IPA") is the trade association and professional institute for UK advertising agencies. Our 247 corporate members are primarily concerned with providing strategic advice on marketing communications. Based throughout the country, they are responsible for over 85 per cent of the UK's advertising agency business and play a pivotal role in advising the nation's companies on how they should deploy their total marketing communications spend of £14 billion.

The IPA has received the inquiry into the European Commission's proposal for a Directive on Services in the internal market, and welcomes the opportunity to respond to it.

A. THE CURRENT STATE OF THE SINGLE MARKET IN SERVICES

The IPA has always lobbied for the removal of barriers to the free movement of commercial communications across the European Union (EU). A true internal market and the removal of regulations and bureaucracy are fundamental aims of our industry that will, in our view, benefit both business and consumers.

Barriers however do still exist, occuring at every stage of the business process. Advertising agencies face particular barriers as a result of very restrictive and detailed rules for commercial communications, ranging from outright bans to strict controls on content, which vary from Member State to Member State. These differences affect many areas, such as the advertising of alcohol, the making of claims about effectiveness (particularly in highly regulated industry sectors such as healthcare) and other disciplines such as direct marketing mailer distribution, sales promotion offers and packaging regulation.

Furthermore, the differences in legislation between Member States also impede pan-European promotional campaigns.

The IPA therefore welcomes any proposal that will assist in setting up a true internal market for Services and which will cut red tape which prevents businesses from offering their services across borders within the European Union.

B. COUNTRY OF ORIGIN PRINCIPLE

It is the Country of Origin Principle that allows companies established in the EU fully to take advantage of the Internal Market. Barriers to the freedom of movement of services deny EU citizens from obtaining the quality of service and choice that they deserve and restrict competition within the EU.

The IPA therefore wholeheartedly agrees with the principle that a company registered to provide services in one country should automatically be qualified to provide these services in any Community country on the basis of home country regulations. The IPA certainly considers that this is a reasonable and realistic starting point.

Advertising agencies throughout Europe provide services that are legal, decent, honest and truthful. Such principles are embedded in self-regulation, to which all IPA members subscribe. It is perfectly acceptable for these strict rules of self-regulation to be the adequate basis for any pan-European provision of services.

By relying on the Country of Origin Principle, agencies would be in a position to produce advertisements in compliance with the regulations in one State and, without further editing, translating or legal advice, the advertisement could be published on a pan-European basis. Obstacles inherent in other Member States' laws and regulations would thereby be removed. This would give rise to significant cost efficiencies in respect of both manpower and expenses in seeking legal advice.

The Country of Origin Principle is workable in practice. The Television Without Frontiers Directive, which works on a similar basis to this Principle, has not been found to cause any problem.

The IPA would therefore vigorously oppose any moves to remove or water down the Country of Origin mechanism as it relates to the commercial communications sector.

C. THE FUTURE

The IPA believes that the implementation of the proposed Directive would allow for a significant increase in the amount of cross-border advertising, thus giving rise to greater competition, innovation and quality, as well as increasing consumer choice. This would therefore benefit both consumers and business.

February 2005

Memorandum by Transport and General Workers Union

The Transport and General Workers Union (T&G) is Britain's largest General Union with members in most sectors of the British economy. In common with the British and European Trade Union movement the T&G had some serious concerns about the potential impact of this Directive when it was originally drafted. This Directive was ill thought through and leaves too many questions unanswered, particularly in relation to the impact of the Country of Origin Principle.

On a more general point the T&G believes that the European Union must retain a clearly social dimension if it is retain legitimacy with the general public and working people in particular. The Services Directive, as originally drafted, was a clear example of the trend towards deregulation with little regard for social consequences. The Country of Origin Principle is likely to favour companies from Member States with the least amount of regulation, whether that is in terms of employment or health and safety legislation—raising the inevitable danger of a "race to the bottom".

The T&G was pleased to see that the European Commission has recently decided to redraft the Directive. The comments made in this response take into account The Presidency clarified text of the proposal, published on 10 January 2005.

Our concerns about the proposed Directive on Services in the Internal Market stem from a lack of clarity in the proposal as to how domestic employment and health and safety regulations will be affected by the Country of Origin Principle. The T&G is particularly concerned about the Directive's potential impact on the recent Gangmaster licensing legislation. We also believe that the Directive needs to be absolutely clear as what sectors it may apply to. The T&G understands that the UK Government has supported the view that health and social care should be excluded from the Directive and we fully support that view.

HEALTH AND SAFETY

Further guarantees are required in the Directive in relation to Health and Safety, particularly in the area of effective enforcement.

Construction is a particular concern of the T&G. It is one of the most dangerous sectors to work in and as such, effective health and safety regulation is paramount. The wording of the Services Directive must make it absolutely clear that the Country of Origin Principle will not lead to a situation whereby companies apply different quality standards, employ workers on different terms and conditions and apply different health and safety standards. Construction should therefore be derogated from the Country of Origin Principle.

The T&G would emphasise the response of the Health and Safety Commission to the draft Directive.

> "The country of origin approach threatens health and safety standards and offends the principles of good regulation. Temporary service providers would be subject to their home state's laws and authorities through new liaison procedures which will cause confusion and make a nonsense of criminal enforcement to deal with risks in services.
>
> HSC is very concerned about the impact on victims and bereaved families. If people are seriously injured or killed by a temporary service provider, country of origin would mean huge uncertainties about whether enforcement and prosecution was possible. HSC asks how people aggrieved by an enforcement decision could hold the other Member State's enforcing authority to account". (response to DTI consultation July 2004)

We believe that the Directive itself should spell out clearly that the Country of Origin Principle will not apply to any health and safety legislation, provisions or practices, across all sectors. There must be a thorough impact assessment on health and safety issues across the EU and comprehensive measures to harmonise European health and safety standards before any Directive should be allowed to impact on this vital area. The T&G would like to draw to the Committee's attention the recent publication of worker death statistics by the Centre for Corporate Accountability. This shows that in 2002 Poland had 1,588 workplace deaths, Italy 1,388, and Spain 1,177 whilst the UK had 225 (ILO estimates).

There remain considerable differences between the regimes of different Member States, for example, UK health and safety law extends protection to the public, EU health and safety law does not. There are many issues relating to authorisation schemes for work such as asbestos clearing, gas installation etc, and to the whole inspection regime which would be rendered ineffective if the Country of Origin rules were to apply in this area.

The Directive also restricts the ability of Member States to require membership or registration with a professional body or association in their country (Article 16 (3)). The T&G believes that there needs to be absolute clarity that this will not affect the ability of public service bodies for instance to require certain standards when awarding contracts.

Derogations 16 and 17 of Article 17 of the Directive state that the Country of Origin Principle will not apply "for reasons of public policy, public security, or public health or the environment". The interpretation of this needs to be as wide as possible. The Directive needs to make clear that local and national authorities retain the right to define service requirements, regulations and standards which are in the public interest.

GANGMASTERS

The Transport and General Workers union was a sponsor of the Private Members Bill promoted by Jim Sheridan MP, to regulate gangmasters in the agricultural sector (agricultural work, gathering shellfish and the process or packaging of any produce derived from agricultural work or shellfish, fish or products derived from shellfish or fish). The successful passage of this Bill, resulting in the Gangmasters (licensing) Act 2004, was given extra impetus by the death of 21 Chinese cockle pickers in Morecambe Bay. This has led to the recent formation of the Gangmaster Licensing Authority.

All Gangmasters operating in the sectors covered by the Act must now obtain a licence to operate. This legislation was a significant step forward in dealing with the exploitation and abuse of migrant labour. The T&G believes that in some other sectors a similar licensing arrangement may be the best way of avoiding abuse.

The current draft Services Directive could not only potentially render the gangmasters licensing legislation redundant but also close off any opportunity to introduce similar measures in the future.

The T&G understands that the UK Government is seeking to ensure that gangmasters licensing is excluded from the provisions of this Directive. The T&G would also like to ensure that the Directive derogates any similar measures which are designed to prevent the exploitation of workers. Any derogation should allow national governments full scope to define such measures as falling into the current "public policy, public health and environment" derogation, or preferably introduce a specific "protection of workers" derogation.

EMPLOYMENT LAW

All workers employed in the UK, temporary or not, should be entitled to all UK statutory employment rights and should be covered by any terms and conditions set by UK collective bargaining arrangements in that sector, bargaining unit or workplace.

Article 17, recital 41(b) of the Directive attempts to provide some reassurance by specifying a number of derogations from the Country of Origin Principle in the area of terms and conditions, particularly by specifying that this area will be covered by the Posting of Workers Directive (96/71/EC). The T&G does not, however, believe that the UK is in full compliance with this Directive because collective agreements are not legally binding under UK law. There is also no mechanism in the UK for extending collective agreements across sectors. This potentially means that any company trading cross-border would not have to abide by the terms of national agreements in both the construction and electrical engineering sectors where there are currently national agreements in place in the UK.

The T&G would also emphasise that vitally important issues such as unfair dismissal, redundancy, trade union related protections (detriment, statutory recognition) and transfer of undertakings (TUPE) regulations are not included within the scope of recital 41(b). Some of these issues are covered by other European legislation (such as TUPE) but others are not. There are still a number of areas of uncertainty in the area of enforcement. The application of the Country of Origin Principle to this area will make the enforcement and monitoring of labour law far more dificult, particularly if details of any employment relationship will only be held in the country of origin. The T&G does not believe that it is feasable for service providers to monitor employment issues from their country of origin.

To create clarity on these issues the T&G believes that there must be a specific derogation for all employment law matters.

TEMPORARY AGENCY WORKERS

Under the current wording of this Directive, the use of agency workers across Europe will be deregulated. It is entirely inappropriate for the issue of agency workers to be dealt with under the terms of a Directive such as this, particularly since there is a draft Temporary Agency Worker Directive currently under negotiation at European level. The draft Temporary Agency Worker Directive allows for derogations relating to specific labour market needs and the need for Member States to take action to protect agency workers from exploitation. It is absolutely essential that there is a derogation for temporary agency worker issues in the Services Directive so that those issues can be dealt with properly under the current discussions taking place on the Temporary Agency Workers Directive.

SUMMARY

The Transport and General Workers Union regards the following derogations from the Country of Origin Principle as essential:

— Health and Safety issues;

— Employment law issues, including all issues relating to the use of temporary agency workers; and

— Gangmaster licensing.

We also call for a clear derogation from the Directive for health and social care services.

The Directive needs to make clear that local and national authorities retain the right to define service requirements, regulations and standards which are in the public interest.

15 February 2005

Memorandum by Which?

ABOUT WHICH?

1. Which? is an independent, not-for-profit consumer organisation with around 700,000 members and is the largest consumer organisation in Europe. At EU level we are members of BEUC, the Bureau Européen des Unions de Consommateurs. We are entirely independent of Government and industry, and are funded through the sale of our Which? range of consumer magazines and books. Which? was formerly known as Consumers' Association.

THE CURRENT STATE OF THE SINGLE MARKET IN SERVICES

2. Consumers are losing out because of the lack of a single market in services. Their opportunity to use more competitively priced services from other Member States is reduced, and barriers to the provision of business-to-business services impose additional costs that are passed on to consumers. Which? therefore welcomes the draft Directive, subject to the reservations set out in this submission.

EVALUATING BARRIERS TO CROSS-BORDER SERVICES

3. Member States frequently claim that barriers to the provision of services are necessary for consumer protection. However, quantitative and location restrictions often have much more to do with economic protectionism than with consumer protection. We support for example the proposed removal of all total prohibitions on commercial communications by the regulated professions, which restrict competition and choice and make it difficult for new entrants to markets.

4. Which? is not opposed to market entry restrictions provided that they relate to legitimate issues of quality, safety and consumer protection: we have for example called for stricter entry requirements for the car repair trade and for estate agents. Where it is necessary to ensure the operation of certain commercial services for social reasons, this should be done through appropriate targeted, transparent and accountable measures and not by artificial restraints on competition.

5. However, not all barriers are protectionist, and legitimate consumer protection concerns must be addressed. We are for example concerned to see the retention of the high level of protection provided in the UK by the CORGI (Council for Registered Gas Installers) scheme, under which certain gas installations and repairs must be carried out only by a CORGI-registered provider. Similarly, we would welcome some

clarification on how UK financial guarantee or insurance schemes for professions such as law or accountancy might be affected.

6. We support the proposals for evaluation on matters such as non-discrimination, but we would welcome some detailed guidelines and criteria for assessing grey list issues, to encourage consistency. Member States should be encouraged to involve consumer organisations in dialogue on the "grey list" issues, to help distinguish genuine consumer protection from economic protectionism.

THE COUNTRY OF ORIGIN PRINCIPLE

7. We recognise that there are concerns about possible "regulatory arbitrage" and that companies may move to the Member States with the weakest regulatory regimes. However, we believe that businesses trading cross-border with other businesses will be sufficiently aware of the potential pitfalls.

8. Most consumers however will be poorly placed to assess the consumer protection regimes of other Member States. We see consumer confidence as crucial if consumers are to be able to drive the single market by shopping cross-border, but surveys shows that UK consumers are not yet confident about using services from other Member States.

9. Mutual recognition generally works for consumers in the product sector, because of EU legislation on product safety and product liability, the role of technical standards, and the prevalence of brands. In the case of services however, there are relatively few brands and scarcely any standards: there is little EU legislation on the safety of services and none on the liability of suppliers of defective services. Another key difference is that while products can be sold at a distance, most services have to be provided in the country of the consumer.

10. We propose therefore that the Country of Origin Principle should not apply to consumer protection, and that consumers should be able to buy in their own Member States services from other Member States under their own national consumer protection rules.

CO-REGULATION AND SELF-REGULATION

11. We support the proposal for voluntary initiatives to ensure the quality of services, including codes of practice. However, while self-regulation can offer improved protection beyond what the law requires, the basic needs of consumers such as economic and legal protection and safety requirements must be assured by legislation and not by other forms of regulation.

INFORMATION AND REDRESS

12. We are concerned that the proposals on the provision of information to consumers would place the onus on the consumer to request certain key information. We would welcome further initiatives to provide cheap, rapid and accessible systems of cross-border redress.

CROSS-BORDER MEDICAL TREATMENT

13. We support the principle of cross-border medical treatment which would extend consumer choice. A survey for Which? shows that UK consumers have a positive attitude towards going to another EU Member State for medical treatment, with 72 per cent very or quite likely to accept medical treatment in another country, paid for by the NHS, if it meant that they could be treated sooner. However, patients will need clarity about issue such as charges, prescriptions and the availability of complaints mechanisms and redress.

THE FUTURE

14. We believe that the potential benefits of the proposed Directive, and also of any liberalisation of the international trade in services, will depend to a great extent on the energetic application of EU competition laws. A much more pro-active EU competition policy is therefore essential.

15. Which? is calling for a European "supercomplaints" procedure, on the lines of that which already operates within the UK. It is interesting to note that so far all the supercomplaints submitted by Which? to the Office of Fair Trading have concerned services (dentists, care homes, and banking in Northern Ireland). Under an EU supercomplaints procedure, qualified bodies could bring complaints about infringements of EU competition law to the Commission's Competition Directorate-General and would receive a formal response

within a set period. We have also proposed Community-wide price surveys in key sectors to identify whether anti-competitive practices are taking place.

16. The Directive needs to be supported by robust enforcement of the regulation on cross-border enforcement co-operation and the (soon to be adopted) Directive on Unfair Commercial Practices. We would welcome Commission proposals to ensure safer services, to underpin consumer confidence.

15 February 2005